Finger Pointing to the Moon

Osho taught philosophy at the University of Jabalpur before establishing the commune in Poona, India, which has become famous all over the world as a mecca for seekers wanting to experience meditation and transformation. His teachings have influenced millions of people of all ages and from all walks of life. He has been described by *The Sunday Times* as one of the 1000 Makers of the Twentieth Century, and by *The Sunday Mid-Day* (India) as one of the ten people – along with Gandhi, Nehru and Buddha – who have changed the destiny of India.

FINGER POINTING TO THE
MOON

Discourses on the Adhyatma Upanishad

OSHO

ELEMENT
Shaftesbury, Dorset • Rockport, Massachusetts
Brisbane, Queensland

© Osho International Foundation 1994

This edition published in Great Britain in 1994 by
Element Books Limited
Shaftesbury, Dorset

Published in the USA in 1994 by
Element, Inc.
42 Broadway, Rockport, MA 01966

Published in Australia in 1994 by
Element Books Limited
for Jacaranda Wiley Limited
33 Park Road, Milton, Brisbane 4064

Editing: Swami Yoga Pratap Bharati
Ma Kamaal
Design: Ma Deva Sandipa
Typesetting: Swami Sambodhi Prem
Production: Swami Krishna Prabhu
Photography: Osho Photo Services
Cover design: Max Fairbrother

Printed and bound in Great Britain by
Hartnolls, Bodmin, Cornwall

British Library Cataloguing in Publication
data available

Library of Congress Cataloging in Publication
data available

ISBN 1-85230-598-3

*Spontaneous talks
given by Osho
to disciples and friends
in Mount Abu,
Rajasthan, India.*

Contents

Introduction

The word upanishad means seed – seeds of the ancient Eastern art/science of learning to observe the mind and its processes in a relaxed and non-judgmental way, thus enabling one to transcend a life of slavery to the senses and find the perception and clarity of self-realization.

In these seventeen discourses Osho uses the ancient wisdom of the Adhyatma Upanishad as a jumping board for his message for a humanity moving faster and faster towards who knows what, at the dawning of the twenty-first century. "...The Upanishads have, for the first time, used a scientific language and have left aside the anthropocentric language of man."

These ancient sutras are usually presented in the format of master-disciple dialogue. The Adhyatma Upanishad varies this format in that it is the disciple himself who is speaking prior to self-realization and detailing his understanding and the steps on the way to enlightenment.

Osho says, in speaking of the unnamed seeker, "This is why I have chosen this Upanishad. This Upanishad is a direct encounter with spirituality. There are no doctrines in it; there are only experiences of the fulfilled ones.... In it there is no discussion of that which is born out of curiosity or inquisitiveness, no; in it there are hints to those who are full of longing for liberation from those who have already attained liberation....

"I will say only that which I know, which I have lived. If you agree to put all at stake, whatever is my experience can also become yours. Experiences do not belong to anyone; they come to whosoever is ready to receive them. Nobody has any monopoly over the truth; whosoever is willing to disappear inherits it. Truth belongs to one who shows the readiness to ask for it—who opens the doors of their heart and calls for it....

"I will say to you only that which I know, because only in saying that lies some value; because only that which I know can, if you are willing, vibrate the strings of your heart too with its living impact."

When once the question, "There must be something more than this?" has arisen in your heart, you become a seeker. This book is the story of one such seeker and his path, climaxing with a song in his heart and a dance to his being: "I am that which I have been seeking, I am the ultimate, the divine." This dance, this song is also your birthright.

Ma Kamaal

THE
DIVINE IS YOU

CHAPTER 1

INVOCATION

Om, may the sun god give us his benediction.
May Varuna, the god of water,
give us his benediction.
May Aryama, Indra, Brahaspati
and Vishnu give us their benediction.

✻

My salutations to Brahman, the absolute reality.
O Vayu, god of air, salutations especially to you,
because you are the Brahman manifest.
I shall call only you the manifest Brahman.
I shall also call you the truth, call you rit – the law.

✻

May they protect me. May they protect the speaker.
Protect me. Protect the speaker.
Om, peace, peace, peace.

I will say only that which I know. I will say only that which you can also know. By knowing I mean living it. One may know even without living it, but such knowledge is a burden; one may sink because of it, but one cannot be saved by it. Knowing can be alive also. Such knowing renders us weightless – light so that we can fly in the sky. Only when knowing becomes living do wings grow, fetters break and the doors to the infinite become wide open.

But knowing is difficult; accumulating knowledge is easy. Mind chooses the easier and avoids the difficult. But the one who avoids the difficult will miss religion as well. One who wants to avoid not only the difficult but the impossible too will never ever come close to religion.

Religion is only for those who are ready to enter into the impossible. Religion is for the gamblers, not for the shopkeepers. Religion is neither a business deal nor a compromise. Religion is a wager. A gambler puts his wealth at stake; the religious person puts himself at stake because that is the ultimate wealth.

One who is not ready to stake his very life will never be able to know the hidden mysteries of life. Those secrets are not available cheaply. Knowledge is available very cheaply; knowledge is available from books, from scriptures, in education, with the teachers. Knowledge is available almost for free; you do not have to pay anything for it. In religion you have to pay heavily. It is not right even to say "heavily," because only when someone stakes everything do the doors to that life open. The doors to that life open only for those who put this life at stake. To put this life at stake is the only key to the door of that life. But knowledge is very cheap, so the mind chooses the easier and the cheaper way. We learn things – words, doctrines – and think that we know. Such knowledge only enhances ignorance.

The ignorant person at least knows that he does not know; at least that much truth he has. But more untruthful people cannot be found than those whom we call knowledgeable. They don't even know that they don't know. Something heard, something committed to memory, deludes them into thinking they have also known.

I will say to you only that which I know, because only in saying that lies some value; because only that which I know can, if you are willing, vibrate the strings of your heart too with its living impact.

What I myself do not know, and what is only skin deep in me, cannot go much deeper in you either. Only that which has entered the depths of my own heart has the possibility; if you cooperate, it can reach your heart. Even then your cooperation is a must, because if your heart is closed there is no way of thrusting the truth forcefully into it. And it is good that it is so, because if truth can be forced on you it cannot become your freedom, it can only become your slavery. All compulsions become slaveries.

So in this world, everything can be given to you through force; only truth cannot be, because truth can never become slavery. The very nature of truth is freedom. So truth is the only thing in this world which nobody can give you forcefully, which nobody can thrust upon you, which cannot be put upon you from the outside like clothing; for which your willingness, your openness, your receptivity, your invitation, your heart full of gratitude, are the prerequisites. If your heart becomes like the earth before the rainy season when it is thirsty for water and develops wide cracks due to the parching summer heat – as if it has opened up its lips here and there anticipating the rains – then the truth enters you. Otherwise the truth turns back even from your very doorstep. Many times it has turned back, in many, many lifetimes.

You are not new – nothing is new on this earth; you are all very old. You have sat at the feet of Buddha and heard him, you have seen Krishna, you have also been around Jesus, but still you have missed, because your heart was never ready. The rivers of Buddha and Mahavira have flowed past you, but you have remained thirsty.

The day Buddha was about to leave his body, Ananda was

weeping and beating his chest in desperation. Buddha asked him, "Why are you weeping? I have been near you for long enough ...forty years! And if it has not happened even in forty years, what is the point of weeping now? And why are you feeling so troubled about my death?"

Ananda replied, "I am so distressed because I could not manage to disappear while you were here. Had I disappeared, you would have been able to enter me. For forty years the river was flowing by my side and I have remained thirsty. Now I am weeping because I do not know when and in what lifetime I shall be able to meet this river again."

You are not new. You have cremated buddhas, you have cremated Mahaviras – Jesus, Krishna and all; you are living after cremating them all. They lost the battle against you. You are very old. You have been here since life is. It has been an infinite journey. Where are we missing? It is just that you are not open, you are closed.

I will say to you only that which I have known. If you can make yourself an opening, you will also know that. And it is not that there is some great difficulty in it. There is only one difficulty, and that is you.

Some people move only with curiosity, just like small children asking while they are on a walk, "What is the name of this tree?" And if you don't reply, they immediately forget that they had asked anything and they start asking something else: "Why is this rock lying here?" They ask just for the sake of asking and not in order to know. They do not ask in order to know, they ask because they cannot remain without asking.

Those who are living out of curiosity are still childish. If you ask, "What is God?" just as casually as a child would ask on seeing a toy shop on the road, "What is this toy?" you are still a child. And the child can be forgiven, but not you.

Curiosity will not do. Religion is not a child's play. Even if you are given a reply, it serves no purpose. The child's fun is in asking. He could ask, that is his fun. Even if you give him a reply he is not very interested in it. What is the matter?

Psychologists say that when children learn to speak for the first time they are only practicing their speaking by asking, just as when a child learns walking for the first time he tries every now and then to get up and walk. So children repeat the same sentence again and again only because they have acquired a new experience, a new dimension through speaking. So in that new dimension they are floating and rehearsing; that is why they ask just anything, they say just anything.

In the world of religion, if you are also asking just anything, saying just anything, thinking just anything without any deep desire to know – only out of curiosity – then you will still cremate some more buddhas; then who knows how many more buddhas will still have to work hard on you!

Truth has no relationship to curiosity.

Some people move a little ahead of curiosity and become inquisitive. There is a little more depth in inquisitiveness, but just a little more. Inquisitiveness is also not very deep, it is shallow as well, for it is only intellectual. The intellect is the same as scabies: if you scratch it a bit, it feels good. So the intellect goes on itching: Is there God? Is there any soul? Is there any salvation? What is meditation? – not that you want to do it. What is God? – not that you want to know it, but just for discussion, just for conversation. It is a mental exercise, an intellectual entertainment. So people only talk big, they never stake anything. Whether God is or is not, it is not truly their concern; and they remain untransformed whether God does exist or does not.

It is very interesting: one person believes there is a God, another believes there is no God, and the lives of the two are identical. If someone is abused, the one who believes there is a God gets angry, and the one who believes there is no God, he also gets angry. Sometimes it happens that the one who believes there is a God gets even more angry. The one who believes there is no God, how much can he do to you? At best he may abuse you in return, hit you or kill you. But the one who believes there is a God can send you to rot in the agonies of hell. He has more ways of becoming angry.

If belief in God or no belief in God does not bring about any change in one's life, it only means that it has no relation to God, it is only intellectual talk. Such inquisitiveness makes a man a philosopher. He goes on contemplating and deliberating, he learns the scriptures, accumulates too many doctrines, is able to think of all the pros and cons, holds debates, but he never lives.

If you are also only full of inquisitiveness there will be no journey at all. People full of inquisitiveness are those who sit near the milestone and ask, "What is the destination? How far is the destination?" They continue asking this but they never get up and begin to walk.

You know so much! What is there that is lacking in your knowing? You know almost everything – whatever Buddha knew or Mahavira or Krishna knew you also know. While reading the Gita, don't you feel you know all this? Yes, you also know, but this is all only in your head. The seed has not yet reached your heart. And the ideas that are only in the mind are like the seed lying on a stone. The seed is there, lying on the stone, but it cannot sprout. To sprout, the seed will have to fall down off the stone and seek the soil. And the surface of the soil is not suitable either, because more moisture is needed. So it has to move underneath the surface to where there is some water, where there is some juice flowing.

Seeds remain in the mind like those lying on the stone. Until they fall down into the heart the wet soil is not available. In the heart some juice flows, some love; there is some water there. If a seed falls there it sprouts.

Inquisitive people have a lot within them; everything is there, but it is like the seeds lying on the stone. The soil is not far off, but even this little journey is difficult for them. They are averse to moving, so the seed remains sitting on the rock. This small journey will have to be undertaken – that the seed falls down from the stone to the soil, seeks a place in the soil, finds some moisture, and hides itself a little inside the soil.

Remember, whatsoever is to be born in this world needs a deep silence, solitude and darkness. Those things that are kept in the mind are kept in the open light. Sprouting is not possible there. The heart is the wet soil hidden within you. There something can sprout.

Therefore those who live only in inquisitiveness become scholars and pundits; knowledgeable, but nothing sprouts within them – no new birth, no new life, no new flowers, nothing at all.

There is one more dimension of seeking: we call it *mumuksha*, a deep longing for liberation. Here there is no concern for knowing, the concern is for living. Here there is no concern for knowing, the concern is for being. The question is not whether there is a God or not, the question is whether I can *be* God. There may be a God, but if I cannot become God then there is no point in it all. The question is not whether there is any liberation, the question is whether I can also be liberated. If there is no possibility of my becoming liberated, then even if there is a liberation somewhere it is meaningless for me. The issue is not whether there is a soul within or not – there may be, there may not be – the real issue is whether I can become a soul.

Mumuksha, the longing for liberation, is a search to be. And when one wants to be, one has to put oneself at stake. This is why I say religion is a gambler's affair.

I will say only that which I know, which I have lived. If you agree to put all at stake, whatever is my experience can also become yours. Experiences do not belong to anyone; whosoever is ready to receive them, they come to him. Nobody has any right over the truth, whosoever is willing to disappear inherits it. Truth belongs to one who shows the readiness to ask for it – who opens the doors of his heart and calls for it.

This is why I have chosen this Upanishad. This Upanishad is a direct encounter with spirituality. There are no *siddhants*, doctrines, in it; in it there are only experiences of *siddhas*, the fulfilled ones. In it there is no discussion of that which is born out of curiosity or inquisitiveness, no; in it there are hints to those who are full of longing for liberation by those who already have attained liberation.

There are some people who have not attained, yet they are unable to drop the enjoyment of guiding others. Giving guidance is a very enjoyable thing. In the whole world, the thing that is given the most is guidance, and the thing least accepted is also guidance. Everybody gives, nobody takes.

Whenever you have an opportunity to give advice to someone you do not miss it. It is not necessary that you are capable of providing this advice; it is not necessary that whatever you are saying is your knowing at all, but when it comes to giving advice, the temptation or the joy of being a teacher is very difficult to overcome.

What is the joy in being a teacher? You suddenly, free of cost, are on the upper side and the other is on the lower side. If someone comes to you for a donation, how difficult you find it even to give a penny! The difficulty is that you have to give something from what you have. But in giving guidance you have no difficulty, because what difficulty can there be in giving what you do not have? You are losing nothing. On the contrary, you are gaining something: you are gaining joy, you are gaining ego-enhancement. Today you are in a position to guide, and the other is at the receiving end. You are on the top, the other is below.

This is why I say that, in this Upanishad, there is no pleasure of giving any advice or guidance; rather there is great pain, because what the seer of this Upanishad is giving, he is giving after knowing it. He is sharing something very intimate, very inner.

The hints are brief but deep. The hits are very few, but deadly. And, if you are willing, the arrow will pierce your heart directly and will not leave you alive. It will kill you. Therefore, be aware and be alert, because this very business is a dangerous one. You will have to lose what you think you are. In it, there is no way of achieving without losing yourself. Here only those who lose are the achievers.

That is also why I have chosen this Upanishad. In fact I can tell you directly, there is no reason for bringing the Upanishad in – but I will use it as an excuse, a shelter. If you shoot an arrow directly, the person can escape; but if it is hidden behind the Upanishad there are less chances of you missing it. I have selected the Upanishad so that you may not know that I am directly aiming at you. This way the chances of escape are minimized. All hunters know that better hunting is done from a hiding place. This Upanishad is only a hiding place.

I will say only what I have known, but then there is no difference between that and the Upanishad, because whatever the seer of this Upanishad has said, he also has known it.

This Upanishad is the manifestation of the subtlest mysteries of spirituality. But if I go on talking on the Upanishad only, there is a fear that the talk may remain merely talk. So the talks will be only a background, and along with it there will be experiments. Whatever is said, whatever the seer has seen, or whatever I say, and I have seen – there will be attempts to turn your face, to raise your eyes towards that. The attempt to raise your eyes towards that will be the main thing; the talk on the Upanishad will be only for creating a milieu. Such vibrations can be created all around you so that you forget the twentieth century and arrive in the world of the seer of this Upanishad, so that this world which has become so lusterless and ugly may disappear and the memories may arise of those days in which this seer lived. An atmosphere, a milieu – the Upanishad is only for that. But that is not enough; it is necessary, but not enough.

So whatever I say, if you just stop at hearing it I will know you have not heard it at all. Whoever does not set out on the journey after hearing this, I don't believe he has heard. If you think you have understood just by hearing...don't be in such a hurry! If it was possible to understand something only by hearing we would have understood long ago. If it was possible to understand something only by hearing there would be no shortage of people with understanding in the world and an ignorant person would be difficult to find. But as it is the world is full of only the ignorant.

Nothing is understood only by listening. By listening we only close our fists on words. Not by listening but by doing one understands. So listen to find the way of doing, not for the understanding. Listen in order to do, do in order to understand. Do not come to the conclusion that just by listening you have understood; that intermediary link of doing is necessary. There is no other way. But our mind says, "I have got it; now where is the need to do?"

Destinations are reached by moving towards them. You may have understood everything, the whole route of your journey may have been memorized by you, you may have a detailed map in your pocket; still, without moving no one ever comes to their destination. But it is possible to dream of having arrived. A person may be asleep right here and can dream of having arrived anywhere.... The mind is an expert in dreaming.

Don't think that only you see such dreams; even those whom you call very intelligent also go on having these dreams. Your saints, your monks and sannyasins – those who have been searching for years – have not come even an inch closer to anywhere. They have not even begun their journey at all and they have been searching for years! Their whole search has been circular. In the mind a circle has been created – a sort of whirlpool. And in that whirlpool they move round and round, and ultimately everything gets lost. All the Vedas, the Upanishads, the Korans, the Bibles – everything gets lost, but there is not even an inch of movement.

We will discuss the Upanishad not to make you understand the Upanishad, but for you to *become* the Upanishad. If by listening you memorize something and begin to repeat it, it means I have harmed you; I did not prove to be your friend. Your repeating what you have heard is of no value. When I can see that the same happens to you as has happened to me, that your eyes also open up, only then have you become the Upanishad.

Understand it this way: a poet sings a song about some flower. There can be a great sweetness, rhythm and music in this song – songs have their own beauty – but howsoever much the song may sing of the flower, yet the song is just a song, it is not the flower, it is not the fragrance of the flower. And if you are satisfied only with that song, then you have gone astray.

This Upanishad is a song of a flower that you have not yet seen. The song is wonderful: the singer has seen the flower. But do not be satisfied by the song, the song is not the flower.

It also happens that sometimes you too come close to the flower – only sometimes. Sometimes you too get a glimpse of the flower – accidentally, suddenly – because the flower is not foreign to you, it is your very nature. It is very close to you, just by your side. Sometimes it touches you, in spite of you. Sometimes the flower gives you a glimpse, a glimpse like a flash of lightning. In some moment it abruptly enters your experience: you feel that there is something more in this world, that this world that you know is not all that is. In this rocky world there is something else which is not a stone but is a flower, alive and blossoming. And if you have seen it in some dream, or a lightning flash in the dark of night…. You see something and it disappears again – thus it happens sometimes in your life. It often happens in the lives of the poets, it often happens in the lives of the painters, that a glimpse of the flower comes close by.

Yet, however close to the flower, however great a glimpse you may have had, this closeness is still a distance. No matter how close the flower may come to you, still the distance remains. And even if I can actually touch the flower with my hands, still it is not certain that the experience I am having is that of the flower, because the message is coming through my hand. The hand may give a wrong message. There is no certainty of my hand giving the right message: there is no reason to trust my hand implicitly. Again, the message that the hand will give will be less about the flower and more about itself.

If the flower feels cold, it is not necessary that the flower *is* cold; maybe my hand is feverish and that is why the flower is felt to be cold. The message is more about the hand, because whenever a message comes through a medium it is always relative. One cannot be absolutely certain about it.

I was reading a memoir written by Popov. Popov was a seeker, and an ardent seeker. She was practicing spiritual disciplines with Piotr Dimitrovich Ouspensky. Once she was sitting with Ouspensky and a gentleman came and asked him whether there is a God or not. Ouspensky exclaimed, "God? No, there is no God." Ouspensky paused a little and then said, "But I cannot say with any guarantee, because whatever I have known is through a medium. Sometimes I have seen through my eyes, but the eyes cannot be relied upon. Sometimes I have heard through my ears, but the ears can hear wrongly. Sometimes I have touched through my hands, but touch cannot be relied upon either. So far I have not seen directly, I have never been face to face. Therefore I cannot say with any guarantee. Whatever I have known so far, it has not given me any experience of God. But that does not prove that there is no God, it only informs you about what my experiences are. So I cannot give you any guarantee that God is not. But do not drop your search and believe me, go on searching for yourself."

Whenever something happens through a medium it is not trustworthy. Even if we come very close to a flower, still it is the eyes that see, the hands that touch, and the nose that gathers the fragrance. These are all experiences through our senses. Thus it is that sometimes a poet comes so close to that ultimate flower that its echo descends into his songs. But still he is not a Buddha, not a Mahavira.

Who is Buddha? Who is Mahavira? Buddha is that consciousness which has become the flower itself; even that much distance, that of seeing the flower, does not exist. Consciousness has become the flower.

Only by becoming the flower can one fully know what is.

These are statements of a seer of the Upanishad. It is like a song about some flower. Go on humming it – there is a lot of sweetness and an exquisite taste in it, but it is not the flower, it is only a song. If you make the effort you will sometimes see the flower.

People come to me and say, "There was a great light during the meditation, but I lost it again. Infinite light was there, but it disappeared again. There was immense bliss, but where has it gone now?" Now they are searching for it again and cannot find it.

A glimpse means you had come close. But glimpses are bound to be lost. Meditation can, at the most, give only a glimpse. But do not stop there; do not get stuck looking for that same glimpse again and again. The only purpose of meditation is that one gets a glimpse. Then one has to go ahead, into *samadhi,* into enlightenment, so that one becomes the very flower.

In meditation is a glimpse; samadhi is being it.

Do not stop at glimpses. They are very lovely: the whole world starts looking stale – just one glimpse of that living flower, that flowering which is within, and the whole world becomes insipid and meaningless. But then some people catch hold of the glimpses and start repeating them and think everything has happened. No, until you are the divine yourself, do not believe that God is.

You can be it, because you already are it. You have only to open up a little, to uncover a little. You are present here and now, just hiding. There are only a few layers of clothes covering you – and they too are very thin – so that if you so desire you can throw them off right now, be free of them, and be the divine. But your clinging is very strong; though the clothes are thin, your grip is very tight. Why is this clinging so strong? The clinging is strong because we think that these clothes are our being, that this is what we are. Besides that we do not know of any other existence.

In this Upanishad there will be hints of that existence which is beyond these coverings. And along with this Upanishad we will meditate, so we can get a glimpse. And we will hope for samadhi, enlightenment, so that we become that without which there is no contentment, no peace, and no truth.

The Upanishad begins with prayer. The prayer is addressed to the whole universe.

May the sun god give us his benediction.
May Varuna, Aryama, Indra, Brahaspati
and Vishnu give us their benediction.
Salutations to that Brahman.

O Vayu, salutations especially to you,
because you are the Brahman manifest.
I shall call only you the manifest Brahman.
I shall also call you the truth, the rit – the law.
May they protect me, the speaker –
and my master.

The Upanishad begins with this prayer. The journey of religion has begun with a prayer. It has to be so. Prayer means trust and hope. Prayer means our feeling of being one with the whole universe. Prayer means, "How would I be able to manage alone?"

If it were possible that you alone could make this happen, it would have happened long ago. But by yourself even the trivial could not be achieved. You had desired money, you could not achieve even that. You had wished for position, you could not manage even that. You had all sorts of wishes, large and small, but none were fulfilled. Alone you could not even manage the world: would this great journey of truth be possible by yourself alone? By yourself, you are even defeated in the world.

Everyone is defeated in this world. Even those who appear to be victorious are also defeated. They only appear victorious to others; in themselves they are utterly defeated. You also appear to yourself as defeated, but to others you appear victorious. There are people behind you who feel that you have achieved, that you have won in the worldly battle. But if we look within man, everyone is defeated.

This world is a long story of defeats. Here victory just does not happen, here victory just cannot happen; it is not in the nature of the world. Defeat is the destiny here. Defeat is not of any individual, not of any person, but the destiny of being in the world is defeat. You will have to accept defeat there. Nobody ever wins there.

We could not win in the world where the only concern was with petty things, where it was just a dream – Shankara calls it *maya*, an illusion. When we were defeated even in that illusion, in that dreamlike happening, how then can we hope to win on our own in the world of truth?

Prayer means the realization of a person who has been defeated in the world. When even after trying for lives upon lives he has been defeated in the mundane, what capability can he claim in matters of the sacred and the absolute?

Hence the prayer. Hence the seer has invoked the whole universe to help him. He has invoked the sun, he has invoked Varuna. All these names are symbolic of the powers of the universe. The sun has been invoked first because the sun is our life. Without him, we wouldn't be. Within us, it is the sun that lives, burns. If the sun is extinguished there, we will be extinguished here. The sun is our life, hence he has been invoked.

The seer says: *Salutations to Vayu, the god of air* – Vayu has been especially saluted in this prayer – *because you are the Brahman manifest*. It is a bit strange. Think a little. It is very interesting, because Vayu is absolutely unmanifest; all other things are manifest. Had the seer said to the sun, "You are the manifest Brahman" – radiant, burning, hot, living – it would have been understandable. But the seer did not call the sun "manifest Brahman"; he said that to Vayu, whom we cannot see at all, who is really unmanifest.

Where is that Vayu manifest? We only infer that it is, we only feel that it is, but it cannot be seen. Where is it available to the eye? Manifest means that which can be seen by the eyes. Now, Vayu is not at all available to the eyes. Rocks, mountains, they are all visible, but not Vayu.

But the seer says: *Oh Vayu! Salutations to you, because you are the manifest Brahman*. He said so because Vayu, the air, is not visible but still is; it is not seen by the eye, nevertheless it is touching the eye each moment – and the same is the situation with the supreme truth. It is not seen but it is touching us every moment.

Vayu is not seen because we do not have the eyes to see it. Vayu is simply there. Without Vayu we cannot exist. Vayu is in our breath, protecting us, and our very life depends on its inhalation and exhalation. Something which is so near us, which is our very breath, we cannot see because our eyes are very gross. Whatever is very gross, that is what we see. Whatever is subtle, we are unable to see.

Vayu, the air, is very subtle. It is present before us; it is within us and without us. It is present in every cell of our body, but not visible. That is why it is said: *You are the manifest Brahman* – you are just like the Brahman.

Brahman is present here but not visible. And it is present in our every fiber; in fact, it *is* the fiber and yet we see no trace of it. That is why Vayu has been saluted – because we know the Vayu but not the Brahman. A thread of relationship has been attempted, that Brahman is just like Vayu, the air.

"I will call you the manifest Brahman," the seer says, "I will also name you the truth and *rit*, the law, because you are just like that which is and is not known to us; who we ourselves are and yet whom we do not know; who is now and here since eternity and not known by us. But this search may be fulfilled, if all the gods protect us."

What is meant by gods is the endless number of life-forces since eternity. And life is a vast network of endless numbers of forces. Your existence is also a vast network of these endless powers. Within you meet the sun, Varuna, Indra, Vayu; Agni, the fire; Prithvi, the earth; Akash, the sky – they all meet. If we can know one individual in his totality we have known the whole of the existence in seed form. Everything is there in the individual, everything has united in him, and in their meeting the individual exists.

So prayer is for the help of all these. But will the sun help? That question does arise. Even if the prayers are done, will the sun help or will the Vayu help or will the earth help? The question is not of the earth's help or the sun's help, but that you prayed – that is the great help! Let this be understood properly.

No sun is coming to help you, but you prayed and it will affect you, not the sun, because a prayerful mind becomes humble, a prayerful mind becomes helpless, a prayerful mind accepts the fact that alone it cannot accomplish anything; a prayerful mind is ready to dissolve and give up its ego and the feeling that it can do it. And these things bring results. The whole outcome of the prayer is on you. The prayer does not change the sun, but you. And the moment you change, you enter into another world.

Normally, when you pray you think that someone is going to do something for you, and that is why you pray. No, prayer is only a device. Certainly you join your hands in prayer towards someone else, but its consequences happen within you – in the one who has joined hands in prayer.

Thus there are difficulties in understanding it. If you pray in the presence of a scientist, "Oh sun, help me!" the scientist will say, "What nonsense! How can the sun help you? When has the sun ever helped anyone?" Or you pray, "O Indra, bring rains!" and he will say, "Have you gone mad? Have rains ever fallen by prayers?" The scientist is right.

Neither the sun nor the clouds nor the winds will listen to you. None will listen to you. But the fact that you called out will transform you. How intensely you called will create an equally deep intensity within you. If your whole being calls out, you will become a totally different person.

This is what prayer is for.

Enough for today.

WE ARE IN IT!

CHAPTER 2

In the cavity of the heart, which is situated within the body, an unborn eternal lives.

❋

Earth is its body, it dwells within the earth but the earth does not know it.
Water is its body, it dwells within the water but the water does not know it.
Light is its body, it dwells within the light but the light does not know it.
Air is its body, it dwells within the air but the air does not know it.
Sky is its body, it dwells within the sky but the sky does not know it.
Mind is its body, it dwells within the mind but the mind does not know it.
Intellect is its body, it dwells within the intellect but the intellect does not know it.
Ego is its body, it dwells within the ego but the ego does not know it.
Reasoning mind is its body, it dwells within the reasoning mind but the reasoning mind does not know it.

The unmanifest is its body, it dwells within the unmanifest but the unmanifest does not know it.
The indestructible is its body, it dwells within the indestructible but the indestructible does not know it.
Death is its body, it dwells within death but death does not know it.

✳

It is the innermost self of all these elements,
its sins are all destroyed,
and it is the one divine god Narayana –
the sustainer of all human beings.

✳

The body, the senses, etcetera, are non-soul matter, and the feeling of 'I-myness' over them is adhyas – illusion.
Therefore, an intelligent person should drop this illusion through allegiance to Brahman –
the absolute reality.

A fish in the sea remains as a stranger to the sea, not because the sea is far away from the fish but because the sea is too close. Whatsoever is at a distance is seen but what is very near becomes invisible to the eye. It is not difficult to know the distant, it is difficult to know what is close. And it is impossible to know that which is the closest of the close. Let this be understood properly, because it is something that must be known for the inner journey.

People ask where to seek God. They ask, "How did we forget that which is hidden within? How has that been separated which is nearer to us than our heartbeats, which is nearer to us than our breathing? How has that been forgotten which I myself am?" And their question seems to be logical. It appears that what they are asking has validity and that it should not have happened like this.

If I am unable to know even that which is hidden within me, if even what I am remains unknown, then who else will we know, who else will we recognize? When even the near slips out of the hand, how could we achieve that which is far? And it is not that it has only come close to us today; it has always been close to us, since endless time. Not even for a single moment have we been separated or away from it. Wherever we run, it runs with us; wherever we go, it goes with us. It travels with us to hell as well as to heaven; it stands by us in sin as well as in virtue. It is not right to say that it stands by us, because even in 'standing by' there is some distance. Actually our being and its being are one and the same thing.

If this is true, then it is a great miracle in the world that we have lost our own selves – which sounds impossible. How can one lose one's own self? It is not possible even to lose our shadow, and we have lost our souls. How it is possible? But this has happened. How this losing of the self takes place, that is the essence of this sutra. Before we enter into the sutra let us understand its basic foundations.

Eyes have a limit of vision, a range. If an object is beyond that range the eyes cannot see it. If an object is within that range but too far to either side, then too the eyes cannot see it. Eyes have a range of vision. A thing brought too close to the eyes cannot be seen and taken too far away also it cannot be seen. Beyond either side of a certain range of vision the eyes cannot see, they are then blind. Now, you are so near yourself that you are not only near the eyes but you are behind them – and that is the problem.

Let us understand it this way. If you are standing before a mirror, at a certain distance your image is very clear. If you move too far away from the mirror there will be no image. If you come too close to the mirror, so much so that you put your eyes against it, then you cannot see your image at all. But here the situation is that you are standing behind the mirror; thus there is no possibility of there being any image of you in the mirror – the eyes are in the front and you are behind them.

Eyes see that which is in front of them. How are the eyes to see that which is behind them? Ears hear that which is outside the ears. How are the ears to hear that which is within the ears? Eyes open outwards, ears also open outwards. I can touch you, but how can I touch myself? And even if I am able to touch my body, it is just because I am not the body – the body too is the other, hence I am able to touch it. But how can I touch the one that I am, the one that is touching? With what can I touch?

Therefore the hands touch everything but cannot touch themselves. The eyes see everything but cannot see themselves. In regard to our own selves we are blind; none of the senses that are known to us are of any use. Unless some other senses open up – some eye that can see withinwards, backwards, in the reverse, or some ear that is affected also by the inner sound – there is no way we would be able to see and hear and know ourselves. Till that happens there is no way of touching our own selves. What is near is missed; what is nearest of all is not possible to be known. This is why the fish is not able to know the sea.

The second thing: a fish is born in the sea, it lives in the sea; the sea is its food, the sea is its drink, the sea is its life, the sea is its everything. Then it dies and dissolves into the sea, but it never gets the opportunity to know the sea because it does not have any distance from the sea. A fish, however, comes to know what the sea is if someone comes and lifts it out of the sea. This is a very contradictory thing: the fish comes to know the sea when it is away from the sea – when it is struggling for its life on the sand under the hot sun, then it knows what the sea is. For knowing, this much distance is necessary.

How can we know the one that existed even before we were born and that will remain even after we are dead? How can we know the one in which we are born and in which we shall disappear? For knowing, some separation is a must. That is why the fish does not know the sea; only when someone throws it out onto the shore does it come to know.

Man is in a greater difficulty. The divine is the ocean that surrounds us. It has no shores to it where you can be thrown out, where you may start writhing with pain like a fish. It would have been very easy if there was such a shore, but there is no such shore. God is the ocean. This is why those who look for God as a shore are never able to find him. The shore is available only to those who are ready to drown in the ocean of the divine.

There simply is no shore so there is no way to find it. How can there be a shore? Everything else can have a shore; the whole cannot have a shore – because something else is needed to form the shore. The bank of a river is formed of something other than the river. The shore of the sea is formed of something other than the sea. But there is nothing other than God which can form the shore.

The very meaning of God is that there exists nothing other than it. God does not mean someone sitting somewhere up in the sky and administering the world from there. No, these are stories for children. What is meant by God is that element other than which nothing exists. This is the scientific definition of God.

God means the whole, the total, everything – whatever is. What is cannot have a shore, because there remains nothing else to form the coast. Therefore God is everywhere; there is no shore. One who is ready to drown is saved. One who tries to be saved, drowns.

We are in it. We are in what we are trying to find.

There is no need to call who we go on calling, because there is not even that much gap that one has to call. That is why Kabir asked, "Has your God gone deaf that you shout your *ajan* so loudly?" God is so near that there is no need even to call him. Even if there is silence within, that too will be heard – he is so near. If you have to call the other, you have to speak. But for calling oneself, where is the need to speak at all? One can hear others only when words are spoken, but even one's own silence is heard.

Being so near is the difficulty. Let this be understood properly: we have missed the truth because we are born in it. Our flesh, the marrow, the bones, the whole body is made of it. It is our breath, our life, everything. In numerous ways, through numerous doors, we are combinations of it – we are its play. There is no gap at all, therefore there is no memory; therefore its remembrance has become impossible. Therefore we see the world, but the truth is not seen at all. The world is at a distance, there is a gap between the two; this is why the passion for the world arises.

What is the meaning of passion? Passion means an attempt to close the distance between you and the object from which you have a feeling of distance. There is no passion for God because there is no distance between you and God. Or even if someone seems to be searching for God, it looks like a false passion. The person seems to be searching for something else in the name of God. He is making God an excuse but he wants something else. Maybe he wants power, maybe he wants prestige, wealth, position or something else.

A friend came and told me, "Since the time I began to absorb myself in meditation experiments in your camps, I have been benefiting greatly."

I asked, "What benefit are you getting?"

He replied, "Spiritual benefit there is none, but financial benefit has begun!"

Very good! Where is the haste for the spiritual? – it can be post-poned. Monetary benefit is the immediate need!

We search for something while we call it something else. Wher-ever we have put the label God, if we tear the label off we will find something else underneath. We want something else. A person who wants something else in the name of God is more dishonest than the person who is openly seeking worldly pleasures. At least there there is honesty, an authenticity. One person says, "I want money," another says, "I want sexual pleasures," still another says, "I want position, I want ego fulfillment," and there is one who says, "I want God," but in this desire for God is also his feeling that one day he will show to the world that God too is in his fist.

Therefore, watch the seeker of God carefully. If his ego is increasing, understand that his search is for something else; if his ego is decreasing, shattering, disappearing, then his search is really for God.

The conceit of sannyasins and your so-called saints is well known; even the conceit of big politicians stands nowhere against it. At least the politician's very search is for that conceit, so it is fine; it is a clear-cut matter, there is nothing much of a fabrication in it. The fun of being something special is the whole game for them. But for a saint the matter is different. He says that he is in search of being nothing...and he then goes on becoming some-thing. If two saints meet, they cannot be made to sit on the same dais because there will be problems as to who sits where, higher or lower. So usually saints simply do not meet each other, because many problems arise.

There is a friend who is a little crazy – crazy in the sense that he tries to arrange for saints to meet with each other. He told me once that great problems surfaced. Even such questions arise as to who should join hands first in greeting. A difficult situation. Even worldly people do not look so worldly. They may not be wanting to greet somebody with folded hands, yet they do it. In their minds they may think that it would have been better had the other folded hands first, but they hide such feelings; it looks ungentlemanly.

To some saints it does not appear even ungentlemanly – these saints do not even respond to greetings, they have stopped the very arrangement. They only give blessings.

That friend was busy arranging a meeting of such a saint with another. The other saint said, "Everything else is okay, but if I do not greet him and he immediately gives me blessings, that will spoil everything."

Our search is for something else, it has nothing to do with religion or with the divine. We are desiring something else, we are asking for something else, but we are dishonest and we have covered ourselves with claims that are different. How can the search for God begin? – because there is no distance. If there is a distance, a passion arises. If there is a distance, one feels like running. If there is a distance, a desire arises to win. If there are difficulties, ego becomes interested to defeat, to win. But as far as God is concerned, there is no distance. The situation is that God is already with us.

When Tensing and Hillary climb Mount Everest, what is their joy? They are the first in human history to stand on the highest peak. There is nothing else on Everest. But the first man on Everest! – history is created; the ego finds importance in the act. Now as long as there is Mount Everest in the world, the names of Hillary and Tensing cannot be effaced.

There was so much competition to reach the moon until recently. It is very interesting to know what we have left behind on the moon. Those who reached the moon were Christians, but they did not leave a statue of Jesus there, they have left the flag of America. Just think: flags are real, Jesus is unreal! Even the idea did not cross the minds of the Americans to take at least a small statue of Jesus. They took the flag! The flag is the real ego of man. And if the name of Jesus is remembered sometimes, that too means a kind of a flag, it does not mean anything else. When it is a question of fighting, of keeping the flag aloft, at those times Jesus, Rama, Krishna, Buddha are all remembered; but their use is also not more than that of a flag. They are also a flag on the ego of man.

On the moon we have left behind flags. Man is busy desiring to find something which only he can do so that his ego acquires importance. But if you were born on Everest then you would be in great difficulty as to where to hoist the flag.

Man is born in God; only he is. You are already there, you have never gone away. That is your land on which you are already standing. Therefore, in attaining God there is no scope for any ego. Ego is not interested in it. Then how can any longing or thirst arise when there is no desire for God?

A thirst for the divine arises in a very strange way. Understand this properly, because there is no other way than this. A thirst for the world arises because of the distance. If the distance is impassable, the attraction becomes tremendous. And this is why, in the world, whenever things are achieved one's interest in them is lost, because the distance is covered. You desired a woman, you found her; you desired to build a house, you built it; you desired to raise a gold spire on your house and you put it there – what next?

So whatever is achieved, it then becomes worthless because it has come close to you, it is not distant anymore. If it is distant and there are difficulties in the way so that not everyone can achieve it, only then you feel the thrill, the joy of it.

The joy of richness is not in the richness itself, it is in the poverty of many others. If everybody becomes rich, the whole thing is spoiled. That is the problem in America: the joy of being rich is becoming less and less. The poor are wearing the same type of clothes as the rich, driving the same type of cars, living in similar houses. There is not much basic difference between the rich and the poor. The fun of the rich is getting spoiled. The rich are feeling troubled due to it; they are searching for new tricks which only they should be able to enjoy.

We are in God, hence there is no call, no invitation in it for the ego; there is no challenge, no motivation for the ego. How then can the longing for the divine arise? The longing for worldly things arises due to their distance and due to their challenge and calling. The longing for God arises from the failure of worldly things.

Let this be understood. When you have run in all the directions and are defeated everywhere; when you have achieved everything and it has all proved worthless; when your search for things is complete, and with the completion arises their negation, everything comes to a zero; then only arises the longing for God. All things appear gold from a distance, but they all prove to be a lump of mud as they reach your hands. The longer the distance, the purer the gold. As it starts coming closer it starts becoming more impure. Even more close and it starts turning into clay.

There is the story about Midas of Greece – there is a great satire in it. Midas was blessed with a supernatural power; the gift from the deity was that whatever he touched became gold. We are all the reverse of Midas: whatever we touch becomes a lump of mud!

But it is very interesting.... Even Midas was in great trouble – how can there be any end to our troubles? Whatsoever Midas touched became gold. He touched his wife, she became gold. He touched his food, it became gold. He picked up a glass of water, before it reached his lips it became gold. Poor Midas! He was in great difficulty. You cannot quench your thirst with gold. No matter how much we may talk about "a body like glittering gold," no satisfaction will arise from such a body. No matter how much a lover may praise the body of his beloved as "a body of gold," he should realize what happens if that body really becomes gold. He would beat his head if that ever happened. He would feel that the earlier body was better.

So Midas was in a great difficulty. He was attracted to gold by the talk of the poets. Now what? Everything became gold – his wife, water, food! People began to run away from him. His own children started keeping a distance from him – who knows when he may touch you! No friends would come near him. Midas became very lonely. He was a king, and he became lonely. His ministers would not come too close to him; they would keep a safe distance so they could run away if necessary. Midas started dying of hunger. He could not take any food, he could not take any water. He started shrieking and shouting, "Oh, God, take back your gift! I was better as I was before! This blessing has turned into a curse."

Midas was in such a state – everything that he touched was turning into gold. Just imagine what our condition would be if whatever we touched turned into a lump of clay. The wife appears to be beautiful and golden when she is at a distance; the day the marriage takes place she begins turning into dust. Within four or five years she becomes as good as dirt. Everything turns into dirt.

The day you realize that all running is futile you come to a dead stop right where God is. The day you come to know that you have not gained anything by running, you do not run anymore. And because of not running, now you see what was not seen before because of running.

When the mind was engrossed in running, things that were far away were seen. When the running becomes useless, the eyes return to the nearer scene. And if the running ceases totally, the eyes start seeing in reverse. Until now they were seeing only outside, now they begin to see inwards. The mirror performs an about-turn. Then you do not find anything worth seeing in the world, or worth getting and worth searching for in the world. Now the world does not remain a desire anymore. That is why Buddha, Mahavira and the Upanishads have laid so much stress on the fact that desirelessness is the door.

Desire is a door to go far away; desirelessness is a door to come near.

Let us now understand this sutra: "Within the body is hidden the unborn and eternal."

It is never born, it is there forever and ever. The eternal and unborn is hidden within the body but the body does not know it. Body is part of the earth; it is hidden within the earth but the earth does not know it. In this sutra the same thing is repeated from different angles.

The unborn and the eternal is hidden within fire, but the fire does not know it. It is hidden everywhere, but the one behind which it is hidden does not know it because the one behind which it is hidden is running outside. Have you ever realized this? If you can experience the inward running of your body you will attain *samadhi*. You have experienced only the outside running of the body – a beautiful body is seen and a thrill runs through your body; every cell of your body begins to run after it. A beautiful flower is seen and the eyes begin to run. A sweet melody is heard and the ears begin to run.

The body is always running outwards. Have you ever experienced the body running inwards? No, you have not. Then how is the poor body to know who is hidden within? Where the body never goes, where the body never looks, never hears, never explores...how can the body know what is there within? Therefore the body remains a stranger to the one whose body it is. All the running is outwards, hence an ignorance prevails inside. This sutra is a repetition of the same thing from different doors.

What is hidden within the air, the air does not know. Mind does not know the one whose body it is. The ego is unaware of the one whose body it is. The reasoning mind, the imperishable, the un-manifest – they all do not know the one whose body they are and who is hidden within them. Even death remains unacquainted with the one whose death happens. This statement is a little strange: Death remains unacquainted with the one who dies. Nothing dies when one dies.

When death happens, who actually dies? Nobody. Body does not die, because it has always been dead; there is no question of its dying. The one who is hidden within the body is eternally immortal; there is no question of its dying either. Only the relationship breaks. In death the relationship between the dead and the immortal breaks. But death itself, even after coming so close, remains ignorant of the one that is immortal.

How many times have we died, and yet so far we have not come to know that the one which is immortal is within us. This very situation means that even in coming close we are unable to look inwards; our seeing continues to focus itself outwards. See a man lying on his deathbed: he still goes on looking outwards. Even now he does not feel like looking within. Death is pulling and dragging him from the body, but he still clings to the body – clings more forcefully, more than ever before.

This is why old people become ugly and the young look beautiful. If we look at it deeply, the reason for this is not the body alone. The young person does not cling to the body, he is still confident of it. The old person begins to cling to the body; and because of that clinging, all sorts of ugliness is born. The old person begins to be afraid: here comes death...now comes death ...death is close by. The more the old person is afraid of death, the more strongly he clings to life. And the more strongly the person clings to life, the more ugly he becomes.

How lovely children look! They simply do not cling at all. They have no idea that death exists. Look at the birds and the animals: however old they become they look the same. I am talking of those animals and those birds who are not yet spoiled through the company of man. Man just spoils everything. So it appears very strange that in the jungle the birds and the animals do not appear to become old. The kind of old age that catches man does not seem to catch birds and animals. They remain like children. In some deep sense they are not aware at all that death will be coming, therefore there is no clinging to the body.

The freshness that is in children is because life is natural, there is no fear of death. It becomes difficult in old age; death becomes clearer. Life is an effort now, the old man lives by effort. Every inch of the journey he is conscious of death now. That creates an uncertainty; tension grows within him and anxiety and anguish catch hold of him permanently, and that turns the mind ugly.

Death itself does not come to know the immortal hiding within the body. The only reason for this is that the phenomenon of looking inwards happens only when the looking outwards becomes futile and meaningless. Let this be understood properly. It seems to become meaningless many times, but it does not really become so. It is not that the meaninglessness does not dawn upon you – it *does* dawn upon you. You were thinking of buying a car and you bought it. When you had not bought it you were dreaming about it in the night. The night before the day of its delivery you could not even sleep well – the whole night!

Someone has written about his friend who purchased a very beautiful car, a Ferarri. It was a costly car. On the very first day he was driving it, the car was a little scratched.

That friend was not a child, he was a fifty-year-old man; and he was not an illiterate, he was a professor in a university – and a professor of philosophy at that. But he was seen weeping that day, resting his head on his mother's shoulder. Just because the Ferarri got scratched! The car was costly. How much he must have dreamed about it. That scratching of the car must have entered deep into him, to his very soul; that is why he wept.

Weeping you all do. That man must have been more honest. On the open road, resting his head on the shoulder of his mother, he started weeping. But how long will this state last? In a few days the Ferarri will become old. After a month or two this man will be sitting in the same car and he will not even feel in what car he is sitting. He will get bored with this car – but not with cars. Dreams of some other car will catch hold of him. He may think of owning a Rolls Royce now, or some other car. Mind will get bored with one woman or one man, but it will not get bored with woman as such or man as such.

We all get bored, but our boredom remains tied to particular things. But the very reality of this boredom does not become a part of our experience. When we are tired of one thing we just select another new one of the same type, and this process continues forever. This is the only difference between you and a buddha.

You get bored with one woman but your interest continues in another woman. If you are bored with your wife, your interest continues in someone else's wife. Whatever is near and available becomes useless, but what is at a distance sustains your interest. That thing at a distance will also become useless tomorrow when it comes close to you. But it is not possible that all things can come near one. Some things continue to remain at a distance; thus the interest continues, the desires go on racing.

Getting bored with one woman, a buddha is bored with all women. Living in one palace, a buddha has lived in all palaces. For a buddha, just one happening is enough. This is a scientific approach. If one drop of water has been known, then the whole sea has been known. He would be a mad scientist who continues to go on testing all the oceans and saying, "When I complete the tests of all the drops of all the oceans, I will make a statement that water is made up of hydrogen and oxygen." We are in a similar kind of madness. A scientist tests just one drop, discovers that water is made up of hydrogen and oxygen atoms, and that H_2O is the equation for its constituents, and the matter is over for him. All the water of all the seas is now known. Wherever there is water, even on any other planets – and the scientists say there are at least fifty thousand earths like ours – or anywhere in the universe, it will be made up of the same arrangement of atoms: H_2O.

All water is known by knowing one drop.

Understanding the pattern and the behavior of one desire, he comes to know the whole nature of all desires and becomes a buddha. Knowing one desire, he who sees its futility – the compulsory futility – and its unavoidable failure, his desires simply drop. The desires drop like the crutches of a lame person falling down suddenly. He was walking with the help of the crutches; he had no feet to walk, he had wooden feet. Suddenly the crutches fall down and the lame person collapses. A similar thing happens when the crutches of desires drop. There are no real feet to walk on in the worldly life; they are artificial, wooden, made of desires. Desires falling away are the crutches falling down, and one suddenly finds oneself there – from where he had never moved, where he has always been, in his true nature. That is God, that is soul.

The end part of the sutra explains this:

> Death is its body, it dwells within death but
> death does not know it.
> It is the innermost self of all these elements,

its sins are all destroyed,
and it is the one divine god Narayana.
The body, the senses, etcetera, are all non-soul
matter, and the feeling of 'I-myness' over them is
adhyas – illusion.
Therefore, an intelligent person should drop this
illusion through allegiance to Brahman –
the absolute reality.

The last thing is this sutra. The race after desires is due to the fact that some dream always appears to be coming to its fulfillment somewhere in the far distance. A person looks in the desert, sees a lake of water near the horizon, runs for the water, and on reaching there discovers that there is no water, that there is nothing but sand and sand. But then the lake appears somewhere else. This is called an illusion.

When the sun's rays become hot and are reflected on sand, the vibrating rays create an illusion of ripples and waves. The ripples and waves are so continuous that a sort of vast, reflecting stretch of surface appears. If a tree is nearby, even that tree will be reflected in that surface, which acts like a mirror. When from a distance you see not only water but even the reflections of the passing clouds in water, how can you disbelieve? If there are also reflections of rows of birds flying in the sky in the so-called water, and if the nearby trees are also getting reflected in the water, your confidence as to the existence of the water is confirmed. Not only waves are seen, even the reflections in the waves are seen. But as you go nearer the reflections cease to appear, and on reaching the spot you find nothing but sand.

Adhyas, or illusion, means seeing what is not there. Shankara loved this word very much, and for the Upanishads it is very fundamental. Adhyas means projection, seeing what is not there: what is seen is not really there, you are projecting it from within. You are the cause of the projection.

A face appears beautiful to you: is that beauty there or are you projecting it?...because tomorrow the same face can appear ugly to you. Maybe it did not appear beautiful to you yesterday. Today suddenly your divine eye has opened up and the face has begun to look beautiful to you. To your friends it still does not look beautiful.

It is said that Laila was not beautiful, it was only to Majnu that she looked beautiful. The whole village was troubled, and people tried to persuade Majnu: "You are naive. There were many other more beautiful girls in the village; you are unnecessarily obsessed with Laila." Majnu replied, "If you want to see Laila, you have to have the eyes of Majnu." This is adhyas, illusion. The question is not of Laila but of the eyes of Majnu. The question is not of what is being seen but of the one who is seeing her. So Majnu said, "See with my eyes, then you will be able to see Laila." There is no doubt that with the eyes of Majnu she will look beautiful. If it were possible to borrow Majnu's eyes, then Laila would appear to you as beautiful as she appeared to Majnu.

Eyes are also a type of spectacles. The colors of the spectacles get projected onto the objects seen. All your senses are projecting. You are creating a world all around you. Your mind is not only a receiver, it is a creator as well. You are creating a world all around you – of beauty, of fragrance, of this, of that.

This world is not as you see it. It is dependent on you. If you change, the world also changes. A young man sees one world, an old man sees another, and children see yet another. What makes the differences? The world is the same. But the children do not have the same eyes that the young man has. Children are still interested in collecting stones and pebbles – just the colorfulness of things is enough. The young man says, "Throw them away! What is in them? What value do they have?" For a young man money has become valuable. He has started understanding the value of money. Now collecting stones and pebbles won't do. Now it is no use running after butterflies.

Children are catching butterflies; they look heavenly to them. The young man takes children to be ignorant, but when the man becomes old his senses get tired, his experiences turn sour and bitter, and he feels as if his mouth is full of a kind of tastelessness. Now even young people appear like children to this man. For him, young people are running after different kinds of butterflies. Only the kind of butterflies has changed, but not the butterflies as such.

Old people go on saying, explaining, that these are butterflies, but no young man listens to them. They themselves had not listened to their fathers and grandfathers. There is a reason for not listening, and that is that they have different eyes. If the young man receives the eyes of an old man he will see the same. And remember, the interesting thing is that if the old man can receive the eyes of the young again, he will forget all these experiences. He will forget all this wisdom he is displaying; the world once again will become colorful to him.

I have heard: a chief justice of the Supreme Court of America had come to Paris when he was young and got married. After thirty years, when he became old, and after his children had also got married and had visited Paris, the chief justice came again to Paris with his wife. His name was Peare. He saw Paris, and said to his wife, "It is not the same Paris. Its colorfulness has gone. Beautiful were those days in Paris when we came here for the first time. Everything was incomparable; Paris was different!"

His wife replied, "Excuse me, you have forgotten. The first time we came Peare was different; Paris is still the same. If you can see Paris with the eyes of a young man, it is still the same. How can Paris change?" People change and their vision changes.

If the world appears changed with the change in your vision, understand well that what you had seen and thought it to be was only adhyas, an illusion. It was created by your projections, it was not the world as it is. Is there any way that the world can be seen without your projections? If there is, only then one would see the world as it is.

Projections are illusions. Therefore, remember, seeing does not mean just seeing with the eyes. Seeing means such a state when all your projections cease, when you have no viewpoints. When you do not have your individual eyes to impose conditions, when you have no emotions and desires to project, then seeing happens.

See the desert when you are not thirsty: the desert cannot deceive you then. Deception happens because of the thirst. You want water, and when you do not get it the desire becomes more intense. And when desire is too intense, your mind goes insane and it wants to believe even in that which actually is not there.

But there is a state where all visions cease and seeing arises. When do the visions cease? Visions cease only when all desires cease, because every vision is a game of your desires, an extension of your desires.

The sutra says:

> *The body, the senses, etcetera, are all non-soul*
> *matter, and the feeling of 'I-myness' over them*
> *is illusion.*
> *Therefore, an intelligent person should drop this*
> *illusion through allegiance to Brahman,*
> *the absolute reality.*

Through allegiance to Brahman – allegiance to the self.

Our allegiance is always to the other, to somebody else, not to our own self. We are running after other things, not towards our own center. We are always going somewhere else, avoiding the one which is within.

Allegiance to Brahman means that the race of desires is gone, one has arrived at one's self. One has come to the place where there is no mind, no senses, no body, but only pure consciousness. In being rooted there, all illusions are at once shattered; then there is no world but only Brahman, the absolute reality.

When I am speaking in Hindi – many people do not understand Hindi but they can also utilize this occasion. Those who do not understand Hindi should close their eyes and listen just to the sound. They should sit in silence as if in meditation. And many times the truth that one does not understand through the words one comes to understand merely by listening to the sound.

When I am speaking in English, friends who do not understand English should not think that this is of no use to them. They should close their eyes and meditate on the sound of my words without attempting to understand the language. There is no need to try to understand a language which you do not know. Sit silently, become like an ignorant person, and meditate upon the impact of the sound. Just listen. That listening will become meditation and it will be beneficial.

The real question is not the understanding, but to become silent. Hearing is not the point, becoming silent is the point. So many times what happens is that what you have understood becomes a barrier, and it is good to listen to something that you do not understand at all; then thinking cannot interfere. When something is not understood there is no way for thoughts to move; they simply stop.

Therefore, listening sometimes to the wind passing through the trees, to the birds singing, to the sound of running water, is better than listening to the seers and sages. The real Upanishads are flowing there, but you will not understand them. And if you do and you can just listen, your intellect will soon quiet down because it is not needed. And when your intellect quiets, you are transported to the place you are in search of.

Enough for today.

THE
WITNESS AND
THE ILLUSION

C H A P T E R   3

Knowing oneself as sakshi pratyagatma,
the inner witnessing soul of one's intellect and all
its dispositions, and acquiring the disposition that
"That am I," giving up the claim of 'mine'
over all things.

❊

Giving up following lok, the society, he gives up
following the body also.
Giving up following the scriptures,
he gives up the illusion of the soul also.

❊

Being rooted in his own soul, and through
techniques, through listening and through self-
experiencing, the yogin comes to know himself as
the soul of all and his mind is annihilated.

❊

Without giving opportunity to sleep, to society's
talks, to sound, touch, form, taste, and smell –
the objects of the senses – and to forgetfulness of
the soul, contemplate the soul within you.

ow may one enter into that supreme truth, how may one know that supreme mystery which is so near and yet remains unknown? – which is forever with us and yet is lost? How may we reach it? How has anyone ever reached it? In these sutras is the explanation of that science, the process of that path.

Let us first understand a few things about illusion. Illusion means to see as it is not. Truth means to see as it is. Whatsoever we see is illusion, because we involve ourselves in our seeing; our experience does not remain objective, it becomes subjective. Whatsoever is out there, it does not reach us as it is. Our mind distorts it, embellishes it, ornaments it, prunes it, making it bigger or smaller and changing it into many, many forms.

The biggest change, the deepest delusion, is that we associate ourselves with everything, which in fact we are not associated with at all. As soon as we are associated the reality is lost and the dream projection starts appearing true. For example, we call a thing 'mine' – *my* house...the house which was there when we were not and which will still be there when we will no longer be. Something that can be before I am, and will continue after I am not, which does not disappear with my disappearance – how can it be 'mine'? If I die this moment my house does not collapse or disappear; in fact it will not even know that I have died. Then what kind of association can there be between myself and that house? What is the relationship? Tomorrow someone else will live in that same house and call it 'mine'. Yesterday somebody else was living in it and he was calling it 'mine'. Who knows how many people have stuck their 'I' on that house, and have passed away? But that 'I' never sticks onto the house, and that house does not belong to anybody; the house belongs to itself.

In this world everything belongs to its own self. If we can understand this properly, we shall be able to shatter the illusions easily.

There is a piece of land. You call it *my* field, or *my* garden. If not today, tomorrow there will be claims advanced about the moon – America will say it is 'ours', Russia will say it is 'ours'. Until yesterday the moon did not belong to anybody; it simply was, it simply belonged to itself. But now someone or other will claim the moon and sooner or later there will be struggles and confrontations. Up to now the sun belonged to itself, but tomorrow the sun may also be claimed.

Wherever man sets his feet he labels it with his 'I'. Nature does not accept his labels, but other human beings have to, otherwise there will be confrontation. Others have to accept the labels because they want to put their own labels on things. So the house becomes somebody's and the piece of land becomes somebody else's. Why are we so impatiently eager to stick this label of 'I' somewhere? The eagerness is because the more places and things on which we stick this label, or make our signatures, the bigger the circle of 'mine' grows and the bigger the 'I' is developed within us.

'I' is as big as the number of things that carry its label. If someone says that he has one acre of land, how can his 'I' be as big as that of another person who says, "I have one thousand acres of land"?

With the expansion of the 'mine', the 'I' feels as if it is growing bigger. If the expanse of 'mine' decreases, the 'I' also shrinks. So every brick of 'I' is made up of 'mine'. Thus the more ways I can say 'mine', the higher rises the palace of 'I'. Hence our whole life we remain in only one race: how many things we can stick our labels on and say, "It is mine." While doing so, while we continue to label things, one day we die, and wherever we had put our labels, someone else begins to stick his labels on the things we had called 'mine'.

Things belong to themselves, not to any person. They can be used, but there can be no ownership. Ownership is an illusion, and while we are using them we should have a sense of gratitude because we are using something that does not belong to us. But when we say 'mine', all sense of gratitude disappears and a new world of 'mine' is created. That includes money, position, prestige, education and everything. For these things it may be okay, but what is more surprising is that things which have nothing to do with 'I' also get included. We say: *my* religion, *my* god, *my* deity, *my* temple – with whom 'I' can have no relationship whatsoever. And if it can, then there is no possibility of freeing oneself from the world. If religion can also be mine and thine, if God can also be mine and thine, then there is no hope. Where shall we then find a way out of 'mine'? If God also falls within its jurisdiction, then there remains no space left anywhere for the 'I' to go away to. But we put the label of 'mine' on temples and mosques and on God as well.

Wherever man goes he reaches there with his 'mine'. Try to understand the implications. 'I' actually becomes bigger through 'mine', but the greater the expanse of 'mine', the greater the unhappiness. The increase in 'I' is the increase of unhappiness, because 'I' is a wound. And the greater the 'I', the bigger the area vulnerable to hurt, so that more hurt can be inflicted upon it. It is like someone having a large physical wound which tends to get hurt every now and then; any move the person makes and it gets hurt. The wound is big, its area large, and any little touch becomes a hurt. The bigger the 'I', the bigger the hurt and the greater the pain.

With the expansion of 'mine', the 'I' expands. As the 'I' grows, the pain also grows. On one hand one feels that happiness is on the increase, on the other hand the unhappiness also goes on increasing. The more we increase this happiness, the more unhappiness goes on increasing – and between the two an illusion is carried on. Where there is no possibility of saying 'mine', there too we go on saying 'mine' falsely, unmeaningfully. This hand you call 'mine', this body you call 'mine', are also not yours. When you were not, even then the bones, the skin, the blood of this hand existed somewhere; and they will exist even after you. The bones in your body, they have been bones in so many other earlier bodies. The blood in your body has flowed in the body of some animal yesterday and in some tree the day before. Who knows how long, how many billions and trillions of years, the journey has been? Even when you won't be, not a single particle of your body will be annihilated.

It will all exist. It will flow in some other bodies.

Understand it this way: the breath you took in just now, a moment ago it was inside the person sitting next to you. A moment ago he was calling it *my* breath, and a moment later it does not belong to him anymore, it has become somebody else's.

Life does not accept anybody's claim over it and goes on flowing each moment. But we go on claiming. This illusion of claim, this is man's deepest illusion.

So whenever a person says 'mine', he is falling in ignorance. This sutra is to break this very illusion. Not only the land is not mine, the house is not mine, the money is not mine – even the body is not mine. Your body is made up from the atoms of your parents. Those atoms existed before you were, and they are coming to you after a long journey. Before your parents, they were in the bodies of their parents. These atoms have had a long journey of millions of years; now they constitute your body. That body too is a field, a land in which you are rooted, but you are not it. You are not the body, you are separate from it.

This sutra says a man is not only not the body, it goes even deeper and says man is not even the mind, because mind is also an accumulation.

Do you have a single thought which may be yours, which you can say is yours? There are none. Some have come from tradition, some from scriptures, some from hearing someone, some from your reading – they have come from one or the other external sources. If you search for the birth-chart of your every single thought, if you look at the journey of every single thought, you will find you don't have a single thought of your own, they are all borrowed; they have come to you from somewhere.

No thought is ever original, all thoughts are borrowed. But we claim even a thought to be 'mine'.

Remember, even a breath cannot be called 'mine'; thought is a much more subtle matter. Going deeper and deeper into this analysis, where does one come to? Where have the Upanishads come to? Where does Buddha come to? Where does Mahavira come to?

Continuing this analysis, using the negation, "I am not this, I am not this"; when in the end nothing remains to be negated, when nothing remains about which I can even think whether it is mine or not, that which remains even then.... When there is nothing left to cut, when all relations are broken and none remains that can still be broken, that which remains even then is what the Upanishads have called *sakshi,* the witness.

There is a big world around me – it is not mine. Shrinking, I come closer – this body is not mine. Descending deeper into it – the mind is not mine. Then who is there whom I can call 'I'? Or is there nothing in me which I can call 'I'? Am I, or am I not? Cutting away 'mine' in its entirety, what purest thing remains within? Only one thing remains which is not discarded; there is no way it can be discarded.

In the West there was a philosopher named Descartes – a deep thinker. He decided not to accept anything until he found the truth which cannot be doubted, so he began to reflect. He labored hard and he felt everything was doubtful. One may say "God is," but a doubt can be raised about it. God may or may not be, but a doubt can always be created. "There is heaven," "There is liberation" – it can all be doubted. Descartes said, "I will believe only in a thing which cannot be doubted, not something that can be proved or argued in favor of, no. Something that cannot be doubted, something which is inevitable, indubitable...only then I will accept it."

He searched and searched. However he too stopped at one point. He denied God, heaven, hell, and everything else, but he got stuck at one point: "Am I or am I not?"

Descartes said, "This cannot be doubted, because even if I say 'I am not,' then too I am needed to be able to say this." It is like a person who is in the house and who answers the caller, "I have gone out," or "Right now I am not in the house. Come back in a little while and then I may meet you because by then I will be back home." His very telling this will be the proof of his being at home. So the fact of my being is indubitable. This much is clear, that I am, though what I am is not so clear. Am I a body, or a mind, or what? – this is not so clear.

This is what the Upanishads are in search of. One after another everything is eliminated, just as one would remove layer after layer of an onion. If you go on peeling an onion, finally nothing will be left of it in your hand. An onion is nothing but layers upon layers of skin – clothing over clothing – and there is nothing to be found if you go on undressing it. It is as if someone may have made a cloth-doll and we remove the cloths one by one. The first layer removed, the second layer is revealed; the second layer removed, the third layer is revealed; and so on, until all the layers of cloth have finally been removed, and there remains no doll anymore, just a nothingness in your hand.

So the biggest search of man is to find out if he too is nothing but an accumulation of many, many layers that we can go on peeling off and in the end there is nothing in our hand. If we go on denying and saying, "I am not the body, I am not the mind, I am not this, I am not that," it may turn out to be the story of the onion, and in the end nothing may remain of which one may say that "This is me."

But the Upanishads say that even if it is so, yet it is necessary to know the truth; even if it is true that there is nothing within, yet it is worth knowing it, because the outcome of knowing the truth is very significant. But on searching deeply, however, it is found in the end that no, man is not just an accumulation of clothing, man is not just layers upon layers upon layers; there is something within the layers which is different. But we only come to know of that when by removing all the layers we arrive within ourselves. That element which remains in the end is called by the Upanishads sakshi, the witness.

This word sakshi is very beautiful and very valuable. The whole philosophy, genius and wisdom of the East is implied in this small word. The East has contributed no other more important word than sakshi, the witness, to the world.

What does sakshi mean? Sakshi means the seer, the witness. Who is this who is experiencing that "I am not the body"? Who is this who is experiencing that "I am not the mind"? Who is this who goes on denying that "I am not this, I am not this"? There is an element of seeing, of watching, of the watcher within us which sees, which observes everything.

This seer is the sakshi, the witness. What is seen is the world. The one who is seeing is who I am, and what is being seen is the world. *Adhyas,* the illusion, means that the one who is seeing misunderstands himself to be all that is seen. This is the illusion.

There is a diamond in my hand: I am seeing it. If I start saying that I am the diamond, that is an illusion. This illusion has to be broken and one has to come, finally, to that pure element which is always the seer and is never the seen. This is a little difficult. The one who is the seer can never be seen, because by whom will it be seen? You can see everything in the world except yourself. How will you see yourself? – because two will be needed for seeing: one who sees and the other who is seen. We can grab everything with a pair of tongs except the tongs themselves. That effort will fail. We may find it puzzling that when the tongs grab everything, why can they not grab themselves?

We see everything, but we are not able to see ourselves. And we will never be able to do so. Whatsoever you can see, know well that that is not you. Thus take one thing to be certain, that whatsoever you are able to see is not you. If you are able to see God, then one thing has become certain, that you are not God. If you have seen light within you, one thing is conclusive, that you are not light. If you have an experience of bliss within you, one thing is determined, that you are not bliss. Whatsoever has been experienced, you are not that. You are that which experiences.

So whatsoever becomes your experience, you are beyond it. Therefore it will be useful to understand one difficult point here: spirituality is not an experience. Everything in the world is an experience, but not spirituality. Spirituality is reaching towards that which experiences all, but which itself never becomes an experience. It always remains the experiencer, the witness, the seer.

I see you: you are on one side, I am on the other side. You are there, the one who is being seen; I am here, the one who is seeing.

These are two entities. There is no way of dividing oneself into two so that one part sees and the other part is seen. Even if it was possible to divide, then the part that would be seeing is myself, the part that would be seen would not be myself. The matter is finished.

This is the whole process or methodology of the Upanishads: *neti, neti* – neither this nor that. Whatsoever can be seen, say that you are not that. Whatsoever can be experienced, say that you are not that. You can go on stepping backwards until nothing remains that can be denied or eliminated. A moment comes when all scenes are lost. A moment comes when all experiences are dropped – all!

Remember, all! The experience of sex is of course dropped, the experiences of meditation are also dropped. The experiences of the world, of love and hate are dropped, the experiences of bliss and enlightenment are also dropped. Only the pure seer remains. Nothing is there to be seen, only emptiness remains all around. Only the watcher remains, and the empty sky all around. In the middle stands the seer, the watcher, who sees nothing because everything has been denied and eliminated that could be seen. Now he experiences nothing. He has removed all experiences from his way. Now he remains alone, the one who was experiencing.

When there is no experience, there is no seeing; there is nothing seen and there is no object to be seen, and the witness alone remains. It becomes very difficult to express in language what really happens, because we have no other word except 'experience' in our language; therefore we call it 'self-experience' or 'self-realization'. The word experience is not right. We say "experience of consciousness" or "experience of the Brahman, the absolute," but none of these expressions are right, because the word experience belongs to that same world which we have eliminated. The word experience does have a meaning in the world of duality, where there was 'the other' too. Here it has no meaning at all. Here only the experiencer remains, the witness remains.

The search for this witness is spirituality.

Remember: the search for God is not spirituality. In the ancient yoga sutras God is not discussed, not even mentioned; there was no need. Later, even when the sutras mentioned God, they called God a means in the journey of spirituality and not a goal. It is said that God is useful in the spiritual practice, in the spiritual search, hence it is good to accept it; but it is only a means, a device, that's all.

Buddha and Mahavira also denied God. They invented new devices. This device is not needed, they said. If God is nothing but a device, then other devices will serve the purpose as well. But both Buddha and Mahavira cannot deny sakshi, the witness. They can deny God, they can deny everything else, but when it comes to sakshi, it is religion. If there is no mention of the witness, understand well that the whole thing has nothing to do with religion. Everything else is secondary. Everything else may be useful, may not be useful; there can be differences of opinion about everything else, but not regarding the witness.

Therefore, if someday in this world a science of religion is created, there will be no mention of God, soul or Brahman. These are all local matters – some religions believe in them, some do not – but the sakshi will certainly be mentioned because it is not a local issue.

There can be no religion without the witness. So the witness alone is the scientific basis for all religious experiences – of all religious search and journeying. And it is on this and around this sakshi that all the Upanishads revolve. All principles and all indicators are for pointing out the witness.

Let us try to understand this a little further. It is not difficult to understand the meaning of the word witness, but it is a complex thing in actual practice.

Our mind is like an arrow, sharpened on one end. You may have seen an arrow: it cannot be shot from both its ends, an arrow will only go in one direction. It can't travel in opposite directions simultaneously, it will go only towards its target in one direction. So, when the arrow is on the bow and then it is shot, there are two aspects to be considered – when it leaves the bow on which it was set it begins to move away from it; and it begins to come closer towards the target, where it was not earlier. One state was that the arrow was on the bow, and far away on a tree was sitting a bird.

The arrow was still on the bow and had not yet pierced the bird. Then the arrow left the bow, started moving away from it and coming closer to the bird. And then comes the state when the arrow has pierced the bird; the bow remains vacant and the arrow is in the chest of the bird.

This is what we are doing with our awareness the whole time. Whenever the arrow of our awareness leaves us, the bow within becomes vacant and the arrow, on reaching the object, is attached to it. A face looked beautiful to you, the arrow of your awareness is released. Now that arrow is not within you, the awareness is not within you. The awareness raced away and attached itself to the beautiful face.

There is a diamond lying on the road; the arrow is released from the bow. Now the awareness is not within you, now the awareness moves and, reaching the diamond, pierces its heart. Now your awareness is with the diamond and no longer within you. Now the awareness is somewhere else. So all the arrows of your awareness have reached out and pierced somewhere else – and somewhere else, and somewhere else. You have no awareness within you anymore, it is always going out. An arrow can only go in one direction, but awareness can be bi-directional – and when that happens the witness is experienced. The arrow of awareness can go in both directions; it can be two-edged.

When your awareness is drawn somewhere, if you can manage only this much, then one day the witness will happen within you. When your attention is drawn outside – say a beautiful young woman passed by or a beautiful young man passed by, your awareness was caught there and now you have completely forgotten yourself. The awareness is no longer within. Now you are not conscious: now you have become unconscious, because your consciousness has traveled to someone else. Now your consciousness has become the shadow of that person or object – now you are no longer conscious.

Now, if you can do this one thing.... You see someone beautiful, your awareness is drawn there. If in that same moment you can be aware of the bow within from where this arrow has been shot, if you can simultaneously see them both – the source from where the awareness is shooting forth and the object where awareness is going to – if they can both come into your attention simultaneously, then you will experience for the first time what is meant by the witness. From where the awareness is arising, from where the awareness is shooting away – that source has to be found.

We see a tree – we see its branches, its foliage, its leaves and flowers, its fruits, but we are not able to see the roots. The roots are hidden in the darkness underneath. But the tree is taking its nourishment from the roots. Your awareness expands and travels all around; a big tree of the world is created, but the source from where the awareness emanates, that oceanic consciousness, remains unnoticed. What is needed is that the roots are also seen at the same time, both the roots and the tree are seen simultaneously.

Understand it this way: when I am speaking, your awareness is on my words. Make this a double-pointed arrow...it can become so right now, this very moment. When I am speaking, do not only listen to what I am saying, also remain aware simultaneously that you are listening. The speaker is someone else, he is speaking; I am the listener, I am listening. If even for a moment, now, here, you can manage both things simultaneously – listening as well as remembering the listener, this remembrance within that, "I am listening" – then there is no need to repeat the words. If you repeat the words, "I am listening," you will not be able to listen at the same time, you will miss what I say. There is no need to form the words inside, "I am listening, I am listening." If you do that you will be deaf for that period of time to what I am saying. In that moment when you hear your own voice saying, "I am listening," you won't hear what I am saying.

It is a simultaneous experience of listening to what I am saying and also being aware that you are listening. The feeling, the realization, the experience that you are the listener, is the second aspect. Achieving awareness of the second aspect is difficult. If you can manage it, becoming aware of the third aspect is very easy.

The third aspect is this: if the speaker is A, the listener is B, then who is the one that is experiencing them both, the speaker as well as the listener? That one is the third, and this third point is the witness. You cannot go beyond this third. This third one is the last point. And these are the three points of the triangle of life: the two are the object and the subject, and the third point is the witness of these two, the experiencer of these two, the seer of these two.

Now we may understand the sutra.

Knowing oneself as sakshi pratyagatma,
the inner witnessing soul of one's intellect and all
its dispositions, and acquiring the disposition that
"That am I," giving up the claim of 'mine'
over all things.

The seeker, the explorer of this truth, the aspirant for liberation, having experienced that "I am the witness" and never a doer, that "I am ever a witness" and never the indulger, drops the feeling of 'mineness' and the desire over everything. He goes on receding within to that point beyond which it is not possible to recede any more.

Giving up following lok, the society...

Such a man stops following the society. The word *lok* means the society, the culture, the civilization, the people who are around you, the crowd. To give up following the society before you have the experience of the witness is dangerous also, because with society are associated its morals, its rules, regulations, limitations, organization and discipline. So society will certainly become the master for one who is not yet his own master. Somebody has to control one who is not his own master; some discipline is needed, otherwise all systems will go berserk, will become anarchic. But the one who has experienced his own being, the one who has experienced his witnessing, is himself his own master in this world.

It is very interesting that one who drops all mastery over everything becomes his own master; and the one who goes on accumulating all kinds of mastery, he only indicates that he has no mastery of his own self yet. This means that one who is busy making efforts to have more houses, more land, a kingdom, this and that – one thing is certain, that he does not yet belong to himself, because to one who acquires his inner kingdom, all other kingdoms become insipid and worthless.

The one who acquires his inner kingdom does not have any desire for any other kingdom. Even if he has an outside kingdom, it becomes worthless. If his desire for the outside kingdom is strong, it only indicates that he has no idea at all of the inner master, the witness; he is trying to substitute for it. There is no master inside, so through gaining mastery over things he is trying to convince himself that he is a master: "Look! I have so much land, so much money, so many possessions!" By so doing, he is trying to create a confidence within himself that, "Who says I am not a master? I am a master of many things!" This mastery is false, because nobody is ever a master of things in this world.

Bhartrihari renounced his kingdom: he left his kingdom, went to a forest and began to meditate deeply. Later, a very interesting event happened. He was sitting near the mouth of his cave; suddenly a horse rider came along the road that ran in front of the cave. Almost simultaneously another rider appeared from the other direction and swords were instantly drawn for a deadly battle. Bhartrihari could not understand this sudden happening. As they pointed their swords towards something on the road, Bhartrihari saw that there was a diamond lying there. The first rider claimed that he had seen the diamond first, therefore it was his. The second rider said, "Do you see the sharpness of my sword? Do you see the strength of my arms? How does it matter who saw it first? Whoever is fit to be the owner is the owner. Naturally, I am the owner!"

A deadly battle ensued and within moments both the riders' heads were rolling on the ground; both the blood-soaked bodies were lying on the ground, and the glittering diamond lay where they had seen it.

Bhartrihari thought how strange the incident was! The diamond of which both riders had claimed ownership and had perished for, wouldn't even know what had happened around it, because of it. And who knows what else might have happened in the past around this same diamond? And the diamond is just lying there. Many more may perish for it in the future, and the diamond will still be lying there, unconcerned.

The efforts for mastery over things is an indication that the person making them has no mastery over himself. Whenever a person starts experiencing the witness he becomes his own master. His desire for mastery drops; he no longer wants to become the master of anybody or anything else, because now he knows that there is simply no way to become a master of the other. Let me repeat it: There is no way of becoming a master of the other.

If a husband thinks he is the master of his wife, he is insane. If a wife thinks she is the master of her husband, her mind needs medical treatment. Nobody can be anybody's master, because everybody is born as his own master. In the very nature of things, everyone's mastery is hidden within oneself. On no account can it be revoked. And unless it is revoked, how can anybody else become its master?

Therefore, a very interesting thing happens. A husband thinks, "I am the master." The wife laughs inwardly and she knows, "I am the master." That is why there is friction twenty-four hours a day. That friction is for this very reason, that each moment it has to be decided as to who is the master, who is in power. There is no certainty. There never is certainty. Since there is no certainty even in relation to things, there can be absolutely no certainty in relation to individuals. There can be no mastery even over a diamond, how can there be mastery over a living individual?

One who is the witness drops all kinds of mastery, because he has become his own master. The mastery that can be, it becomes his; the mastery that cannot be – he does not bother to fall into that madness. In such a state he drops bothering about society; he drops it because now there is no control over him, he is his own controller. Now he can walk on his own feet, now he can walk in his own light, now he does not need any borrowed light anymore.

Giving up following lok, the society, he gives up
following the body also.

Not only does he stop following others, as the realization of the witness deepens he drops the slavery of the body too. Then he does not do things because the body is saying so, now he does what he wants to and the body follows him like a shadow.

Right now your body does not follow you like a shadow; on the contrary, you follow the body like its shadow. The body dictates to you to do things or not to do things, and you have to act accordingly. The body is the master, and it has its own indicators which control you.

It is bound to be so, because whosoever is not his own master, the society will be his master, his biology will be his master. Society is the group of human beings around us, and our body is connected with the earth, with nature. One who becomes his own master becomes free of the systems of the society and also of his biology. Then the body does not tell him, "Do this"; then he moves on his own and the body follows.

The phenomenon of the body following you is very valuable. We cannot even conceive how the body can follow. Only when the body is hungry...even if it is the body of a Mahavira, he too will feel hunger only when the body is hungry first; and it is only when the body indicates its hunger that Mahavira will go out in search of food, begging for food. So how can the body follow one? Does it mean that suddenly Mahavira will say, "I am hungry," and the body will become hungry?

What is the meaning of the body following? It is a deep alchemy. Certainly the body will not be hungry unless Mahavira agrees. Whatever happens to the body, whatever it feels, it will be able to convey it to Mahavira only when he is ready to listen. It is Mahavira who decides that he will fast for a month. If you decide that you will go on a fast for one day, for twenty-four hours you will go on eating food in your mind, because the body will protest, "Who is the master? Without consulting me...fasting? I will see to it!" The body will go on sending the message around the clock: hunger, hunger, hunger; and your whole consciousness will be covered over by hunger. Ordinarily the body will not trouble you very much if you just could not eat, even if it is for a whole day, but you make a decision one morning that you will not eat that day, and...!

A very interesting thing happens which is worth noting. If you take your meals daily at one o'clock in the afternoon, normally your body will not report hunger till about one o'clock. But if early one morning you get up at six o'clock and decide that today you will fast, your mind will start having lunch right from six o'clock that day. The body should have waited at least until one o'clock! But no, the body has received the hint that you are trying to establish your mastery. One o'clock is a far-off matter; your body will begin to agitate right from the morning. It has never before happened like this – you used to feel hunger only around one o'clock, but today it will start happening right from the morning.

The mastery of the body is ancient, thousands upon thousands of lifetimes. And whosoever is the master, no one ever wants to relinquish the mastery so easily.

If Mahavira says he will fast for a month, the body becomes silent for one month; it does not communicate any message of hunger until then. The body follows, which means that it does not report. It will report only after a month whether it is hungry or not; for the whole month it will remain quiet. But what does this mean? Will it happen through practicing? If you go on practicing every day – just as one takes daily exercise, similarly if you go on practicing fasting every day – then will a habit slowly be formed? No, do not fall in this fallacy. It is not a question of practice and habit, it is a matter of the experience of the witness.

If the experience of the witness is there, if a Mahavira decides to fast not only for a month but even for a year.... The body may become just a skeleton of bones and die and be finished, but it will not need to send any message to Mahavira. It will not dare to communicate the message to Mahavira that it is hungry. It is none of the body's business to send the message. It is a matter of settling once and for all who is the master. As long as the body knows that it is the master it does the mastery, but once the witness is experienced the mastery of the body is immediately gone. The inner law simply changes. The body starts following you. And then there are unique experiences.

After Mahavira thousands of people have fasted – so many Jaina monks are engaged in fasting – but Mahavira's fasting was unique. Have you looked at Mahavira's body, his statue? If you put the bodies of these Jaina monks in front of Mahavira's statue you will know what I mean. Where is the difference? Monks' bodies are continuously reporting hunger, not only to them but even to you. Mahavira's body does not report any hunger – neither to Mahavira nor to you.

It is very difficult to find a body as beautiful as Mahavira's. That handsome body is saying that now someone has become the master inside and the body has no capacity to disturb. Now the body cannot say anything like "Do this," or "Do not do that." Now it is of no concern for the body; now everything is in the hands of the knower within. Now whatsoever he decides, howsoever he decides, he may do; the decisions are in his hands. He may live if he chooses to live, he may die if he chooses to die, but the body cannot interfere. The body will only follow like a shadow.

Giving up following lok, the society, he gives up
following the body also.
Giving up following the scriptures,
he gives up the illusion of the soul also.

Thus one goes on giving up: the society, the body, the following of the scriptures. For one who is the witness, all scriptures become meaningless. This is a little complex. We can say this in the opposite way also, that to the one who is the witness, the scriptures also become meaningful. And this is the same. The reason it is the same is that as long as you have not become the witness, no scriptures can be meaningful to you. You may learn them by heart, you may have learned all the Vedas by heart, but they are not meaningful because the meaning is not in the words but in the experience. The experience is not your own. You may go on repeating the word witness like a parrot, but even while you are repeating it there is no witness within who may be listening to it.

Until you are a witness all scriptures are useless. But they will appear to be meaningful until you have your own knowing. The day you have your own knowing, you yourself become the scripture. When you yourself have become the scripture, what use have you now for scriptures? Thus the day the scriptures become meaningful they become useless too. You now know that which the scriptures express. Now what value are the scriptures? You have arrived at the destination; the journey is completed, so what is the use of that map that you have been carrying up to now? Now you can throw the map away. What will you do with it now?

Buddha used to say that when someone crosses a river in a boat, the moment he has crossed the river the boat is of no further use. The person leaves the boat there and moves on. But Buddha told the story: It once happened that four idiots crossed a river in a boat. Upon crossing the river they lifted up the boat and started carrying it on their heads. People of the village said to them, "We have seen many people crossing the river, but they all leave the boat there at the river. What are you doing?"

They replied, "How can we leave the boat that has been so helpful? We are not so foolish."

Now they were stuck. The boat had helped them to go beyond the river, but now how to go beyond the boat? So they started carrying the boat wherever they went. Now it was becoming impossible to get rid of the boat.

Do not think that such people existed only in the past. They may have died, but their children are there and they continue to carry ·the boat. They say, "Our father used to carry this same scripture and we shall also carry it. Our father's father also did the same; so what can we do now? – we are helpless. This has always been on the heads of our forefathers, so we too will keep it on our heads. Moreover, this scripture is a kind of boat, and how many sages have been able to cross over due to these boats!"

The day one experiences oneself, nothing remains to be learned from the scriptures – and this is also true, that that day the scriptures also become meaningful. It is then that we come to know that what is written in the scriptures is correct. This will appear to be a paradoxical statement: the day you know firsthand that what the scripture says is right, from that day on the scripture becomes useless, and one drops it. The real spiritual traveler drops all the scriptures.

And the last thing said in the Upanishads is miraculous. Only Buddha gathered that much courage and said, "I am not a soul either." This sutra of the Upanishad is wonderful. It contains the whole essence of what Buddha has said. Finally:

> Giving up following the scriptures,
> he gives up the illusion of the soul also.

Then he does not even say, "I am the soul."

"I am not the society," this is where the thing began. It went deeper when it said, "I am not the body, I am not the mind." Now this is the last jump: "I am not even the soul." What would this mean? It means that now it will be foolish on my part to create any boundaries for myself.

When we say "I am the soul," my soul and your soul become different entities. When I say "I am the soul," I become an individual, and the whole universe becomes separate from me. This last illusion also disappears, that I am separate, I am an individual. Then all distance and all boundaries between me and the universe disappear. The drop becomes the ocean. How can the drop even say "I am a drop"? The drop has become the ocean.

In the end, when everything has disappeared, even the idea that "I am a soul" drops – and what does this mean? This does not mean that there is no soul. It means that "I am God." Being a soul is not enough! This is a very difficult declaration. Whenever this declaration is made, trouble arises.

Al-Hillaj Mansoor declared to the Mohammedans, "I am God." They immediately killed him. They said, "What a sinful thing you are saying. What a sin you are committing! You and God! Whatever heights you may attain, however great a *siddha,* fulfilled one, you may become, you cannot be God, because being God means the last thing." Man is made of earth...and Mansoor is talking of such lofty flights. No, it is not possible.

So they cut Mansoor to pieces limb by limb. While Mansoor was being butchered he was laughing. Somebody from the crowd asked him, "Why are you laughing?" Mansoor replied, "I am laughing because I have already said, from the beginning, that I am not that which these people are cutting up. Who do they think they are cutting up? I have already said, 'Oh fools, I am not that which you are cutting up.' Only when I could say that, I came to know that I am God." Until his last breath, from the mouth of Mansoor the words, *"Ana'l haq, ana'l haq,"* meaning, "I am God, I am the truth," were resounding in the whole atmosphere.

There was a fakir named Sarmad. He is looked on with great respect by Sufis. He is among those chosen few who can be counted on your fingers. Aurangzeb, the Moghul king of India, came to hear some complaints about Sarmad, that he was saying some strange things. There is a mantra of the Mohammedans, "There is no God except Allah, there is one Allah only." But Sarmad was only repeating half of the mantra, "There is no God, there is no God." Now this changed the whole meaning. It meant there is no Allah. It was a very serious matter!

Aurangzeb summoned Sarmad and said, "You call yourself a Sufi fakir, a lover of God! and you go on repeating 'No Allah.' This is too much."

Sarmad replied, "I have attained only this far. I have yet to travel the rest of the territory. You are saying the whole mantra 'There is no God except Allah, there is one Allah only.' I have not yet reached the experience of the full mantra. Let me move further; slowly, slowly perhaps I may attain. But so far I can only say that much. And I am not ready to tell a lie. Up until now I have known only this much, 'There is no God.' The remaining part – 'except Allah, there is one Allah only' – I have not yet understood. Wait a little, I am working towards it. If you have understood the mantra fully, say so."

Undoubtedly it was a sin...and this man was an atheist. How many more people are being spoiled by him? Sarmad had a great prestige in Delhi. Millions of people were touching the feet of this man who was saying, "There is no God." This is called a miracle – when somebody says, "There is no Allah," and millions of people see Allah in him!

It has happened so; it happened so with Buddha, it happened so with Mahavira, it happened so with Sarmad. Mahavira asserted, "There is no God," and millions of people called him *bhagwan*, the blessed one. Buddha said, "There is neither any God nor any soul," and millions of people bowed down to his feet and asked him to indicate the way, and how to reach that place where there is no soul and no God.

Sarmad was given three days by Aurangzeb to correct his mistake and start repeating the complete statement of the mantra; otherwise he would be beheaded.

Sarmad said, "What is the guarantee of the three days? I may be alive, I may not be alive, and you may be deprived of the opportunity to behead me. It is also not certain that in three days' time I shall be able to attain to the complete mantra – and as long as I do not attain to the truth of the whole mantra myself, I am not going to repeat it the way you want it. I will say something only if it is my experience. So it is better that you behead me now."

Sarmad is reported to have said further, "It is also possible that on being beheaded my remaining journey may be completed, the

last part that I have not been able to know up to now. Perhaps it is
my head that is the hindrance."

It is doubtful that Aurangzeb would have understood. Emperors
and intelligence do not have much relationship anyway. Aurangzeb
had Sarmad beheaded that very day. In Jama Masjid, in Delhi, Sarmad was beheaded. And when his head fell on the steps of Jama
Masjid and started rolling down the steps, it was heard to say,
"There is no God except Allah, there is only one Allah." Thousands and thousands of witnesses heard it.

Aurangzeb repented very much, but it was too late. When he
asked Sarmad's disciples, they laughed and said, "Sarmad told us,
'As long as I survive, even in the tiniest way, how can there be any
talk of the second part of the mantra? Allah will be on the day
when I am not. This head is a small hindrance. It is good if it is cut
off. It is very kind of Aurangzeb that he is having it cut off. I
would have managed it myself, but that would have taken time.
Aurangzeb is getting the job done faster.'"

When a person dissolves himself completely, he does not even
say that he has a soul. Then even the last illusion drops. As long as
you do not know that you are God, know well that the illusion is
still surviving. As long as you do not have the very experience, "I
am Brahman, the ultimate," understand well that ignorance still
prevails – and go on discarding it. Become free of the society,
become free of the body, become free of the scriptures, and finally
become free of your own self too.

Being rooted in his own soul, and through
techniques, through listening and through self-
experiencing, the yogin comes to know himself as
the soul of all and his mind is annihilated.

The mind can be suppressed – though even that is difficult. The
mind can be hidden – though even that is difficult. But the annihi-
lation of mind – that is the last thing that can be managed.

Even if your mind becomes quiet, it becomes unquiet again the next day. It arises again and again, it revives again and again; it sprouts again and again – somehow its seed remains. However much we may meditate, pray and remember God's name, one moment it feels that everything is alright and the next moment it feels that everything has gone topsy-turvy; sometimes it feels that the destination has come, this is the place, and then again everything gets lost.

This whole game appears like snakes and ladders which children play. There are both ladders and snakes in it. Up the ladders you climb and then suddenly you come to the mouth of some snake and immediately you have dropped down to a lower level. This goes on happening – climbing up, falling down. A similar thing goes on with the mind. Sometimes it feels one has climbed, everything is fine, perfectly okay; one feels one has arrived. "So this is what the saints have been talking about – this is the very place, this is the very state – and I didn't get it until now!" But just as you remember the saints, you fall in the mouth of the snake and drop down headlong to discover that you are again back where you started from. You feel those saints must have been telling lies, or "Probably I hallucinated; I just imagined everything was alright, but in fact everything is wrong."

Around me are many who have been climbing ladders and coming down through the snake's mouth. One day they come and report to me, "How wonderful, fantastic! Now there really remains nothing to be done." And the next morning they come back, beaten, down. Against every ladder a snake is awaiting you.

Many times you will feel the mind is gone for good, and it will be back again. You will get glimpses. Even if it disappears for only a little time, you will have a small glimpse of beyond the mind. Even if it moves out of your way for a while, a space is created; the sky is cleared, a window has opened up and you see the stars in the sky. But this does not last long. A yogi becomes a *siddha*, the enlightened one, when the mind is annihilated. The mind is annihilated when one experiences that, "I am not even a soul."

As long as I feel that, "True, I am not the body, I am not the mind, but I am the soul," as long as there is any support left for my 'I', my mind will survive in its seed form. As long as there is any support whatsoever left, even that of the soul, my mind will remain in its seed form. Whenever a drop of rain will come, the seed will break open, sprout and start growing into a tree.

Only when I no longer remain does the mind cease. It is easy to give up money, it is easy to give up position, it is easy to give up attachment to the body, it is easy to give up attachment to the mind, but it is the most difficult task to break the attachment with my very self, with my very individuality, with my very existence. But as soon as this is broken, the mind is annihilated.

Sariputta came to Buddha. He asked Buddha, "How can I be liberated?" Buddha said, "Do not come to me, go elsewhere – because I cannot liberate you, I can only liberate you from this 'you'." Buddha said further, "'I' is never liberated. One is liberated from the 'I'. So if you are looking for *your* liberation, go somewhere else. But yes, if you want liberation from yourself, you have come to the right place. I will make you free from yourself. So do not ask how you will be liberated. You will not survive in your liberation. You should ask how to be free from this 'I' – how to be liberated from this 'I'."

Therefore Buddha did not choose the word *moksha,* liberation, he chose the word nirvana. With the word moksha there is a feeling of 'my'. At least this much will remain, the soul will remain – and sitting on *siddhashila,* the seat of the liberated one, one will enjoy liberation. The same person, the same man who was running a shop here, now sitting on a seat of the liberated one in the world of liberation is enjoying there!

This interest remains lurking in your mind, that you will remain. But what is there in you that is worth keeping? And what is there in you worth saving? Have you ever thought about it? Have you ever considered what you have that would be worth saving for eternity? What kind of fragrance have you that you could say that it should remain forever? What kind of melody have you that you would want to make it immortal? What is there in your personality which you would want to remain forever? There seems to be nothing of the sort within you.

Buddha says, "This too is a sort of desire, a lust for life – that one should survive, for no reason at all. There seems to be no reason why you should survive. What is in you which, if saved, may be beneficial to the world? There is nothing."

So, Buddha says, "No, this word liberation is not right"; and he chose the word nirvana.

This sutra is a sutra for nirvana. Nirvana means the extinguishing of the lamp. When a lamp is extinguished, can you tell where the flame has gone? The flame does not go anywhere, it simply ceases to be; it disappears, it simply merges. Now you will not be able to find that extinguished flame anywhere. Nowhere in all the worlds, nowhere in the vast infinity, will you be able to locate that extinguished flame. It has merged, it has merged so utterly that it cannot be called back from the infinity. It has moved so deeply into the formless that it cannot take any form anymore. It is annihilated.

So Buddha says that you will also get annihilated, just as a lamp is extinguished. Hence he chose the word nirvana. He says, "You will attain to nirvana – not moksha but nirvana. The flame that is faintly flickering in you will be extinguished."

This seems to be a very frightening thing. What, then, is the purpose of all this? To put more oil in your lamp and keep the flame burning? What really is the essence? But Buddha says that when you are annihilated, only then will you know what you are. And when you have disappeared, only then will you know that you are not lost; you have gained all, you have become all.

So the soul is also dropped.

Without giving opportunity – at any point – *to sleep,*
to society's talks, to sound, touch, form, taste and
smell – the objects of the senses – and to forgetfulness
of the soul, contemplate the soul within you.

Everything goes on dropping. Sleep is dropped, unconsciousness is dropped. We have forgotten our self – this the Upanishads call sleep. This forgetting of our own self, who we are, this not knowing of the truth that "I am God" – this the Upanishads call sleep. The day this sleep does not possess us even for a moment, that day there remains no way for the unconsciousness to take over. When this smoke no longer surrounds us, these clouds no longer hang around and the sky becomes spotless and clear and a darkness due to the clouds never descends, then there is a constant remembrance.

Remembrance is not the right word. All words are wrong for expressing what the Upanishads want to say. But one is helpless – there is no other way but to use words.

It is not right to say 'remembrance', because the word remembrance implies something which is past and forgotten also. Constant remembrance implies something that is never forgotten.

It happened once: There was a mystic in Tibet called Naropa. Many people used to come to him and they were puzzled, because it was well known that he was totally merged in the divine and they never heard Naropa ever remembering God's name. His disciples often asked Naropa, "People say that you are merged in the divine, but how come you never remember God?" Naropa is said to have replied, "How am I to remember when I never forget? And the day I start remembering God, know that Naropa has fallen. The day I remember, the day I call God's name, you may understand that Naropa has fallen, that he has forgotten and has fallen asleep. When I do not fall asleep, when I never forget God, how am I to remember then?"

In such a state is entry into that absolutely secret cave which is within us all.

Enough for today.

REFLECTIONS
IN A MIRROR

CHAPTER 4

This body is made from the excreta of your
mother and father and is full of excreta and
flesh. Therefore, moving away from it as from
a chandal, the lowly untouchable, and becoming
Brahman, the absolute reality, be fulfilled.
O seeker of the truth! By knowing the oneness
of the soul and the supreme soul, just like the
oneness of ghatakash, the sky within a pot,
and mahakash, the sky without a pot,
undividedly be always peaceful.

✳

Becoming the self-illuminated, self-created
sustainer of all and the eternal soul, Brahman,
the absolute reality, drop the sense of your body
and also of the universal body, as if these were
containers of excreta.
Investing the sense of ego that has controlled the
body into the ever blissful conscious self, give up
the gross body and be your immortal lone soul.

✳

O innocent one! Just as a city may be seen
reflected in a mirror, I am that Brahman,
the absolute reality, in whom the reflection of
this world is seen – knowing this, O sinless one,
be fulfilled.

We know the body only from the outside. Just as a person may go around a palace, see the outside form and beauty of its walls and conclude that this is the whole palace, similarly we see our body only from the outside.

The body is not only that which is seen from the outside. Seeing the body from the inside, one is at once freed of it. The form of the body that is seen from the outside is only the covering. The reality of the body is seen from the inside, the way the body really is.

Buddha used to send his disciples to the cremation ground to see the dead bodies, to see the bones, to see the skulls. That is how the body is: everything is covered by the layer of skin, otherwise you would be revolted by it and it would not be possible to have so much lust, so much attachment, and the feeling of 'my-ness' for it. Try sometime to visualize the body from the inside; then you will be able to understand this sutra. Go sometime to a hospital; see the surgeon performing operations in the operating theater. What you will see inside the body, that is the reality.

This sutra is very helpful for meditation. Let it be very clear to you that there is no condemnation of the body in this sutra. Religion is not interested in condemning anything, or in praising anything. Religion is only interested in knowing what *is*.

So when it is said that the body is an accumulation of flesh, bones, blood, marrow, excreta, etcetera, remember there is no intention of any condemnation at all. It is not an attempt to disgrace the body; the body is just so. The whole thing is just a revelation of the facts the way the body is, nothing else.

This sutra says:

This body is made from the excreta of your
mother and father and is full of excreta and flesh.
...Moving away from it as from a chandal,
the lowly untouchable, and becoming
Brahman, the absolute reality, be fulfilled.

The words *chandal* and *sudra* are very valuable. Ancient Indian psychology says that whosoever believes himself to be the body is a sudra; 'sudra' means the one who has believed himself to be the body. 'Brahmin' means the one who has known himself to be the Brahman, the absolute. One is not a brahmin just by being born in a brahmin family, nor is one a sudra just by being born in a sudra family. Sudra-ness and brahmin-ness have nothing to do with houses or families; sudra is a state of being, and so is brahmin.

All are born as sudras, only a few die as brahmins. The whole world is sudra. Sudra means, all those people in the world who live believing themselves to be the body. It is very difficult to find a brahmin. It is not difficult to take birth in the house of a brahmin, but to *be* a brahmin is difficult.

I have heard, Uddalaka said to his son Svetketu, "Go to the ashram of a seer and come back after becoming a brahmin."

Svetketu said, "But I am already a brahmin, I am the son of a brahmin."

Uddalaka then lovingly but firmly told his son, "It has never happened that just by being born in our house a person becomes a brahmin. We have actually been *becoming* brahmins. So you go to the ashram of a master and come back having become a brahmin. Where in the world has brahminhood been received from a father? It is received from a master! And in our family there has never been a nominal brahmin, we have always actually become brahmins. You go and come back when you have become a brahmin."

This sutra says: Move away from your body as if you are moving away from a chandal or a sudra. It is not that one has to move away; the moment one understands it is stinking filth, it is excreta, it is flesh, blood and marrow – as soon as this is realized, moving away begins on its own. We are attracted, we are pulled, to where we think is fragrance. We start moving away, we are repulsed from where we feel is stinking. Our inclination to be near the body is because of our ignorance of it. We have no idea what our body actually is.

So visualize the inside of your body. Become your own surgeon and open up your own body. The skin is not very thick, it is thin. We have developed so much attachment to all the things that are hidden behind this skin, and we start living as if that is all there is to our being. So we get attached to it, tied down to it.

If you start realizing the exact reality of your body you will find that a moving away has already begun; you do not have to move away, moving away begins on its own. Then if we have to re-identify with the body it will require effort. But our being attached to the body means only one thing, and that is that we have never looked at the body from its inside.

We know our body by seeing it in a mirror – but what is seen in the mirror is the outside cover of the body. It will be very good if someday science develops such a machine – like the x-ray machine – that if one stands in front of it, it shows everything on the inside of the body just the way it is: bones, flesh, marrow, excreta and all. Such a machine will be very useful.

Once you come to know the real situation of the inside of your body, you will immediately find that a distance has developed between your body and yourself; all those connecting bridges will have collapsed, all the identifications will have disappeared and the gap will start increasing. The seers of the Upanishad have tried to create that eye through which you can glimpse within – behind the skin, behind your own skin.

Truth is liberating. If we come to know the truth of our body, our mind starts becoming free of it. Lack of truth is bondage. Whatever we do not know in its reality becomes a bondage.

> O seeker of the truth! By knowing the oneness
> of the soul and the supreme soul, just like the
> oneness of ghatakash, the sky within a pot,
> and mahakash, the sky without a pot,
> undividedly be always peaceful.

When the futility of the body is seen and the worthlessness of the body is realized, the body feels to be a heap of filth and pus.

And when the distance from the body begins to increase, then only the nearness with God begins to develop. The nearer one is to the body, the farther away from God; the farther away from the body, the nearer one is to God. The stronger our bond with the body, the greater the distance from that bodiless consciousness. When the bond becomes less and when distance from the body starts growing, this has only one meaning – that closeness with the soul is increasing.

The soul is one pole and the body the other: we are between the two. When we are too close to the body we are far away from the soul; as we start moving away from the body we are coming closer to the soul. This is why the act of moving away from the body has been taken as a process of meditation. This was very much misunderstood also.

When the Indian scriptures were first translated into Western languages, people thought that these scriptures were enemies of the body. But it is not so. They are only devices. Knowing the reality of the body, our consciousness immediately moves on to the journey within. Realizing the actual truth about the body, the connection with the body loosens. In order to loosen that connection, it is necessary to intensify this realization.

Reflections on death, contemplation on the realities of the body, uncovering the actualities of the body and seeing them clearly – these are methods of meditation. Through them a person begins to move withinwards. And that moving happens easily, there is no effort required for that. If you want to move withinwards without understanding the body it will be very difficult, because the mind will remain interested in and bonded with the body.

One of Buddha's *bhikkhus* is passing through a village. He is very handsome, and meditation has added a dignity, a grace to his beauty. Silence has crystallized within him and its rays are emanating from his eyes and his face. An aura of light has graced him. One very famous prostitute sees him and is enamored of him. Rabindranath Tagore has written a beautiful poem about this event.

That prostitute comes to him and requests the bhikkhu to rest for one night in her palace. The bhikkhu replies, "There is no rule about this so I will not refuse your invitation. I will come, but the time is not yet right. When the actual reality of your body is revealed to you, that's when I will come. Right now you are mistaken. The day you awake to the reality of it, I will come."

The prostitute could not understand this. The very meaning of a prostitute is one who does not understand any other language but the language of the body. So do not think that just because a woman is somebody's wife she is not a prostitute. If she understands only the language of the body she is a prostitute. As long as the language of the soul is not understood, nobody can rise above prostitution.

And don't think that the word prostitute applies only to women; no, it applies to men too. Only the language of the body is understood; all transactions are carried out at the body level. The whole mind is focused only on the body, the body itself is the trade – this is all that is meant by the word prostitute.

The bhikkhu said, "I will certainly come, but only when the reality of your body is revealed to you."

The prostitute said, "Are you mad? This is the time for you to come – while I am young and at the peak of my beauty. My body will never be in any better condition."

The bhikkhu replied, "The concern is not for the better, the concern is for the real. When your body manifests its reality, then I will come."

The prostitute said, "I am unable to understand what you say. Please make it clearer to me."

The bhikkhu said, "When nobody comes to you anymore then I will come, because at that time your body will be showing its reality. Then the body will look the same from the outside as it really is inside. Right now it does not look the same on the outside as it really is inside. So when nobody comes to you, then I will come."

Many years passed, and the prostitute became old, leprosy had spread all over her body, every limb had started wasting away, and the people threw her outside the village.

These were the same people who used to hover around her door! These were the same people who used to be dying for entry into her palace, who used to consider themselves lucky and were grateful even to get a distant glimpse of her. The same people threw her out of the village.

It was a dark night with no moon. She was in agonizing pain and thirst. There was nobody even to offer her a cup of water. That night the bhikkhu came; he laid his hand on her head and said, "I have come. Now your body is in its real condition, now nobody comes near you. Now the outside body has become the same as it is inside. Now the distance between the outside and the inside has disappeared, the illusion that the skin was maintaining is no longer there. Now the inner filth and pus is manifest outside also; now you are the same inside and outside. Now I have come. This is the day I had promised I would come when I said that when nobody else comes to you, I will come."

The bhikkhu further said, "As far as I am concerned, even at that first meeting I could see in you what has now manifested. Yes, then you couldn't see it. I could have become your guest even on that day, there was no difficulty, but your illusion would have increased: 'Now even bhikkhus have begun to be my guests.' I had no difficulty, I could have come on that first day, because I could see your body as it is today. What the whole village can now see, I had seen that day."

But that prostitute, now lying on the outskirts of the village, was not looking at her body. With closed eyes, she was still remembering those days when she had a beautiful body, when she had dignity and lived with pride in the village.

Even in old age people reflect about their days of youth. When the body manifests itself in its true form, they continue to cover it up with their mind. When even the skin cannot hide their old age, they close their eyes and delight in brooding over the past.

When an old man derives delight in thoughts of his youth, he will die a sudra. And when even a young man sees the old age in his body before it actually occurs, he will die a brahmin. When even a dying person is carrying the lust for life, know well he is a sudra. When even in the peak of youth someone begins to see his death, understand that the brahmin is being born in him. And it is necessary that this reality of the body is seen by us, so that the bonds are loosened and we can turn towards where consciousness is.

> *O seeker of the truth! By knowing the oneness*
> *of the soul and the supreme soul, just like the*
> *oneness of ghatakash, the sky within a pot,*
> *and mahakash, the sky without a pot,*
> *undividedly be always peaceful.*

Just turn away from the body and look towards that *mahakash*. That mahakash, that vast existence, is very near.

If an earthen pot is on the ground and we turn it over and place it upside down, and if the pot then looks up, it will see only its earthen body, not the sky. Kept upside down, even if the pot looks upwards what will it see? All it will be able to see is its own base, its own layer of mud – its body – but not the sky. Then we place the pot the right way up, its face towards the sky. Then when it looks up toward the sky it will be able to see, "I am not the body." Now the pot will also be able to see, "The small sky which is within me is the same sky that is outside; and between the two of us nowhere is there any gap, we are inseparable. It is me who has expanded into the sky above, and it is the sky above that has come all the way down into me; nowhere is there any obstacle, any boundary, any wall in between."

A similar thing happens when you are looking towards your body; you are like a pot turned upside down – you see only the body. When you turn away from your body you become like a pot kept right way up – now you are facing the sky. As a person turns away from the body, immediately he is focused towards the sky and sees for the first time that there is not even a grain of difference between him and this vast existence spread all around. He has become the vast existence, the vast existence has reached out to him.

*O seeker of the truth! By knowing the oneness
of the soul and the supreme soul, just like the
oneness of ghatakash, the sky within a pot,
and mahakash, the sky without a pot,
undividedly be always peaceful.*

As soon as this unity is seen, peace happens.

What is the unrest, in fact? What is our restlessness? Our restlessness is that we are too big and imprisoned in the tiny. Our restlessness is like that of a person who has been made to put on a child's clothes and cannot move freely, he feels restricted. And again, if these clothes are made of iron, how much greater will the difficulty be? Our difficulty is similar.

We are big – not only big but vast – and we are imprisoned in a small body. The house is small and the resident is very large. It feels inconvenient on all sides; everywhere there seems to be a boundary and everywhere inconvenience. There seems to be no place where one can get out. And the difficulty has multiplied because what we think is our house is our prison. We are busy decorating it, furnishing and developing it. We are arranging for gold and silver decoration inside the prison, we are beautifying and ornamenting the prison walls – and this is the same prison we are trapped in. We are facing towards the walls, not towards the door.

It will be so, because you turn towards what attracts you. The face is towards where the attraction is and the back is towards where the repulsion is. As long as you are identified with the body you will be facing the wall. And the moment there is repulsion towards the body, you have found the door.

In your body too there is a door. But that door will only be seen by you when your attraction to the body disappears. That door in the body is called the heart. It is not the real heart that you call the heart; what you call the heart is the organ that is beating near the lungs. There is no door there, that is only an arrangement for pumping the blood. This is not the heart.

The heart, in the language of yoga, is the name of that door where you suddenly find yourself standing when you have turned away from the body, when you have no interest in even looking at the body – when there remains no attraction to the body and the infinite is born in you. It is here that the door is – where the pot opens towards the sky.

There are many types of doors in your body, but you come to know of them only when you arrive at them, not before that.

Look at a small child: a child does not know that there is a sex door in his body. But when the child grows and becomes a young man, suddenly one day he will become aware of that door. Through that sex door he can enter into the world; that too is a door for going out of the body. And, remember, this is the reason why there is so much yearning for sex. Because of it we are able to flow out of our body for a moment, but only for a moment. For a moment the body is forgotten and we drown in nature.

One of the doors of man is towards nature – downwards – and one is towards godliness – upwards. When our mind is filled with sexual desire we are closest to the body. And when we are closest to the body, then the door opens through which we enter into the world of other bodies. When we are disinterested and far away from the body, then the door opens from where we enter into the world of souls. Both these doors are there in the body.

In the body is the door that leads towards matter, and also in the body is the door that leads towards godliness. But disinterest in the body will not happen just by thinking so. If you go on just thinking that the body is only flesh, bones and marrow and nothing else, this won't help; thinking only indicates that you do not know – and that's why you are thinking.

Many people go on saying to themselves for lifetimes, "What is there in the body?" But they know that there is something in the body, otherwise why the necessity for this auto-suggestion? otherwise where is the need for repeating this suggestion to yourself? They are only attempting to persuade themselves, their minds, not to fall for what the body says because there is nothing in it. But who is this mind that is getting involved in the body? – it is they themselves. And the mind's interest in the body is still sustained, that is why it needs to be persuaded.

This sutra is not meant for persuasion. Do not repeat it; do not start chanting it sitting with your eyes closed. This sutra is for revelation. Understanding this sutra, try to search within your body with closed eyes to see whether it is true, as the sutra says, that this body is nothing but bones, flesh and marrow.

Don't just believe it. Believing it will be dangerous because you will start repeating it. No, explore it, search for it. Maybe the seer is simply joking, maybe he is telling a lie. Whatever the seers have said is not for you to believe in, but for knowing through your own search.

Search within yourself. Grope within for your bones. Press your fingers in your flesh and feel. Touch your skull and feel what is in there. Try to become acquainted with your body from all sides. The day this acquaintance is complete.... And why delay? – it can happen today. You have already been given your body, but you have never bothered to explore it, you have never bothered to examine it. But the behavior of man is so unbelievable that perhaps you may be forgiven.

I know of doctors whose whole education and study is of the bones, flesh and marrow, but they too are equally infatuated with the body. A doctor being infatuated with the body is a miracle! It means their blindness is unequaled and unaccountable. As surgeons they cut and dissect bodies on their operating tables, and yet, like Majnu, they go on singing songs in praise of Laila. This is a *real* miracle; the producing of amulets, etcetera from the air by Satya Sai Baba is no miracle at all. The miracle is that a doctor, who daily cuts open the body and knows all the flesh, marrow and excreta, who closes his nostrils so that the stinking smell from inside the body may not enter his breathing, who is familiar with every bone and each vein in the body and knows there is nothing in the body that can be called beautiful, also becomes mad with desire for someone's body.

A very interesting thing happened.... I was saying all this to a doctor – he is my friend. He said, "Now, while you are telling me this, I remember an incident. Once I was operating upon a woman's belly. When it was opened, I was nauseated because of all I saw there; it was very unsettling. While all this was happening," the doctor told me – he is an honest man – "side by side, my attraction to the beautiful nurse standing by my side was also asserting itself. The open stomach was there in front of me, and I was thinking how to complete the operation as soon as possible as I was later going to see a movie with this nurse."

Now this is how man's mind is! We are so skilled in deceiving ourselves. This man too will do the same things. Soon he will be out of the operating theater, he will hold the hand of the nurse, and forget completely what, in reality, a hand is.

So an average man can be forgiven – but I am saying so only in comparison to the doctor. Otherwise no man can be forgiven, because we have our own body and we have not been able to acquaint ourselves with that body either. And people set out in search of their soul! Unable to even acquaint themselves with their bodies, they set out in search of the soul.

People ask me, "How to attain to the soul?" Be kind enough to first know the body well. First get acquainted with what is so near you. And acquaintance with it becomes a ladder for rising towards the soul, because whosoever becomes acquainted with the body disidentifies with it; and whosoever turns away from the body faces the soul – his opening is towards the soul. And when the sky meets with this ghatakash, this little sky within the pot, what happens then is called peace.

To remain imprisoned in the body is the cause of unrest, and to experience being one with the all-pervasive, the vast space outside of the body-prison, is the advent of peace. Without meeting the ultimate, no one has ever become peaceful. Therefore, all other attempts to become peaceful will fail. At the most there can be only more or less unrest. Sometimes more unrest, sometimes less, that is all. What you call peace is nothing but less unrest, nothing more than this – just normal unrest. When there is normal unrest people say everything is peaceful, everything is going fine! When the unrest increases a little one feels troubled.

Psychiatrists say that their whole business is to keep people normally abnormal, normally mad. There are two types of mad people in the world – in fact there are only two types of people as such: one, the abnormally mad, they have to be kept in madhouses; and the normally mad, they are sitting in houses, offices and shops everywhere. The difference between the two types is only of the degree of madness. Anyone of the second type can at any time abruptly take a jump from his shop to the madhouse. There is no difficulty in it, it is only a question of a rise in the degree.

And several times every day you come very close to the madhouse. When you are full of anger, just for a few moments you have become mad. At that time there is no difference between you and a mad person. You will do the same things that a mad person does. The only difference is that this happens to you occasionally, this madness of yours happens only occasionally, whereas someone else's madness has settled; it just does not leave them, it has become stationary. You are a little liquid in your madness, it keeps itself flowing. Somebody else has solidified in it, frozen in it like ice.

Psychiatrists say that their whole work is to pull back those who have gone a bit too far in their madness and to bring them back alongside the normally mad crowd. They say they cannot do anything more than that; that somehow, through persuasions and seductions, treatment and therapies, possibly in a year or two, at the most we can bring them back to their shops or offices where they came from. They are allowed just that much madness which does not interfere with the day-to-day work they are doing.

Unrest has become our nature. And it is only natural to be so because there is only one meaning of being peaceful: when your river of life falls into the ocean of life, in that moment of meeting there is peace. Without meeting the universal life, there is no peace.

Becoming the self-illumined, self-created
sustainer of all and the eternal soul, Brahman,

the absolute reality, drop the sense of your body
and also of the universal body, as if these were
containers of excreta.

Not only has this body to be given up, but this vast body that we see as the universe has also to be given up. Man is a miniature form of the universe. There is this body surrounding you, and within it you are the immortal flame of soul. Similarly, the body of the whole is this universe, and within it is hidden Brahman, the universal soul. The sense of this body has to be given up, but even the sense of this vast universal body spread all over is to be given up also – it becomes meaningless too.

When a person disidentifies with his body, he experiences his soul. Try to understand this clearly. When a person drops attachment to his body, then the luminosity that comes to his eyes for the first time is that of his own flame, his own soul; it is that of the ghatakash – the sky within the pot. And when somebody becomes free even from the universal body of the whole, what he experiences then is that of the flame of Brahman, the absolute.

This is the only difference between the soul and the universal soul. Soul means, you experienced just the tiny flame. Universal soul means, now you are standing in front of the super sun. Being free from one's own body one experiences the soul, being free from the universal body one experiences the universal soul. But the difference is only one of degree. So for one who has reached up to the soul there are no obstacles, no hindrances; he can easily take the second jump also.

Investing the sense of ego that has controlled the
body into the ever blissful conscious self,
give up the gross body
and be your immortal lone soul.

The meaning of sannyas is that our face constantly remains toward the sky. The *grihastha,* the householder, once in a while gets a glimpse of the sky through effort, but soon returns again to his home, the body.

Be clear about the meaning of grihastha; grihastha means one who keeps falling back to his body. The word *griha,* the house, does not refer to that house in which you live, it refers to the house – the body – with which you are born. And one who became settled in this house is a grihastha. Sometimes he gets glimpses of the sky too, but he keeps coming back to the body. Sometimes the pot faces the right way up, but it soon turns back down again – gets stuck again. To remain upside down has become its habit. And because of habit, to remain upside down feels to be the right thing – because of the habit, the long-time habit.

If a person is made to remain in a headstand from the time of his birth, and is brought up in the same posture, then if one day he is asked to stand the right way – on his legs – he will ask why he is being made to stand in a wrong way! Naturally, because now he has become habituated to standing on his head.

I have heard.... There is a small tribe in South America; it is a tribe of some three hundred persons living on a small hilltop, and on that hill there is a type of fly whose bite makes people blind. All those three hundred people of the tribe are blind. All the children are born with sight but they become blind within three months, because by that time the fly has bitten them. Therefore nobody in that tribe is even aware that there is anything like sight. How much can a child of three months know about eyes? Before he is more than three months old he turns blind. And all the others are already blind.

Now if by chance some child grows with sight intact, the doctors of that tribe will certainly label that child abnormal and have his eyes operated upon. Such an operation to destroy the eyes would seem a completely normal thing to do. They will say, "Is there such a thing as eyes? Who has ever had eyes? No one. This case is certainly some mistake of nature!" Destroying the eyes through an operation will become an absolute necessity. To be blind is natural to them; it has become a habit.

What we are ordinarily, appears as natural. But it is not necessary that it be natural. Try to understand this. A habit can appear
to be your nature, but habit is not nature. What is the difference
between the two? Habit means a thing which we have been doing
and we are therefore continuing to do it. Nature means a thing
which will continue to happen even if we drop all our doings; it is
something that does not need to be done.

It is our habit for life after life to be bound to the body, a habit
of countless lifetimes; it is not our nature. So once you have the
right experience of the true nature, this habit will break. One may
go on getting glimpses, but that makes no difference. A glimpse is
like lightning that suddenly happens and then again darkness settles, then we settle back into the old habit.

A sannyasin is one who takes the decision, "Now I will break
the mind's identification with the house, the body, and I will continuously keep awareness of the open sky. And my effort will
continue ceaselessly – sitting, moving, in waking and even in sleep
– so that as far as I can manage I will be aware that my mind does
not identify itself with the body, that my soul keeps flowing in the
vast ocean of the whole."

And when I say "keeps flowing," I am not just using words.
When you do this experiment, you *will* experience that you are
actually constantly flowing. As you will face towards the soul, you
will feel that you are continuously being emptied, that like the
Ganges you *are* falling into the ocean. This remembrance should
remain continuous.

> O innocent one! Just as a city may be seen
> reflected in a mirror, I am that Brahman,
> the absolute reality, in whom the reflection of
> this world is seen – knowing this, O sinless one,
> be fulfilled.

Just as a reflection is seen in a mirror.... But the reflection that
is seen in the mirror is not the actuality; the actuality is the mirror

in which the reflection is seen. Are you aware that when you look into a mirror you see the reflection and not the mirror? When you are standing before a mirror, have you ever found yourself seeing the mirror? No, you are always seeing your face, not the mirror. And the face which is not there in the mirror is seen and the mirror which is there is not seen.

If a mirror can be made in which the reflection of your face cannot be seen, then you will not notice that there is a mirror there at all. Because your face is seen, you infer that there is a mirror. The mirror is only inferred because you are able to see your face; so only the face is seen, not the mirror. Yes, if there is some flaw in the mirror that is another matter. The more flawless, the purer the mirror, the less it will be seen. If we can make an absolutely flawless mirror it will not be seen at all.

The whole story of the Mahabharata happened because of the making of such a flawless mirror. It was just a joke, but the joke proved to be very costly. Duryodhana and all his brothers were the sons of a blind man, so a joke was played on them. The joke was not in good taste anyway, because a joke which may hurt someone is more of a violence than a joke.

The Pandavas had built a new palace and had invited their cousin-brothers to see it. Absolutely flawless mirrors had been fitted in that house; the mirrors were so flawless that they were not visible as mirrors. So if a mirror was fitted opposite a door, the door appeared in the mirror and the mirror itself could not be noticed. Poor Duryodhana, in trying to pass through such doors, smashed his head in the mirrors and fell down. Draupadi saw this and laughed: that laughter gave birth to the whole Mahabharata. It was the revenge for that laughter.

In a way it was not such a serious thing, but sometimes even a small laugh can bring out so much violence! The satire behind the laughter was deep: "You are the son of a blind man, so naturally how can you see? It is bound to be so, because you are the son of a blind man." Hence the laughter: "You are bound to fall, son of a blind man – you are seeing doors where there are no doors!"

Completely flawless mirrors had been used, thus the reflection in the mirror is seen, but not the mirror.

The seer says:

> O innocent one! Just as a city may be seen
> reflected in a mirror, I am that Brahman,
> the absolute reality, in whom the reflection of
> the world is seen – knowing this, O sinless one,
> be fulfilled.

The soul within us is a clean, flawless mirror; the whole world is seen reflected in it. So we run to catch hold of the world but we do not see the mirror in which the world is seen reflected.

If a diamond is seen, a Kohinoor, you run after it. However, you do not even consider finding out who this is in whom the diamond is reflected, the one who is seeing it. What is that mirror within me which reflects the diamond right to the depths within? The moon is seen in the sky. Who is there within that is reflecting the moon?

There is a revolving mirror within us that goes on reflecting the whole world in it. As long as you are running to catch the world you are trying to catch the reflections. The day you begin to be aware of the mirror you have entered the world of truth. And the one who sees the mirror does not become infatuated with the reflections. It does not mean that there will no longer be reflections in the mirror; no, they will form, but the insistence to catch hold of them is dropped.

And a mirror is never polluted by reflections. No matter in how many worlds you may have been wandering, your mirror has always remained pure and innocent. Understand this properly. This is why it is said in the sutra: "O innocent one!" It is addressed to you, "O, innocent one!" Even you will suspect that the seer has probably made some mistake in addressing you thus. "Me? Calling me innocent?" But no, it is said with a reason. No matter how many faults may happen, the mirror always remains pure and innocent.

You may put anything in front of a mirror – even stinking excreta – it will reflect it. But do you think the mirror was polluted by
that stink? No, remove the excreta you placed before it, and the
mirror is the same as ever before; there won't even be a trace of
that filth left behind in the mirror.

So a lot has been happening in front of your mirror, but it only
happens in front of it, nothing enters within it. Nothing can enter
it. This is why it has been said: "O innocent one."

This is a very fundamental difference between Christianity and
Hinduism. Christianity asks you to stop committing sins, Hindu
thinking asks you to know that you are already innocent. Christianity says, "Efface all sins, drop all wrong doings"; Hindu thinking says, "What is there to be effaced? You are a mirror; just know
this much and everything is already effaced – then you are already
pure and innocent."

It is one and the same thing. Even if one is engaged in effacing
everything, by the time all wrong has been effaced from in front of
the mirror, the mirror will look pure – it already was. So it can be
begun from this end also.

There is the same difference between Jaina and Hindu thinking
also. It is a very interesting thing. Jainas' emphasis also lies on the
removal of sins: remove all sins, so that when all sins are removed
you will be able to see the pure mirror – although the mirror was
pure in the first place. Hindu thinking emphasizes: Why make
meaningless efforts in removing sins? Just realize the truth, that
you are a mirror; then even if the sins continue to remain before
the mirror, you still are innocent, sinless. Therefore Jainas as well
as Christians have always felt that Hindu thinking is a bit dangerous; it does not leave much room for your concepts of morality
and sins and virtues.

It *is* dangerous. The deeper the truth is, the more dangerous it is,
because the deeper the truth is, the more powerful it becomes. And
in power there is danger. If it falls into the hands of the wrong people, then there is great danger. Often the wrong people are in
search of power, so it does fall into their hands. But Hindu thinking

is very, very deep. The whole point is that your consciousness within is just a mirror. Whatever you have inside, it is outside your consciousness. Nothing has ever entered inside your consciousness, though it feels as if this has happened.

If you put something in front of a mirror, it appears as far inside the mirror as it is away from the mirror. It is a simple law of the rays of light and their ratio: the farther a thing is from the mirror, the deeper inside the mirror it appears. So take note of a very interesting principle: the deeper inside you something appears to be, know that the further away from you it is. If something appears to be totally inner, you can be absolutely sure that there can be nothing else more outer than it. As it often happens, people say, "This love is very deep within me." It means it is something far away from you. When you say that somebody's love has entered very deep in your heart, you should know that you are attempting to touch something that is far away from you. It means that someone is far away from you and therefore is being seen deeply within your mirror.

The things that are nearer appear shallower, and the things that are far away appear deeper in the mirror. Again it is not necessary that if a thing appears deep in a mirror, the mirror itself should be really as deep within. Even in a small lake the moon appears as deep inside the lake as it is far away in the sky, and the lake is not so deep as that. How deep are your mirrors? Put a mirror on the ground and the moon will appear in it as deep as is its distance far away in the sky.

Howsoever deep the reflections may go inside, they actually never penetrate. Nothing has ever gone inside you, it cannot. It only appears to be going within because there is a mirror within. Our consciousness is a mirror, the purest mirror, so pure that…. Because no matter how pure glass may be, it is still glass; that much matter is there. But the purest consciousness…!

Even if we make a mirror out of air, that too won't be as pure as the mirror of consciousness. If we make a mirror of air, and something is reflected in it, we will set out in search of that reflection through the mirror, because the mirror will not obstruct us in any way. It is a mirror of air; you will just go through it.

The mirror of consciousness is much purer, because consciousness is the subtlest phenomenon in the world. It is the subtlest energy. The whole world is reflected in it.

The seer says, "O innocent one! Just as reflections are seen in a mirror so does the world appear within you. Knowing this – recognizing that 'I am Brahman,' that 'I am the mirror, not that which is reflected but that in which everything is reflected' – be fulfilled."

There simply is no fulfillment other than this. As long as one does not recognize the purity of one's consciousness one is unfulfilled. He may go on doing anything, he may go on achieving anything, but all that achievement will be useless. All that is done will be undone; all running about will be as good as drawing lines on water – they disappear even before one has finished drawing them. One may go on drawing these lines again and again, but they will just go on disappearing.

At the end of life, at the moment of death, people who have been searching for reflections come to realize that they have been drawing lines on water. Everything disappears: all reputation, all positions, all wealth, all accumulations – everything disappears. It is discovered in the moment of death that it was all a great mistake, that one was drawing lines as though on granite but actually one was drawing lines on water. But it is only discovered when nothing can be done about it.

But if it can be known today, if it can be known now, then something is possible; drawing lines on water can come to an end. And a person who chooses to stop drawing lines on water enters a different world, a world in which nothing ever dies.

There is one world of death, there is another world of the deathless. Whosoever moves away from death attains to the deathless.

Enough for today.

LET GO
AND FLY

CHAPTER · 5

Only a person free from holding onto
the ego attains to self-nature.
Therefore, becoming spotlessly clean like the
full moon, one becomes ever blissful and
self-luminous.

✳

On cessation of the sense of doing, all anxieties
cease. On cessation of the anxieties, all desires
cease. The cessation of desires is emancipation –
and this is called jivanamukti,
liberation while living.

✳

Seeing all, everywhere, in every direction, as
Brahman, the absolute reality – on the ripening of
the feeling of such goodwill do desires cease.
Never be negligent of your allegiance to Brah-
man, the absolute reality, because that is the only
death, say the ones who are well-rooted
in Brahman.

✳

Even if shifted aside, the algae do not lose time in
covering the water again. Similarly, if a wise man
swerves from his allegiance to Brahman even for
a little while, illusions cover him.

n this sutra many valuable things are said – not only valuable but original also.

Only a person free from holding onto the ego attains to self-nature.

A very deep truth is revealed in this. The ego has not caught hold of you, it is you who has caught hold of the ego. The world has not caught hold of you, it is you who have caught hold of the world. Sufferings are not clinging to you, they are your very own creations. Sufferings are not chasing you, they have not taken any resolve to give you trouble; they come to you only at your own invitation.

Normally we do not think this way. We think: Why are there sufferings? Why is there this worldly anguish? Why this cycle of birth and death? Why does this ego torment me? How to be free of it? Constantly this thought runs within us: How to be free of it? You must have all encountered this question sometime or other – how to be free of it? – otherwise it would have been impossible for you to come here.

But this sutra will disappoint you greatly, because it says the very question of becoming free does not arise because the ego is not holding onto you, the world is not stopping you in any way; your births have not invoked you, it is all due to your own will. So it is wrong to ask, "How to be free of all these?" The right thing to ask is, "How, in what manner and with what trick, am I holding onto all this misery and trouble?"

One should not raise the question of becoming free of all these. The question should be: What is our methodology, what is the pattern with which we catch hold of sufferings? We go on catching hold of sufferings, and with our own hands we go on imposing upon ourselves more worlds, more births, more incarnations. The question should be: Why do we go on creating newer and newer expanses and skies of desires? This is what is needed to be understood.

This will have several implied meanings. One meaning will be that liberation is not some attainment which is to be achieved. The world is certainly to be lost, but liberation is not to be achieved. If you are ready to drop the world, then you will find that your liberation is already the case. You are already free, but you have managed to remain in bondage through great self-trickery.

If you have seen how parrots are caught in the jungles you will understand. A rope is tied across two supports. The moment a parrot comes and sits on the rope, he immediately hangs upside down because the rope has turned due to his weight. Now the parrot feels that he is caught. The upside-down hanging parrot feels that he is caught, badly caught; his feet are entangled, now there is no way to get away. It is the parrot who is clutching the rope tightly, the rope is not holding him at all. But what the parrot feels also appears logical: "The rope which has turned me upside down has caught me, it must be holding me!"

So the parrot stays hanging. He tries in all possible ways to straighten himself up so he can fly away, but he is unable to manage to do that because the rope is very light compared to the weight of the parrot – so no matter how much he tries, he always swings back to his upside-down position. Thus, the more he tries, the more convinced he becomes that there simply is no way of release.

If the parrot could understand, it could undo its grip and fly away the same moment. But it tries first to sit upright. Even if it leaves the grip in its upside-down position it can fly away because the rope has not caught it. But the parrot has never flown in an upside-down position; whenever it has flown it has been standing upright. It knows only one way of flying. It thinks that perhaps flying has some unavoidable connection with standing right side up on two feet.

How is the parrot hanging upside down to understand that it can also fly here and now, and that it is not caught at all? But because it is hanging upside down it fears that if it leaves the rope it will fall on the ground and die. So it clutches the rope tightly.

And howsoever late its catcher may come, he will find the parrot hanging there.

Man's consciousness is more or less in the same situation. Nobody has caught you. Who is interested in catching you? This world has no interest in holding you. What could be the purpose, what would the world achieve through holding you? No, nobody is interested in catching hold of you. You have caught yourself. But there are some illusions which give you the idea that you are caught by others.

The greatest illusion is that you think yourself to be so valuable that the whole world is interested in catching you. This is egoistic to feel that all the miseries are rushing towards you only; that so many miseries pay so much attention to you; that all the hells are created just for you – they are all just for you, and you are sitting in the center! As if this whole cosmic arrangement goes on running just for you – and you are nothing but a parrot hanging upside down on a rope! But the reasons for the creation of this illusion are more or less the same as those for the parrot.

As soon as a human child is born, many tragic events take place side by side. They are a must, that is why they take place. A human child is born the most helpless of all animals in this world. The child of no other animal is born so helpless. Children of other animals can walk and run and can set out in search of their food soon after they are born, but a human child will require twenty-five years after its birth to be ready to set out in search of its own food. Twenty-five years!

A human child is the weakest of all animals at birth. Biologists say that something has gone wrong somewhere. They say that for a mature birth, the human child should remain in the womb for twenty-one months. But the human female is weak, she cannot keep the child so long in her womb. Thus, according to some biologists, the whole human race is an abortion. No human child is born fully developed, all are born partially developed. By contrast, children of all animals are born fully developed.

But for the human child this partially developed birth is a

blessing as well as a curse. In this world there is nothing that is one-sided, there are always two sides to everything. It is unfortunate that the human child is weak, but this is a blessing also because it is due to this weakness that man became superior to all other animals. There are some deep reasons for that. Because the human child is born very weak – he requires great assistance, otherwise he will not survive – just to provide that assistance the unit of 'family' came into existence; otherwise there is no need for a family. In animals there is no family life because it is not needed. A human child will simply die without a family; hence the mother, the father, and the sacred institution of family. It is all born out of that weakness of the child.

On the basis of the family, the society, the nation, the whole network of civilization was born. And because a human child is born helpless he does not possess the basic instincts. The animal child is born and it comes with intelligence – just enough to live its life. But the human child does not arrive with such intelligence; if we leave him unattended he will die. There is no way he will survive. This is why the human child has to be trained.

No animal child needs any training. A human child needs to be taught. He does not come prepared with anything, everything has to be taught. Therefore there are schools, colleges and universities. These are institutions born due to this human weakness. We have to impart all education, everything; one thing after the other has to be taught. A great effort has to be made, and still there is no certainty that the child will learn! Thus all arrangements of education and conditioning are developed because of the weakness of the human child. This sutra has some relationship to this reality.

Because the child is helpless, the parents have to pay a lot of attention to it. Because of this attention the child feels, "I am the center of the world, the whole world is revolving around me." A child cries a little and the mother comes running. A child becomes slightly ill and the father is in immediate attendance along with a doctor. The small child knows that everything moves at his slightest bidding. A slight noise, a slight crying, a slight indication of trouble calls the whole family to his service. And for the child, the house is the whole world; he knows no other world. So a natural illusion is created in the mind of the child that, "I am the center of the world, all arrangements are just for me; everything is happening just for me, everybody is looking just toward me."

This illusion settles deep in us, and then for the rest of our lives we go on living with the assumption that we are the center. This brings tremendous pain; this is why the ego hurts – because it is not true, you are *not* the center of the world. The world runs very happily without you. It faces no obstacles at all because of your absence. But somewhere in some corner of your mind you go on feeling, "I am the center." And you are always waiting for this world to accept that you are the center. This is the very search of the ego.

The sutra says: *Only a person free from holding onto the ego...*one who is prepared to give up that concept of ego which has grown and deepened from childhood...*attains to self-nature.*

This is inevitable; this creation of the ego from the very birth of the child is inevitable. This is an unavoidable evil. But to get stuck there and not to move on destroys our whole life, because then we remain deprived of knowing that entity which is hidden within us. We will be able to know it only when we drop our ego. Why? Why in religion is there so much emphasis on dropping the ego? The emphasis is because one who feels that he is the center of the world remains deprived of knowing his own center. That man lives believing a false center to be his center. A man who believes that he is the center of others' eyes never bothers to seek if he in reality has any center of his own, and thus a pseudo center is born. This pseudo center is dependent on others, and therefore one only gains unhappiness from the ego.

When you say, "You are a good man," you are reinforcing my ego. Tomorrow, if you say, "No, it was a mistake, you are not a good man," then you have just withdrawn the brick you lent to my ego and with which I had built up the castle; it then comes to the verge of collapsing.

The ego is created through the eyes of others, through the ideas of others; ego is dependent on others. And remember, whatever is dependent on others cannot be your center. So we worry too much about who says what, who says good things about us and who says bad things.

A friend had come to me who said, "This is my problem"...he is present here. He said, "This is my very problem, that somebody says something, a small thing, a quite insignificant thing, and I am so hurt that I cannot sleep the whole night." For example, he said, "I had gone to a shop to buy some material. I wanted to buy some material, but I did not like what the shopkeeper had showed me. The shopkeeper said, 'Leave it. I knew when I first saw your face that you would not buy any.' I could not sleep that night, trying to work out why this shopkeeper spoke like that."

Our ego is dependent on what others say. The people all around us either contribute to our ego or they take away some of it. This is why we are concerned the whole time as to what people are saying or thinking about us. That is our capital. Collecting others' opinions contributes to our pride – but what is the reliability of others' opinions? Their opinions are in their hands. Today they may be extending it in our favor, tomorrow they may not. Today they may have a good opinion of us, tomorrow they may have a bad one – and they have their own motivations.

That shopkeeper had his own motivations. He gave a hit to the ego. Now two things could have happened through it. One was that this man might have purchased the material, just to save face if for nothing else. And it would have been better if he had made a purchase, for at least he would have saved himself from a whole night's sleeplessness. But then another worry would have gripped the mind: "Why did I buy the cloth which I did not want?" And you all have bought many such items that you never wanted to buy, but on many occasions your ego goads you to buy.

In the West, salesmen are slowly being replaced in shops by saleswomen. Now there are no more salesmen, only saleswomen! Now there is no sense in keeping the word salesman in use. When a male customer enters a shop to buy a pair of shoes and a beautiful salesgirl approaches him, fits a pair of shoes on his feet with her own hands, ties the laces carefully and smilingly adds, "Beautiful! This pair looks so beautiful on your feet," now, howsoever much that pair of shoes may be pinching him, it is his compulsion to buy them. He will have to buy them. Now it is no more a question of shoes, now you are buying something else, the shoes are just an excuse.

We have all bought many such things which we never wanted. Our whole life is a similar collection of things, and the ego is the total collection of all this. We have stolen the shine from the eyes of others, put it all together and that has become our flickering light. But it is always the others who are the masters, any day they want to they can pull back the support.

Even the biggest of leaders is not bigger than his followers. He cannot be, because his whole leadership is in the hands of others. Today they have given it, tomorrow they can take it away.

Therefore, however great a leader may be he is a follower of his followers. He has to follow them. He has to watch in which direction the followers are going, then he runs and stands in front of them. He has to mark the direction of the wind, the direction of his followers, and his whole expertise is in then running and standing in the front. And this is why, all the time, every day, the leader goes on changing his statements. He has to change. That is what is called keeping the follower's views in mind. You have received your ego from them. Your prestige, position, everything you have received from them – it is all borrowed. And whatever is a borrowed thing, it is not you. You were there before all these things were received. When death snatches all this away from you, you will still be there.

You have created a false center, and if you have taken yourself to be this center, why then will you then search for your real center? You have taken it for granted that this is the real center.

What is your image in your own eyes? It is an image created by others. It is others who have created it – somebody has given color to it, somebody has drawn its eyes, somebody has drawn the feet, and that is all you are. But this is only a paper image, one small shower of rain will wash off all its colors. But this situation is born out of the inevitabilities of life.

Psychologists say that a child becomes aware of others first, not of himself. Naturally, when a child opens his eyes, he sees his mother. How can he see himself? The other, the 'thou', is seen, not the 'I'. Slowly his acquaintance enlarges. He sees his father, his brothers, sisters, and the family, and this way he is slowly learning to experience the other. And it is in contrast and relation to this other that he begins to experience his 'I'.

It is very interesting to note that the experience of 'I' is not the first. I am, but I do not experience myself first, I experience others first. Naturally when I experience the others first, then the 'I' that I will create will be based on the opinions of these others.

Therefore, the psychologists say, a child who has received love from the mother and the father and has received the appreciation of the family has got a feeling of self-love. But a child who has not received any love from the parents, any appreciation of the family – a kind of pathetic personality develops in him, because if the people through whom the child first became aware of his 'I' did not express their joy and happiness about him, the 'I' of that child becomes poor and destitute forever. He did not receive the nourishment.

Psychologists say that something is missing in a child that is brought up in the absence of a mother, and this can never be compensated for because the child's very first experience of 'I' remains crippled. The person from whom that first understanding of 'who I am' was to be born, the 'thou' from whom the first glimpses of 'I' were to come, was never there to give those glimpses. That person was never there to reflect the experiences of dignity, respect, pride, honor and love.

If a mother had not danced within herself on the birth of her child, if a mother was not overwhelmed with joy and if her whole being was not thrilled all over, then the 'I' of that particular child will remain crippled forever. He will suffer a lot. He will have to find crutches. He will be in great difficulty.

We get our first experience of 'I' from others, and we continue to get it from others all along. Slowly, slowly we accumulate opinions, approval, certificates, views of others, a prestige and a respect from the society. On this false center we remain hanging, whereas our real center is hidden behind it.

'Thou' cannot be first, 'I' is first – it is another matter that we only come to know it much later. When a child is born, he is born with his 'I', with his soul. But that center remains hidden and another new center gets created. Then we hold onto this new center. We do so because we do not know any other center, and we are afraid that if we let go of this center we may be hanging in mid-air, and if we do not take care we may be lost. We are afraid that everything may go topsy-turvy, chaotic. Hence we hold on fast to it like that parrot holding fast to the rope, because of the fear that it may fall down and be hurt.

We also go on holding onto this 'I' because we do not see anything else that can be held for support. We move on its support and keep holding tight lest it may slip out of our clutches. This brings misery because it is not the true center.

This situation of ours is like a person who is born with a treasure, but who mistakenly thinks it buried in a ditch and goes on digging for it fruitlessly. Our real center is an emperor; our soul is sheer bliss and a treasure. But this 'I' is a false ditch where, however much we may dig, we will find no treasures whatever. Digging there we can never reach to our self-nature. Therefore, the sutra says:

> Only a person free from holding onto
> the ego attains to self-nature.

What is to be done then?

Gurdjieff was a remarkable mystic. When his grandmother was on her deathbed he asked her, "Do you have any life experiences and conclusions that you think are worth passing on to me?"

His grandmother then said a very strange thing to him. She said,

"If you can remember one thing throughout your life that will do. That is: Never do anything as others do it – never do any work as others do it, always try to do it differently." Gurdjieff later on developed a whole philosophy around it and formed "the law of otherwise" – always doing things differently from others.

Gurdjieff made great efforts to apply this advice and a unique person was born in him, because not doing anything as others do it brings tremendous results. The first outcome is that, as one's ego is nourished only when one does things the way others do them, naturally there is nothing to nourish your ego. On the contrary, people will laugh at you.

Gurdjieff has said, "My grandmother told me, 'I am nearing my death and I will never know whether you followed my advice or not. So give me a demonstration before I die.' An apple was there near her bed; she gave it to me and asked me to eat it, but making sure that I did not eat it the way others do."

This child Gurdjieff must have found himself in great difficulty: what to do? But children are very inventive. If the parents did not kill their inventiveness completely there would be many inventors in the world. But inventions seem to be dangerous, because anything new brings uneasiness.

Gurdjieff took the apple and, bringing it close to his ear, he first tried to hear it, then bringing it near to his eyes he looked at it, he kissed it and touched it with closed eyes, then danced while still holding it in his hands, jumped and ran, and then he ate the apple. His grandmother said, "I am satisfied."

"Later," Gurdjieff said, "this became a principle in my life – not to do anything the way others do but to bring some originality of my own to it." People used to laugh at him and call him mad. They would say, "What sort of man is this? What is he doing – hearing an apple with his ears?"

Gurdjieff said, "I did not realize it then, but another outcome was that I was no longer worried about others. What others are saying or what their opinions are about me, or what others think about me – this concern simply dropped. I just became alone, absolutely alone on this earth. Because of this," Gurdjieff writes further, "I did not have to undergo that suffering all others go through. No false center was ever created within me and I never had to make any effort to destroy my ego. It never formed in the first place."

What is to be done? Drop bothering about others. I watch you in the morning when you are meditating. You are meditating, but an idea remains lurking, "Someone must be watching me...what will the others say?"

Just today a friend came to me. He said, "Whatever you say, I will do it alone. But doing it here in front of so many people...." There will be no benefit in doing it alone. There will be no benefit, because the benefits of meditation are multidimensional. Your courage to go mad in front of so many people simply knocks down your ego. Your childlike behavior in front of so many people suddenly removes you from your ego and throws you to your center. This will not happen in your aloneness. In aloneness, everybody is a singer in his bathroom, and everybody can make faces in the mirror in the aloneness of his bathroom – not only children, but grownups too. Such stories are luckily not told by the mirrors. But these things are of no value, and are no help – no help at all.

Drop worrying about others, stop thinking about the opinions of others; start reducing your craving for others' attention. The search for others' attention is the food for the ego. The others' attention is food, the ego gets nourished by it. Therefore, the more people pay attention to you the juicier it feels to you, the more you feel you are something. But if nobody pays any attention to you, you are in a house and nobody even looks at you....

Gurdjieff was experimenting with his disciples. He and his thirty disciples lived in a big house, and he told them to live there in such a way as if the other twenty-nine did not exist. They were not to speak with anyone, not to make any signs, not to make any gestures which might create any communication. Even if one passed by someone else, he had to remember that he was all alone there, nobody else was there in the house. Knowingly or unknowingly, nothing was to be done by anyone that might indicate the presence of the other. If someone stepped on somebody else's toes he was not to make any apology, for there was no one else present there. Even if because of somebody's mistake an ember from the fire was to fall on someone's hand, no one was to ask for any forgiveness – for there was no one else present there. No one was even to express through their eyes, "I am sorry."

Gurdjieff asked these thirty disciples to stay like that for three months. Twenty-seven disciples ran away after some time; only three remained to the very end, but those three were transformed into totally different persons.

What was the purpose of this experiment? Let us understand it. It is very easy not to pay any attention to others, or not to apologize, even if you kick someone! This is very easy, there is no difficulty in it. This is how we always want it to be. But this is not the significant point. So what meaning does this experiment carry?

Remember, its meaning is deep and hidden. Gurdjieff had asked you not to pay any attention to the fact that there is someone else present, but then also to understand well that others also will not pay any attention to you. That is where the catch is. You will not pay attention to others, you are alone; others will not pay attention to you, they are twenty-nine. You will not receive twenty-nine other people's attention, for three months, at all!

All transactions are mutual. I give you attention, you give me attention. It is a business. I am fulfilling your ego, you are fulfilling mine. But in this experiment the exchange will cease at both the ends. What was the reason for those twenty-seven disciples running away? Many of them said later, "We felt as if we were suffocating, that we would die, that we were choking."

Actually their throats were not choking, it was their ego's throats that were choking. They were thinking, "Three months! And there will be no food for our egos! By the time we are out of this place we will be empty." Those three courageous disciples who stayed, came out after three months as different persons altogether. What had changed in them?

Ouspensky was one of those three disciples who had stayed through the experiment. Later he said, "This man Gurdjieff was amazing, because in three months.... And we had no idea that this was a device to kill our egos. We had thought that the experiment was being carried out to bring peace and silence to our minds. We were not even told that our egos will be killed. After three months we became as though we did not exist; only our being remained. There was no tune of 'I' arising anywhere in us."

The day no 'I' arises within you, that day you are standing at your real 'I'. That real 'I' is called the soul. And naturally then your individuality becomes spotlessly clean like the full moon – ever blissful and self-luminous.

The light already exists there, the bliss already exists there; it is only a question of a small jump from your 'I' to the soul. The spotless cleanliness is already there, it has never been disturbed.

Another important sutra, equally original and wonderful. Many times words hide the real meaning and it is not seen. And because those words are familiar it becomes difficult to dive deep into them. You all must have heard these words before; none of them are unfamiliar, but their arrangement here is totally unfamiliar.

> *On cessation of the sense of doing, all anxieties*
> *cease. On cessation of the anxieties, all desires*
> *cease. The cessation of desires is emancipation –*
> *and this is called jivanamukti,*
> *liberation while living.*

On cessation of the sense of doing, all anxieties cease.... We all want to destroy anxieties. Who is the man who does not want to be free from anxieties? But we do not want to be free from being the doer. We want to be free from anxieties but we do not want to be free from the doer – and anxiety is the shadow of the doer. A person who thinks, "I am doing this," cannot save himself from anxiety. The anxiety will go on piling upon him. The more he thinks, "I am doing," the more anxious he will become.

The people of the East have invented ingenious devices. One of them was to feel, "I am not doing, God is doing." This was a technique of meditation. The technique was: "Not even a leaf of the tree moves without the permission of God." There is nothing like this in actuality. If God had to issue permission to every single leaf, by now he would have gone mad. Imagine telling every single leaf, "Now move, now stop!"

No, there is no such God anywhere to move and stop every single leaf. But this statement has nothing to do with God anyway, it is simply a technique of meditation, a device, because a person who believes that not even a leaf moves without his permission slowly starts dropping the notion of "I am doing." "*He* is the doer," such a man believes; "I am nothing at all. I may be instrumental at the most. If he makes me move, I move; if he makes me walk, I walk; if he makes me get up, I get up."

Thinking that everything is happening through God and we are just puppets in his hands has allowed a great phenomenon to take place in this world; the people in the East have become totally anxiety free. The anxiety-free time that the East has known has been known nowhere else on the earth, and the anxiety-laden time that the West is experiencing presently has also never been known before anywhere. But the cause originates from the same source. In the West God became a doubtful entity, the concept of destiny lost all meaning.

I do not say that the concept of destiny is right, but the device in the concept of destiny – "Everything is happening as per destiny" – ended in the West. Neither God survived nor fate nor destiny; the whole responsibility fell on man. "I am doing. Whatever I am doing, *I* am doing." The 'I' remained, because there is no way of denying it.

It makes no difference whether God is or is not, but if you can leave aside your doer in favor of God – even if he may not be – it begins to have an effect on you: you become anxiety free.

In the West, anxiety has deepened. American psychologists say that three out of every four people are mentally sick...three out of four! How long can that fourth person remain unaffected amongst these three? These three are trying in every possible way to drown the fourth. It is a big figure if three out of four persons have become mentally disturbed and sick. What is the reason? The East has never produced so many mad people as the West.

In the West the madness goes on increasing and slowly, slowly is taken for granted. Even Freud eventually accepted after a lifetime of research on the mind that there was no way of curing man; man will remain more or less mad. He accepted his inability. And if Freud accepts his inability it is very meaningful, because this man devoted fifty years of his life to exploring the human mind and he has done some deep research. He says there is no way man can be made fully healthy.

But Freud is not aware that fully healthy people have lived on this earth and fully healthy societies have also lived. But those societies had concepts altogether different. The deepest of those concepts was, "I am not the doer." They had found a device: the doer is God, fate, destiny – somebody else. "I am just an instrument and am like a leaf – moving when moved, not moving when not moved, winning or losing when made to win or lose. I am nowhere in it."

This had a twofold effect. One was that when you are not the doer, then there arises no reason to worry about anything. Then defeat is accepted as well as victory. When victory is none of your doing, it does not create an ego; and since defeat is also none of your doing, it does not give one sleepless nights, nor does anxiety overtake one, neither does it pain one's heart. And another more interesting thing also happens: if someone else wins there is no envy in your mind about it, because if he has won it is not his achievement, it was God's will that it should happen that way. Neither is he bigger because he has won, nor are we smaller because we are defeated. It is all God's will.

A very peaceful mental state develops if the feeling of being a doer drops. It is not necessary that one should believe in God for this. Buddha dropped it without believing in God, Mahavira dropped it without believing in God. This is a little more difficult.

If one has to drop the doer without believing in God, one has to deepen his witnessing very much. Just remain a watcher; whatsoever is happening, just remain a watcher. If there is defeat, just watch that you are witnessing the defeat; if there is victory, just watch that you are witnessing the victory. Neither you lose nor you win, you are only the witness. When it is morning, you witness that morning has come; when it is evening, you witness that evening has come. When the darkness of the night gathers, you witness that the darkness has come. When the sun rises and there is light, you witness that the light has come.

You remain a watcher in your own place – whether it is day or it is night, whether it is happiness or unhappiness, whether it is defeat or victory. Thus when a person settles in witnessing the doer dissolves; the doing no longer remains yours. You no longer remain the center of doing, you become the center of seeing, witnessing, knowing. The doing goes on happening around you in existence.

Mahavira says, "My stomach is hungry, I watch it; a thorn pierces my foot and the foot is in pain, I watch it; the body becomes sick, a sickness has come, I watch it." Even at the time of death, Mahavira will go on watching that the body is dying. You will not be able to watch that the body is dying; you will feel that *you* are dying. If you have been the doer your whole lifetime, then you will have to do the dying also. When you have done everything, to whom can you leave the act of dying? One who disowns life also disowns death. One who has kept watching life as a witness watches death also as a witness.

If the doing dies, in other words if the doer disappears, the anxieties die. The second statement is an even deeper truth than this:

On cessation of the anxieties, all desires cease.

It appears as if there is some mistake in this sutra. In the scriptures it is always said: when desires die, all anxiety dies. And this is what you may have heard also, that if there is no desire there is no anxiety. This sutra is saying just the opposite. It says: if the anxiety ceases, the desires cease. On the death of doing, anxiety dies, and on the death of anxiety, desires die. Why?

Have you ever observed? – when you are more anxious you are more full of desire, when you are more tense sexual desire arises more in you, because with sex that tension can be released and one can become lighter. When your mind is in anger, then too sexual desire arises more in you. When your mind is in a joyous, blissful state, sexual desire is less. If the mind is totally and constantly in a blissful state, there simply will be no sexual desire. There are reasons for this. When the mind reaches a certain limit of tension due to anything, the sex center functions like a safety valve; it *is* a safety valve. When your anxiety increases and becomes too much, when you are not able to tolerate it and so much energy is flowing around in your body that it makes you uneasy, your body finds a way of throwing that energy out.

The sex center is a safety valve. Wherever any energy is functioning, safety valves have to be there. Nature has done the same.

If you are heating up a kerosene pressure stove, some arrangement has to be there so that if you pump in too much air, the excess gets released. When you have electrical fittings done in your house, fuses have to be provided so that if excess current is drawn into a circuit the fuse will burn out, disconnecting the flow of electricity. The fuse does not permit more than a certain amount of energy to pass through it. As soon as too much current begins to be drawn, the fuse will burn out because of the excess energy trying to flow, and everything will be safe again.

The body has a biological safety valve through the sex center. Whenever excess energy accumulates in your body and uneasiness grows and anxiety grips you, there is a struggle within you; then it is necessary that either you become a witness and all this trouble subsides, or the second possibility is that the energy flows out of your body and you become weak. Then under the influence of that weakness all this trouble cools down – because one needs strength even for the troubles to continue.

Therefore it is often the case that weak people are gentle people. It does not mean that they actually are gentle people, all it means is that they do not possess that much energy which is necessary for doing evil.

Have you ever observed that fat people are usually cheerful, very sociable, and usually not quarrelsome. Why? If you ask a physiologist he will say that a fat person cannot fight; if he does he will be beaten; hence he becomes so sociable, because he cannot afford this fighting business. If he attempts it, he is bound to be beaten. So they are always smiling. This smile means, no fighting, please; everything is alright, no need to move into fighting.

A fat person cannot run. And in a fight there are only two alternatives: either you fight or run away – and he can do neither. So he becomes non-quarrelsome. But it does not mean he has transcended fighting. No, in man everything lies deep within, and it is useful to become aware of these things.

So whenever you are full of anxiety, unhappiness and misery, desire will arise in your mind. Either you become a witness, in which case the energy that is entangled in anxiety will be released and, riding on it, you will set forth on the upward journey.... Or, if you cannot become a witness, the energy which is making you restless, which has created a cyclonic turmoil in you will be released through the safety valve of the sex center; you will become weak and you will feel you have become lighter, relieved.

Freud has described sex as a natural tranquilizer, a soothing drug. Man returns home tired and weary from the whole day of problems of all sorts and engulfed in anxieties. If he is able to release the energy through sex, he falls asleep peacefully in the night.

This is the reason why women do not take much interest in sex, because they very soon come to realize that they are functioning only as a safety valve to the man. They soon discover that there is no love or anything of the sort in it, it is all instrumental. They soon come to realize that slowly, slowly they have become an instrument for this man through whom he releases his energy and goes to sleep. And it often happens that after intercourse the man turns over and falls asleep, whereas the woman remains weeping because for her there cannot be a bigger insult than just being used like a thing.

An unaccountable number of women come and tell me that they have no interest at all in sex. The reason for this is not their lack of interest in it, the whole reason is that man has used them as a thing and their interest has turned sour. In fact the reality is just the opposite: women are more sexual than men, they have more energy for sex. But they do not appear sexual, instead they appear quite disinterested in sex. Their attitude towards man appears to be, "Okay, take what you want and be done with it. One less problem for me!" But they seem to have no more interest than this. The reason for this is not that they do not have any sexual desire within, but because they have a feeling of hurt at being used as a thing. They are pained at being treated like a thing and not as individuals. But all of this brings other results.

A man is able to release his energy through sex, but what is the woman supposed to do? So women turn quarrelsome, nagging, overbearing. They throw out their energies through these other routes twenty-four hours a day, because the sexual safety valve device is not functioning for them, and they come to think this device is only for men.

Now this is a very paradoxical thing. Women should be more sweet, but it does not happen that way; they should be more gentle, but it does not happen that way; they should be more harmonious, but it does not happen that way. What is the matter? Somewhere, some mistake is happening in the natural arrangements. And the mistake is that what could have been the natural outlet to their energies is blocked and they have lost interest in it. To become a witness is arduous, so all those energies go on circling within and they come out in different forms.

The woman will drop utensils from her hands – usually it has to be chinaware, so it falls and breaks. In this breaking, her energies are getting an outlet. You can prepare a complete chart of such events to find out yourself as to when such things happen more in your household. And you will inevitably discover that they break more during the days when the energies of the woman do not get released – then through so many methods like anger, tension, etcetera, the woman will throw out her energy.

When there is great anxiety of the mind, it runs toward indulging desires. Therefore, this sutra says that on the death of anxieties, all desires die.

This is a very unique and ancient sutra. And it is only now that the psychologists are discovering this. If you become anxiety free, your desires will become very weak. If you become completely anxiety free, your mind will not even move towards desires. Desires become inevitable to release the storm when it arises within you beyond a certain limit. When there are no storms of that intensity, the desires become very weak. But the energy does not get weakened; the desires weaken, but the energy goes on accumulating.

Everything gets transformed at a certain limit. Water turns into steam when heated up to one hundred degrees. On the accumulation of one hundred degrees of heat, the water then becomes steam. When your semen, your energy, continues to become accumulated within to a certain point – without any storms happening and with no necessity arising for uselessly throwing the energy out – then suddenly, when the energy accumulation reaches a certain level, which is like the hundred-degree point, it begins to rise upwards instead of flowing downwards.

Have you observed: water flows downwards and steam rises upwards. Water, whose nature is to flow downwards, suddenly at one hundred degrees becomes steam and starts rising upwards, towards the sky.

This is the phenomenon that happens within you too: there is a point, a level, an evaporating point, where evaporation happens. When the energy accumulates up to that point, suddenly you find that what used to flow outwards has begun to flow inwards, what was a sin till yesterday has turned into a virtue, and what looked like an enemy till yesterday, now there is no greater friend – all this comes to be realized.

The cessation of desires is emancipation.

When there is no desire you are liberated. And one can be liberated while living, there is no need to be liberated after dying. One who is unable to be liberated in life should not hope that he will attain it on death, because one dies the same way one was living. As you lived, so will you die; nothing different is going to happen in dying. Death is the ultimate culmination of life. Only to a *jivanamukta*, one who has known liberation now and here, death becomes liberation while living too.

> *Seeing all, everywhere, in every direction, as*
> *Brahman, the absolute reality – on the ripening of*
> *the feeling of such goodwill do desires cease.*
> *Never be negligent of your allegiance to Brahman,*
> *the absolute reality, because that is the only*
> *death, say the ones who are well-rooted*
> *in Brahman.*

> *Even if shifted aside, the algae do not lose time in*
> *covering the water again. Similarly, if a wise man*
> *swerves from his allegiance to Brahman even*
> *for a little while, illusions cover him.*

So it is necessary to keep constant awareness. Losing awareness even for a moment will not do. To remain aware is necessary up to such a time as there remains not even the smallest quantity of algae or grass within. When all algae and grass are burned in their very seed form, then there is no need for remaining aware, because awareness at that stage becomes your very nature.

Enough for today.

LIFE IS AN OPPORTUNITY

CHAPTER 6

One who has attained oneness with Brahman,
the absolute reality, while living,
will remain so even after leaving the body.
Therefore, O innocent one! becoming awakened
be void of all choice in duality.

✳

When one sees the nondual soul through
nirvikalpa samadhi – the choiceless awakening –
that is the moment when the knot of ignorance in
the heart dissolves completely.

✳

Consolidating the self-ness, dropping the I-ness
etcetera, exist with indifference to them,
like with pots and clothes, etcetera.
All titles – from Brahman, the creator god,
to a stone – are false. Therefore, rooted only in
the soul, see your own soul everywhere.

✳

I myself am Brahman – the creator;
I myself am Vishnu – the sustainer; I myself am
Shiva – the destroyer; I myself am Indra – the
chief of all gods; I myself am this universe, and I
myself am all. There is nothing other than myself.

hatsoever is worth achieving in life can be achieved only during the lifetime. But many people go on waiting until after death. Many people think that how can truth, the divine, liberation be achieved while still being in the body, in life, in the world? However, what cannot be attained during life cannot be attained ever.

Life is an opportunity to achieve, whether you spend it in collecting pebbles or in attaining to the divine. Life is a completely neutral opportunity. Life does not tell you what to achieve. If you collect pebbles, accumulate worthless things, or waste your life in increasing and inflating your ego, life will not prevent you from doing so. Or you may dedicate your life to attaining the truth, the self and the ultimate depths of life; then too life will not object to your doing so.

Life is merely a neutral opportunity – you may use it the way you like. But many people have made arrangements to deceive themselves. They think, "Life is for worldly pleasures." They have created such divisions: "Life is for *bhoga*, indulgence." But then only death remains for *yoga*, union with the divine. But death is not an opportunity. Let this be understood properly. Death is an end of all opportunity.

What is the meaning of death? Its meaning is that now there is no more opportunity left. Life is an opportunity, death is the end of the opportunity. So nothing can be achieved through death, because for achieving anything there should be a span of opportunity.

But we have divided: we say life is for indulgence. But when life will be exhausted, then?…then yoga. We have created all these stories that you utter into the ears of the dying person at the time of death – when he will not even be able to hear. When living persons do not listen, how would a dead or dying person hear a *gayatri* mantra, or recite the name of the divine, or chant "Rama, Rama"?

The person could not hear the gayatri mantra his whole life, and even if he heard he did not listen, and even if he listened he did not grasp.... That person at the time of death – when all the senses will be failing; when the eyes won't see, the ears won't hear, the hands won't touch; when life is disappearing back into its source – will he be able to hear gayatri? No, he will not be able to hear. But then why do people go on uttering such things into his ears? There is a secret in it. That dying person is unable to hear anything, but the living ones who are uttering it for him remain under the assurance that at the time of their death somebody will utter it for them, and the goal will be achieved. So they have invented stories of this sort.

These dishonest people have invented stories. It is said: One person was dying and he had a son named Narayana, one of the names for god, and he shouted aloud "Narayana" to call him. Hearing this, the god Narayana, who is in heaven, was tricked. He thought that he was being remembered. The dying man was calling his son, perhaps to advise the son in his last moments as to how to do black-marketing or how to keep double accounts! But due to the god Narayana's misunderstanding the dying man went to heaven. He himself was surprised as to how he arrived there. But his utterance of the name of Narayana at the time of his death had managed the miracle. No, things cannot be managed so cheaply. And a Narayana who can be so easily deceived will also be only a bogus Narayana.

Deceptions don't work in real life; it is another matter that you may console your mind with such ideas.

Death is the end of opportunity. Understand this meaning properly. Death is not yet another opportunity for doing something.

Death is the end of all opportunities; you won't be able to do anything. There simply is no way of doing anything in death. Doing means life, so whatsoever is to be done has to be done during life.

In this sutra some beautiful words have been used.

One who has attained oneness with Brahman,
the absolute reality, while living,
will remain so even after leaving the body.

Only the one who has known his self during his lifetime will remain as Brahman, the ultimate one, when his body drops. Someone who has believed his whole life that he is the body will become unconscious while dying – he will go totally unconscious. Very few people die consciously. Death happens in a kind of sleep, in an unconscious state. You are not conscious while dying, otherwise you would be able to remember your previous death. Whatever happens in unconsciousness does not remain in the memory. That is why people do not know that they have been born many times and they have died many times, because whenever they died they were unconscious. And whosoever dies unconscious is born unconscious, because birth and death are two polarities of the same thing. A person dies here, this is one end of the phenomenon; then the same person enters a womb somewhere, that is the other end. Death and birth are two sides of the same coin.

One who dies unconscious is born unconscious. Therefore you do not even know that you had died earlier. You also do not know of your birth. This news of your birth is also given to you by others. If there is no one to tell you that you were born, you will have no remembrance of your own that you have been born. It is very interesting. That you were born is definite – you may have died before or not, but the fact that now you are born is definite. But you do not even have any memory of this. This too you have heard from your parents, from others.

The news of your own birth is a rumor to you, you do not have any proof of it. There is no memory of it in your consciousness. What might be the reason for it? You were born; birth is a big event, and you have no knowledge of this big event.

Remember, one who does not know about his birth will have great difficulty in knowing about his death while dying. They are interconnected. Death has happened many times, but you have died unconscious. Leave death aside; you are sleeping every day, the phenomenon of sleep is happening every day, but do you know that just before sleep comes you are losing your consciousness? Do you have any awareness of encountering sleep? When sleep descends, are you able to see it descending? Up to the point of sleep you are able to notice anything; you are still awake, sleep has not descended yet. And the moment sleep descends you are lost. At the very descending of sleep you lose consciousness.

When you are unable to remain aware even in sleep, how are you going to remain aware in death? Death is a very deep sleep, the deepest sleep: it is very difficult to remain aware in it. You will die unconscious. And in that unconsciousness, whoever is reciting the gayatri mantra, whoever is chanting "Rama, Rama," you will know nothing of it. And this unconsciousness is actually necessary.

Only those people are freed from this unconsciousness who become free from their identification with the body. Why? If a surgeon is operating on your stomach he will have to make you unconscious because there will be so much pain that you will not be able to tolerate it. You will shout, cry, shriek and shake, and it will be almost impossible to carry out the operation. The pain will be so much that you may even go insane, your mind will never again be normal. This is why the surgeon administers anesthesia first and makes you unconscious, and then does the surgery. Your body is cut, but then you do not know. And because you do not know, you do not feel the pain.

Understand this properly. Pain is not experienced because of pain, it is experienced because of knowing. When the surgeon is operating the pain is there, but the only difference is that you do not know it. The surgeon will cut you open and take out unwanted things, but you will not know it. You will know the pain only when you regain your consciousness. And when you know, you will experience the pain happening. In your unconsciousness, even if limb after limb is cut – you are cut to pieces – you will not know.

However, the surgeon is doing a small operation, whereas death is a very big operation. There is no bigger operation than death. The surgeon is merely cutting away a limb or two, but death has to cut away and separate your body from you. You cannot be kept conscious in such a big operation, therefore death has forever used the natural anesthesia. As soon as death approaches you fall unconscious. In that unconsciousness, the world's biggest surgery happens, the separation of your body from your soul.

But a person can die without becoming unconscious. Nature allows a person to die consciously who has come to know that he is not the body. Why? – so that then, when the body is being cut off, he does not identify with the body. He goes on watching from a distance. He can watch from a distance because he knows that something else is being cut: "I am not being cut, I am watching it, I am only a witness." Whenever such a realization becomes crystallized, nature gives such a person the opportunity to die consciously. But this happens at a much later stage. First one has to learn to sleep consciously, and that too comes later; first one has to learn to be conscious while awake.

One who is conscious while awake slowly learns how to sleep consciously. One who lives consciously one day dies consciously. One who dies consciously is able to know that he has become one with Brahman, the ultimate reality. But first one has to know this in the consciousness hidden within one's own body. Then one day this outer pot also breaks and the inner sky merges with the vast sky.

One who dies consciously passes through wonderful experiences. Death does not feel like an enemy to him, death feels like a friend to him. Death feels like a great union with the divine, with the vast. One who dies consciously can also take a new birth consciously. One who is born consciously, his life is altogether different because he does not repeat the same things over and over again which he has repeated many times before. All that becomes foolish and meaningless to him. His life becomes something new, his life enters new dimensions. And his witnessing is continuous; one who was a witness at the time of birth, one who was a witness at the time of a previous death, he remains a witness throughout his life.

Thus in only one death you can die fully conscious, and in only one birth you can be fully conscious; thereafter the cycle of birth and death ceases. Thereafter you disappear from the world of bodies. For this phenomenon of disappearance, in India we have devised a very beautiful word: *kaivalya*. This is a wonderful word.

Kaivalya means, "I am alone. Only I am and there is nothing else; only I, only consciousness, only the soul, nothing else; only the watcher, only the witness, nothing else. All else is a game, all else is a dream. The truth is only the witnessing consciousness. Only the seer is the truth, the seen is not the truth." Kaivalya is the name given to this experience.

Let us understand this a little. You were a child, then you became a youth, and then you became old. Childhood went away and youth came, youth went away and old age came. This means you are nothing but a constant change. Neither childhood remains, nor youth, nor old age – everything changes. But is there anything within you that does not change? You were miserable, then you became happy; you were happy, then you became miserable; you were peaceful, then you became unpeaceful; you were unpeaceful, then you became peaceful – everything changes. You were rich, you became poor; you were poor, you became rich – everything changes. But is there any one thing within you that does not change?

If there is not such a thing within you, then you simply are not there at all. Then what is the meaning of your being there? Who will then thread together your childhood, your youth and your old age, like a string of a necklace? A necklace is a necklace only when its beads are threaded together on a string. If there is no string inside to thread them all together and only the beads are there, then not only the necklace will not be there but also all the beads will be scattered.

Your childhood is there like a bead, your youth is there like a bead, your old age is there like a bead – but where is the string on which these are all threaded together? Where is that continuity factor? And that continuity factor is the truth. All else changes. India's definition is that whatever changes, we call it a dream. Let this be understood properly.

We have our own definition of the word dream. Whatsoever changes, we call it a dream, and what never changes, we call it the truth. So the childhood passes off like a dream; youth passes off like a dream; happiness comes and goes, unhappiness comes and goes; just as dreams disappear, everything goes on disappearing. Therefore, the seers of India say, it is a vast dream spread all around you.

There are two types of dreams. One type is your personal dreams, the ones you see in your sleep during the night. The other type is the common dream which you see while awake during the day. But there is no difference between the two, because they both are changing. The dreams of the night are falsified by the morning, and the dreams of life are falsified by death. A moment comes when all that was seen becomes useless. Is there any truth then? But even for the existence of dreams there has to be the base of truth. Even for change there has to be some base which does not change; otherwise change is not possible. Where is that base? It is within us. The sutra of the sage says: witnessing is the base.

You saw your childhood; the childhood has changed but the seer within you is unchanged. Then came youth and you saw it; then the youth also went away but the one who saw it is unchanged. It is the same seer who saw the childhood, who saw the youth, who saw the old age; who saw the birth, who saw the death; who saw the happiness, who saw the unhappiness; who saw the success and failure. Everything changes, only the one who goes on seeing, who goes on experiencing everything, does not change. It is this seer whom we know as the soul; it is the truth. To know this one, the unchanging, is kaivalya.

Kaivalya is experienced the day a person, separating himself from all the dreams, separating himself from all the beads, comes to know himself as the string running through them all. The day he comes to know that, "This uninterrupted consciousness, this witnessing spirit, this is what I am; I am only this conscious-ness"...when such a realization becomes a crystallized experience – not a thought but an experience, not a word but a realization – we call such a person the one who has attained to kaivalya. He has known the one that is worth knowing, he has achieved the one that is worth achieving. And in achieving that one alone one achieves everything; and in losing that one alone one loses everything.

We try to catch dreams, but even before we have any grip on them they are lost and our fist remains empty. In the night we saw that we were emperors; in the morning our hands are empty. In life we see we have become this, we have become that; at the time of death our hands are empty. Whosoever we had held as our own – on whosoever we had closed our fist – they disappeared like the air from one's fist. The fist closes and the air disappears from it. Everything proves to be a dream.

Remember, our very meaning of 'dream' is only this, that wherever there is change there is no truth. What is that which is non-changing and uniform? You go on searching in this world and nowhere will you find that uniform, unchanging truth. Only when you search within yourself will you find in the watcher that continuity, that integrity which is uniform. That is known as kaivalya. If you know that one while living, then at death, on the dropping of the body, the oneness with Brahman, the absolute reality, is experienced.

Therefore, O innocent one! becoming awakened
be void of all choice in duality.

How shall we be able to know the one? The process is: be void of all *vikalpa*, all choice in duality. This word vikalpa is also worth understanding. Vikalpa means all the things that have their opposites – those opposites are the vikalpa. For example, happiness: its opposite is unhappiness. If you want happiness, you will also get unhappiness. You will have to bear it. That is the price one has to pay for the happiness. If you want love you will have to encounter hate also, that is the price. If you want success, failure will also come your way; it is the shadow of success, it comes along with it. Vikalpa means the world of duality, where everything is in two parts; you desire the one and you are bound to be entangled in the other too. There is no way to be saved from this situation.

The only way to be saved from it is to give up both, to become choiceless. That means wherever there is duality do not choose, drop all choosing. Understand this a little more, because it is a matter that takes one very deep. Wherever there is a possibility of two – whenever...! If you want peace, you will continue getting caught up in peacelessness. This is a little difficult to understand. We can understand dualities of happiness and unhappiness, success and failure, respect and disrespect; but I say peace and peacelessness too. It is the same thing, a matter of duality. Not only this: if you want liberation, you will go on falling in bondage because duality is the same here too, the opposites are facing each other here too; the possibility of choice is the same. So a person who says he wants liberation, he will be entrapped.

Liberation comes to one who does not choose between dualities; peace belongs to one who does not choose between the dualities – who does not ask for peace. Who says, "Peace or turmoil, I am not going to choose between the two" – such a man becomes peaceful. The flower of love blossoms in the life of one who does not choose love against hatred, who says, "Neither do I want love nor hatred, I am indifferent to both; I beg to be forgiven for both, I do not want to meddle in either of the two." The flower of love blooms in the life of such a person.

Wherever there is duality, wherever there is vikalpa – the option – wherever there is the possibility of choice, do not choose. But we always choose! And we are unable to understand that our choice is the very entanglement. When you choose happiness you have also chosen unhappiness, the unhappiness has already arrived, the unhappiness also has already entered your door. Why?

Understand the process. I desire happiness – this desire implies several things. One, it implies that I am unhappy now. Only the one who is unhappy wants happiness. Why would a happy person desire happiness? We ask only for that which we do not have, we do not ask for that which we already have. This is why nobody asks for unhappiness, because everybody already has it. People ask for happiness because they do not have it. So the day you say you want happiness you have made at least one thing clear – that you are unhappy.

Secondly, whatever happiness you are asking for, if you don't achieve it you will slip into deeper unhappiness – and there is no guarantee of achieving this happiness. And if you do achieve it, still you will later slip into unhappiness because now you have come to know how many dreams you had arranged around it and none of them were fulfilled.

All happiness appears to be in the distance, in the future, but as you come closer it disappears. As long as happiness is not yours it is happiness; as it becomes yours it turns into unhappiness. Happiness is in the distance. Happiness is not in things, it is in the distance, it is in your hope, it is in your waiting. When it comes, or as it comes closer, it begins to disappear, and by the time it is in your hands it becomes unhappiness.

Neither happiness nor unhappiness is inherent in anything. The greater the distance, the greater appears the happiness; as it comes closer, the greater the unhappiness. This is a very complex trap. Whatsoever we bring close, unhappiness begins to breed out of it. The more we ask for happiness.... One, you will not get it, because nothing is received by asking; and when you will not get it, you will be frustrated. Second, even if you did get it you would also be encountering failure, and an emptiness will surround you, that all your efforts have turned futile, nothing really has been achieved; one rushed around, labored hard, and all that is received is this? What appeared to be so glittering from a distance.... Any music at a distance sounds celestial.

If you make a choice you will become entangled in the world. The world is in choosing, liberation is in non-choosing. Just do not choose! When happiness comes, accept it; when unhappiness comes, accept it. But do not have any choice within that, "I want this." One who does not put forward any demand in this world becomes free of this world. Let this sink a little deeper in you. One who does not ask for anything from the world cannot be entrapped by the world. If you ask for anything from this world you are entrapped. If you get what you ask of the world you are entrapped. If you do not get it, then too you are entrapped. You are entrapped because of the very asking; it has nothing to do with gaining it or not gaining it.

Fishermen attach bait to their fishing hooks. Only that fish will be safe from the hook which will not open her mouth at all. The fish that opened her mouth is hooked. A fish will open her mouth only for the bait; no fish is so foolish as to open its mouth for the hook. All fish will open their mouth for the bait, and that is why a fisherman will just sit waiting after putting his line in the water. A fish is entrapped because of the bait.

Everybody wants happiness, and the hook of unhappiness comes out of the happiness. Everybody desires respect, and the hook of disrespect appears out of the very respect. Everyone wants peace, and the very peace becomes turmoil. Think of the fish which does not choose either of the two – the bait or the hook; which simply swims past this bait indifferently. It is impossible to catch this fish.

Be in the world like this fish which does not choose, which does not ask. Then there can be no bondage for you, you cannot be trapped.

To become a sannyasin means giving up all choosing of options. So remember, sannyas is not a choice against the world. And those people who have given sannyas a meaning of being against the world will remain entangled in the world.

There are people who say, "Sannyas is against the world; and we are in the world – how can we take sannyas? We shall take sannyas when we renounce the world." Their sannyas is also a duality. Sannyas and the world for them are two sides, opposites. They say that if they choose the world, how can they choose sannyas also? Or if they choose sannyas, how can they choose the world also? If sannyas too is a duality, then all meaning of sannyas is lost. The very meaning of sannyas is to become non-dualistic. Now we do not choose! Whatsoever happens is accepted, what does not happen is not demanded. Such a state of being is sannyas. Then you can be a sannyasin anywhere. Then sannyas is a state of being, not an alternative choice.

This sutra says:

*Therefore, O innocent one! becoming awakened
be void of all choice in duality.*

Awakening happens only when one becomes void of all choice in duality.

*When one sees the nondual soul through
nirvikalpa samadhi – the choiceless awakening –
that is the moment when the knot of ignorance in
the heart dissolves completely.*

There are two types of awakening. One is *savikalpa samadhi,* the choiceful awakening. It is awakening just in name. Savikalpa samadhi – choiceful awakening – means that someone chose to become peaceful. Understand this properly.

Often this is what people choose first. When they are too hurt by the world they become disturbed, restless, and then they think to attain peace through meditation. They choose peace against the turmoil. They do begin finding peace through meditation, but deep within this peace remains hidden the face of peacelessness. That alternative will always be present there, because in the first place you have chosen peace against turmoil. You cannot be free of the opposite of that which you have chosen; it will remain present. At the most what can happen is that the side you have chosen may come out on top and the side you have not chosen may remain at the bottom – but it cannot be destroyed.

Choice can never take one out of a duality; the duality will remain there. You may choose, but because of the very fact of choosing its opposite remains present. So you may even become peaceful, but your peace will be only on the surface. Your being peaceful will be on the surface and the turmoil will remain hidden within. And you will always be in fear of the turmoil exploding any moment. The seed of turmoil will remain and the fear of its sprouting will also remain.

This is why people run away from the world, because in the world they are afraid of the turmoil that remains hidden within themselves, which is likely to explode at any moment if somebody provokes it a little. A person escaping toward the jungle is not running away from you, he is running away from the turmoil hidden within himself. If he appears to be running away from you, it is just because of the fear that you may expose the inner layer of his turmoil. A husband escaping toward the jungle is not running away from his wife but from the celibacy that he has imposed upon himself. The sexuality is still hidden inside him, because anybody who understood celibacy to be against sexuality cannot be free from the seeds of sexuality. One who chooses will remain tied to the opposite.

The very meaning of choosing is that we are choosing *against* something. And whatsoever we have chosen against will continue to follow us. Whatever we have arranged on the surface, below it is present that against which we have chosen – because that too is part of it.

In fact, we have divided life into two parts – one we have chosen, the other we have not – whereas they are both integral parts. Where will the part we have not chosen go? It will remain with us. And then you will be afraid that if you are with people, if you have a family, a business, and are in the marketplace, the part which is hidden within you will pop out just at the slightest investigation by somebody. Hence, run away! Run away to a place where nobody can make you see what is hidden within. But that will not destroy it. One may live in the Himalayas for a thousand years, but the day he returns to the marketplace he will find that those thousand years have been wasted. The marketplace will again provoke what is hidden inside and it will come out in the open.

Choiceful awakening means you have become silent by choice.

Choiceless awakening means you have dropped all choosing. Only the choiceless awakening – which means one does not divide things in two parts – is an awakening. The choiceful awakening is nothing but a deception of awakening. But one first comes toward the choiceful awakening; one chooses sannyas frustrated by the world. It is only natural, tormented by the world one chooses sannyas.

The second thing will happen only when one will get tired of sannyas also, when one will experience that like any two opposites, sannyas and the world are also two parts of the same symphony. That day the real sannyas will flower. That day one will not choose. That day one will drop choosing as such. That day one will understand, "In choosing is the world, and hence I do not choose anymore. Now whatsoever happens, I accept it; what does not happen, I am not concerned by it. Now I am willing – in whatsoever way existence cares for me I am willing.... Now there is no voice of mine whatsoever against existence. Now if unhappiness comes, the right thing is happening. If happiness comes, the right thing is happening. Now I do not separate myself and say that it should happen only in a certain way. Now I have no expectations, demands and claims of my own. I have given up claims."

The day one gives up claims the choiceless awakening happens. That day there remains no bondage for you in this world. Even if the whole world becomes an imprisonment and tightens itself around your body like an octopus, there will be no bondage, because you accept that too; it is okay.

If someone puts chains on my hands, remember the chains are not a bond because the one who puts them on my hands believes it so; it is a bondage only if I believe it to be a bondage. It can be a bondage only if I believe it to be so – it will all depend on my belief. I can stretch my hands forward and ask to have the chains put on my hands.

There is a very interesting and beautiful event in the life of Ramakrishna. From his very childhood Ramakrishna was a person with a mind drawn towards the divine. It was difficult for him to reach home if he had to pass by a temple. He would dance there, lie down there flat on the steps of the temple, and if someone uttered the name of Rama he would be in a sort of trance. So the members of his family thought that this boy would not live a worldly life, there was no such hope.

However, it was the duty of his parents, when he came of age, to ask him whether he would marry. They asked him, "Rama" – his real, given name was Gadadhar – "will you marry?" They had thought that Ramakrishna would refuse. But Ramakrishna was delighted at the question and said, "What is marriage and what is it like? I will certainly do it!" The parents were taken aback. They had thought that the boy was of a sannyasin nature and that he would not marry, but what is this? They began to search for a bride.

A bride was selected; she was quite young in age still, she was about eight to ten years younger than Ramakrishna. Ramakrishna went to see the girl, and the members of his family also accompanied him. Ramakrishna's mother had put three *rupees* in his pocket in case he may need them for anything, although the bride's village was not very far away. Ramakrishna was given new clothes and was groomed for the occasion. On reaching the village he saw the girl; she was very lovely. Ramakrishna put those three rupees at her feet and touched her feet. All who saw that happening were embarrassed and said, "Are you mad? She is going to be your wife, and you are touching her feet! And why have you presented her with those three rupees?"

Ramakrishna said, "She looks as lovely as my mother." Ramakrishna knew of only one love, the love of the mother. He said, "She is so lovely, just like my mother! I shall only call her 'mother'. What difference does it make if she is also a wife?"

Later they were married, but Ramakrishna always addressed Sharda as "Mother" and he continued to touch her feet. And when the day for the worship of the mother goddess Kali arrived, Ramakrishna would seat Sharda on a throne and worship her. He would say, "When there is the living mother, what is the need of an idol?" Having a wife was not a bondage; he never looked on her as a bondage. He just stretched forward his hands and took the fetters.

Everything depends upon your attitude. Unhappiness is unhappiness because you reject it and you desire happiness. Unhappiness is because you desire its opposite, otherwise what is the unhappiness? Unhappiness is hidden in your demand for the opposite. What is peacelessness? Peacelessness is because you desire peace. Our world lies in our choice.

This sutra says: Whosoever becomes choiceless sees the nondual soul, because the one who does not choose in the outside world – neither happiness nor unhappiness, neither love nor hate, neither the world nor liberation, neither matter nor God – who simply does not choose, with whom all choosing has ceased, he immediately reaches within himself.

It is in the choosing that the consciousness becomes stuck. We get stuck in what we choose. When one simply does not choose, all blockage is destroyed; his contact with the shore is broken and his contact with the midstream begins; he merges with the stream within.

He who attains to choicelessness sees the soul, and then the knot of ignorance in the heart is completely destroyed.

> Consolidating the self-ness, dropping the I-ness
> etcetera, exist with indifference to them,
> like with pots and clothes, etcetera.

Understand this word *udasin*, indifferent, also. Udasin, indifferent, does not mean remaining *udas*, sad. Udasin means to live unconcerned, to live without purpose. The word udasin has done a lot of harm. There is a sect of udasin sannyasins; they remain in self-imposed sadness because they think *udasinata*, indifference, means *udasi*, sadness.

Indifference has nothing to do with sadness; the relationship is only in the sound of the words. Indifferent means, "I keep no choices. Whatsoever is happening, let it happen. Not udasi, sadness, but udasinata, indifference. It is all fine, whatsoever takes place is fine." It is just as if one lives in a house – the examples taken in this sutra are pots, clothes, belongings, etcetera in the house – and one goes on moving in and out of the house with ease.

If a pot is lying around it is lying around, one does not need to take note of it. If clothes are hanging in the house they are hanging; one passes by these things, one does not need to pay special attention to them.

Similarly, within us our egos are hanging, along with unhappiness, happiness, agonies and anxieties, memories of happiness and unhappiness – they are all lying there within us. These are like inner household goods – pots, vessels, clothes, etcetera. Pass through them in a way that all is fine; whatever is, is fine. No need to pay attention to them, no need to choose from them, no need to be attracted to one thing and repulsed by some other – this is what is meant by indifference.

An indifferent person is very cheerful, not sad. But keep in mind the meaning of being cheerful. Being cheerful means that nothing now disturbs him, and hence the inner flower begins to bloom; nothing now bothers him, hence he remains in bliss within himself.

If you forcibly impose sadness upon yourself you will never be able to be cheerful. One has to become indifferent. Try it out by experimenting....

You are walking down a road: decide to remain indifferent to everything you come across for five minutes. Then which house is beautiful, which is not, it is all the same. Then whoever passes by – whether he was a rich man or poor, he was a respectable person or a disreputable person, he was a political leader or a thief – whoever he was, you have nothing to do with it. A beautiful woman passed by, a handsome man passed by, somebody's dress was elegant – you are not concerned with any of these matters. Walk down the road for five minutes as if it is totally empty, or you are passing through a jungle and there is nothing to attract you. Try this out – just remaining indifferent – and you will immediately notice that the road has lost all meaning. Its meaningfulness was in your inner attachments.

In a memoir that Vidyasagar has written he has said that one evening he had gone for a walk and he saw a Mohammedan gentleman walking ahead of him. He too was going for a walk every day. Suddenly a servant came running – Vidyasagar was walking just behind – and said to that Mohammedan friend, "Mir Sahib! Your house is on fire, please come fast." Mir Sahib replied, "I am coming." But he kept on walking at the same pace; the same movement of the legs, the same unhurried steps – nothing changed in him. Hearing the news of the fire, even Vidyasagar's walking speed changed, his breathing became faster. But Mir Sahib continued to walk in the same indifferent way.

The servant was puzzled, he said again a little louder, "Didn't you hear? Your house is on fire!" Mir Sahib said, "I have heard," and he continued walking in the same nonchalant manner.

Vidyasagar then came forward and said, "What are you doing? Do you understand what the servant is saying, that your house is on fire?" Mir Sahib told Vidyasagar, "That is alright, but what can I do now after the house is on fire? Why should I also spoil my walk? And I have this one opportunity – if I can carry on my walk unhindered by the fact of my house being on fire, I shall have a taste of indifference. The house is on fire, okay, but I shall walk in the same way as I was walking before the house was on fire. If I change my gait even slightly, that will be a change in my consciousness...so it is alright." And Mir Sahib continued walking in the same way.

Vidyasagar has written further that he and Mir Sahib's servant ran to the burning house, leaving Mir Sahib with his walk. "We had become very upset and on reaching the house we helped to extinguish the fire." And Vidyasagar says he could not sleep well that night. But by the unperturbed attitude of Mir Sahib that he had seen that day, it is very clear that Mir Sahib must have slept peacefully that night too. What difference would there have been? A person whose walking speed was no different – how could there be any difference in his sleep?

Indifference means a neutral attitude. Whatsoever is happening is alright, it is accepted; there is a state of suchness, there is no choosing of any kind. Restlessness is not caused by the fact that the house is on fire. Try to understand it: restlessness is caused by the expectation that, "My house should not be on fire." There is this hidden expectation that your house should not have been on fire. You may not even be aware of it, it is hidden in the unconscious mind that your house should not have been on fire. So when the house *is* on fire, that inner expectation is shattered and that unsettles your gait, that unsettles your consciousness. But those who have no expectations of any kind, and whatsoever happens they have no attitude and insistence against it, their consciousness does not become unsettled. This unwavering of the consciousness is udasinata, indifference.

> *All titles – from Brahman, the creator god,*
> *to a stone – are false. Therefore, rooted only in*
> *the soul, see your own soul everywhere.*

All positions, all titles and all reputations are false and artificial. Whether it is a stone lying on the roadside or the god installed by us up in the sky, all are useless.

Remain attentive only to one that is not false, remain absorbed in that witnessing alone. So even if you are a stone, remain absorbed in the same witnessing, and even if you are Brahman, the creator god, remain absorbed in the same witnessing. Then no choosing will be necessary between becoming a stone or Brahman, because the witnessing is one and the same. If you are poor, remain absorbed in the witnessing; if you become rich, remain absorbed in the witnessing. Then poverty and richness will make no difference to you, because within you the same stream of witnessing will be flowing.

All titles are futile. All that is received from the outside is futile. Only what is attained from within is meaningful. But nothing other than the witnessing consciousness is attained from within. In all conditions, in every situation, go on seeing the soul residing within.

> *I myself am Brahman – the creator god;*
> *I myself am Vishnu – the sustainer god; I myself*

am Shiva – the destroyer god; I myself am Indra –
the chief of all gods; I myself am this universe, and
I myself am all. There is nothing other than myself.

The same kaivalya attitude – the one who experiences this consciousness, the one who knows this witnessing, 'the other' disappears from him. The other is no longer there, only I am; everything is my own extension. Because the day I come to know my own consciousness, I also come to know that your consciousness is not separate from mine. As long as I know only my body, you are separate from me, because my body is separate and your body is separate.

Understand it this way. There is an earthen lamp burning, there is another silver lamp burning, and a third gold lamp is burning. Now if all these three lamps look to their bodies of clay, silver and gold, then the three of them are different. The silver lamp will look down upon the earthen lamp and the gold lamp will look down upon both the silver and the earthen lamps. But if any one of these three lamps experiences the flame – "I am the flame" – would that lamp be able to say to the other lamps, "You are different from me"? No, because now it will see the other lamps as flames too. Now for this lamp the bodies have become meaningless, whether they are of clay, silver or gold. Now only the flame has remained meaningful, which is neither clay, nor silver, nor gold, but simply a flame. For the lamp that has experienced that it is the flame, all the lamps of the world have become one with it: "Now wherever there is flame, it is me."

As long as we see the bodies, we are separate. But when we have seen the witness within, which is our eternal flame, we all become one and inseparable. Then the witness hiding within that bird flying near the tree, that too is me. And the witness hidden within Brahman, the creator of the world and the controller of the world, that too is me. Then the one who is begging on the street is also me and the emperor sitting on the throne is also me. Once the experience of the inner flame has begun, forms become meaningless; then body, matter, become meaningless, only the flame becomes meaningful.

One more interesting thing is that whether the lamp is made of clay or gold, there is no difference in the flame. Does an earthen lamp have an earthen flame, or a gold lamp a gold flame? No, there is no difference – the flame is a flame, the same everywhere. The body makes no difference to the flame. It is the same flame shining in the most ignorant as in Buddha. But Buddha knows it and the ignorant do not. And what really is the difference in knowing? Buddha has stopped bothering about the outer form of the lamp and has discovered the inner flame; the ignorant person is still influenced by the outer form – in the clay, silver or gold body – and has not yet been able to know the flame within. But the flame is there.

It is 'I' spread over all – such a realization is *adhyatma,* spirituality.

There are two or three important things to be mentioned. The very first day I asked you to remain cheerful, joyful, happy and laughing; to laugh as much as you could – even without any reason. But one thing I had left out knowingly. I had not asked you not to laugh without any reason while I am speaking. This part I had left out knowingly. I wanted to discover those three or four so-called intelligent ones that must have certainly come here – they would laugh even while I am speaking! And due to their laughter, they would be deprived of understanding what I am saying and would hinder others also. And my inference is not incorrect.

Three or four 'intelligent' people are here – one or two of them are from Punjab. I used to hear that people in Punjab have a little extra intelligence, but I had never believed in it. Even now I do not believe it, though those two Punjabi friends are trying hard to make me believe in it! That is alright, but I had never thought that in their company two or three Gujaratis would also do the same! There was no hope for much intelligence from the Gujaratis, but they are competing with the Punjabis.

Even in idiocy there is competition! And remember, it is always easy to move to one extreme, but the question is of staying in the middle. Either people will sit keeping their faces and features corpse-like, or they will start expressing cheerfulness idiotically. That too is not cheerfulness.

If you make loud sounds without any reason while I am speaking, you have no idea what you are doing. You are only attracting people's attention, telling them that you are also here. That is not showing wisdom and it is not going to benefit your meditation in any way. When I am speaking, that is the time to become silent and quiet, putting aside all the activities of your mind so that what I am saying may penetrate you. If I am saying something and you laugh loudly without any reason, then whatsoever was entering in will be pushed out by the force of your laughter. You threw it out. So move a little thoughtfully. If you don't move thoughtfully you will never be able to go deeper.

The second thing: yesterday I had sent instructions that only during morning meditation you can undress completely if you feel like it – it is useful. But it is not useful at all during the afternoon *kirtan*, devotional singing and dancing, and the meditation at night. For me, neither clothes nor nudity are of any significance – take note of it. Many times it is misunderstood. Many times it is felt that perhaps I am saying that if you become naked you attain liberation. It is not so easy, otherwise all the birds and animals would have been liberated by now. And if liberation is just withheld because of wearing clothes, then there is not much difficulty in making the whole world liberated by making it naked. No, it is not so easy and so cheap.

When I say that in some moment during meditation, if you feel that your clothes are obstructing you – in the movements of your body, in the expression – remove your clothes; then nakedness will be helpful. But there might be some fools, in fact there *are*.... Some fools cling to clothing, and some fools start clinging to nudity. They think that now that they are standing naked nothing else remains to be done. So I see some one or two persons, who do not do any steps of the meditation either, just standing naked – and they think this is enough.

Nothing is going to happen just by becoming naked. And I have no emphasis on nakedness – both the emphases are the same. Some people think that if you remove all the clothes from your body, your life is finished; and some think that if you remove all your clothes, you attain everything – their minds also attach great value to clothing. The types are similar. People covered by clothes and the naked monks – they are similar, their minds are the same, there is no great difference between the two. They both believe that clothes are important.

I do not tell you to remove your clothes because in being naked you will attain liberation. Naked you already are – under your clothes you are naked. What difference is it going to make whether you are naked without your clothes or you are naked within your clothes? When I permit you to take off your clothes, it means if and when, during meditation, you feel the usefulness of removing clothes, when your body energy awakens, when your bioenergy awakens due to the deep hammering from your breathing and you feel that clothes are hindering you in any way, only then take off your clothes; otherwise there is no sense in doing so. And there is no need at all to take off your clothes in the afternoon kirtan, nor is there any need to do so in the meditation at night. And if anybody persists during afternoon kirtan or the nighttime meditation, we will have him removed from the campus.

In the morning meditation it has a scientific basis. When there is deep breathing and the body energy starts arising vigorously, the clothing may create a hindrance. Then it is fine to remove your clothes. And then during the second step of this meditation, where I am telling you to drop all kinds of suppression and not to refrain from anything your body-mind feels like doing, then if it feels like taking off the clothing, do so. But there is no need in the kirtan or in the night meditation.

Do not make nudity a doctrine; nudity is a device.

The third thing: some Western men and women sannyasins might be taking a bath naked at the well, then some Indian friends crowd there to watch them. Don't be so foolish. If you want to bathe naked, do so. But when someone else is taking a bath naked and you go to watch them, you are only demonstrating your numerous suppressed and sick attitudes.

There are two types of mad people. One mad type is made up of those who want to watch others naked; and there is also the other type who want to show themselves naked. Psychology has different names for the sicknesses of all these mad people. In the West, they have many cases in the courts against such people who suddenly expose themselves to somebody. They are called exhibitionists. Two or three such friends have arrived here; their whole joy seems to be that others should see their bodies. And usually these are people whose bodies are not worth seeing. If they were worth seeing people would come to them to see their bodies. Those whose bodies are not worth seeing are the people who stand naked in a crowd; nobody goes to see them, but they think at least this way someone may see them. Such people with these sicknesses have no reason to be here.

And then there are some people who engage themselves in watching others when they are naked. They are also sick! If you have a liking for someone, if you are in love with someone and there is such a close intimacy, then the clothes drop on their own and they are naked. But in that love they do not feel naked, they feel closer; the obstruction of the clothes has gone. But to just go and watch someone who is naked and with whom you have no loving intimacy is very dirty and mean and speaks only of your hidden sickness.

While I was coming here, with me in the car was one English sannyasin, Vivek. When the car stopped at a corner, four or five donkeys came and stood by the car. I asked Vivek whether in England there were bigger donkeys than these standing here or were they the same as these? She replied, "Slightly bigger." I did not say anything else to her, because I was just joking. But then yesterday I was informed that people are gathering in a crowd near the well when people are bathing. So I am going to tell her today that she was mistaken, it is difficult to compete with India; the donkeys are bigger in India.

The fourth thing: after the thirty minutes of the meditation, when I ask you to be quiet, to be silent, then if you are unable to become quiet and silent it only means that you are not doing any meditation, you are just hysterical. Understand this difference clearly. When I say, "Breathe fast and intensely for ten minutes," you should be your own master and be able to do so. When I say, "Go mad for ten minutes," you should have the mastery to go mad also – you are being mad decisively, madness is not taking you over. You are throwing out the suppressions from within yourself, at your will. And when I say, "Make the hammering sound of 'Hoo-Hoo' for ten minutes," *you* are doing it – it should not catch hold of you, otherwise you have become a slave. And then when I say, "Stop completely!" one who cannot stop is hysterical. It means that the matter is not under his control, now he is unable to stop it; he is going on shouting, he is going on crying. It means crying has overpowered him.

This will not do. Such a person is sick, he is not meditating.

Meditation means, you are to establish your mastery. And if this mastery cannot be established then there would be no difference between hysteria and meditation. So when I say "Stop!" you are to stop at once. Even a moment's delay in it shows that you have lost your mastery, and whatever you were doing in that moment has become the master. If you were shouting, it has caught you and you are unable to stop it. If shouting catches you and you are unable to drop it, then you won't be able to enter into peace.

Mastery leads you into peace.

There are three or four persons who simply do not stop even after I have asked everyone to stop. They think that they have gone so deep in meditation, now how can they stop? You have not gone into meditation! And if this is done again today I shall ask for them to be removed, because they need medical treatment, not meditation. And after thirty minutes, when you think that now a cough is coming or something else like that, please don't be confused. Coughing is an infectious phenomenon. One person coughs, and then five to ten idiots follow him. The first person's coughing may have been genuine, but the other five to ten persons are simply following him. Did you notice last night – the coughing also stopped? Now how did this happen? When I asked you not to even cough, how did it stop? Because it was false.

Coughing is also not permitted. Just try experimenting with it; you won't die by not coughing for ten minutes. You have no idea how many tricks your mind plays. The mind says, "A really bad cough is forcing its way, I will cough just slightly." You succeeded in hindering it slightly, but you coughed. You thought, "But what can I do? – coughing is compulsive." No, it is not compulsive.

Do you notice that when I speak here for one and a half hours that you do not cough even once, and when I ask you to be quiet for ten minutes, you are suddenly overpowered by coughing? If the coughing was genuine, it should have been present in the same proportion throughout the period. But it is not so. You are sitting in a movie house, and there will be no coughing for three hours. What really happens? Then you go to a temple and the coughing takes over! Are there some cough germs sitting in the temple or what? Coughing in a movie house can be understood, there certainly are germs there in abundance. But it happens in the temple, where everything is spotless, clean.

The reason is psychological. This coughing that comes to you is not physical, it is mental. Stop it! Stop it absolutely! What can really go wrong in ten minutes? At the most you may die...although it has never been heard of that someone did not cough for ten minutes and died because of it. One may have died because of coughing for ten minutes, but never because of not coughing for ten minutes. Please be kind, stop it completely. Just be a corpse for those ten minutes.

When I say, "Stop!" stop completely; just freeze. Otherwise all is useless. The energy arises but it does not get an opportunity to work on you; and you, having happily dissipated it in coughing and the like, return home. Then you come to tell me that nothing happened! You coughed – is that not enough to happen? They come to tell me that meditation did not happen to them, and I know that they were coughing the whole time. Now even the poor meditation is being blamed!

Establish a little mastery. When I say, "Quiet," then there should be such a pindrop silence here as if not a single person is here, as if all have disappeared. Only then the results....

Also, when I begin to speak in English you are not to get up. Just sit down where you are. Behave at least with some understanding. When I am speaking in Hindi, those who do not understand Hindi are sitting peacefully. And when I begin to speak in English, those who do not understand English simply get up and leave. This indicates great impatience and idiocy.

There are about fifty Western friends here. They are also here sitting and listening. Just look at their faces. When I am speaking in Hindi, just look at their faces. They seem to be understanding even more deeply than you are. Why? They do not understand the language at all, but they have this much patience – "We may not be able to understand, but something significant is being said; so let us just sit quietly and hear it." They are not able to understand, but this silence of one hour will definitely be beneficial. They will not be able to understand, yet being patient for one hour is nothing but meditation. But no sooner do I begin to speak in English than you are up and moving. It means that neither you have any patience, nor is silent awaiting happening, nor have you any concern about the disturbance you cause to others. Please think!

A poet friend of mine, an Urdu poet, had been to Sweden. He was telling me that when he would recite his poems in Urdu nobody would understand, but thousands of people would be sitting silently. He told me, "I was very surprised. I had thought that nobody would come to listen to me, or if they did, they would soon go away." So he asked them, "You don't understand the language, so how can you sit so silently while I am reciting?" They replied, "This is true that we don't understand what you are saying, but when you are reciting with such feeling we do understand your eyes, your gestures, the movements of your hands, and we know that something very significant and deep is being said. At least we can show that much courtesy so as not to disturb you in that feeling, that state of yours."

So this won't do! At night, I see some outsiders come here, and the moment I begin to speak in English they start leaving. Tonight no one will be allowed to leave like that. If someone gets up to leave near you, immediately ask him to sit down. And if they still leave, from tomorrow night onwards I am not going to allow them in here. I shall announce before I begin to speak in Hindi that those who want to leave during the English part should leave now.

Life needs to be given a discipline, an orderliness, otherwise nothing will happen.

Enough for today.

YOU
ARE THE KNOT

CHAPTER 7

The delusion of things being in one's soul
is an imposed phenomenon. Dropping it,
one is oneself the perfect, nondual and actionless
Brahman – the absolute reality.

✳

The world that appears as a different thing
from the soul is almost untrue.
Where is the division in a pure,
formless and organless entity?
The conscious-soul is free of the notions of seer,
seeing and the seen, etcetera.
It is immune and utterly full like the ocean
at the time of deluge.

✳

Even as darkness dissolves in light,
the cause of illusion dissolves in the unparalleled
absolute reality which is without organs –
so where is the division in it?

✳

The supreme reality is one singularity;
how can there be division in it?
The state of sushupti – deep, dreamless sleep –
is blissful; who has seen divisions in it?

very important question has been raised in this sutra. This question has been arising in man's mind for centuries, since the beginning of time: how to be free from this world in which we are entangled, this world in which we have become encompassed by sorrow and anguish? And what actually is this world and what is the nature of this darkness in which we are drowned and lost?...because without knowing its nature, there cannot be any way of being free from it.

Whatsoever one wants to be free from, one will have to know it well. The bondage is created by our ignorance. So if the bondage is to be opened and loosened, it is only through knowing that the knots can be opened.

One day, when Buddha came amidst his disciples, he was holding a silk handkerchief in his hands. The disciples were surprised, because Buddha never carried anything in his hands when he came to address his disciples. Then he sat before them and tied one knot in the handkerchief, then a second knot, then a third – five knots, one upon the other. Then he asked his disciples, "When I came here with this handkerchief there were no knots in it, and now there are five knots. Now I ask you, whether anything is changed in the handkerchief or if it remains the same handkerchief I came with?"

Certainly the disciples must have been in difficulty. It is incorrect to say that the handkerchief has changed, because the handkerchief remains exactly the same. Tying knots in a handkerchief does not make even an iota of difference in the nature of the handkerchief – how large it was and what it was still remains the same. But it is also not right to say that the handkerchief has not changed at all, because previously it was an open handkerchief and now it is full of knots. That much change has certainly taken place.

One disciple stood up and said, "You are asking a very difficult question. The handkerchief has *almost* changed."

Understand this a little, because this word almost will soon be coming up in the sutra and then it will be imperative that you understand it. "Has almost changed" – it means that it is changed and it is also not changed. It is changed if we look at the body of the handkerchief, and it has not changed if we look at the nature of the handkerchief. It is changed if we look at its body. It is not changed if we look at its soul. A change has taken place externally because of the knots, but it is not changed on the inside. The shape and form are changed. It is not changed if we look at its real nature, but it is changed if we look at the practicality of it, because the handkerchief that was open can be used as a handkerchief, but the handkerchief that has five knots in it cannot be used as a handkerchief. It cannot even be called a handkerchief, because 'handkerchief' is the name of a utility.

Remember, when we give a name to something it is in fact naming a utility. It is a compulsion of language to use the same name even when the utility is not there. For example, a fan: when one is fanning with it in hot weather it is called a fan; but when the fan is not in use and is put away it should not be called a fan. A fan means something that is already being used to fan, which is presently functioning as a fan. But when it is lying idle, when it is not fanning the air, it should not be called a fan.

Legs are something with which you walk. But when you are not walking, they should not be called legs. The name should be of the function, of the action. But language would become too difficult – a separate name for a walking leg, a separate name for an idle leg – it would all get too complicated; so somehow we carry on.

Thus the word fan has two implied meanings. One, a fan which is already fanning the air; and the second, a fan which can fan the air, which has the potential to fan the air. We use the same word in both the senses. There are uses for a handkerchief: something can be tied up in it. But a handkerchief which is itself tied up, now nothing else can be tied up in it.

Buddha said, "I want to ask one more question, and that is, that if I want to untie this handkerchief, what shall I do?" Saying this, Buddha began to pull the handkerchief from both its ends; the knots became even smaller and tighter.

One disciple shouted, "Excuse me, but what you are doing is going to make the knots even tighter and render its untying almost impossible."

Buddha said, "One thing is now clear, that the handkerchief cannot be opened up by doing just anything. I am doing something, but you are saying that this is making the situation worse. So what will have to be done to open up the handkerchief?"

One disciple replied, "First of all we shall have to know how the knots have been tied. As long as the nature of the knots is not understood, it is not possible to undo them. So first we would have to see how the knots are tied. The manner of undoing the knot is just the reverse of the manner of making the knot. And as long as we do not know the manner in which the knots were tied, it is better not to do anything than to do something, because by doing something the complications may increase and the knots may get tighter, rendering the solution more troublesome."

In our consciousness there are also knots. And the situation is exactly the same: we are not changed at all and yet we are changed. Our nature is exactly the same as that of the supreme Brahman, but there are some knots in us. And as long as these knots are not undone, we cannot be that ultimate nature which is knotless.

Jainas have given a name to Mahavira which is very lovely. The name is: *Nirgrantha*, the knotless one. Whenever Buddha refers to Mahavira he always calls him *Nirgrantha Natputta*, that son of the Natha family, that boy born in the Natha community, who became knotless; whose knots were cut, opened.

This word nirgrantha is very valuable. Brahman, the absolute, is knotless, and we are full of knots – that is the only difference. But how were the knots tied and what are they? It is necessary to understand their nature. This sutra is about the nature of the knots. Let us understand this sutra, there are some very valuable hints in it.

The delusion of things being in one's soul
is an imposed phenomenon. Dropping it,

one is oneself the perfect, nondual and
actionless Brahman, the absolute reality.

When a knot is made in a handkerchief it is not separate from the handkerchief. Have you ever seen a knot alone without the handkerchief? Have you ever seen a knot alone without any string? Did you ever see a pure knot – a knot all by itself? Whenever there is a knot it will be in something, it can never be all by itself. It shows one thing clearly, that a knot cannot be separate from that from which it is constructed. When it cannot exist all by itself, how can it be imposed from outside?

No, the knot does not come from the outside. And even in the handkerchief the knot was not there until it was tied. So it is a very interesting question. The knot cannot just come from outside – nobody has ever seen a knot all by itself, nothing of the sort exists. It is always in something, never alone. And the handkerchief itself was knotless just moments ago, it was not carrying any knots in it. Then where did the knot come then? Did it come from within the handkerchief? How can it come from within the handkerchief when there was no trace of it in the handkerchief just moments ago? It did not come from outside, because on the outside no knot is ever found. Neither has it come from outside nor has it come from within; the handkerchief has imposed it upon itself, the handkerchief has created it. 'Created' means it was not in the nature of the handkerchief, it has achieved it.

The world is our achievement; we have created it with great effort, through many devices. The knot does not exist somewhere in existence, the handkerchief has imposed it upon itself with great effort.

Whatsoever appears to be in the consciousness is an imposition. Whatsoever comes to be experienced within, it is all imposition.

As we were discussing earlier, things come before a mirror and they are reflected in it. If the mirror commits the same mistake that we do, thinking that it *is* these reflections, it will be in the same trouble that we are in. But the mirror does not commit such a mistake, though some other mirrorlike things – photographic plates or photographic films – do commit such mistakes.

A film hidden inside a camera and a mirror are similar. An image forms in a mirror as well as in the film in a camera, but the mirror does not catch hold of the image, whereas the film does. Thus, whatever image forms on a film is caught by it, and because of this catching the film becomes useless. Now no other image can form over its surface, it is full.

A mirror is never full. However many images may form in it, it always remains empty. Images come and go, the mirror goes on letting go of them. The renunciation of the mirror is continuous. It goes on letting go of its indulgences, it never holds on to them. Your face is seen in the mirror, and it lets go of it. No sooner do you move away than the mirror has forgotten you, as if you had never come before it.

The consciousness of man is like a mirror and the mind of man is like a photographic film. The inner consciousness of man is like a mirror, nothing sticks to it. But man has another mechanism called mind. Mind is like a film: whatever is reflected in it gets caught by it.

In fact if the mind does not catch hold of things it loses its utility. This is why we say that a good memory is a valuable thing. The society, the education, is all based on a good memory system. To whom does that good memory belong? It belongs to the mind which holds onto things.

Mind is a mechanism like a film. It goes on retaining like a film; whatever comes in front of it, it retains. Whatever is of no use is also retained; what is useless, rubbish and meaningless, is also retained. What is not needed at all is retained. A film cannot choose. Anything exposed to it – it cannot choose what to retain, what not to retain. Whatever comes in front of it is caught by it.

Your mind goes on catching hold of things: you have no idea how much mess you accumulate during the day. Psychologists now say that your mind does not catch hold of only that of which you are aware, it also catches hold of that of which you are not aware.

For example, we are sitting here; I am speaking and you are listening to me. You are not even aware that a bird warbled and flew away, that there was a sound of a horn on the road – you have no idea of all this, but the mind is catching hold of all of this too. If you are later asked whether a bird had flown by while you were listening to the talk, you may say you do not remember this at all. However, if you are hypnotized and then asked what other things had happened, you will admit both: the bird had flown by and the horn was also sounded on the road.

Psychologists call it subliminal memory. Hidden behind the conscious mind is the subconscious mind which is taking in things the whole time – even those of which you are not aware. While you are sleeping at night, then too your subconscious mind is absorbing; it goes on absorbing even what is happening outside.

You will be surprised to know that the latest scientific discoveries reveal that a child gathers memories even in the womb. The child goes on gathering impressions of whatever is happening on the outside. Yoga has recognized this since ancient times, that whatever takes place in the mother, or around her, the child catches it and his growth is influenced by it. And the science of the West is coming closer to recognizing this now.

As our understanding grows, things are becoming more complex. Now the psychologists say that by the age of four the child has gathered fifty percent of his knowledge. Fifty percent! The total knowledge he will have when he dies at the age of eighty years, fifty percent of it he has gathered by the age of four; the remaining fifty percent is gathered later. From the point of view of knowledge, you have completed half your life within four years; you have become half old! But yoga says that when we understand what the child gathers while in the womb, perhaps the situation will be even more strange: perhaps the child gathers a greater percentage in the womb itself. But the child himself has no memory, everything is subliminal; it is there in his mind.

Governments in the West are very concerned about it, because the information is caught by the subconscious mind and this phenomenon can be exploited, and dangerously exploited. The advertisements at the movies that say smoke such-and-such a cigarette, or use such-and-such soap, or do this, do that – all this still needs to be displayed on the screen. In this displaying, there is still a subtle resistance. Because you know this is an advertisement you are not influenced as much as it is possible to be. A beautiful woman holding a cake of soap in her hand and telling you that the secret of her shining beauty lies in this soap – now everybody knows that it is not something to be believed. Still, through repetition it works, it catches your mind.

But now subliminal advertising has been discovered. Now, "Use Lux toilet soap," won't be visible on the screen. The movie you have gone to watch will continue and at some point during it, in a flash, in the one-thousandth part of a second, the advertisement for Lux toilet soap will pass. Your eyes won't be able to catch it because it will pass so quickly, but your mind will catch it.

This is dangerous. Governments of many countries are thinking of putting a ban on such a thing, because it is too dangerous. You are not even aware of it, you have not been able even to read it, you have not even sensed that something else took place in between the film images. You were busy watching the movie, and in between two sequences of the movie an advertisement has passed in a flash.

After much investigation it has been established that one in a thousand persons will get a faint inkling that something happened, that something else was there in between – but he too won't be very sure of it. The remaining nine hundred and ninety-nine will have no idea of it; they will be happily there in their seats and their subconscious mind will catch it. This is dangerous.

This means that someone may be running for a seat in an election and his advertisements may go on flashing in this fashion in the movies – and you will go and vote for that person without even realizing why you are doing so. This is dangerous. This can be misused. The dictatorial governments can misuse it badly because you can be victimized so easily.

But the mind is catching things the whole time, catching everything. Thousands of suggestions are being caught each moment,
they are accumulating. Mind is like a film, or like a tape in a tape
recorder; it goes on accumulating everything. And in everybody's
brain there are some seventy million cells, and each cell can store
millions and millions of units of information. A man, given a long
enough life, can memorize all the books of all the libraries in the
world. It is a question of life being long enough; on the mind's part
there is no problem. Mind has a long enough film, it is life that
falls short. If a man has a hundred or two hundred thousand years
to live, in this very tiny skull all the libraries of the world can be
accommodated.

The mind accumulates. It is a collector. There is no bigger
hoarder than the mind. All safes are too small, and all the rich are
poor compared to the accumulation the mind can have.

Hidden behind this mind is the consciousness. That consciousness is spotlessly clean like a mirror, it does not hold onto anything.
Whatever comes in front of it, it sees it; when the object moves
away, it is over – the mirror is once again clear and empty. Whether
it is a moon reflected in the consciousness, or a thorn or a flower,
whether it is a beautiful face confronting it or an ugly event, it is
seen in the consciousness only for those moments when it is facing
it. As soon as it moves away it disappears from the consciousness.

Mind is a mechanism. You are not the mind, you are the consciousness. But we have all believed ourselves to be the mind. We
do not have any idea of that mirror which is spotlessly clean and
pure.

This sutra says:

> *The delusion of things being in one's soul*
> *is an imposed phenomenon. Dropping it,*
> *one is oneself the perfect, nondual and actionless*
> *Brahman, the absolute reality.*

Nothing is to be done, you already are the Brahman – this is what Vedanta declares. You have not to become Brahman, you already are the Brahman. You do not have to go anywhere to achieve the truth, it is always with you. What has gone wrong then? The mind is in front of the consciousness, so whatever gets accumulated in the mind, all that accumulation goes on shimmering in the consciousness.

Let us understand it this way. The moon rises and is reflected in the lake. Then, when the moon sets, the reflection disappears from the lake also – for it is seen in the lake only as long as it is in the sky. When it is not in the sky, it disappears from the lake also. Now if we hang an artificial moon in the sky so that it never moves away, then its reflection will always be there in the lake. It will never disappear from the lake, because as long as the moon does not move away, its reflection in the lake will not move away.

Try to understand this. It is subtle, and a complete understanding of man's inner mechanism is necessary.

If this situation continues for a long, long time, the lake itself may begin to suspect that the image is its own and not a reflection of the moon, because it never disappears. The sun rises in the morning every day and the moon rises in the night, but they also set and their reflections vanish from the lake, leaving it empty. Thus there is an interval every day, and the lake can come to remember that the sun came and it has gone now, the moon came and it has gone now, and that "I am merely a mirror, a lake."

The consciousness is deep within you; in front of it is the mind and in front of the mind is the world. In the world everything is changing, changing every moment. In the mind nothing changes; mind is photographic, static. So whatever picture from the world is imprinted on the mind, it remains stuck in the mind forever. That stuck picture appears stuck in the consciousness also – it is always there. This creates an illusion that consciousness and the mind are one and the same. They both appear to be one, because no distance between the two is visible. Whatever is seen in the mind, it is also seen in the consciousness; there seems to be no boundary line between the two. Therefore this illusion: the world seems to be superimposed in the consciousness, and it appears as if the world has entered into the soul.

Nothing ever enters into the consciousness, everything enters into the mind. So as long as we have not learned the art of removing the mind from in between so that the consciousness and the world can come face to face without the mind being there as a middleman, so that the world of mind does not come in between, so that the projections of the mind are not there – until then we shall not come to know that everything was imposed from the outside. "I am the Brahman, not the world, and I am the consciousness, not the body. It only appeared that I was the body because the picture was imprinted in the mind that I am the body." The same picture was reflecting in the consciousness. Nor is there in reality any greed, or anger, or sex in the consciousness. These are all in the mind and all the images in the mind are reflecting inside, and they have been reflecting for so long, for such an eternity, that it is only natural to fall into the illusion that it is not a reflection or an image, that it is your very nature.

Remember, your body is destroyed in every life. But what about the mind? The mind is not destroyed, and your mind transmigrates from one life to the other. When you die your body is left behind, but not the mind. The mind is dropped only when you are enlightened.

Even death is not capable of destroying the mind; death destroys only the body, not the mind. Mind goes beyond death also. Only *samadhi,* enlightenment, is capable of destroying the mind. Therefore those who know have called samadhi the great death, because in death only the body dies, but in samadhi both the body and the mind die and only the one survives – that which is deathless and cannot die.

Thus the mind goes on forming, accumulating and increasing over the endless span of time, and all the time, always, whether there is body or there is no body, the mind remains attached to the soul. The shadow of the mind remains constantly on the soul. And slowly, slowly the soul also begins to feel, "Whatsoever is there in the mind is what I am."

This is our world, this is our knot. The only way of opening this knot is to be without the mind for a while; to move the mind aside and come face to face with the world – not to have a broker, a middleman in between.

If we can have even a single glimpse of the world directly, without the presence of the mind in between, we shall come to remember clearly that nothing has ever entered the consciousness, that the inner mirror is ever clean and spotless, that no images have ever stuck to it. All images have come and gone; the events of lives upon lives have happened, but no trace, no scratch has ever been left on the consciousness.

The experience of that spotless nature is the *Param Brahman,* the supreme ultimate reality. When Brahman, the ultimate reality, associates with the mind it becomes the world; when Brahman dissociates from the mind it becomes Param Brahman, the supreme ultimate reality. And when the soul associates with the mind the body becomes inevitable, because satisfaction of the passions of the mind are not possible without the body. Mind impels and excites passions, but they cannot be fulfilled without a body.

You may have heard, and it is now fast becoming a scientific reality, that some ghost has entered into the body of a person. Some would call it a superstition, some would call it an illness, some would call it this or that, but you may have never thought that even if ghosts are there, why do they enter into other human bodies? You may perhaps think that it may be some old enemy who has entered to torture the person. You may think perhaps it is a matter of some revenge, some fruition of karma, of past actions, some settlement of past deeds. No, nothing of that sort.

A ghost is a consciousness whose body has dropped but not the mind. And the mind demands a body, because all desires and passions of the mind can be fulfilled only through a body. Its mind wants to touch some lovely body, but the ghost cannot touch it because it has no hands; its mind wants to taste some delicious dish.... The ghost still has the mind which desires to taste things, but it does not have the tongue. So the problem of a ghost is that it has a mind, but no senses through which to fulfill these desires.

The whole complex of desires is intact with the mind, but all the means for their fulfillment are missing.

The whole meaning of a ghost-soul is one who has not yet received a body. There are two types of souls which have difficulty in getting a body. Ordinary persons get a new body easily; one died here and is conceived there, there is no gap. Sometimes there is at the most a gap of a minute, two minutes or five minutes. Normally you died here and are conceived there immediately. But the extreme souls, the most evil souls or the most noble souls, do not find conception easily because they need suitable wombs. If a Hitler dies, it would not be easy for him to find parents, because to give him birth equally evil parents are needed. So for years, sometimes for centuries, they have to wait. The difficulty is similar for a noble soul also.

The noble souls that wander without a body we have called *devas*, gods; and the evil souls that wander without a body we have called *pretas*, ghosts.

Whenever there is a moment when a person is so weak that his soul shrinks in his body, some ghost enters in him – neither for harassing him nor for torturing him, but for satisfying its own desires through his body.

If you are weak and without any will, some ghost can push his way inside you, because it does not have a body and its desires are burning. That ghost will touch some woman through your hands, will taste some food through your tongue, will see some beauty through your eyes and will listen to some music through your ears. It is for these reasons that ghosts enter into someone's body, not to harass the person. You are harassed in the process, but that is a by-product, not the motive of any ghost. But certainly when two souls are residing in the one body, trouble and harassment are bound to be there.

This harassment is like that of a guest coming to one's house and then staying for good, not even thinking of leaving. Slowly the guest starts expanding his territory in the house and the owner of the house begins to shrink into a corner; and slowly, slowly there comes a time when it is no longer clear who is the guest in the house and who is the owner of the house. And the guest? His conceit goes on welling up because the owner serves him, for he is a guest and "a guest is God." Thus the guest starts falling into the illusion that he is the owner; and one day he asks the actual owner to leave, for it has been too long that he has stayed in his house. A situation of suffering may arise. The mind demands a body immediately after the death, hence the new birth. The soul is associated with the mind and the mind is associated with the body.

There are two types of spiritual discipline. One is of separating the body from the mind, which we often call asceticism. This is a very long journey, arduous, and the outcome is uncertain. The other is of separating the mind from the consciousness, which we call vedanta, the path of knowledge. If we want to assign proper names they would be: separating the mind from the body is named yoga, and separating the mind from the soul is named *sankhya*, knowledge. These are the only two disciplines.

Sankhya means that knowledge alone is sufficient, nothing else is required to be done; and yoga means, much would have to be done, and only then something would be possible.

This sutra is of sankhya, knowledge. It says,

> *The delusion of things being in one's soul*
> *is an imposed phenomenon. Dropping it,*
> *one is oneself the perfect, nondual and actionless*
> *Brahman – the absolute reality.*

Nothing else is to be done.

> *The world that appears as a different thing from*
> *the soul is almost untrue.*

Hence I was saying that the monk told Buddha that the handkerchief was *almost* changed. This sutra says that this whole world of divisions which is seen is almost untrue. Because...

Where is – and how can there be –
the division in a pure, formless and organless entity?

Almost untrue – this is a very valuable philosophical concept. And it is necessary to understand it a little, because what is meant by 'almost untrue'? Something can be untrue, this is understandable, but what is meant by *almost* untrue? Something is true, this can be understood, but when someone says 'almost true', what would that mean? This 'almost' disturbs everything. It is like you say to somebody, "I almost love you." Now this disturbs everything. If there is love, say, "Yes, there is love"; if not, say, "There is no love," but what is this "almost in love"? What to call it: love, non-love or what? If you say a certain person is "almost a saint," what would it mean?

This word almost is precious and valuable in Indian philosophy. India has created a new category, a new level of thinking. In the philosophy of the whole world there are two categories of thought: of truth and of untruth. In Indian philosophy there are three categories of thought: of truth, of untruth and of almost truth – a third, in-between category. This 'almost true' or 'almost untrue' we have called *maya*, illusion, or *mithya*, the false. Thus we have created three words: *satya*, truth, *asatya*, untruth, and mithya, the false. Now, what is meant by this mithya? Ordinarily, people understand that mithya means untrue, a lie. No, mithya does not mean untruth; it means something in between the truth and the untruth. In between the true and the untrue? It means that which is untrue but appears as true.

It is dark and there is a rope lying on the road and it appears to you as a snake. In the darkness you lose all courage. You are on the run, sweating profusely, your heart racing fast. Then somebody says, "You are frightened and troubled unnecessarily. Take this lamp and go back and see for yourself; there is no snake, it is only a rope lying there." You then see it in the light and find it to be a rope. Now what will you call that snake you had seen? It certainly was not a true snake, but you cannot call it untrue either, because it worked as if it were true. You ran away from it just the way you would run away from a true snake; you perspired, and the perspiration was real – and it was caused by an unreal snake! Your heartbeat had increased and there was fear of a heart attack. A heart attack was very possible, and you could have died. And this is the puzzle: how does a true heart attack happen due to an untrue snake? But a true heart attack *can* happen due to an untrue snake. Indian philosophy is not prepared to call that snake altogether untrue.

The snake is definitely not true, because on investigation it is discovered that it is a rope lying there. But it is not untrue either, because it brings the same results that a true snake will bring. This India calls, 'almost untrue', or 'almost true'; mithya – false, maya – illusion. This is the third, the middle category. It is difficult to translate it into the English language, it is difficult to find words for this category in other languages. Whatever translations are done carry the meaning of asatya – untruth, and not of mithya – the false. Mithya is purely an Indian word.

Take note of the meaning of mithya. It means what is not but appears as if it is. And there are things which are not but appear as if they are. So, India says, it is necessary to create a third category for such things.

This false world.... You must have heard the vedanta describing this world as false so many times. The Upanishads call it false, Shankara calls it false from morning till evening in his statements. So we come to think that they are all saying that this world is untrue. No, they are not calling it untrue; they are saying that it is like seeing a snake in a rope. This world is not appearing as what it is but is appearing as what it is not. It is an optical illusion, a defect of the vision.

It is like looking at the moon after pressing the eyes and thus seeing two moons. There is no second moon. But if you are asked while your eyes are in that condition which one is the true moon and which one is the untrue, you would not be able to answer correctly. Both appear to be true. But both are not true, and if you stop pressing the eyes you will see only one moon, the second one disappears. What was that other moon? It was, after all, seen by the eyes. If there was a way to keep somebody's eyes permanently pressed in this fashion, he would always be seeing two moons.

Our vision is pressed under the experiences, images and accumulations of the mind the whole time. So we see what mind shows us.

Just imagine for a while that you are a resident of a country where snakes do not exist. You have never seen a snake, or the picture of one – you simply do not know the word snake. Now can you ever see a snake in a rope? It is not possible. How can you see one? If you have no experience of snakes, the rope may be lying there but how can a snake be seen in it?

The snake is seen in a rope because the mind has an association with the snake, an image, an impression of the snake; mind has seen a snake. You may have seen one in a picture, or in reality, or with a snake charmer – but you have seen one somewhere. That image is in your mind; it is hiding within your mind.

A rope is lying in the darkness; suddenly seen, the rope creates several illusions. The darkness creates fear. With this fear gets associated another fear that has arisen on seeing the snake, that it may bite you. With all this you start seeing in the rope even the wavy patterns of a snake's body. Fear, fear of snakes, the similarity of the wavy patterns...the snake within your mind is projected on the rope. You escape. The rope is not even aware what has happened. What has made you run away, and why?

It happened once with me, many years ago. I used to get up at 3 a.m. and go for a walk. It was a lovely night and the roadside was thickly covered by clusters of bamboo groves. There was a slight opening at one point, otherwise it was covered all the way along. I used to run straight from one end to the other of that stretch one way and then run facing backwards the other way. In an hour – from 3 a.m. to 4 a.m. – I would do my exercise there. One day a weird thing happened. While I was running backwards and still under the bamboo-shaded area, a man – a milkman – was approaching me with all his empty containers on his way to collect milk from some dairy. Then suddenly as I emerged from the shaded area – it was a moonlit night – he could see me all of a sudden. A moment before I was not visible, so all of a sudden...and running backwards! Only ghosts are known to run backwards!

That milkman threw the empty containers away and ran off. There was something odd about the way he ran off. I had no idea he had become so scared of me, so I ran after him to help. Now he ran for his life! The faster I ran after him, out of concern, calling him to stop, the more speed he was gaining. I had never before seen anyone run like that! Then I had an inkling that perhaps I was the only other person around here and he had become scared of me.

Hearing the noise of the falling containers and running feet, a man in the nearby hotel woke up. I went to him and asked him if he knew what had happened. He said, "If you are asking me, I know that you run backwards here every day, but still I get scared sometimes. That man must have been new on this road."

I said, "Keep these containers with you, maybe the man will return in the morning." He has not returned even now! Whenever I have passed by that hotel again, I have inquired if that man has ever returned. He never came back.

Now there is no way of telling that man that what he had seen was 'almost false'. There was no ghost there, but he managed to see it! For him the ghost was a complete reality, otherwise he would not have disappeared for that long a time. That man must have had some past experience that he imposed on the scene.

What really is is not what we are seeing; we are seeing what our eyes are showing us. Our mind is imposing things each moment and we are seeing who knows what, and it certainly is not out there in the world.

This whole world is the extension of our mind. What we see is projected by us. First we project and then we see. First we project a snake in a rope, then we see it and run away. This whole world is like that. We ourselves attribute beauty to somebody, then we become infatuated by it and then wander around maddened by it.

The seers of the Upanishads say that this whole world as seen

by man is 'almost false'. In saying 'almost' a very beautiful thing
has been said. What has been said is that it is not totally false, otherwise how could so many people have been troubled by it? Some
reality is there in it. It is a rope, this much is true; it is not a snake,
that much is false. The rope resembles a snake to a certain extent,
that is true; but yet a rope is a rope and it does not become a
snake, that too is true. And the world of fear that has arisen
between these two, the world of seeing a snake in the rope – that is
false, that is illusion.

As long as the mind is not totally removed and we are not able
to see the world directly, we will not be able to see the truth of the
world. As one sees the truth of the world, the world disappears
and only the absolute reality remains. At the moment the absolute
reality is seen divided. Somewhere the absolute reality is a stone,
somewhere a tree, somewhere it is a man and somewhere a woman
– the absolute reality is seen divided. If the whole projection
arrangement behind the eyes is removed, then this whole world
becomes one pure consciousness, one ocean. All divisions fall.

> *The conscious-soul is free of the notions of seer,*
> *seeing and the seen, etcetera.*
> *It is immune and utterly full like the ocean*
> *at the time of deluge.*

Where that inner witness is – that conscious-soul freed of mind
and having become void – there is no division. Seeing, seen, all
these notions have disappeared. Neither is there a seer, nor is there
anything to be seen: all dualities have disappeared. There is only
one expanse of consciousness there. For that expanse a beautiful
simile has been used here, which says:

> *It is immune and utterly full like the ocean*
> *at the time of deluge.*

Our oceans, however big they may be, are limited, and no

matter what their expanse they still have coasts. Whoever or whatsoever has a boundary is incomplete, because it is bounded. A
small pond has a small boundary, a big ocean has a big boundary.
What is the difference between a small boundary and a big boundary? A boundary is a boundary. You are imprisoned in a small
place or in a very big place. What difference does that make? – a
prison is a prison!

Therefore the example does not say, "like an ocean," it says,
...*like the ocean at the time of deluge.*

The time of deluge, *Pralaya kal,* is a mythological theory that
when this creation, this world dissolves, it will be covered in water
– the whole creation. There won't be even an inch of land left anywhere. So the condition of the oceans at the time of the deluge is
that there will be no border, no coast to them...because the very
meaning of coast is that there is still some land left to border the
ocean, and that land becomes its boundary.

The witnessing consciousness is like the ocean at the time of the
deluge. It has no coastline left around it; it is absolutely full – there
is no boundary anywhere to it, it is limitless. But this is true only
when divisions drop. As long as there is division, there are limits.

Even as darkness dissolves in light....
A marvellous thing has been said here:
...the cause of illusion dissolves in the unparalleled
absolute reality which is without organs –
so where is the division in it?

Even as darkness dissolves in light.... A very unique insight.
There is darkness in your house and you light a lamp – did you
ever think where the darkness goes?

When you light the lamp, where does the darkness go? Does it
go out of the house? So do one thing: first light a few lamps outside the house and keep a few people on watch. Then light a lamp
in the dark cellar in the house. If the darkness goes outside, the
people sitting outside will see it coming out of the house. No, the

darkness does not go outside. Where does darkness go then?

It is a very beautiful thing the Upanishad is saying, that the darkness merges into the light. It will be difficult to understand, because we consider light and darkness to be enemies. How can there be a merger? And we believe that they are opposites. There is struggle and conflict between the two and we want to leave darkness and hold on to light.

So it will be very difficult for us to believe that darkness merges into light. Our fear will be that if the darkness merges into light, all light will become darkness. For example, black ink merging into a white cloth: what will it mean in fact? It will not mean that the black ink will disappear in the white cloth, it will mean the white cloth will disappear into the black ink. Make an experiment and see. Merge the black ink and a white cloth and see. Then you will find out that it is the white cloth that has disappeared, not the black ink.

Darkness dissolves in the light. Many other points arise out of this fact. First, it means there is no enmity between darkness and light. What will this mean? This will mean there is no enmity between the world and enlightenment, and that the world merges into enlightenment. It means there is no opposition between the false and the true, and that the false merges into the true.

The darkness merges into the light – it is as if the darkness was just waiting for the light to come so that it can merge into it. Have you ever seen darkness hesitating? When you light a lamp does the darkness think whether to merge or not to merge – "Let me think a little"? Or, "I will come back tomorrow after thinking whether to take sannyas or not." Or, "Should darkness merge or not? Let me think and ponder." No, it does not think. It seems as if it was just ready and waiting, waiting that, "You will appear and I will merge into you." It does not delay a bit, not even a moment. The appearance of light and the merging with darkness happen simultaneously.

What are its implications in spirituality?

Its implications are that as soon as the light arises within, the mind and its illusions, carrying all their situations with them, merge totally in that light. They do not survive, they cannot be found anywhere even with great searching. It becomes hard even to conceive how they were there until yesterday. When you see a rope in a rope, you will have difficulty in understanding how until just a moment ago there was a snake in the rope and where it has gone now. You yourself will start having suspicions about yourself: have you fallen in some kind of delusion to even entertain the thought that it was there?...how could it be?

Those who are awakened find it difficult to even think that there is or there can be a world.

Just this morning I was talking to a sannyasin. She had come and she was asking when she would get rid of all this misery and anxiety: "Sometimes it appears that it has happened, but then again I revert to the same misery."

I told her that I am also in a difficulty. Slowly, slowly it has become very difficult for me to even understand how misery becomes possible, how it becomes possible for misery to occur. It is not that I was never in misery. I was, but now I find it difficult to understand.

It is as if somewhere far away in the past one might have seen a snake in a rope and now, on remembering, one finds it difficult to grasp how it was even possible to see a snake when it was a rope. And if somebody is still seeing the snake, it becomes a very difficult situation for me. The difficulty is that what is appearing to you like a great question is no longer a question at all to me, and it feels that you are carrying all kinds of meaningless things with you. But to say so also feels wrong, because that person is suffering, running fast; he is still seeing the snake. If you say to a person who is running fast in fear, whose heart is shaking and sinking, "Why are you running and talking all this nonsense, it is a rope and not a snake," he will become very angry.

Remember, you have no idea of the difficulties of a Buddha, a Mahavira, a Krishna and a Christ in teaching you, because they have to give you treatment for a sickness which really does not exist at all. The sickness is simply not there, but the patient is trembling; the patient is complaining that he is dying.

In medical science there is the word placebo. This name is used for a medicine which is almost a medicine. Placebo means it is not a medicine at all; it works for a disease which is actually not a disease. It is an 'almost medicine' for an 'almost disease'. It works – it is just a sugar tablet.

Homeopathic medicines are more or less placebos, they are not medicines as such. But they work, because where is the real disease? No problem – medicine was not needed in the first place. Real medicine is needed only if there is real disease, and ninety out of a hundred diseases are unreal – common diseases included. And it is dangerous to give real medicine for an unreal disease because the medicine will then bring harmful effects.

This spiritual disease, this disease of misery and anguish, the disease of worldliness, is one hundred percent unreal. But it is not right to call it one hundred percent unreal – if Buddha says it or Shankara says it, it is a true statement on their part, but out of compassion for the millions and millions of people who are suffering from this disease they have to say 'almost'. These people have to be seduced, persuaded: try taking this medicine, repeat this mantra, recite these chants, do this, do that. Taking the medicine continuously, perhaps you will forget about the disease. Or taking the medicine continuously, perhaps you will become so fed up that you throw both the medicine and the disease away. Or taking the medicine continuously you will say, "Enough is enough, it has been enough taking the same medicine life after life, I will not take it any longer, now I accept the disease." If anything like this happens you will find that there was no disease at all; the enemy you had been fighting with was not there at all – it 'almost was', it only appeared to be there.

Hence all religions have developed false devices, and it is difficult to find bigger liars than Buddha, Mahavira, Krishna and Christ! The reason for this is not that they are liars – there have never been truer people than these – but because all your diseases are false. And those who have to work to treat these falsely sick people, they know what they have to do.

All the big philosophies created by these wise people are false. False means 'almost false'. They are only devices to cut away your diseases.

For example, you have run away from a rope and believe it to be a snake. Now I may say a million times that it is not a snake but a rope, but it is only words and you will say, "How can I trust in what you are saying? Who knows, it may be your experience, it may not be! Even if you do have the experience it may be of some other rope, of some other snake. Who knows whether it is about this snake or this rope?"

Instead of trying to explain to you, it is better that I tie an amulet on you saying, "It is a snake and not a rope, but here, take this amulet – no snake in the whole world dares to face this amulet." This will be more effective. Instead of explaining that it is a rope and not a snake, put on this amulet. There is no real snake there, true, but here too there is no real amulet. But this amulet will give you strength, a confidence will arise in you that this is something real.

And if this miracle can also be staged, that a rope is placed in the darkness of a house and you are taken to it wearing your amulet, and from a distance you see it to be a snake but on your coming closer it turns out to be a mere rope, then everything is solved – the amulet works! Then you may go anywhere in the world, and it may come to such a state that even a real snake appears to be a rope – the amulet!

The mind of man creates illusions. These illusions are self-imposed. All of these illusions merge in the ultimate truth. The moment the witness is experienced, the whole world, the whole panorama of our projections, shrink and merge in the witness – in the endless, boundless ocean.

The supreme reality is one singularity;
how can there be division in it?
The state of sushupti – deep, dreamless sleep –
is blissful; who has seen divisions in it?

Understand this last thing in this sutra: the state of *sushupti*, deep, dreamless sleep. Those who have searched into the inner layers have accepted three states of human consciousness. One we call the waking state, which prevails from the time we wake up in the morning. The second we call the dream state, which prevails during sleep when we see pictures and images of things. And the third state comes sometimes during sleep for a short while when there is neither dreaming nor waking but only a deep sleep – sushupti – remains. Sushupti means, such a deep sleep where not even dreams remain.

The Upanishads believe – no, one should say know – that no divisions remain during the sushupti state. They cannot remain because the very mind from where they were arising.... When you are awake, the divisions are there. This is your house, the neighbor's house is not yours; you are poor, your neighbor is rich; you are black, your neighbor is white – thousands of divisions, they all remain there. These divisions are created by mind. You may have observed one very interesting fact – that the divisions remain in the dream state but the dividing lines disappear.

Understand this a little. In the waking state, the divisions are there and the dividing boundaries are there. There is a friend, there is an enemy; a friend is a friend, an enemy is an enemy; in the waking state A is A and B is B. However, during the dream state the divisions are there but their dividing boundaries in between are lost. Divisions are no longer solid, they become liquid. You are seeing that a friend is approaching and suddenly he turns into an enemy! And you do not even have a doubt, in the dream you do not even question how this can be possible! You were talking to a man, and he suddenly turns into a horse. Still you do not doubt during the dream that a man can suddenly become a horse.

Boundary lines do not remain. Divisions remain – a man is a man, a horse is a horse – but the boundary lines do not remain. Everything becomes liquid, everything is mixed up as if mind is shaken. During the waking state things remain clearly separate, logical, rational and distinct. During the dream state the mind gets unsettled. It is as if a reflection of the moon was there in the water, then somebody disturbed the water and the reflection was divided into thousands of pieces and the moon was spread all over the water. The moonlight remained, but not the moon; it was broken into pieces. In the same way the mind is shaken in the dream state. Thus shaken and unsettled, all boundary lines are lost. Things are mixed up with each other. Nothing is clear anymore as to what is what, what is A and what is B, when A turns into B and no logic is followed.

Dreams do not believe at all in logic, they proceed in a non-understandable manner. Anything trespasses into anything, and you cannot say why it is happening like this. There are no rules in the dream state. The rules of the waking state do not function there.

The third state is sushupti, the deep, dreamless sleep. Even dreams no longer remain here. And remember, where dreams cease the mind also ceases. Where there are no thoughts there can be no mind.

In the waking state the mind is solid, in the dream state it is liquid, and in the deep sleep state it disappears like a vapor. These are the three states of all matter that science recognizes. India has recognized these three states for the mind also.

Science says there are three states of matter: solid, liquid and gaseous. If you make ice of water it has become solid; if you make steam of it, it has become vaporous. So water has three states: steam, water, ice. Every material in the world has three states. But India says mind is also matter and it too has three states. Waking is the solid state, dreaming is the liquid state, and deep sleep is the vaporous state – mind simply vaporized, it simply is not there. In deep sleep no sense of anything remains. No sense will remain, because there remains no sensor. The whole world becomes one.

In sushupti you reach the same place which sages attain in samadhi, the supreme awakening. The only difference is that the sage is fully conscious while you are unconscious. The deep sleep state and samadhi are the same with only a slight difference, but it is a big difference. The sage attains sushupti fully awake and full of consciousness – then it becomes samadhi, the supreme awakening.

Deep sleep plus awareness is equal to samadhi.

You also reach there daily. You report it when you get up in the morning saying, "I had a very pleasant deep sleep." Had there been dreams going on the whole night you would never have said that you had a pleasant deep sleep. Then you would have said, "I had a restless night; there were dreams upon dreams, I could not sleep at all." When dreams cease you have a pleasant sleep. But when you are actually having deep sleep you are not aware that it is pleasant and good, because even that much cannot be sensed while sleeping in unconsciousness. Only after waking up in the morning, you are left with a feeling of pleasantness, of wellbeing – as if a faint shadow, a faraway but reverberating echo of pleasantness is left behind.

It is very interesting to note that so far no man has ever reported, upon waking up, that he had a very unpleasant deep sleep. Have you ever experienced it, that there were dreams and nightmares and...then it was not deep sleep. The deep sleep never came to you then. In the whole history of mankind no one has yet reported, "I had such a deep sleep in the night, with so many nightmares!" Nobody has ever said so, it has simply never happened. How can anybody say so? A deep sleep is a pleasing sleep; no unhappiness can exist there.

Therefore we cannot call that pleasure a pleasure, we call it bliss, because pleasure has its opposite called sorrow, but bliss has no opposite to it. Therefore the deep sleep state is bliss. Only one feeling remains – that of bliss without any division. Just as the deep sleep state is a singularity, similarly the experiencing of the witness is a singularity. Only bliss remains there. And just as the utterly full ocean of Pralaya kal – the time of the deluge, the dissolution of the universe – is limitless, boundless, with no shores, so is bliss without any divisions.

Enough for today.

REALIZE
THE FRUITS

The root of this division is mind.
If there is no mind, there is no division.
Therefore, concentrate your mind on the
universal consciousness which is your interiority.

✳

Knowing that you are the perpetually blissful
soul, always rejoice in this bliss
within and without your very soul.

✳

The fruit of detachment is knowledge,
the fruit of knowledge is relaxedness,
and the peace that descends from experiencing
the self-bliss is the very fruit of relaxedness.

✳

If each one of the aforesaid does not happen in
succession, know that the previous one did not
yield fruit. Abstention from the sense-objects is in
itself the supreme contentment and
incomparable bliss.

The root of this division is mind.
If there is no mind, there is no division.
Therefore, concentrate your mind on
the universal consciousness...

ind and concentration – these two points must be deeply understood. 'Mind' is a must for life. Mind means the flow of thoughts, and all the time your mind is flowing within you. Take note of the first point, that mind is not a thing. Mind is a flow, not a thing. And this distinction is meaningful.

A stone is lying there, it is a thing; a waterfall is flowing, that is a flow. A thing that is lying there is static; what is flowing is changing every moment. Mind is not a thing but a flow, so mind is changing every moment. It is never the same even for a moment. It is like the changing river.

Heraclitus has said, "You cannot step into the same river again," because when you step into the river the second time, the water into which you have stepped the first time must have flowed very far away. Similarly, the same mind cannot be found again – what has flowed away has flowed away. The whole time the current is flowing within, and standing behind this current we are seeing the world.

Thus the shadow of mind is falling on everything we see. And the changing mind, a mind which is divided into thousands of pieces, divides the whole world also.

So, the first thing, mind is an everchanging flow. Therefore it is not possible to know through the mind the one that never changes. If the medium of knowing is changing every moment, we cannot know that which never changes. Anything known through a changing medium will also be seen as changing. It is as if you are wearing sunglasses whose color goes on changing from red to green, from green to yellow, from yellow to white. The color of everything that you are seeing will also go on changing accordingly, because the medium used for seeing is being imposed on all that is seen.

Our mind is changing every moment. So we can only know through the mind that which is also changing; we can never know through mind that which does not change. And the ultimate hidden truth of this life is unchanging, it is eternal, it never changes, so mind is not the medium for knowing it.

All matter in the world goes on changing, it goes on changing like the mind. So through the mind the matter of the world can be known, but the universal soul hidden within the world cannot be known. For example, science uses mind for discoveries; science researches the world through the mind. Science will never be able to say there is a universal soul, it will always say there is only matter. The realization of a universal soul will never be available to science. Not because there is no universal soul, but because the medium that science uses for knowing is able to know only the changing, it will never be able to know the unchanging.

Understand it this way. If music is playing and you try to listen through your eyes, you will never be able to listen to it – in fact you will be unaware of its very presence. Eyes can see, so through the eyes you can know forms; but the eyes cannot hear so you cannot be aware of sound through them. Ears can hear but cannot see. But if somebody tries to see through the ears he will say, "There is no form in the world." Ears can catch only sound. A medium can know only what it is sensitive to.

Mind is change. Mind's nature is change, flow. Mind can come to terms with the changing but it is never able to know the unchanging. So those who set out in search of the universal soul through the mind will, sooner or later, turn atheist. If they do not turn atheist, it only means that they are not courageous enough to fully accept what their mind is telling them. But a man working through the mind just cannot be a theist. His theism will be as false as the claim of a deaf man to have heard music through his eyes, or as the claim of a blind man to have seen beauty or light with his ears. The theism of a person functioning through mind will be as false as these.

So there are so many theists in the world, but it is very difficult to find a *real* theist. You too, if you manage to bring trust, it is coming through your mind; you are bringing it through calculated thinking. Through thinking, nobody can ever be a theist; and if he is he will be a false theist.

If one wants to become a theist through thinking, only atheism will come. Try hard to understand this – because the very medium of mind is incapable of grasping the unchangeable. It is another matter to deceive oneself. Just think about your theism: you believe in God, but it is a calculated entity, it is brought out of your logic, guessing, thinking, scriptures, traditions and doctrines. Such a god is not real and such a god only tells about your dishonesty, because God can never be born out of mind.

In this world, ninety-nine percent of the people called theists are hidden atheists. There is no strength in their theism, it is spineless, it is impotent. Only a slight hit and their theism will wither away. It has no inner root. One becomes a theist only if one sees the world directly, putting the mind aside. Then it is not the world that is seen, because with the removal of the mind that which is changing cannot be seen. When on removal of the mind the consciousness sees the world, it can relate only to that which is unchanging.

Consciousness is eternal, it is unchanging. Consciousness falls in tune only with that which is eternal. What is seen on the removal of the mind is the supreme self; what is seen when bringing the mind in is the world. Let us define it this way – that those who have known existence without the mind have said, "There is nothing but the supreme self." And those who have known existence through mind have said, "There is everything except the supreme self."

So through the mind you will never be able to know. Yes, you will be able to know the world – the world in fact will be known only through the mind – but not the truth. And whatsoever is known through the mind will be changing every moment. This is why science is never stable. Science will never be stable, science will never be able to say that such and such truth is permanent. Science will only be able to say, "Tentatively, temporarily, out of all that we know so far, this is the truth. What will be the outcome of what we will know tomorrow cannot yet be said." Science is changing every day. All that was true yesterday becomes false today.

The difficulty now is such that whatever science teaches in the schools and the colleges, most of it has already become 'almost false', because it takes about twenty years to bring down new discoveries to the level of the schools. During these twenty years it has become untrue. Today no big books can be written on science because, if someone is writing a one-thousand-page book, by the time it is written, printed and published, many things will have been proved to be wrong. So science is gradually coming down to smaller books. Actually even small books are not being written, only small essays and articles, because they can be written immediately and there is no fear of their being outdated by the time they are published.

Science is bound to change, because nothing that is discovered through mind can be eternal. So the thinkers in the West find it difficult to understand how something that was said by Mahavira two thousand five hundred years ago, or something that was said by the seers of the Upanishads five thousand years ago, is still true. Five thousand years! When even things said only five years ago have become outdated and untrue, things which were said five thousand years ago must have become untrue long ago.

What they are saying seems to be rational, because when things said even five years ago are now dubious, it is only natural that things said five thousand years ago should be thought dubious.

But no, what the Upanishads have said is still true – they are true today and will still remain true tomorrow. Now this can mean two things. One, that the intelligence of India has become dull and is not developing any further, that it has become static at the point of five thousand years ago and is standing still, clutching whatsoever had been discovered then. It has not moved any further from there; otherwise all those things would have become wrong by now.

Even in India today, those who do any thinking – and very few people do – they do almost borrowed thinking which is more or less a shadow of Western thinking. So whether it is in the West or in India, according to the manner of thinking of science today it will appear that these thousands-of-years-old statements of India must have become untrue long ago. Because India has stopped thinking any further it has not been able to make any amendments, and so things have remained where they were. And what they are saying is right too – for those who work through mind.

The fact is that these truths have not been attained through the mind. They were attained five thousand or fifty thousand years ago, they may be attained five thousand or fifty thousand years from now – and this attainment is not through the mind. What is not attained through mind does not change. There is no way for it to change, because no sooner is the mind dropped than one enters into a world which is eternal, timeless; where nothing ever changes, where everything is unchanged; where time has stopped, where there is no movement in time, where time has frozen. These truths will always remain truths. As they have been realized in a state beyond mind, no changes of this world can bring about any change in them. Yes, if these had been realized within the scope of the mind, the changes in the world would go on bringing changes in them.

This is the original discovery of India, that existence can also be known without mind. This is the difference between science and religion. Science says that whatsoever can be known, can only be known through mind. Religion says that whatsoever is known through mind is functional, it is 'almost true', but the truth is that which is known by transcending the mind. And it is only beyond the mind that the real knowing is possible.

So how to get rid of the mind? How to quiet or empty the mind? This sutra says that if you can concentrate the mind it will quiet down, it will become empty.

This is the second thing to be understood: the very nature of mind is not to concentrate. If you try to concentrate it even for one moment it will not concentrate, it will seek to flow. If I ask you to concentrate your mind on Rama, you will find that no sooner do you think of Rama than the whole chain of events in the life of Rama will begin to come to the mind. Sita will enter from the back door, Hanuman will begin to peep in, and the whole mess of them will be there. While concentrating your mind on Rama, Dasharatha will come in, Ravana will come in, all of them will come in. Just try and single out Rama – no Dasharatha, no Ravana, no Sita, no Hanuman, no Lakshamana, nobody – exclude the whole company, just Rama alone; then the mind will be in difficulty!

But then there is another way out for the mind, which is to divide Rama into several parts: say, to begin from the feet. First see Rama's feet, then see his body, then the face, then the eyes; this will give the mind relief because the flow has begun again. If you select only the eyes of Rama, the mind will go on moving from one eye to the other eye. So select only one eye, select a half blind Rama having only one eye. Now when you concentrate your mind on only one eye, the thinking will start about the eye and its functions.

To flow is the nature of mind. So no matter what you do, the mind will discover a channel in it for flowing. It will immediately discover a channel and start thinking. This is the difference between meditation and thinking. Meditation means cessation of thinking, stoppage of flow. Concentration means only one point remains, without any thinking about it.

What will happen then? This is against the nature of mind. It is impossible for mind to remain this way. If you do insist and try for the impossible there is only one way: first the mind will struggle hard, and it will try in every possible way to convince you, to persuade you, to trick you into thinking. It will say, "No problem, let us think about Rama; that is good, to think about Rama is a religious act." It will say, "Okay, if you don't want to think about Rama, let us do some chanting: Rama, Rama, Rama, Rama." But "Rama, Rama, Rama, Rama," and the flow has begun. The first Rama, the second Rama, and the flow has begun, the mind has found movement, it has started moving.

At first mind will make effort to seek channels to flow along, because that is its nature. But if you persist and remain aware and you say, "I will not allow any flow at all, I will stick to only one point, I will not move from it this way or that" – and if you continue your insistence, not letting the mind move in any direction whatsoever, then the second way for the mind is that it will drop, because concentration is simply not possible for the mind.

You will probably find it strange to know that mind simply cannot concentrate. This is why you are asked to concentrate, because if you do become concentrated your mind will cease. It is impossible for the mind to concentrate. When you are concentrated there is no mind. As long as there is mind, you are not concentrated.

Concentration means stoppage, cessation of all flow, end of all time, disappearance of all movement.

If you incessantly continue your efforts to concentrate and remain aware and watchful that mind is not searching for a trick that may trigger the flow, a moment comes when, because of the effort to concentrate, the mind ceases. Because of the effort to concentrate, the mind does not concentrate but ceases; it quiets down, it disappears. When you do not listen and remain engaged in the efforts to concentrate it, the mind drops.

Cessation of the mind is in becoming concentrated. So when we say, "Concentrate the mind," we are saying an incorrect thing. This is why I said that Buddha and Mahavira are saying 'almost false' things. They have to. When we say, "Concentrate the mind," we are giving an incorrect statement because mind cannot become concentrated, and if it did the mind would no longer remain.

Concentration and mind are opposite phenomena. In the effort for the opposite, the mind dies. But it is a very difficult thing…difficult because it is necessary to understand concentration. Concentration means not allowing the flow to be born. Thinking is a flow, meditation is stoppage of the flow. A river is flowing. If it freezes into ice so that all flow stops, there is no movement. Similarly, if the mind stops so that all flow ceases, it freezes like ice, then that very moment there is no mind, the mind has disappeared – and what remains then is the consciousness.

This sutra says:

> *The root of this division is mind.*
> *If there is no mind, there is no division.*
> *Therefore, concentrate your mind on the*
> *universal consciousness which is your interiority.*

We do not exactly know if there is any universal soul. But there is no need to know that. The big question is not whether there is a universal soul or not, the big question is to concentrate the mind. Concentrate on anything, even if you can concentrate on an imaginary thing that will do. So the question is not that the problem will be solved only if you concentrate on something real. The sutra does not ask you to first find out the universal soul and then concentrate. It says, even if you feel that a universal soul is imaginary, nothing to worry about; because if the mind can be concentrated even on an imaginary object it will disappear. And as soon as the mind disappears one starts seeing that which is real. So there is no harm in moving with a make-believe object.

A universal soul or God is an hypothesis for meditation. For seekers the universal soul is not something to believe in, it is an imaginary point for concentration of the mind. And when I am saying an imaginary point, do not think that I am saying there is no universal soul. It is just not there for you yet. You are only concentrating your attention on an imaginary point. That point can be anything, it can have any form. Its name may be Rama or Krishna or Allah, any name will do, it makes no difference. It is not important what you are concentrating on, what is important is that you are concentrating. So all religions of the world serve this purpose. If there are differences in their doctrines, it makes no difference for the seeker. All those differences are for scholars, for those who have to indulge in futile discussions. For a seeker these things make no difference; Allah, Rama or Jehovah – any name will do.

The science of religion, the process of religion, does not attach any value to the thing you concentrate upon – it is irrelevant. What is important is that you are concentrating. It may be anything, A, B, C, D, or anything, but you are concentrating. In the very process of concentrating, the mind ceases. And what is known after the death of the mind – its name is not Allah, or Rama or Krishna. It has no name. All names are imaginary; they are utilitarian, they are amulets. They work, and when understanding dawns they can be thrown away. Then they are not needed anymore.

This is a very revolutionary thought. The ordinary religious man finds it difficult to conceive that his Rama, his Krishna, his temples and the idols in them, are all imaginary. Imaginary does not mean false, it means hypothetical. They can be used; the journey can begin from them, though at the end of the journey one discovers that the journey could have been accomplished even without them. Also at the end of the journey one finds that it could have been performed with any other name as well. But that cannot be known at the beginning of the journey nor is it necessary to know it. Let a Hindu proceed like a Hindu, let a Mohammedan proceed like a Mohammedan, and let a Christian proceed like a Christian. On reaching the destination it will be known that Hindu, Mohammedan, Christian – all these were just utilitarian things and had no relationship with the actual ultimate truth.

These divisions have a relationship with our ignorance, not with our knowledge. They have something to do with making us begin the journey from where we were standing in the world, but nothing to do with the destination we reached. After attaining, nobody remains a Hindu or a Christian or a Mohammedan; on attaining, one just remains religious.

So remember, as long as you are a Christian, a Hindu or a Mohammedan, know well that you are not religious. These are only the beginnings of the journey toward religion.

Gurdjieff has said a very valuable thing. Whenever someone would come and ask, "What is the path to the truth?" Gurdjieff would say, "Do not talk big. I can only indicate ways to find the path. After that it is up to you. Right now it is enough that you first find the path. Do not ask what the path is, first ask the direction that may take you to the path. First be concerned about finding the path."

Remember, Hinduism, Mohammedanism, Christianity, etcetera are all small sidetracks to reach to the path. None of them is the path; religion itself is the path. Hinduism is a sidetrack, Mohammedanism is a sidetrack, Christianity is a sidetrack. Religion is the path. Once you reach the path all the small sidetracks disappear.

Being concentrated is valuable, because the effort to become concentrated is against mind. But it is necessary to be very careful, because there are two ways to detour while becoming concentrated. One, you are likely to create a chain of thoughts; and once thinking begins, the whole thing becomes meaningless. The second difficulty is, if the chain of thinking did not happen then you may just go to sleep at once.

You may have observed that some nights, if there are too many thoughts in your mind, you cannot fall asleep. Some thoughts are going on in your mind – there is some worry, some stream of activity in your mind – and sleep becomes impossible because these thoughts are hindering sleep. And the night when there is no thinking, no thoughts in the mind, the mind is empty – then you fall into a deep sleep immediately. As soon as you lie down, sleep descends on you.

A coolie, a farmer has deep sleep. The reason for it is that his work has no concern with thinking, worrying, thought processes or mental gymnastics. He does not need them. He is digging a ditch or working in a field: this is just routine work, no thinking is required. In the evening he comes back home tired and tattered, and he falls on his bed; thoughts are absent, and he falls into a deep sleep instantly.

But with people whose work is mostly mental, sleeplessness becomes their main suffering. Those who are busy thinking and deliberating the whole time, their thinking continues non-stop even at night and they are unable to fall asleep.

I am saying all this so that its opposite also becomes clear to you. While experimenting with the mind on concentration, the danger is that at first the mind will try to induce thinking – which is convenient for it, being its nature; but if this did not happen and you remained insistent upon concentrating, the second thing that can happen is that, in the absence of thinking, instead of moving into meditation you will fall asleep, because as soon as thinking stops, it is an old habit that we fall asleep.

So many people, in the name of meditation, go on sleeping and enjoying a nap. Sitting in the temple they go on dozing. It is not their fault; they do not know what is happening. They are trying to concentrate and in the effort to concentrate two misfortunes can happen: either thinking may begin or, if that does not happen, sleep may begin.

So one has to avoid thinking and sleeping as well. These are the two ditches, and in between the two is meditation.

Zen masters in their monasteries have one monk move about with a stick in his hand while the others are meditating. The moment he sees some meditator has begun to doze, he gently hits him on the head.

Soon we will also make this arrangement. And it is not that it is all useless. No, it is very useful, because the dozing is instantly disrupted. Thinking was going on – that stopped and the dozing began. You avoided one ditch and fell into the other. The dozing begins only when the flow of thinking breaks.

And then came the monk who gave a hit on the head. The flow of thinking had stopped, the dozing had set in; the monk gave a hit on your head – for a moment the dozing was broken. In that single moment a glimpse of meditation happens. And if even a moment's glimpse happens, that is a big support to your meditation. One starts feeling that there is no darkness where one is going, everything is clear there.

It sometimes happens that because there are so many meditators it is not so easy for the master to really see each moment who is dozing and who is not. So there is an arrangement in Zen that if any meditator feels that he is getting sleepy, he brings both hands near his chest. Thus the master can easily see that in that person there is arising a danger of falling asleep. This gesture is an invitation for the hit; that, "Dozing is just about to begin, the waves of sleep have just begun to give me their featherlike touch; the waves are overpowering me and I am afraid that now I will be lost in sleep."

If thinking does not begin and dozing does not happen, meditation will take place. Meditation means the absence of thinking and sleeping. You will then be in meditation.

Keep these two things in mind, whatsoever may be the point of concentration.

> Knowing that you are the perpetually blissful
> soul, always rejoice in this bliss
> within and without your very soul.

This second thing is also very valuable. We rejoice, but never in ourselves, only in others. It is a very curious fact that we find delight, we take interest, we sometimes even get a little happiness – but always in the other. Did you ever rejoice in yourself? You will never have done that. We simply pay no attention to ourselves.

This sutra says that the seeker should slowly give up delighting in others and start delighting in himself. You are sitting unoccupied and feeling unhappy: you think that if some friend arrives then there could be some fun; if some companions turn up then there could be some joy and frolic. Alone, you begin to be sad. Alone you are not happy. In aloneness, boredom sets in, boredom from one's own self.

Nobody likes themselves! The interesting thing is that everybody wants others to like him, and you yourself do not like yourself. You get bored with yourself and you want others to be very pleased when they see you. How is this to happen? It is impossible. You think of giving others great happiness. You cannot give happiness to your own self, how can you give it to others? And what you don't have yourself, you cannot give; there is no way of giving it to others.

This sutra says, rejoice in your own self. You are sitting alone, be joyous. This state has been described by fakirs as *masti,* ecstasy. There seems to be no external reason but one is simply intoxicated with joy, as if some stream of joy is flowing within on its own. One is enjoying oneself on one's own, there is no medium of the other.

There are many different spiritual disciplines using ecstasy. Sufis use and value highly the spiritual practices of ecstasy. Their fundamental principle is that you do not make your happiness depend on the other. Whosoever associates his happiness with others, his sorrow also gets associated with the other.

Do not associate your happiness with others, associate it with your own self. You are sitting unoccupied under a tree – be happy. It will seem difficult: how to be happy, when there are no reasons for being happy? We usually only become happy for some reason...a friend is approaching – you have not seen him for a long time, so you are happy. We are always happy for some reason.

Happiness without any reason is masti, ecstasy. There is no visible cause for the happiness, one is just rejoicing in something from within. Sometimes such a thing happens to mad persons, so it sometimes becomes difficult to distinguish between the mad and the *masta,* the ecstatic one. Those whom we have called masta, many of them...in the West exactly the same type of people are put into lunatic asylums, because there is no way to distinguish them. The West has no idea how to distinguish between a masta and a mad person. To them the man appears mad. In the West they have made it a definition of healthiness that if one is joyous due to some reason his mind is alright, but if one is joyous without any reason he is mad. How can there be happiness without any reason?

The tradition of the mastas says that happiness can only be without any reason: there has never been any happiness because of some reason. Now this is rather a difficult statement! The tradition of the mastas says that there has never been any happiness because of some reason – only a false notion of happiness. From reasons, only suffering has arisen. Let this be understood – it has a complete psychology of its own.

When you seek happiness for a reason – in some person, in some thing, in some event – the end result is never anything but unhappiness. Suffering upon suffering follows. The wife is seeking happiness from the husband, the mother is seeking happiness from the son, the father is seeking happiness from the son, from the daughter. Happiness is always looked for somewhere else – in relations, in money, in position, in prestige, but always somewhere else. We are all seeking happiness everywhere except within our own selves. And the hilarious thing is that the others themselves are also seeking happiness somewhere else. It is as if we are digging a mine we think is a diamond mine, and the mine itself has gone away in search of the diamonds; and the diamonds themselves from this so-called mine have gone searching still somewhere else.

We are like a 'postage unpaid' letter which has no address on it. So the search is on. We have no idea who we are looking for, and again we have not inquired of the person whose place we are going to, whether he himself has not gone somewhere else in a similar search! Everybody is somewhere else, so a meeting never happens with anybody. To whomsoever's place you go, that person is not there. Whomsoever's hand you hold in your hand, that person is not there. Whomsoever you embrace, that person is not there, he is somewhere else.

Everybody has gone somewhere else, so nobody is able to meet anybody – nobody will ever be able to. So whoever is seeking happiness in some cause will go on falling into deeper and deeper misery, because every time there will be hope that this particular cause will bring happiness, and when it is attained the hope will be shattered.

The scripture of the masta sect says that only sorrow comes from others, never happiness; happiness always comes from one's own self. And whenever it feels as if it is coming from the other, the tradition of the mastas says, the other is not the cause, but you.

Understand this also a little. You feel that you are in love with someone. The presence of that person feels to be pleasing. Is it really the presence of the other that is giving you happiness? Or is it your idea that you are in love, and that the presence of your beloved gives you happiness? Now which is giving you happiness? If it was the presence of that person that was giving you happiness, then that person's presence should give happiness to everybody. But that does not happen. That same person's presence can give unhappiness to someone else. If water quenches thirst, it must quench the thirst of everybody. If you say that this water quenches my thirst only, then it is something that has to do with you, not with the water.

One should learn to distinguish between subjective truth and the objective truth. If water is water, it will quench my thirst, it will quench your thirst, it will quench anybody's thirst. It will quench the thirst, it will have nothing to do with different people; whosoever may be thirsty, it will quench their thirst.

Somebody's beauty pleases me but does not please someone else. If it is beauty, then whosoever is in search of beauty, has a thirst for beauty, should get happiness from it. But this does not happen. This beauty pierces someone else like a thorn and they want to run away from it, whereas the same beauty gives you happiness. Some-one derives unhappiness; someone does not seem to even notice that there is any beauty; someone simply laughs and says that you are out of your senses, seeing beauty where there is none!

What does it all mean? It means that the beauty you are seeing is attributed by you. There is nothing there – you are the cause of it. And that is why it becomes possible that from the same beauty that you derived happiness in the morning, you can derive unhappiness by noon and by the evening again derive happiness. Or today you derived happiness, tomorrow you start to derive unhappiness.

An interesting incident happened. One film actress came to me and said, "I am in great difficulty and so I have come to seek your advice. My difficulty is that I had made a love-marriage, but within a year or two it felt that it was a mistake and there was nothing else but quarreling and pain in my life. However, I still carried on for ten years, but the quarreling and the hell went on deepening and there remained no sense or even a possibility to carry on any further."

She was very perplexed, because her husband had loved her and had courted her with great persistence, but then her husband also became weary of the whole thing. So after ten years they divorced, and now it was ten years since the divorce. They had a daughter who was now grown up and had recently married. That is when the husband and wife met again – on the occasion of their daughter's marriage. That film actress had come to tell me that her husband had once again fallen in love with her and asked that they should marry again. Now, what was she supposed to do?

There is difficulty. It is clear that nobody falls in love with anybody; others are only screens and, seeing our own images in them, we go on falling in love. When we feel that we are getting happiness from the other, then too it is nothing but our own illusion. The deeper we go the clearer it will be that the occurrence of happiness is our own projection. And because we believe that happiness is in the other, and since no happiness ever comes from the other, we suffer.

A person who discovers that the source of happiness is within himself does not go anywhere else searching for it; he starts experiencing himself drowned in happiness. He dances not because of any external cause but because of his own existence. One's own existence is enough delight, one's own existence is enough bliss; there is no need to search for any other cause. Breathing is happening, even this is supreme bliss; the heart is beating, even this is supreme bliss.

Experiment with this a little. Just sit under a tree alone and fall in love with your own self for the first time; forget the world, just be in love with own your self. The spiritual search is in fact the search for falling in love with one's own self.

The world is a journey of falling in love with others, spirituality is a journey of falling in love with one's own self. Spirituality is very selfish. It is a search for one's own self, a search for the meaning of one's self. It is to rejoice in your own self, it is to have a taste of yourself. And when this taste starts happening within …wait a little, search a little. Feel your uniqueness, delight in your own existence, because, "What could I have done had I not been born? How could I have complained – and with whom – had I not been here?"

You are in this existence; even this fact, even this much consciousness, this much awareness that, "I am," the very possibility of a glimpse into bliss – just rejoice in all this a little. Let the taste of all this soak into your every pore. Allow yourself to be swept away in the thrill of it. Start dancing if you feel like dancing, start laughing if you feel like laughing, start singing a song if you feel like singing a song, but remember to remain the center of it all yourself, and let the springs of happiness flow from within yourself, not from outside. Slowly, slowly this moves deep into your experience, and the state that it brings about is the state of a masta, the ecstatic one. Masta means one who has become ecstatic in himself.

This sutra is the foundation sutra of the mastas.

Knowing that you are the perpetually blissful
soul, always rejoice in this bliss
within and without your very soul.

The fruit of detachment is knowledge...

This sutra is very valuable.

The fruit of detachment is knowledge,
the fruit of knowledge is relaxedness,
and the peace that descends from experiencing
the self-bliss is the very fruit of relaxedness.

If each one of the aforesaid does not happen in
succession, know that the previous one did not
yield fruit. Abstention from the sense-objects is in
itself supreme contentment and
incomparable bliss.

Try to understand each step. For the seeker each step is worth keeping in mind and examining constantly. This is a touchstone.

The fruit of detachment is knowledge...

Just as I said earlier, realize the meaninglessness of the body. If you look with a piercing eye, you will come to know that the body is meaningless. Come to a clear and deep realization that the world is unable to give any happiness. And there is no impediment; it will become clear if you search because it is so. It is just like asking a man with closed eyes to open his eyes and to see that the light is there. All these are as simple as that. This is the case. There is no happiness through the world, there is no happiness through the body, there is no peace through the other – this is the case, it is only a matter of seeing with open eyes. Out of the fear of coming to know the truth we have kept our eyes closed for lives upon lives. Our closing of our eyes is on purpose. We have fear.

One friend came to me. He wanted to marry as he was in love with somebody. I asked him, "Are you really in love? Just think it over a little more."

He said, "Think? What is there to think about when love is there?"

I still said, "What is the harm? Rather than think afterwards, it is much better to think beforehand. And what is the hurry? Wait for a fortnight." He appeared a little nervous and restless.

I said, "If love is really there, it will certainly last for fifteen days. What is the nervousness?"

He waited for a fortnight. I had told him to come back after a fortnight, and to think during this period if he really was in love.

He came after fifteen days and said to me, "You have confused me. My mind has fallen into great uncertainty. Fifteen days ago I was very clear and certain in my mind. What have you done to me? I had come to you to receive your blessings so that my love-marriage might be a success."

I told him, "Because you had come for my blessings – it was out of fear – I asked you to think again. One goes looking for blessings only when one is not sure of oneself. So if you had not asked for my blessings I would not have said anything. You are not sure within yourself that you will be happy, so you ask for my blessings so that the responsibility shifts over to somebody else, so that you are no longer responsible. You were trying to trap me; you are in love and you were trying to trap me. Now you think some more, and if you are still confused, wait for another fortnight."

He said, "I cannot wait any longer, because if I wait for another fortnight there will be a divorce before the marriage happens."

We are all afraid. And we do not open our eyes and look around to see what the matter is, because we are already in fear that what we are seeing is not really there. We are hiding our wounds. If we uncover them and see, then it will be known that there is a wound. So we have hidden the wound and worn gold bracelets on top of it. The bracelet is seen, not the wound. And seeing the bracelet we think that everything is alright. But have bracelets ever healed any wounds? That wound goes on growing bigger and bigger inside until it becomes an ulcer.

Our whole life is a self-deception where there is nothing worthwhile. We also feel that there is nothing, but we are also afraid that we are living just with the help of these illusions and if we open our eyes and find out that these too do not exist, then how shall we live?

This difficulty has arisen in the West. Try to understand this. During the last three hundred years, the West has tried to see things as they are. Now the West is in difficulty. The difficulty is that this attempt has succeeded in showing that there is nothing in things, objects. What to do now? Only one feeling prevails in the West now, that everything has become empty and useless, there seems to be no meaning. What to do now?

During these three hundred years, the West has thought much about all the relationships in life, and the outcome is that all relationships have become suspect. Today no lover in the West can be bold enough to say to his beloved that his love is eternal, permanent. It has become impossible to say so, because the more research that was done on love the clearer it became that nothing else is more momentary than love. It was only the talk of poets and blind people who used to say their love was eternal.

It needs blind eyes before one can say that love is eternal. It appears so, but in reality it is not so. When you are in love with somebody it seems that this love will last forever and no power on earth can break it. You are in a great illusion. No big powers are needed, in fact no outside powers at all are needed; you will do the job of breaking it yourself, you alone are enough for it.

Love is ephemeral. When a flower blooms in the morning, who can believe that it will fade away in a few hours? Its flowering deceives and makes one feel that it will remain so forever, but it does not happen that way. Whatsoever has blossomed will fade. When love blossoms, that too is a flower and it will fade.

The West has come to know this well, has come to understand this well, and has fallen into great difficulty: to love has become difficult, because to love, that illusion of its being eternal is necessary. Without that illusion there can be no love. If that illusion breaks, love also falls apart.

So only sex has remained in the West. There seems to be no possibility of love, only sexuality has remained. But it is very difficult to give life depth on a foundation of sexuality. And it is very difficult to create the family on the basis of sexuality. And if sexuality is the only reality, then it is worthless to undergo so many troubles, the many responsibilities of the family system.

In the West, husbands and wives are disappearing, boyfriends and girlfriends are increasing. The husband-and-wife relationship has ceased to be of importance. Boyfriends and girlfriends – that means the friendship is still well and alive. If tomorrow it changes then there is no legal headache. But then an emptiness sets in. Love is uprooted, and if meditation cannot be made available there will be serious trouble. The energy is released and there is no other route for it to travel. This is why people keep their eyes closed and feel that where they are walking is heaven – even in hell. When the eyes are open, hell is seen. You also come across occasions every day where you see hell. Life is such that you will choose detachment on your own.

Life is such that detachment is bound to happen, it is not that you have to make tireless effort for it. In fact you are making tireless effort so that detachment does not arise. Just think: look back on your life, take a bird's-eye view and you will find that the whole of life is leading you towards detachment. The whole message of life is detachment, the whole flow of life is towards detachment. Life brings you sorrow from all directions, but still detachment does not arise in you. Life disappoints you in every respect, breaks you down, tears you apart, but detachment still does not arise in you – it is a miracle! Otherwise the natural flow of life is towards detachment.

In attachment is the birth of life, and detachment is the end result. We are born out of attachment, but if we die also in attachment it only means that we have not heard the message of life.

Detachment is the language of life. If you search, if you do not deceive yourself, then all are helpful – a friend as well as an enemy; near and dear ones as well as distant people, all are helpful in leading you towards detachment.

The fruit of detachment is knowledge...

The day you stand firm in detachment and you have no desires about this world, you have no demands from this world, and the futility of this world is revealed to you – the outcome is knowledge. Then you are full of wisdom; then for the first time wisdom arises in you and a lamp is lit within you.

In the state of detachment the lamp of wisdom burns. If the lamp of knowledge does not burn, understand well that the detachment is false. This is the second part of the sutra. If the second step does not follow, then the first step has been false; it has proved fruitless. In our country there is no shortage of people who have renounced attachment – these people are sitting in every temple and monastery – but it is difficult to find the wise.

I have been meeting so many sadhus and sannyasins. They ran away years ago, but they say, "Nothing has happened so far, knowledge has not happened." But even they are not ready to accept that their detachment is false and that is why knowledge has not happened to them. They believe that their detachment is complete; it is only the knowledge that has not happened. If knowledge has not happened, then the first step has gone wrong, your detachment is false. It is not a product of ripe attachment, it has not come out of ripe attachment; you have run away from the world prematurely, you have run away without opening your eyes – let this be remembered.

There is a man walking in hell with closed eyes and cherishing dreams in which he is in heaven. He does not open his eyes lest he see hell. He hears the statements of the seers and sages that the world is hell; he himself feels within that it may be so and he is afraid of opening his eyes. Or sometimes when his eyes open in some accidental happening he sees the hell, and what the seers and sages are saying appears to be true. But he does not keep his eyes open, he goes on becoming more nervous, and the voices of the seers and sages go on hiding deeper inside him. He starts feeling from inside that everything is wrong and he runs away from the world. But he runs away with his eyes still closed. He moves into detachment, but he does not look at attachment with open eyes. With eyes closed he was in attachment; with eyes closed he has moved into detachment.

This will not bear the fruit of knowledge, because there is no change in the state of mind in this man – his eyes are still closed. Until yesterday he was walking like a blind man in attachments; today he is walking like a blind man in detachment.

The detachment that takes place by opening one's eyes within attachment is the ripened detachment, mature. It is in this maturity that the lamp of knowledge is lit.

The fruit of knowledge is relaxedness.

When the lamp of knowledge is lit what is the result? The result is relaxedness, tranquility. The mind, consciousness, body, being – everything attains to relaxedness. There is no effort left anywhere; there is no tension, no strain, not even a trace of any of these left anywhere in the person. A tranquility, a relaxedness happens.

If knowledge does not bring relaxedness, understand well that the knowledge is false. Then each successive step must be false. If a person with knowledge looks tense, if a person with knowledge is not relaxed, if a person with knowledge has to impose discipline upon himself, then know that the knowledge must have come from the scriptures, not through his own experience. He may have attained knowledge by listening to others but it is not through his own knowing. In such a case, the knowledge may well be in the intellect but it has not yet entered the being. Such a knowledge is a weight over the head, it has not become wings with which one may fly in the sky.

The fruit of knowledge is relaxedness, such that there remains no effort at all within oneself. There remains no effort of any kind, one becomes effortless. Whatsoever happens is right – a state of suchness prevails, relaxedness happens. Whatsoever is, is right. There is no effort to achieve anything, there is no fear of losing anything. No fear grips you that something may go wrong, no uneasiness hovers that some mistake may happen, no tension that you may miss, you may fall down, you may go astray – this is called *uparati*, relaxedness.

Uparati, relaxedness, is a very deep thing. You will come across millions of nonattached people, but none with a glimpse of knowledge in them. You will come across thousands of people with knowledge also, but no glimpse of relaxedness in them. There is no shortage of pundits or knowledgeable people.

But it is very interesting to note that sometimes the ignorant and unknowledgeable people appear more relaxed than the knowledgeable. If the brain of a pundit and that of an ignorant person are examined, the brain of the ignorant person will be found in relaxation, and that of the pundit will be found in great turmoil. It all seems to have gone topsy-turvy. Even ignorance is better than this situation because at least the ignorance is yours. This knowledge is borrowed and therefore a burden. What is one's own makes one light, and what is borrowed makes one burdened. What is one's own always brings flowering, what is from others crushes one.

The fruit of knowledge is relaxedness and the fruit of relaxedness is peace. One who has attained to relaxedness, slowly, slowly sinking deeper and deeper and deeper in it, he attains to the center that has been called peace.

When a person is swimming he will be on the surface of the water. Swimming is an effort, a doing. But another person who has left himself loose and relaxed, who is not swimming but just floating effortlessly, moving with the river wherever it takes him – it is fine with him if it takes him somewhere, and if it does not take him anywhere that too is fine – such a person has attained to relaxedness. Such a person who is effortlessly lying there will slowly, slowly start sinking in the river; he will go on sinking till he reaches the ultimate depth, till he touches the rock bottom of the river – that rock bottom has been named peace.

Knowledge through detachment...if the detachment is real, knowledge is bound to follow. If knowledge is true, relaxedness is bound to follow. If relaxedness is real, peace will always follow. And if peace does not arise out of your relaxedness, know well that your relaxedness is an imposed one.

In the West many books have been written which have strange names such as, You Must Relax. Now this title of the book is absurd. In the very word 'must' there is tension. Now this 'you must' will become the problem, it won't let you relax. People are lying down on their beds reading such books and trying all kinds of postures. The book is saying one *must* relax, so they are relaxing!

They can even impose relaxation upon themselves, they can even lie down on their bed stiff like a corpse, but the tension will continue inside them because now they have to think of relaxing also. If you have to think about your relaxation, that too will require effort, energy. And remember, if you have to do this you will come out of it even more exhausted, because that effort is what tires one. You are concentrating on "I am resting, I am not to make any effort at all." This "I am not to make any effort at all" now becomes the effort.

No peace will be attained through such relaxation. Relaxation is an existential happening. Relaxation means your consciousness has nothing worth achieving, your consciousness has no demands of any kind and no desire to become something – no desire to even become relaxed; there is no insistence even for relaxation to come. If it comes it is good, if it does not come it is equally good.

You may have heard Mohammedan fakirs on the road saying, "May one who gives be happy, may one who does not give be happy." The ordinary beggars also repeat this, but this statement is from the Sufis. The ordinary beggar repeats it deceitfully. When he says, "May one who gives be happy," the sparkle in his eyes is remarkable, and when he says, "May one who does not give be happy," there is no sparkle at all. You will come to know the difference by giving to him and watching, and by not giving to him and watching.

There was a Sufi fakir named Bayazid. He had made a little change in this statement. He used to say, "May one who gives be happy and may one who does not give be even more happy." Somebody asked Bayazid, "We had so far only heard 'May one who gives be happy and may one who does not give be happy,' but what does this addition mean?"

Bayazid replied, "When somebody gives I am pleased, but when somebody does not give I am even more pleased. My sense of gratitude becomes more intense. When somebody gives, it is alright, I am pleased; but when somebody does not give, then also the inner pleasure still remains. I feel like bowing down to him. I feel that if he had given, I would have been deprived of this opportunity of remaining happy when not receiving. This is why I say, 'May one who does not give be even more happy.' He is kind that he gave me one more opportunity to see my stream of happiness remaining uninterrupted when not receiving."

Relaxation comes from within, it is not acquired through effort. So the whole process is by steps. Nonattachment is the first step towards tranquility. Everybody wants relaxation, but detachment comes first – that is the first step towards relaxation. But the Upanishads create conditions and make everything difficult. Who is there who does not want relaxation? Everybody is in search of relaxation, everybody is in search of peace. But then its whole science has to be followed. You desire flowers but do not sow the seeds. You sow the seeds but you do not water them. Or if you water them, you do not raise a fence to protect the plants from animals. No, one has to move through each step.

Detachment means to remove one's mind from all sorts of desires. As the mind is removed from desires, the energy that was being destroyed in running after these desires is saved and it becomes a flame.

...the fruit of knowledge is relaxedness...

One who has come to know has no source of tension anymore. One who has come to know has also no reason to be uneasy. There is nothing in this world about which one needs to be uneasy.

...the fruit of knowledge is relaxedness,
and the peace that descends from experiencing the
self-bliss is the very fruit of relaxedness.

If each one of the aforesaid does not happen in
succession, know that the previous one did not
yield fruit. Abstention from the sense-objects is in
itself the supreme contentment and
incomparable bliss.

Enough for today.

THAT –
THE UNIVERSAL
RELIGION

The one who has the attribute of being
the embodiment of maya, illusion,
who is the source of the universe,
who has the characteristics of omniscience,
etcetera, and is the embodiment of indirectness,
multiplicity and truth, etcetera,
is known by the word tat – 'that'.

✳

The one who seems to be in support of the 'I'
as an experience as well as a word and who is
experienced as separate from the conscience,
is called by the word tvam – 'thou'.

✳

There are two attributes: maya, illusion,
to the universal soul, and avidya,
ignorance, to the embodied soul.
On abandoning the two, what is seen is
the perpetually true, conscious and
blissful Param Brahman –
the ultimate supreme reality.

G od has been addressed by many names. Man has established a variety of relationships with God. Somewhere he is the father, somewhere mother, somewhere lover, somewhere beloved, somewhere friend and somewhere something else. In this way man has tried to establish many, many different relationships with the ultimate truth. But the Upanishads are alone on this whole earth in calling God only 'that', *tat*, and thus not establishing a relationship of any kind.

This needs to be understood properly. This is a very deep insight. Out of love we may call God 'father' or 'mother', but in so doing there is less of understanding and more of foolishness. No matter what relationship we establish with God it is foolishness. Why? – because there is one inevitable factor in a relationship: there must be the presence of two persons. A relationship cannot be constituted without two. I am there and my father is there – both are necessary; I am there and my mother is there – both are necessary. No such relationship with God is either right or possible where we can relate by remaining two. With God, it is possible to be related only through losing ourselves, not through remaining as separate entities.

All the relationships of this world are maintained only by remaining separate entities. The relationship with God is established only by merging with God, by losing oneself in God, by being one with God. This is of great complexity. For a relationship two are required, so we can even say that no relationship can ever be established with God. If two are a must for a relationship, then no relationship can be established with God because the very meeting with God is possible only when the two disappear as two and the one remains.

Kabir has said, "I had set out in search for you but I could not find you. I disappeared in the very search, then you were found. The one who had set out in search for you...as long as he was there, there was no meeting with you; when in the process of seeking you were not found but the seeker disappeared, then the meeting happened."

It only means that man never meets God, because as long as the man is there, there is no God; and when God is there, the man is not there. The two never meet.

So none of the relationships of the world are applicable to a meeting with God. We make a mistake by thinking this way.

A father can be met without losing ourselves; losing oneself is not a condition for meeting. A mother can be met without losing ourselves; losing oneself is not a condition for meeting. But to lose oneself is a basic condition for meeting God. Relationships take place between two, but the relationship with God takes place only when there is one, not two. So this relationship is just the opposite.

The Upanishads did not address God as father or as mother – they did not establish any human relationship. Sociologists say that the establishment of all human relationships is anthropocentric, man-centered. Man goes on imposing himself upon everything. Let us understand this view of man being anthropocentric, because modern psychology and sociology are highly influenced by this word and attach a great value to it.

Whatsoever a man sees, he projects himself in it. If the moon is clouded over, we say, "The moon's face is hidden behind a veil." Neither is there any face nor is there any veil. But man, by nature, projects his experiences on everything. If there is an eclipse of the moon we say, "Her enemies *Rahu* and *Ketu* have swallowed the moon, they are after the moon."

Man can think only in man's language. We also go on projecting ourselves on all that we see around us. We address the earth as the mother; it is a projection. We address the sky as the father; it is a projection. If we look deeply, we shall find that whatever relationships man has with the universe, he has imposed his own image and structure on all of them.

Freud says that the whole issue of God is in fact a substitute for the father.

When a child is born he is helpless, weak and insecure; the father protects him and brings him up. The little child grows in his shadow, he takes the father to be the superpower; there is none bigger than him in the world. So small children are often seen to be discussing amongst themselves as to whose father is the more powerful. Every child claims that his father is the biggest, and every child feels this way – that what can there be bigger and more powerful than his father? All power is in his father's hands.

In childhood, the child takes support from his father to grow. His confidence, trust, respect, all are endowed in his father. If while holding his hand his father walks through fire, the child will accompany him laughing, because wherever his father is going there cannot be any danger for him. Neither have any doubts nor has any distrust arisen in the child's mind yet. His father is still absolutely trustworthy. But as the child grows, this trust will start falling apart. Slowly the weaknesses of the father will become visible to him.

As the child grows he will be able to understand a little, and the very first weakness that he will come to see is that in ninety out of a hundred occasions the mother is more powerful than the father, on ninety to ninety-nine occasions out of a hundred. All his father's pomp and show, all his strutting is outside his house – he enters the house a little afraid, a little meek. This will be the first crack in the child's trust. As he grows up and begins to understand things, he sees that his father also has a boss and that he trembles before her.

This trust that had been imposed on the father in childhood now shifts away from the father, leaving a gap. It is this same trust that, according to Freud, one imposes on a God – an imaginary father – so that the mind does not have a gap. So man calls God the father, the supreme father, the most powerful of all.

Remember, whatever qualities a child ascribes to his father are exactly the same qualities religious people ascribe to God. And just as children fight amongst themselves to settle whose father is greater, the Hindus, Mohammedans and Christians fight to prove their god to be the greater. Now, how can a god be greater? These are all childish ideas. But the very imposition of fatherhood upon the concept of God is childish; it is born out of the child's mind.

So Freud went so far as to say that as long as children are brought up with their father it is very difficult for them to get rid of God. God is nothing but another form of father. There seems to be some truth in it, because in matriarchal societies, where the mother is supreme and the father is secondary, God is not addressed as the father but as the mother. It reveals the truth of the matter. For example, the worshippers of mother goddess Kali accept God in the form of mother, not in the form of father. These worshippers of Kali are from a matriarchal society where the mother is primary and the father is secondary. Such societies are still existent on the earth, and in these societies the concept of God is that of a mother, not of a father.

This supports Freud's idea a little that concepts are formed in childhood – and the moments of childhood are valuable, because whatever patterns are formed in the mind during that period, whenever there is any loss of them one feels restless. It becomes necessary for the person to compensate for those losses. And man goes on trying his whole life to complete the patterns created in his childhood.

From this you should take note of one more interesting thing. In societies where the family system has been uprooted – for example, as has happened in America, where the roots of the family system are pulled out, where the children care for neither the father or the mother, nor do the mother or the father care much about the children; where the relationship between the family members has become weak – in those societies the concept of God also becomes weak.

Where the family system totters the God also totters; there spreads atheism. In societies where the father's power is very strong and where the father's orders are supreme and discipline is ensured, atheism is not born. And the conclusions that Freud derives from all this are true, but only half. There is truth in his conclusion that to see the father in God is an attempt by man to fill a psychological emptiness. But when Freud says that God is nothing more than this, this is where he is mistaken.

Man may call earth the mother – this is something to do with the man, but because of this the earth does not cease to be what it is. Man may call God father, mother or anything whatsoever. This may be an extension of his family, his childhood or his mind, but the God on whom this extension is done does not become a falsity because of it. What names we give it depends on us, but its existence does not depend on us.

Had Freud known about the Upanishads he would have been in difficulty, because the Upanishads do not create any relationship with God. Had Freud read the Upanishads the story of modern psychology would have been different. But Freud was an honest man. Had he even a slight inkling that there is some tradition of thought, philosophy, experience which does not establish any kind of relationship with God and which uses a most impersonal word *tat*, 'that' – where God is 'that', and there cannot be any other more impersonal address – Freud would have surely been amazed. 'That' means no name has been given, only a hint. 'That' is not a name, it is only an indication, a pointing finger.

Certainly this tat cannot be born out of any shortcomings of childhood. One may think of mother, one may think of father – but 'that'? It has nothing to do with the psychology of childhood. In fact it has nothing to do with psychology as such. It has to do with the experience of those who have gone beyond mind, who have gone beyond man.

These words *manushya* and *mun*, man and mind, should also be understood. In this country we have called man manushya. He has been called so because he is surrounded by mun, the mind, because he is living in mind, because he is solely mind-oriented and derives nourishment from the mind. The English word man is also the derivative of the Sanskrit word mun, meaning mind.

Mun, mind, is man. Where mind is transcended, the manhood is also transcended. These are the statements of those who transcended man, who transcended mun, the mind, and hinted at 'that'. But there are several things in it worth considering. A father can be worshipped, but how would you worship 'that'? A temple of 'father' can be built, a temple of 'mother' can be built, but how would you build a temple of 'that'? How can you make a temple of 'that'? or can you? One can make idols of man, woman, mother, father, but how can an idol of 'that' be made? There are no scriptures more iconoclastic than the Upanishads, though not a word has been said by them against worshipping idols. This too is worth understanding.

Mohammedans have been busy breaking idols just because Mohammed said, "There can be no idol of 'that'." Mohammed's statement is similar to that of the Upanishads: there can be no idol of 'that'. Mohammedans seem to believe that the idol of 'that' cannot be made but that the idol of 'that' can be broken! How can that be broken which cannot be made in the first place? So one group of mad people are busy making idols and another group of mad people are busy breaking idols.

It is very interesting to see that the iconoclast is also nothing but a worshipper of idols. One who goes to break the idol also believes in idols – at least he believes them to be worth taking the trouble of breaking. He believes in the idol at least that much. Where is the difference? One goes to place offerings of flowers on the head of the idol, another goes to break the head of the idol with a hammer.

It is hammers and chisels with which the idols are made and it is also hammers and chisels with which the idols are broken. There is not much difference between the belief of the two – both believe that there is some importance in the idol. The idol-worshipper believes it to be of importance, the iconoclast believes it to be of importance. Sometimes the iconoclast attaches more importance, because while the idol-worshipper never risks his life in the making of the idol, the iconoclast risks his life for breaking it. The iconoclast puts his life at stake in breaking an idol when the Koran says, "There can be no idol of 'that'." Whose idol are you breaking then?

The Upanishads are neither idol-worshippers nor iconoclasts. The vision of the Upanishads has gone far beyond form, shape and idol. This is why they said, tat, 'that'. What idol can be made of 'that'? No, no idol can be made of 'that'. 'That' is not a form. Is there any form or shape of 'that'? 'That' is not a form, 'that' is formless. Even the word 'that' is formless. If anybody wants to give a form to 'that', it cannot be done. What is tat, 'that'? It is only an indication, as if somebody points a finger and says 'that'!

Wittgenstein is an amazing modern thinker. He is one of those who gave birth to this century's greatest logic. Wittgenstein, in his important book Tractatus Logicus, which is one of the three or four most important books written in this century, writes that there are things which cannot be said but still they can be shown. Nothing can be said about them but they can be indicated.

The Upanishads only indicate towards God, they say nothing. 'That' is just an indication. There are many things implied in this indication, take note of this fact. One implication is that no relationship can be established with 'that'. This is why the Upanishads do not call it 'thou', because with thou it is possible to establish the relationship of 'I'.

Wherever there is thou there will be 'I' also. Thou cannot exist without 'I'. As soon as I call somebody thou, 'I' has entered in, 'I' has made its presence there. It is in reference to 'I' that somebody is thou, and it is in reference to thou that I am 'I'. I and thou exist simultaneously. 'That' is alone. There is no necessity of the other to exist with 'that'. 'That' does not produce any indication of the presence of someone else.

Whenever we say thou, then whosoever has been addressed comes on the same level as we are. 'I' and thou stand side by side. When we say 'that', no relationship is being formed on our level. Where is 'that'? Whether it is above, below or within us, nothing of that sort is revealed. With deep insight the Upanishads have called God 'that'.

Let us understand this sutra now.

The one who has the attribute of being
the embodiment of maya, illusion,
who is the source of the universe,

who has the characteristics of omniscience,
etcetera, and is the embodiment of indirectness,
multiplicity and truth, etcetera,
is known by the word tat – 'that'.

The one who seems to be in support of the 'I'
as an experience as well as a word and who is
experienced as separate from the conscience,
is called by the word tvam – 'thou'.

Tvam, thou, you.... As soon as we call anyone thou, tvam or you, we have already accepted a boundary. This other is seen by us as a separate entity. This entity has a form, a body; you cannot call a bodiless entity thou. You cannot look at the sky and call it thou, it does not mean anything. How could you say thou to the sky? No relationship comes into being. There is such an expanse, without limits; no relationship of thou seems to arise. The relationship of thou arises only where there is some form. But God is even more expansive than the sky; the sky itself is just one event in God. With such a God the relationship of thou is not feasible, because while standing before God there is no remembrance of 'I', that I am. One who still feels that 'I exist' will not be able to see God. The very 'I' is the impediment, the veil.

As long as there is 'I', I will see everywhere only thou. Any relationship with the formless is not possible; relationship is only possible with the form.

Remember, take this as a fundamental principle. What I am, how I am, where I am – my relationships can only be possible within these contexts. If I believe that I am the body, any relationship will happen only with those who also believe they are body. If I believe that I am mind, my relationships will happen only with those who also believe that they are mind. If I believe that I am consciousness, my relationships will only be possible with those who believe they are consciousness. If I want to establish a relationship with God, I also have to become formless and void like

God where there is not even a trace of 'I', because 'I' attributes form. Only when all is void in me will I be able to connect with void. Only when I become formless internally will I be able to connect with the formless outside. There is no other way but to become like the one with whom one wants to connect. There is no other way but to become like the one whom you are seeking.

There are two words, 'that' and thou. The embodied soul we call thou – the consciousness which is encaged in the body, that is limited by the body. And that consciousness which is all pervading – beyond all the limits and is limitless – we call 'that'. To the dew-drop we say 'you' and to the ocean we say 'that'. To the atom, to the tiny atom we say 'you' and to the whole we say 'that'.

Why is there so much insistence of the Upanishads on tat, 'that'? The Upanishads do not have the expectation that you will just begin worshipping and praying to God. Nor do they expect you to just be a devotee of God. The Upanishads expect you to become God yourself. Let this difference be properly understood.

The ambition of the Upanishads is ultimate, absolute; no higher ambition than this has ever been born in the world. The Upanishads are not satisfied just by your worship, prayer or devotion to God. They say that as long as you do not become God the ultimate truth is not perceived. They say that until you become God your destiny is not fulfilled.

'That' means that we are not to establish a relationship of worship or devotion with God – no relationship can be established with 'that' anyway – we are to drop all relationships. In the end we shall drop ourselves also, so that there remains no one to relate and therefore no relationships can be possible. Ultimately we will become only that which we have been addressing as 'that'.

The matter does become difficult to understand, because ordinarily our concept of religion is of worship and prayer, reverence and devotion. The Upanishads' concept of religion is not at all that of worship, devotion and prayer, but of the uncovering and unveiling of 'that' which is hidden within every individual.

The Upanishad is a science of religion. Just as science searches for the truth hidden within matter, just as science breaks matter, splits it into atoms and tries to discover the energy hidden within it and the laws which govern it, in the same way the Upanishads enter into every atom of the consciousness and discover what the laws of consciousness are, how consciousness is moving in the world and how it is static, how consciousness is hidden and how it is manifest.

This Upanishad is using the language of science. If a scientist discovers atomic energy, he does not say that this atomic energy is his mother or father, he does not establish a relationship with it. It is a law that he has discovered, there is no question of establishing a relationship with it. He does not develop a language of attachment around it. If science did develop a language of attachment, it would cease to be science. Attachment, relationship, are non-scientific and they would pervert the truth. So a scientist will have to look at the truth maintaining his distance and neutrality; it is not a question of creating a close personal relationship.

The Upanishads too speak the language of science: they say 'that'. They do not establish a relationship, they keep themselves separate and apart. When the Upanishads say 'that', we do not even notice who is speaking. When somebody says, "God is the supreme father," we know who is saying it – somebody whose desires about their father have remained unfulfilled, somebody whose son-hood has remained incomplete, somebody who has not received the love of father or mother, or somebody who has received so much love that it has caused indigestion. But certainly the person saying this is one who has suffered some kind of abnormality in the relationship with his father. But when one says 'that', nothing is noticed about the speaker, nothing is revealed about the speaker.

The indication is most impersonal and hence very valuable. And the moment we call it 'that', all disputes end.

It is very interesting: if we call God 'that', how will Hindus and Mohammedans fight? What difference can there be between the 'that' of a Christian and a Hindu? If the Christians, Mohammedans and Hindus all call God 'that', there can be no fight amongst the three. No matter what word is used for 'that' – tat or that, it does not make any difference – still there can be no fight. But when a Mohammedan calls it one thing, a Hindu calls it something else, a Christian calls it something else, or when they call it father, the concept immediately alters and adapts for each.

It is a matter worth reflecting on. Freud said that when a person calls God the father, if he searches within himself he will find his father's image in his concept of God. He is bound to find it. When you call God the mother, your mother will appear. What is your concept of mother? With a little refinement, purification, cleansing, painting to it, you can turn your concept of mother into God.

Diderot, a French philosopher, has made a subtle joke. He has said that if horses were to conceive of their God it would have the looks of a horse! No horse can conceive of their God having the face of a man – this is certain, this we know. When a negro pictures God he will have short bushy hair – it ought to be so! Its lips will be like those of negroes, and the skin will be dark, black. When the Chinese paint the face of God it will have high cheekbones, because "Our God, and not looking Chinese – how is it possible?"

It is our concept that we will project. Can an Englishman ever conceive of a black god? There is no such possibility. Do you see the Hindu imagination in their gods? Rama, Krishna...all are swarthy. To the Hindu mind the swarthy color has been a symbol of great beauty – of course it will be so! Do you see their features? The concept of beauty that the Hindu mind has is bound to be projected on Rama and Krishna. It ought to be so.

You may have observed that the ears of Rama, Krishna, Christ and Mohammed are not very big, they are small. But if you have seen the statues of Buddha and Mahavira, you will find that the ears are so long as to touch their shoulders. The Buddhists and the Jainas believe that the *tirthankaras* have ears long enough to touch their shoulders. The whole reason for this seems to be that probably the ears of the Jainas' first tirthankara may have been very long, touching his shoulders – and that has become a continuing concept.

There is no reason to believe that all the twenty-four tirthankaras may have had long ears touching their shoulders. But once a concept has taken root, the statues are made according to that concept and not according to the individual whose statue is being made. If you see the statues of all the twenty-four tirthankaras you will not be able to tell which one is of Mahavira, which is of Parshvanatha and which is of Neminatha. All the twenty-four statues look the same. They can only be identified by seeing the specific symbol engraved at the base of each statue.

A concept is agreed upon and then we move and live according to that. All our gods are created out of our concepts, but there can be no concept created about 'that'. So the day there is a universal religion in the world, that day the Upanishads will be understood rightly for the first time. That day we will understand that the Upanishads have, for the first time, used a scientific language and have left aside the cobwebs of the anthropocentric language of man.

> There are two attributes: maya, illusion,
> to the universal soul, and avidya,
> ignorance, to the embodied soul.
> On abandoning the two, what is seen is
> the perpetually true, conscious and
> blissful Param Brahman –
> the ultimate supreme reality.

This sutra is a little difficult. "God has the attribute of illusion and the embodied soul has the attribute of ignorance." Call it attribute or call it disease.

"God has the attribute of illusion." We need to penetrate this understanding. This is rather complex and subtle; let us try to understand it. There have been many, many apprehensions in man's mind. Let us understand some of the apprehensions, and then we can move into the sutra.

One difficulty that has always been there for any reflective man is that if one accepts God, it becomes very difficult to accept this world; if we accept God, it becomes very difficult to explain this world. For example, if God has created this world, why is it so full of disease, misery, pain and sin? If God has created this world, what is the need to put man in such ignorance? Man cannot be held responsible for all this, only God remains responsible.

A few days back one Christian priest came to see me. I asked him what work he was engaged in. He replied, "We are busy fighting sin." I said, "Sin! Where did this sin come from?" He said, "It is created by the Devil."

So far he was at ease. Normally nobody inquires deeper into such matters, because in doing so embarrassing situations may arise. I asked him, "Who created the Devil?" Then he felt a little uneasy, because now the matter was problematic. He was afraid that if he says that God created the Devil then it becomes difficult, because if God created the Devil, and the Devil created sin, what is this vicious mess all about? Doesn't God possess enough intelligence not to create the Devil? And even if God mistakenly created the Devil, where is the difficulty if you and I mistakenly commit a sin? And if sin is created by the Devil, and the Devil is created by God, and we commit sins, who is responsible? We are just victims, unnecessarily victimized. We have nothing to do with it.

God creates us, God creates the Devil, the Devil creates the sins, we commit the sins – where in this whole circle do we become responsible? Neither do we create God, nor do we create the Devil, nor do we create sin – and we are unnecessarily suffering in this mess.

The priest became a little restless. Christianity has no answer for it. It is difficult to find the answer with any of these people because it is too problematic. Or some people...for example, Zoroastrians believe, as Zarathustra says, that God and the Devil are two elements. Nobody created anybody, both are eternal. Now in this belief the danger becomes even greater, because if both are eternal then neither of the two can ever win or lose. God and the Devil will go on fighting. And who are you – are you the battlefield where they are fighting? Neither of the two can win or lose because both are eternal.

Zoroastrians are also in difficulty if they don't believe them both to be eternal and say that the Devil can be defeated, because then the question arises: How come he has not been defeated so far? So many centuries have passed and he has not yet been defeated. And where is the guarantee of his defeat in the future? In fact, the situation seems to be just the opposite – that the Devil is winning. For him to be defeated is a faraway dream; the Devil seems to be winning every day.

You will be surprised to know that recently, in 1970, in California, America, a new church has been registered under the name The First Church of the Devil. It has its followers and an archbishop, and they have printed their own bible and announced, "We have had enough time to experience that God is being defeated and the Devil is winning."

What is said appears to be right. If we look at the world, their statement does not seem to be wrong. The followers of the Devil win and the followers of God get defeated. The followers of the Devil occupy high positions, and the followers of God wander here and there.

You can try it out yourself – now even the followers of God have learned the trick. They chant the name of God, but get things done through the Devil; they have understood who really wins. In the final calculation it is the Devil who wins. But the fear also lurks in the mind that perhaps, by some mistake, God may win! So they keep chanting the name of God also: Rama, Rama, Rama. They try to remain sitting in both boats – all prudent people are like that. When there is a need they take work from the Devil, and when there is no need and they have free time, they turn their prayer beads to please God. A sort of compromise is maintained, a sort of balance. And then also, who knows who will win in the end?

If the world gives any indication, it is of the Devil winning. The victory of God is not seen anywhere. Neither does good seem to be on the increase nor does evil seem to be on the decrease. Neither does the light seem to be increasing nor does the darkness seem to be decreasing.

So there is trouble in believing the Devil to be eternal. And if one believes that he is not eternal, that the Devil will finally be defeated – no matter how much he wins in the intervening period, that in the end he will be defeated – what is the assurance for it? Where is the guarantee of such a happening? One who is winning now, why should he be defeated in the end? There seems to be no consistency or logic in the belief that the one who is winning all along will suddenly be defeated in the end.

This has remained an enduring question for mankind. Different religions have attempted different methods to solve this problem of duality, but nothing is solved. The concept of the Upanishads seems the least erroneous of them all in comparison – just the least erroneous, but not totally right. But if it is weighed against all the other concepts, the Upanishads' idea seems to be the most correct – not altogether correct, just the most correct.

The Upanishads say that there is no opposition between God and the world: there is no Devil, and there is no power opposing God. How then is this world created? The Upanishads say that God is not creating this world by creating some opponent to do the job. In the very being of God, in the very glow of God – which they call maya, illusion – in the very shadow of God – which they also call maya, illusion – the world is, just as a person stands and his shadow is naturally formed. There is no solid existence of a shadow: a sword cannot cut it, fire cannot burn it, water cannot drown it. Try as you may, it still exists. It does not have a real existence, yet the shadow is. It walks behind you; if you run, it runs after you, if you stop, it stops.

The Upanishads say that whenever something exists, it also has its shadow. And the latest researches in science and psychology also support this fact. Let this be understood. Nothing exists without a shadow. Whatever is, it creates its shadow. If there is Brahman, the absolute reality, it will have its shadow too. That shadow they call maya, illusion. The shadow of the absolute reality is this world.

Jung, a great psychologist, did a great deal of research on this reality from a different dimension and he found that every man also has a shadow existence, a shadow personality. You should also understand this because you too have your shadow existence.

You are a good man, peaceful and patient, and you do not become angry. But one day suddenly, on some minor matter, you become so outrageously angry that it is beyond your own understanding as to what is happening and who is doing this. The matter itself is not so serious that it calls for any anger, and you are not a person who is used to becoming angry – you do not become angry even about big, serious matters! But today, about this minor matter, you are in a rage.

That is why people often say afterwards, "It happened in spite of me. I was not intending it and it happened." Why? How did it happen? You were not intending to do it, then how did it happen?

Sometimes you do not intend to say a certain thing and it pops out of your mouth. You simply did not want to say it and it spurted out of your mouth. You repent afterwards that, "I had never thought I would say it; I had taken the decision not to say it, and yet I blurted it out!"

Jung says that you have a shadow personality of your own in which everything that you deny within you goes on accumulating. Sometimes finding some opportunity, in some weak moment finding some crack in the system, the shadow personality manifests itself. Because of this shadow personality, a serious disease known as 'split personality' is a subject of study in psychology.

A man is divided into two parts. Sometimes it so happens that there become two distinct personalities in the man – it seems there are two men within one. The man says one thing and does another, there is no coordination; he is one man in the morning and another in the evening. His saying, his being – nothing can quite be relied upon. He himself is afraid as to what he is doing and what he is saying, there is simply no harmony. It is as if there are two persons within him. Sometimes he is very peaceful, sometimes very agitated; sometimes silent, sometimes very talkative – he is just split into two parts.

There are thousands of such mad persons in thousands of mad-houses. Their sickness is that suddenly they have completely lost one personality and have become a different person. Till yesterday he was Rama, then suddenly something happened – an accident, or he fell and injured his head – and he became Rahim. Now he simply does not remember that he was Rama; he does not recognize his father, his mother, or his wife. Now he declares himself to be Rahim and gives a totally different account of his life which has nothing whatsoever to do with this family – not even an acquaintance.

What has happened? In the accident the main personality of the man was pushed into the background due to the shock of the impact and his shadow personality has become active, so he has changed his name and everything else.

This assuming of a shadow personality is reversed also by shock treatment. Sometimes when the person is cured he again becomes Rama, the previous person, and his whole behavior changes back to the original personality.

This shadow personality is hidden within every person. If we describe this in the Upanishadic language, it is the ignorance, avidya, that is tied to every person – it is his shadow personality. Just as it is illusion, maya, that is tied to Brahman, the supreme reality – that is its shadow personality. This illusion is not in opposition to Brahman, it is its very shadow, an essential part of its being. This world is not the enemy of Brahman, it is the shadow of the very existence of Brahman. If we try to understand this in the language of science it may become easier to grasp, otherwise it is not easy to grasp at all.

In 1960, one scientist was awarded a Nobel prize for the discovery of anti-matter. This is a very strange word: anti-matter. The discovery by this man is that in this world there is matter and also there is its opposite, anti-matter.

Everything has its opposite. Nothing in this world exists without its opposite. For example, if there is light, there is darkness; if there is life, there is death; if there is heat, there is cold; if there is man, there is woman. The whole world exists through dualities.

Can you conceive of a world where there are only women and no men? It is impossible. Can you conceive of a world where there are only men and no women? It is impossible. The coordination is so deep that when children are born there are one hundred and fifteen boys born and only one hundred girls; but by the age of fifteen, fifteen boys have died and the proportion of boys and girls is equal.

Biologists say that because boys are weaker than girls nature has to give birth to more boys, because by the age of fifteen, the marriageable age, fifteen of the boys will be dead.

You may be surprised to know that according to biology woman is stronger than man. Man's strength is muscular; he can lift a bigger rock but he cannot bear greater pain. A woman's strength is in her forbearance, so women are able to withstand diseases better. And it is necessary, because the greatest tolerance is required in childbirth, and she carries the child for nine months.

If man had to give birth to a child he would have committed suicide long ago. You would not find a single man in the world. Carrying a child for nine months within you – just try carrying a child even for nine days on your shoulders, even for nine hours, even for nine minutes! It is a difficult affair. And then the labor, the delivery pains! Nature makes woman capable of bearing that much pain. She is strong, firm. Her strength is of a different type. She cannot fight, she cannot run very fast, but because of this do not take her to be weak. The dimension of her strength is different. She has greater capacity.

So by the age of fifteen years, the proportion of boys and girls evens out. This proportion is maintained in the whole world. During wars, more boys get killed – certainly, because boys go to the battlefield. Thus the percentage of women increases. And after the time of war the birth-rate of boys increases and that of the girls decreases. Who could be planning all this? And how does all this come about?

During the first world war hundreds of thousands of people were killed. During the first two to three years of the postwar period, the birth-rate of boys noticeably increased and that of the girls decreased. Later on the ratio of their birth-rates settled down to normal. This triggered some thinking. The same thing repeated itself again after the second world war. Then it was realized that nature keeps on balancing the opposites from within.

You need never think that some day on this earth there will be only light and no darkness. This cannot happen. Darkness and light will always remain balanced.

The discovery of anti-matter is based on this same principle that the world is a balance of opposites. So if there is matter, what is opposite to it? And the concept of the physicists is very complex. For example, if a stone is kept on a table, it is seen by us. When it is taken away, nothing is seen there in its place. Now imagine that on that table there is a hollow space exactly in the shape of the stone. When the stone is removed, that hollow space still remains there and that hollow space is the anti-matter. So far nobody has seen it, but the man has received his Nobel prize. And the reason he can receive the Nobel prize is that he cannot be proved wrong, because when everything in this world has its opposite, it is necessary that matter must also have its opposite, which may be hidden somewhere nearby it. It may be seen, it may not be seen, but in principle there is no other alternative but to accept it.

Maya is the shadow of Brahman. Neither Brahman can be there without maya, nor can maya be there without Brahman. And it is on a vast scale that maya is the shadow of Brahman. You could call it the anti-Brahman. On the smaller scale of man, ignorance is the shadow. Ignorance is maya on the scale of man.

Around you exists ignorance. Now what can be done about it? It is there along with man. How to give up ignorance? And if this is destiny, if there is an arrangement in the universe that the opposites will be there and if even Brahman has not been able to drop maya, if even the supreme existence is surrounded by maya, how will we, tiny little individuals, be able to drop ignorance? Brahman is not able to drop maya, so how will we be able to drop ignorance? And if we are unable to drop ignorance, then all endeavor of religion becomes meaningless.

No, we can drop ignorance, but let the process be understood. We can drop ignorance only when we are willing to disappear. If we are not willing to disappear, ignorance cannot disappear; the duality will continue. Either both will remain or both will go. If I say that I want to survive but I also want to destroy the ignorance, then ignorance will never be destroyed. It is your shadow. It is like saying that I want to remain but I want my shadow to disappear. It will never disappear.

There is only one way and that is for me to disappear so that the shadow disappears. Hence so much emphasis on the effacement of the ego. If I disappear my shadow will disappear. When I disappear my shadow also disappears, and I merge and become one with Brahman – not as an 'I' but as a void. What might be happening to my ignorance? When I disappear, when I merge in Brahman, my ignorance merges into the maya. I disappear into Brahman, the ignorance disappears into maya. Whenever I am created I emerge out of Brahman, and ignorance emerges out of maya. Ignorance is our small share of maya given to us, small portions of the land of maya assigned to us.

Maya, ignorance, brings misery and pain. This is why we want to be rid of it. Might it not be giving pain to Brahman? Might Brahman not be wanting to be rid of it? By Brahman is not meant a person but this vast, infinite existence. Might it not be in pain? Might it not be wanting to be rid of it? We feel pain, we want to be rid of it; won't Brahman be wanting to be rid of it also?

On the level of Brahman there is a total acceptance. On the level of Brahman the existence of maya is accepted, there is no denial of it. There is no denial of it, so there is no pain either. On our level there is pain; if we also accept, there is no pain.

When I hurt my hand, the pain is not due to the hurt but due to my idea that the hurt should not have come to me. If I accept that I should have been hurt, that the hurt was bound to happen, that to be hurt is one's destiny, then there would be no pain. The pain is in the opposition, in nonacceptance. The pain is because we are not able to accept it. Some of us do accept – such as a Janaka, or a

Krishna – they accept. Krishna accepts everything. And with acceptance, without doing a thing, ignorance becomes maya, Krishna becomes Brahman.

This is the difference between the paths of Krishna and Buddha or Krishna and Mahavira. Mahavira destroys himself so that all ignorance is destroyed. Krishna neither destroys himself nor his ignorance, he simply accepts. Mahavira destroys ignorance by destroying himself; Krishna becomes Brahman itself through acceptance, at once, because when Brahman is not destroying maya and accepts it, Krishna also accepts it.

For this reason we have called Krishna a total incarnation. There is no nonacceptance there and hence there is totality. Even the slightest nonacceptance and there is no totality.

This is why we have never called Rama a total incarnation. We cannot, because in Rama's mind there are many nonacceptances, many limitations, many limiting concepts. In the story of the Ramayana a washerman says that he doubts Sita's morality because she was stolen away by Ravana. Rama hears of this and is not able to bear this questioning of his wife's morality...a washerman, and questioning his wife's character? Is there a shortage of fools in the world? Anybody may say anything. And it is not certain that washermen in Rama's time would have been very wise people.

But if even a washerman may say, "I have doubts about Sita," and may say to his wife, "You have stayed away overnight, therefore I will not allow you to enter my house – I am not like Rama...." For so many days Sita was forced to stay at Ravana's palace before Rama defeated him and brought her back home. This taunt by the washerman, "What do you think I am? I am not like Rama," was told to Rama and it hurt him deeply, created a thorn in his heart.

Rama has no total acceptance of things. He could not bear the idea of a blot on his name, on his character. He could remove Sita, he could throw her out, because he could not accept this stigma. So the Hindu mind never called Rama a total incarnation. It called him *Maryada Purushottam,* the moral superman; amongst human beings there has been no man of greater morality.

But remember, a moral superman…amongst human beings! But there is a limit! He is very pure, but the emphasis on purity is so much that there is a fear of impurity. But Krishna is a different type of person; he has no fear of any defamation whatsoever. It is as if he makes an effort to become more and more defamed. What might be the difference?

There is no nonacceptance in Krishna. Whatsoever is, is fine. So incredible phenomena took place in Krishna's life. Exactly the same phenomena happened as is happening in the infinity between Brahman and maya – as if the infinity descended in a smaller form on the smaller stage of man, and around it happened the smaller play of maya. In Krishna there was a total acceptance.

When ignorance is accepted, it is not necessary to destroy it. Where there is no acceptance, ignorance will have to be destroyed. But there is only one way of destroying it and that is by destroying one's own self. Then only will it be destroyed.

So the path of Mahavira and Buddha is arduous. It is of cutting, smashing, destroying the ego. Everything has to be smashed, destroyed, bit by bit, from the roots; only then will the shadow be destroyed and one will be rid of it.

The path of Krishna is that of acceptance. Nothing is to be destroyed anywhere. But this is not easy either. It appears easy, but searched deeply perhaps it may prove to be even more difficult, because mind never agrees to acceptance. Mind says, "This should be, that should not be"; "This is how it should be, that is how it should not be" – mind just goes on chattering about what should be, what should not be. Mind goes on dividing.

There are only two paths in the world: one path is to destroy both and the other path is to accept both. Liberation comes on either path.

There are two attributes: maya, illusion,
to the universal soul, and avidya,

ignorance, to the embodied soul.
On abandoning the two, what is seen is
the perpetually true, conscious and
blissful Param Brahman –
the ultimate supreme reality.

On abandoning the two.... I told you there are two paths for abandonment. One path is: you cease, the ignorance ceases. The second path is: agree, accept, drop the idea of going beyond what is – do not think of making even the slightest change in it as it is. Then too what remains is the perpetually true, conscious and blissful supreme reality.

Enough for today.

THE FOUR STEPS

CHAPTER 10

Thus, through statements like Tattvamasi,
That art thou, to pursue the meanings such as
oneness of jiva, the embodied soul,
and Brahman, the absolute reality, is shravana,
listening. And to reasonably pursue the meaning
of whatever has been listened to is manan,
contemplation.

✳

Establishing your mind in the indubitable
meaning attained through this listening and
contemplation, attunement with it is
nididhyasan, assimilation.

✳

Dropping the meditator and the meditation
respectively, when the meditated-upon,
the goal, remains as the only objective and
the mind becomes still like the flame of a lamp
in a windless place –
this is called samadhi, enlightenment.

our words have been used in this sutra. Each word is a world within itself. The four words are: *shravana*, listening, *manan*, contemplation, *nididhyasan*, assimilation, and *samadhi*, enlightenment. In these four words is contained the entire journey to the truth. For the one who may complete these four steps rightly, nothing else remains to be done. It is around these four words that the whole spiritual discipline is developed, so it is useful to understand each of the four words minutely, deeply, with all their subtleties.

The first word is shravana, listening.

Listening does not mean mere hearing. We can all hear, to have ears is enough for hearing. Hearing is a mechanical phenomenon. There was a sound, it fell on your ears and you heard it. But listening is not just this. Listening means that it has not been heard only by the ears, the vibrations have penetrated to the consciousness deep within you. Try to understand this a little.

You are going along a road, your house is on fire and you are running towards it. Somebody passing by on the road greets you. Your ears will hear it but you will not. The next day you will not be able to even recall that somebody greeted you on the road. When your house is on fire, if somebody is singing on the road your ears will hear it but not you.

Hearing with the ears is not listening. It is not necessary that if your ears heard, you also listened. The ears are necessary for listening but are not enough; something more is required within. When your house is on fire, the greetings given to you are not heard by you. Why? The mechanism of your ears did not change but the attention to the ears is broken from within. The attention is with the house that is on fire. The ears are hearing, but the bridge of attention that is necessary to bring the contents to the consciousness is missing. That bridge has been removed. It is in use where the house is on fire. So the ears are able to hear but not you. The connection, the bridge of attention between you and the ears, is broken.

Listening means both you and your ears are present, connected – then listening happens. It is a difficult matter. To create the connection with the ears is a matter of spiritual endeavor. Listening means that when you are hearing, your whole consciousness becomes the hearing; only the hearing remains, nothing else. No thoughts move within, because if there are thoughts moving within, your attention is diverted into thinking and removed from the ears.

Attention is a very delicate and subtle thing. Any slight thinking going on inside and the attention moves to it. You are listening to me and an ant is biting your leg – it is not necessary for your house to be on fire – then for a period of time you become aware of the ant bite and your listening is lost. Your hearing continues but attention is diverted.

Another problem with attention is that it cannot be on two things simultaneously, it is always on one subject at a time. When it moves onto another subject it is immediately removed from the first. It can go on jumping from one to the other – and that is what we do. The ant bit the leg, the attention jumped there; attention came back again and you listened. You felt the sensation of itching, your attention jumped to it; afterwards it came back to hearing again. So there are gaps in the listening when the attention moves elsewhere, and therefore not much clarity in meaning can be found from what you hear because much is lost. Many times the meaning derived by you is your own, because much has been lost; and what you conclude after filling in the gaps is entirely your own.

I have been looking through a book written by a female disciple of Ouspensky. She has written: "When I started working with Ouspensky on spiritual discipline, I was very troubled by one thing that he used to emphasize repeatedly, and I was unable to see the point because there appeared to be nothing in it worth emphasizing. I was also unable to understand why a man like Ouspensky put so much emphasis on such a small matter as this. The man is so wonderful that if he emphasizes something, there has to be some meaning behind it. But my intellect was unable to grasp the meaning. And he would repeat this fifty times a day.

"A disciple may be referring to something Ouspensky had said the day before, saying, 'Yesterday you said so and so,' and Ouspensky would immediately stop him and ask him not to say this; at the most he could say that this is what he had understood him to have said yesterday. 'Don't say that this is what has been said.' He would make this remark about every statement – never to say, 'You said so,' but say, 'I understood this from what you said.'"

This disciple has written, "We used to be very troubled. To have to say before every sentence, 'This is what I had understood; this is what I had understood from what you had said.' What is the need to do so? Why not simply say that you had said so, and the matter is over." Slowly she came to understand that these are two separate things.

Only those who have attained to the art of listening can understand what has been said. If you are only hearing, you will understand only what you can understand and not what has been said, because a lot will be lost in between. And that which is lost, you will fill the gaps for yourself – because empty space always gets filled up. You hear, but in between, when your attention moves away, who will fill up those empty spaces? You will do that. Your mind, your memory, your information, your knowledge, your experience will penetrate those gaps. And you will be the creator of the final shape, which is not what has been truly said. The one who said it originally is not responsible for it.

Listening means that the consciousness shifts to the very ears, with no thoughts, reasoning or arguing within. This does not mean that you accept everything that is said without understanding. But acceptance has no role in the process of listening. Listening means just listen; acceptance or nonacceptance are matters for later on – no need to be in a hurry.

What are we doing? We are hearing and at the same time we go on accepting or rejecting. Our heads continue to nod in agreement or shake in disagreement. One goes on saying, "Yes, it is perfectly true." Somebody else says, "No, it doesn't appeal to me." They themselves are not aware of this continuous nodding and the mental process, but I can watch it.

It means that as I say something, while hearing it you also go on making decisions about it internally. For the period of time you are making decisions the listening will be missed. You yourself are not aware that your head nodded, but inside you agreed with something, hence the nodding. When I say something which does not appeal to you, your head goes on shaking in denial, "No, it does not appeal to me." It is not your head moving, it is your attention inside moving. It is because of the moving attention that the head is also moving. In that little movement your listening is lost.

When it is said that you should not think while listening, it does not mean that you accept everything blindly. No, at this point there is no question of acceptance or rejection, at this point one has only to listen well as to what has been said. You have to listen exactly to what has been said; only after that will you be able to decide whether to accept or reject. To bring the process of acceptance or rejection in while hearing is to miss the listening. Hearing means only hearing.

Right now we are listening. Right now we will not go on thinking simultaneously. Mind cannot do two things at a time; either you listen or you think. Those who think are unable to listen, those who listen have no way of thinking at the same time. But there is no hurry either – thinking can be done later on. It is also just and proper that first one listens and then one thinks...because what will you think about? If you have not heard rightly, or if you have added something of your own onto what you heard, or if there are gaps in what you have heard, what will you think about? Whatever you will think, it has no value. If something is not heard rightly, thinking about it is futile. So the first step, the seers have said, is shravana, listening.

When somebody would come to Buddha or when somebody would come to Mahavira, they used to ask the person to first become a *shravaka*, a listener. To become a shravaka means to become a listener. Even now Jainas go on categorizing in the same manner: *sadhu-sadhvi* and *shravaka-shravika*. But there are neither really any shravakas nor any shravikas, because those terms imply

listening. A shravika is one who has attained to the art of listening.
But there are neither really any shravakas and shravikas – listeners –
nor is there now anyone worth listening to.

You go and look at the shravakas and shravikas in the temples.
Often you will find them asleep – listening is far away. Tired and
tattered from the day's work, they rest and sleep there. Even if they
do not sleep they for sure do not listen. They are busy in their own
mental uproar and thoughts.

Your mind should completely stop, its movement should stop;
only then does listening happen. Listening is the first step. And the
more significant the things discussed, the deeper the listening has
to be, only then can it be understood. So the sutra says:

> Thus, through statements like Tattvamasi,
> That art thou, to pursue the meanings such as
> oneness of jiva, the embodied soul,
> and Brahman, the absolute reality,
> is shravana, listening.

Tattvamasi is a supreme statement. There are only three or four
supreme statements of the truth in the world but none is loftier
than this. Tattvamasi means, That art thou, you are that. 'That',
tat, we were discussing yesterday as being the description of God.
This is the meaning of Tattvamasi, that 'that' is not anything out
and away from you, you are that. What we have called tat, 'that',
gives the impression of distance – 'that' is the indication of distance. Tattvamasi means, 'that' is you, 'that' is not far but very
near, nearer than near. Your very existence is 'that'. This is a
supreme statement. A supreme statement means that if one
explores it fully it will lead one to the ultimate state. This is why
they are called supreme statements. Then no other scriptures are
needed – no Vedas, no Koran and no Bible are needed – Tattvamasi
is enough.

If one does the right listening, contemplation, assimilation and
experiencing of this one statement, no other scriptures are required.

A supreme statement means a condensed statement which covers all – just like formulas in chemistry, or just like Einstein's formula of relativity, where the whole thing is covered in two or three words.

This supreme statement is a formula of spiritual chemistry. Three things are in it: Tat – that, tvam – thou, asi – you. They are the same, 'that' and 'thou' are one – this is the whole of this sutra. But the whole of Vedanta – the philosophy of the Vedas – the entire experience of the seers, is covered by those three words. It is like a mathematical formula: 'that', the existence, God, and 'thou', the hidden consciousness within you, are not two things, they are one. And this is the essence of all the Vedas, everything else is just an expansion of this.

So in the Upanishads such statements are described as supreme statements. From this one statement, the philosophy, spiritual discipline and experience of the whole of life can be derived.

Such statements should be heard in total silence. Such statements should not be heard as one may hear a song. The quality of hearing has to be very different, only then might these statements enter within you. These statements cannot be heard the way one hears things passing by on a road.

That is why for thousands of years the seers in India were insistent that the supreme knowledge should not be written down. Their insistence was valuable. But it was not possible to carry this out forever, it had to be written down. But the insistence in not writing down the supreme knowledge persisted for thousands of years. Many people, particularly the linguists, think that because there was no script, no means for writing things down, that is why the Vedas and Upanishads were not written down for so long. But their thinking is wrong...because it seems impossible that the people who could attain to an experience of the caliber of Tattvamasi, those who could make such supreme statements their living experience, were incapable of devising the art of writing.

That the people whose genius could touch such lofty peaks of experience were not able to devise such an ordinary thing as the art of writing does not feel right. The art of writing was there, but they were not willing to use it. Why? – because if such supreme statements were written down, anybody could have read them under any inappropriate conditions. And by reading them, the person could have formed the illusion of having understood them – because someone can also read these statements without having the certain kind of mental state which is necessary for reading or hearing them.

Where is the difficulty in reading 'That art thou'? Even a grade-one student can read it. And having read it, he will fall into the illusion of having understood it: "Okay, I am also that. This is what the sentence means, and that is that." Then he memorizes it, and he goes on repeating it for his whole life – and the whole thing is missed. The whole purpose of the statement is missed, the essential point is lost.

These statements deserve to be listened to only in a certain state of mind, with a certain quality of mind, in a certain milieu. Then only do they penetrate your being. There is danger in hearing it just anytime, anywhere. The dangers are two: one, that it will get memorized and one will feel one has known it. And the second danger is that due to this false sense of knowing, one will perhaps never make an effort to create that state of mind in which it should have been listened to.

There is a season, a special time, and a suitable, auspicious moment for sowing any seeds. And this is an extraordinary seed – it cannot be just thrown about anywhere. This is why the master used to whisper it in the disciple's ear. Try to understand this.

We have all heard that initiation mantras used to be whispered into the ear of the seeker. What we think is that the masters must have been whispering such mantras into the disciple's ears. That is nonsense. The master used to give these ultimate seeds to his disciple only when the disciple had become just the ears, when the disciple's whole being was ready to listen, when he was not listening only through the ears but with every fiber of his body, when his whole being was there gathered behind his ears, when his very soul, fully withdrawn from all other senses, was attuned behind the ears – then

the master would pass it on. He was saying this only: Tattvamasi –
'That art thou'. The words were the same, there was no change in
the words, but the disciple in front of him, the quality of his consciousness, the capability of his consciousness....

And what does it mean to initiate people by whispering a
mantra in the ear? Even now, so many fools go on whispering initiation mantras in the ears of so many other fools. They pass on
these mantras in one's ear without bothering even to know what
'the ears' means. It has nothing much to do with the ears which are
attached to your skull. What was meant by the ear was a way of
being, an openness in your being, a presence of a kind of peace, a
readiness to listen, an eager thirst, a longing where one's whole
being is ready to listen. Then the master used to simply pour such
supreme statements into the ear. And sometimes it happened that
the very penetration of such supreme utterances in the disciple
instantly became the ultimate explosion of realization.

There are many people who have attained self-realization only
by listening. The other three steps were not needed for them. You
will be surprised to know that the other three steps were not
needed, that only by listening have people become enlightened.

But the matter is not so easy. You might think, "If it is possible
to become enlightened just by listening, then why should I bother
to do anything else? Here we are, just utter it for us and we will
become enlightened!"

Only those can become enlightened by listening whose totality is
invested in listening, when not even a fraction of them is held back,
when the listener does not exist at all and only the act of listening
remains; when even that feeling does not remain that 'I am listening', even the feeling of 'I am' is no longer there; when one has
become only the listening.... When only the process of listening
has remained, when everything else within has become utterly
silent, a nothingness, in that nothingness, just this much impact –
Tattvamasi, 'That art thou' – causes the explosion of the being
...only this much impact!

But one more thing is to be kept in mind in this connection –

that the whole preparation on the part of the disciple or the seeker is that he should be a nothingness; but at the same time, just anyone coming and uttering Tattvamasi, 'That art thou', in his ear won't do. Anybody can utter that; even a human being is not required for it, a tape recorder can do the job of uttering it.

But no, this won't do. Words have power, but that power is dependent on the speaker, it is not in the words. It all depends on from what depth the words are emanating, and how much life energy is contained in the words, and how much juice of direct experience there is in them. And the speaker of those words should also have disappeared at the time of uttering them. The speaker simply should not be there, the echo should have arisen directly from the soul: Tattvamasi. And the listener also should not be there, the echo should have gone directly to the soul: Tattvamasi, 'That art thou'. At this point of meeting, even without doing much, enough would have been done…and a revolution takes place, an explosion happens, and the one who was ignorant suddenly becomes a knower.

There are such happenings in recorded history, when it has happened just by listening. We find it difficult to believe, because even with a lot of effort and doing it does not happen to us; we attempt in many ways, but still it feels that nothing is happening.

When the meeting of two such consciousnesses takes place – where the speaker is not but the words are revealed, and where the listener is not but the listening happens – the listening is sufficient to trigger the journey.

But such a coincidence is hard to find. Even if such a coincidence is found, it is difficult to utilize it. Such a coincidence is a subtle affair. So the disciple used to be near the master for many years awaiting such a coincidence, when the time for such an opportunity may present itself and when he may also be ready. So for many years the only spiritual discipline for the disciple used to be how to remain quiet and silent.

Svetketu went to live with a master. For years the master did not even ask him why he had come. Svetketu also felt that when the time was right the master would then ask, so he waited. The master did not ask him for years. The story is very beautiful: the master's *yagyagui,* the sacred oblational fire that used to burn around the clock, and the vessel that held the fire – even they became impatient.... The story is really beautiful: Svetketu had come and even the *havankunda* – the dug-out vessel for the sacred fire – started taking pity on Svetketu. So many years had passed since he came and the master had still not bothered to even inquire, "What brings you here?"

Svetketu would chop and bring wood, light the fire, milk the cows, massage the master's feet, and when night fell he would go to sleep near the feet of the master. Rising in the morning, he would get busy again with the chores of the day. Even that sacred fire which would be burning twenty-four hours a day began to feel pity: "What is going on here? Svetketu won't say from his side why he has come and Uddalaka, the master, won't ask why he has come."

Such a waiting, such a patience, such a quietness makes one automatically a listener. Slowly, slowly not only the words of the master but even the breathing of the master comes to be heard; even the heartbeat of the master comes to be heard in such an awaiting and in such a silence. It is not necessary that the master should speak, even his movements come to be heard. And when the right moment comes the master speaks. When the right moment comes the speaking happens; neither the master has to make an effort to speak, nor the disciple has to make any effort to know anything. At the right moment the event happens.

Listening is a very valuable step. You may remember these two or three things: one, be the listening itself while listening; forget the listener, be just the ears – extended all over your body – so that your whole body becomes ears listening from all directions. Another, let there be no thinking; just let the mind be fully absorbed in listening and let no thoughts move.

We are all afraid that if we do not think, perhaps someone may put some wrong things in our mind. Who knows, someone may shatter our beliefs. So we are constantly engaged in self-defense: I will let in only things that may be useful to me; if they are not useful to me, I will not let them in.

You will be surprised to know, psychologists say that if one hundred things are said to you, your mind hardly lets five of them in. The remaining ninety-five things it returns, does not let in. And why? Because your beliefs are based in the past, they are pre-determined. Somebody is a Mohammedan, somebody is a Hindu, somebody is a Jaina and somebody a Christian. It is all inside you, it is your mind accumulated from the past, sitting there within you. The whole time it is keeping watch: if there is something in tune with some of your ideas, strengthening them, then let it in. If it is not in favor of your ideas, if it is not strengthening them, then just don't allow it in; stop it on the outside, or hear it in a way as if you have not heard at all; or if you have heard it, oppose it immediately and vehemently so it cannot enter in.

Just pay a little attention to your mind and you will see that you go on saying yes or no inwardly all the time. Who is this saying yes or no within you? It is not you, it is your mind that you have accumulated from the past.

So the mind chooses what is favorable to it and rejects what is against it. It is a difficult task: this is the mind that is to be dropped and this is also the mind that chooses what is the favorable and opposes the unfavorable – so how is this dropping to be accomplished? This is the mind that is your enemy and your controller, and this is also the mind you have set out to drop – and if you set out to drop it with its own help, then you will never be able to drop it. Just the smallest apprehension, that this thing does not appeal to you in the light of your beliefs, and your mind immediately shuts its doors. It says, "Do not hear anymore," "Ignore that," or "Go on opposing from within."

We are constantly engaged in defending ourselves as if some battle is going on. In that case there will be no listening possible, rather, a conflict is triggered. But listening does not mean blind acceptance either. Listening has nothing to do with acceptance. Listening has to do with right hearing of what has been said.

The second step is manan, contemplation – after hearing what has been said, to contemplate over it. To contemplate over what has been said after hearing it in its authenticity is the first condition for contemplation. But if you choose what you like and contemplate over only that, it is not contemplation, it is only deception.

So the first condition for contemplation is that you hear without saying yes or no – no condemnation, no praise, no acceptance, no rejection, no nothing; no evaluation, no judgment – neither in favor nor against. You only hear silently and naturally what has been said, and let it sink into the deepest corner of your heart so that there may be an acquaintance with it, because contemplation can happen only about that with which one is acquainted.

This is the difference between thinking and contemplation. Thinking is done about something with which we are not properly acquainted. Thinking is an intellectual activity with the new – mental gymnastics. Contemplation is a reflection on something that has been absorbed, that has been taken deep within oneself. There is a great difference between the two. Thinking contains conflict within itself, contemplation contains sympathy. In thinking there is confrontation, in contemplation there is reflection. And these are big differences. Thinking means you are fighting with something. If you are unable to win then you will agree with it, but there will be pain in that agreeing.

When you debate a point with somebody and you are unable to logically argue your point of view and you have to concede, have you watched the pain you feel inside? You concede because you cannot argue any further...but inside? Inside you have a feeling that if not today, then tomorrow, eventually you will turn the tables against that person and be able to reject their point.

Thus it is not possible to transform anybody in this world through argument, because argument implies defeat. Even if you are able to prove something to that person through argument he will feel defeated – not transformed, but defeated. He will experience defeat: "Okay, I am not able to reply properly or to search for the right argument today, but the day I have the right arguments I will come and see you." He feels defeated.

And remember, a defeated person is not a transformed person. You can make somebody silent through argument but you cannot transform him that way. And it is right also that no one should become transformed through argument, because when two persons debate something it does not necessarily mean that the one who lost the debate was wrong or the one who won was right. All it means is that the one who won can argue better and the one who lost the debate cannot argue so well – nothing more than this is proved.

So it is natural that nobody is ever transformed and no revolution happens in one's life by argument. Loss of an argument only hurts one's ego, and that injured ego wants to take revenge. Argument is a struggle.

In thinking there is an inner struggle. Whatever you are thinking about, you are fighting with it; an inner struggle is going on. You line up all your past memories and all the past thoughts that go against it. If you are still defeated you accept, but in that acceptance a pain, a bite, a piercing thorn is experienced. This acceptance is out of your helplessness. There is no joy happening in this acceptance; your inner flower does not blossom due to this acceptance, but withers. So because of all the thinking the thinkers are doing all over the world, you will not see the joyousness of a buddha on their faces.

Why, what is the difference?

You will not find the pleasant personality of a Mahavira in the thinkers. On the faces of thinkers you will see the wrinkles of anxiety, not the flowers of contemplation. On the forehead of a thinker the wrinkles will go on increasing with time. Every single line of the forehead will be profoundly pronounced – after all he has worked hard his whole life. But that which happens to a Buddha or a Mahavira, that flowering will not be seen. Thought is burdensome, you are bent over with it. A thinker looks anxious. There is no qualitative difference between thinking and worrying. All thinking is a form of worrying. A restlessness is hidden behind it, a tension, because there is an inner struggle, a conflict, a battle. So a thinker, by the time he grows old, is bent over by the weight, by the sheer weight of his thoughts.

A contrary phenomenon happens with Buddha and Mahavira. As they go on growing older, something within them goes on becoming younger; their look of freshness increases.

This is the difference between thinking and contemplation.

Thinking begins with logic, contemplation begins with listening. Thinking begins with struggle, contemplation begins with listening. Listening is receptivity, where there is no struggle. This is the difference between thinking and contemplation. Thinking begins with conflict because its base is in logic. There is no sympathy there; opposition, enmity, argumentation are its basis. The very fact that contemplation begins with listening shows sympathy is the basis there.

What is meant by sympathy? – sympathetic consideration. Whatsoever we are thinking, or in whichever connection we are thinking, we do so with great love and sympathy.

What is the qualitative difference between thinking and contemplation? When you are considering something with sympathy, your whole inner desire is to feel that, "Whatsoever I have heard may be right. And if it is right, can it be beneficial to me?" So you first try to search for those points which are right. When you think, you begin from a belief that whatsoever you have heard is wrong, so you first try to search for those points which are wrong.

Understand it this way. A person is standing near a bed of roses: if he is thinking he will first count the thorns; if he is contemplating he will first count the roseflowers. This makes a fundamental difference – from where you begin. The one who first counts the thorns, his opposing attitude is evident. He will first count the thorns, and thousands of them will be found. And in counting the thorns, a number of thorns will pierce his hands, blood will flow out. That piercing by thorns, the number of thorns and the bleeding of his hand, will all become the basis for opposition to the roseflowers. And when he has counted thousands of thorns and maybe one or two flowers are seen, his mind will say, "These flowers are only a deception, they cannot be real, because where there are so many thorns, how can the flowers there be so delicate? This is an illusion."

It is natural, it will feel right. Where there are so many thorns, thorns capable of causing bleeding, how can these delicate flowers blossom there? It is impossible. And even if he agrees that the flowers are there, he will say, "They are of no value; amid thousands of thorns, what is the value of a flower or two? It rather appears as a conspiracy of the thorns, so that thousands of thorns can remain in the world with the pretext of just one flower. This is a deception. This flower is a mask for the thorns. This flower is a participant in their conspiracy."

A person who begins contemplation with flowers will first touch the flowers. His hands will be full of the fragrance of flowers, his eyes will be filled with the colors of the flowers. The delicacy of the flowers will be available to his touch, the beauty of the flowers will encompass him from all sides. Then he will approach the thorns – after having seen the flowers, after having known and lived with the flowers, he has fallen in love. Now when he approaches the thorns they will have a completely different quality.

A person who approaches the thorns after understanding the flowers will understand that the thorns are for the protection of the flowers – they are not enemies of the flowers, they are not against the flowers. The same juice that is flowing in the flowers is also flowing in the thorns. And the thorns are for the protection of the flowers. One who is seeing the flowers, one who has been able to see even one flower rightly...thousands of thorns will lose all consequence for him, because the presence of even one flower is enough to render thousands of thorns inconsequential. And if a flower can blossom amidst so many thorns it is an impossible miracle; then the impossible can also happen. And if a flower can blossom amidst so many thorns, that person would see the point that if he sought deeper, perhaps these thorns might also prove to be nothing but flowers.

Contemplation begins with sympathy, thinking begins with opposition. If the condition of listening is fulfilled sympathy is aroused. If sympathy is aroused, the very stream of thinking takes a one-hundred-and-eighty-degree turn and becomes contemplation.

Contemplation does not mean blind acceptance.

So the seer has said: ...*to reasonably pursue the meaning of whatever has been listened to, is manan, contemplation.*

Nobody needs to think that contemplation means accepting blindly. Neither listening means accepting nor does contemplation mean accepting; reason has to be used.

But the use of reason also changes. Reason in itself is neutral. For example, there is a sword in my hand.... Now, the sword is neutral: if I want I can take somebody's life or I can save somebody's life – the sword is neutral. Reason is neutral, but there are different patterns, and the effect of reason can change. If the mind is full of enmity, opposition and confrontation, reason becomes violent. If the mind is full of sympathy, listening, love, search and longing for the truth, reason becomes a protecting sword. Reason in itself is not bad.

So in this country we have accepted two types of reasoning: one, positive reasoning; another, negative reasoning. Negative reasoning is also reasoning. Sometimes negative reasoning appears even more logical than positive reasoning, because negative reasoning has an edge, a sharp edge, that is capable of cutting through and killing.

So negative reasoning sometimes appears to be deeply logical. How would you distinguish what is positive reasoning and what is negative reasoning? This is the difference: that if reasoning is in the search of the good and the truth – is full of sympathy, begins from the flowers and then moves to the thorns....

When I say something to you, just watch from where you are beginning. I am amazed so many times: I speak for an hour, then afterwards somebody comes to me and whatever I have said in this hour has not reached him, he is caught up in the fight against just one single thing. He picks up just one point and comes to oppose it. Whatever else has been said in this one hour he does not remember, just this one tiny matter. And that too he takes out of its context. It had meaning in its context; torn out of its context it takes on an entirely different meaning. But he heard only that. He must have been ready for only that. He must have come prepared to find out something wrong somehow.

If you are here hearing me only to find something wrong you will never be able to move into contemplation.

Remember, howsoever many wrongs you may discover, that will never become a help to your inner growth. No matter how clearly you may establish the location of all the faults – you may come to know of all the faults in the whole world – still no inner growth can happen to you through it.

One who is seeking and is interested in his growth does not bother to find out what is wrong, he bothers to find out what is right. He begins with the right. And he who begins with the right may someday arrive at a point from where he realizes that what was appearing to be wrong also has some meaning, also has some value. Thus what appeared wrong earlier may appear right afterwards. The difference is only of the emphasis.

The negative reasoning seeks the wrong, it begins the journey from there. The positive reasoning begins with the right.

You give the Koran to someone to read; if he is a Hindu he will not see any of that which is significant in the Koran, all that will go unnoticed by him. He will underline all that is not right according to him, and bring it to you saying, "See! I always said that the Koran is not a religious scripture!" Or give the Gita to a Mohammedan and he will pinpoint exactly what is wrong in it. And if you want to learn this art, learn it from the Hindu fundamentalist group, the *Arya Samajis*. They are experts in finding out what is wrong and where. No others are such experts. Save the mind from becoming an Arya Samaji; only then can contemplation become possible. Otherwise contemplation cannot be possible because you are on the lookout for what is wrong, and the wrong will be found in plenty. After all, where is the scarcity of thorns? But what purpose is served by the thorns? Are you going to prepare garlands of thorns, and wear them around your neck?

The purpose, the concern is with flowers, not with the thorns.

So if there is positive reasoning, flowers will be picked from the Koran also – and these flowers are in no way inferior to those of the Gita. If there is positive reasoning, flowers will be picked from the Gita also – and these flowers are in no way inferior to those of the Koran or the Bible.

A contemplating person is in search of flowers, a thinking person is in search of thorns. You have to decide yourself. But remember one thing, that you will become surrounded by that for which you are searching. If you search for thorns you will be surrounded by thorns, if you search for flowers you will be surrounded by flowers.

So remember, that by searching for thorns you are not harming anyone but yourself, because you will get what you search for. Life becomes hell because you are surrounded by all the wrong people; no one seems to be a right person. And not because there are no right people but because your search is for the wrong people.

You tell somebody that a certain person is a very good flute player. He says, "What flute could he play? He is a thief, a charlatan. How could he play the flute?"

Now what contradiction exists between a thief or a dishonest person and flute-playing? He may be dishonest, but who says that a dishonest person does not or cannot play the flute? Who is making this connection? In a thief a flower of flute-playing can also bloom. Theft will be a thorn, the flute-playing will be the flower. When flowers can bloom amidst thorns, why cannot a thief play the flute?

But no, it hurts to accept that someone can do anything good. We would immediately condemn him: "He is a thief, a dishonest man – how could he play the flute?"

The attitude of a person who contemplates will be different. If you say to him that such and such a person is a dishonest man and a thief, he will say, "Maybe, but he is a wonderful flute-player."

This is a difference of choice. And when a person plays a flute so wonderfully well, even his being a thief or a dishonest person begins to become doubtful. When a person is such an amazing thief and a dishonest person, his ability at flute-playing begins becoming doubtful. Whatever we adhere to, it affects the other thing too.

What is the need to determine whether a person is dishonest or a thief? If we want our neighbor to be a thief and a dishonest person, then we will find him to be so. Or if we want our neighbor to be a good flute-player, we should look out for that. In life both things are there. Night is there, day is also there; and the good is there, the bad is also there.

Do not think that heaven is somewhere apart from this earth or that hell is somewhere away from this earth; it is in your eyes. On this very earth people live in heaven, and on this very earth people live in hell. What you seek becomes your world.

Contemplation begins the journey with flowers – with sympathy. It does not hurriedly attack the wrong, first it assimilates the right. And when the right is fully assimilated, only then does it reflect upon what had appeared wrong in the first observation.

And remember, the real differences of this transformation in attitude only begin to be seen later on. A contemplating person slowly grows, sprouts; assimilating the right, he himself becomes right. And the one constantly searching for the wrong, constantly assimilating the wrong, becomes wrong himself. One who sees only dishonesty, theft and wrong in others cannot remain honest for long. The truth is that such a person cannot be honest in the first place.

Actually a thief cannot believe others to be non-thieves – or can he? No, he can never believe others not to be thieves. The very pattern of a thief's thinking becomes that of theft. He immediately searches for and sees the qualities of theft in others too. A debauched person cannot believe that there is any person of character. He just cannot accept it. His very experience becomes a hindrance in believing that.

This is a very interesting thing: no debauched person can believe that someone is a celibate. He simply cannot believe it! This is alright, because if somebody is really celibate, he too cannot believe that somebody else can be debauched. But what is interesting is that not only a debauched person never believes that

anybody is a celibate, but a celibate also does not believe that anybody is a celibate.

Then it is a very problematic issue. A debauched person not
believing that anybody can be celibate is logical, because "When I
have not been able to be one, how can anybody else be?" But
when a celibate also is not ready to believe that another person can
be celibate, his situation becomes dubious; then he too is not a celibate. His own inner experience is that all talk about celibacy,
etcetera is just superficial, there is debauchery within. He, therefore, does not believe.

If you come across any saint who takes others to be non-saints,
you can be sure that he himself has not yet been able to become a
saint. The very meaning of becoming a saint is that, for him, the
whole world would have become saints at once. For him the whole
thing has changed, because his angle of vision has changed. When
one becomes a saint inside, everywhere in the world he sees saintliness, goodness, because what is within is what is seen without.

If you are seeing bad in everybody, if in everybody you see theft,
dishonesty and evil, then leave them aside and worry about yourself at once. What is seen outside is within you. That is what you
are able to see. That is what is seen at once, because that falls in
tune with the inner at once.

Contemplation begins with the bright side of life. Thinking
begins with the dark side of life. If you can remember this, reasoning is then a wonderful thing; thoughts and logic are then very
helpful. Reasoning can then be used wholeheartedly. And reasoning
is then not harmful, it becomes helpful, friendly.

Establishing your mind in the indubitable
meaning attained through this listening and
contemplation, attunement to it is
nididhyasan, assimilation.

You listened to the supreme statement 'That art thou' – you
are the Brahman – you listened to it wholeheartedly. Then with

sympathy you thought it over, reflected upon it, searched for the true meaning of the statement, its many, many conclusions. You groped for its inherent depths from many, many angles, touched them, tasted them, drowned yourself in them, contemplated, and then found that it is true.

It will certainly be found to be true because those who said it have said it after having attained it. These are not conclusions arrived at by thinkers, these are the words of those who have experienced. This is not a statement of those who thought and thought and then decided it to be so, these are intimations from those who knew it, drowned in it and found out.

They are bound to find out. If listening and contemplation run well, they will definitely find it to be right. If it is right, then to become attuned to it is nididhyasan, assimilation. If it is right that "I am Brahman," then to begin to live like Brahman is nididhyasan, the assimilation. In your doings, in your behavior, become attuned from all sides; then make efforts so that there remains no separation between you and what is right, because if the statement is right, then "I am mistaken."

There are only two possibilities: either you are right, then this statement is wrong; or if the statement is right, then you are wrong. And what is our usual assumption? Try to understand this a little. Our assumption is always that "I am right." This is our problem. The biggest trouble, worry and anguish of our lives is that we move with the belief that "I am right." This is our beginning point in everything, that "I am right." We test everything on this basis. This is our touchstone, that "I am right." Now whatsoever does not fit with you is wrong.

This matter must be decided, a seeker must decide, that this foolish thought "I am right" does not become the initial step. If you are right, no search is necessary.

This is very interesting. One woman came to me yesterday: she told me that some twenty years ago she had been initiated by some swami, that her kundalini had also awakened but there is no peace at all, she is very restless.

If the kundalini has awakened, how is this restlessness there? And if restlessness is there, please accept that the kundalini is asleep and not awakened.

But no, people make simultaneous claims from both sides. If you are right, if you think you know, then there is nothing left to seek, the matter is over. Every person moves with the presumption of "I am right," and then says, "I want to seek the truth." If one is to seek the truth, the decision must be clear before the consciousness that "I don't know." Only then is the search possible. When I don't know, my entry into some truth is possible; if I know from the very beginning, the truth itself will appear to be wrong, because when a person who does not know believes that he knows, he can never see the truth as it is.

The very working of the mind is to move with the assumption that "I am right" – my idea, my viewpoint, my religion, my scripture. If you have to begin from "I am right," there is no need to begin at all; you have already arrived at the goal, you are unnecessarily taking the trouble now. And where would you find the goal? You are already standing on the goal. You *are* the goal.

This must be made clear: if that madness of "I know" has taken possession of one the matter is over, no search should be undertaken. The very meaning of search is "I don't know." There is suffering, anguish, pain and tension: "I am in trouble, in disease, and am surrounded all around by my diseases; I am nothing but a combination of all these diseases." Moving with such a belief is the search.

And this is the reality also. You are nothing more than a combination of diseases – a bundle containing all sorts of diseases. And every man is an inventor, he invents his own diseases. And even amidst all these diseases, he persists in the feeling that "I am right."

Assimilation means: one saw that this supreme statement was right. One listened, reflected upon it and saw that it was right. The mind has seen the fact of its being right, the consciousness has begun to realize the fact of its being right; now to mold yourself in accordance to that is assimilation – to start living that which has appeared right.

And remember, once something is seen to be right, then there is no difficulty in living it. The moment it is seen the living begins. Who knowingly puts his hand into fire? Only in ignorance are hands put into fire. Who knowingly does evil? Only in ignorance is evil done. Who knowingly invites insanity? Only in ignorance is insanity invited. Once what is right begins to be seen, the very glimpse will begin to transform you from within. All your vibrations will slowly begin to harmonize with what you have seen.

This attunement, this harmony is called assimilation.

Even after this, if the attunement does not happen or it seems to be difficult, the seeker now knows that the difficulty is on his part. So he melts himself further. If the journey seems to be complex, he knows that it is his complexity. So he tries to untangle himself.

But if the person who proceeds with the notion of being right takes two steps and sees no fruits coming, he thinks that the notion of 'Thou art that' itself is wrong...so leave it.

People come to me...yesterday one friend came: he did meditation for the first time yesterday, and yesterday he said to me that nothing has happened. Is there a limit to the foolishness of man? In this world foolishness and Brahman are the only two things that seem to be limitless; there seems no limit to them. He had arrived only yesterday, for the first time. In the morning he must have jumped up and down a little, and in the afternoon he approached me saying that nothing has happened so far. He said, "There seems to be no substance in this method. Nothing has happened to me up to now."

I asked him how many lives he had been doing this method.

He said, "I have just arrived today. There is no question of life-times."

Give the method at least a little opportunity to work. Have some mercy on the method, give it some opportunity.

Man is on the move always assuming himself to be right. So wherever any difficulty appears, the other must be wrong. He keeps his rightness intact and proceeds on the journey. You will have to wander then for birth after birth; nothing will ever fall together, because attunement is a great effort. It will not happen just like that, because the conditionings of lives upon lives are in the background; you will have to break them. Even if you came to see today – suddenly, clearly, in a split second – what is right, still your feet are in the habit of walking; your body has habits, your mind has habits, there is a long network of habits. That network would not be broken suddenly today. One will have to work hard to break that network.

It is not a question of the methods, the question is about you. Any method can work, but you.... Take note of it. Our whole life is a habit. From small things to big things, everything is a habit. There is a long line of these habits, and our consciousness is habituated to flow sticking to and following the same groove. Even if it is seen suddenly, today, that the old path is wrong, a new path has to be created in order to follow it. And remember, you will have to create a deeper groove than the older one for the stream to take this new route, to alter from the other one. But just by your thinking that a certain thing is right, nothing is going to be solved.

Assimilation means that whatsoever is listened to and understood to be right, one's life has to be transformed accordingly. It will take time to be in accord with it. The mind will create hindrances, the body will create obstructions – all this will happen. But once the right way has been seen then the courage to throw yourself completely, in every respect, into this journey is also necessary. Then sitting back will not do.

If the guiding star has been seen – however far away it may be – if the star has been seen, then plunge forward on the journey. And do not begin to think that now you have taken one step and you have not yet reached the star, that you have taken two steps and you have not yet reached the star. Do not be concerned. Even with these two steps you have come closer; these two steps you have taken are not a small matter. There are many who have been simply sitting down for lifetimes; they have not yet even stood up, they have simply forgotten that one has to even stand up, that one has to even walk.

Buddha has said, just walk. There is no concern about the number of mistakes you may make; that you walked is sufficient. You walked, you made mistakes, we will correct them. You went astray – don't worry, at least your feet made some movement. Today you wandered off the path, tomorrow you will come back towards the right way. There is only one mistake, said Buddha, and that is that you do not walk at all and just go on sitting – although one who remains sitting will never make any mistakes. How can one make a mistake by just sitting idle? In this world mistakes are made by those who move, who do something. How can those who do not do anything and who are just sitting make any mistake? They are absolutely mistake-free. But the only real mistake in this world is to remain sitting.

Get up and proceed on the journey of what feels to be right. Even if it proves to be wrong tomorrow, at least there will be one benefit, that you would have learned to walk. And once you have learned to walk, tomorrow the right direction can also be found. The direction is not the real thing, the real thing is move-ability, the capacity to walk.

Nididhyasan, assimilation, is an effort to become attuned. It is a wonderful word.

> Establishing your mind in the indubitable
> meaning attained through this listening and
> contemplation, attunement with it is
> nididhyasan, assimilation.

Now our mind should become attuned with whatsoever has been understood through the listening. It should not remain only as a glimpse, it should become our total mind. It should not remain just one thought among many, it should become our very mind.

For example, a man takes sannyas. Now sannyas can be taken when it is an intellectual decision, an idea; it seems right, it makes sense – so one takes sannyas. But it is still only a thought in the mind, just as there are a thousand others, so no attunement will be born yet. Slowly, slowly the color of what has entered one as a single thought will spread over all the thoughts.

What is meant by spreading over all the thoughts is that even while eating your meals...there should appear a marked difference between a sannyasin eating his meal and a worldly person eating his meal. That tinge of sannyas should even spread over the act of taking meals. A sannyasin should take meals in such a way as if he is not taking meals, a sannyasin should walk in such a way as if he is not walking, a sannyasin should get up in such a way as if he is not getting up; he should drop all doing.

One form of sannyas is that which is taken by way of a thought, and another is when one's entire life becomes attuned with it; then the very mind becomes a sannyasin.

So Buddha said, even when a sannyasin sleeps...one should be able to distinguish between a sleeping sannyasin and a sleeping worldly man. The very quality, the very manner of a sannyasin's sleep should change, because whosoever's mind has completely mutated, its shadow, its tinge, its vibrations should spread over all his actions. It is bound to spread.

Thus assimilation occurs not as a thought but as attunement. And...

> Dropping the meditator and the meditation
> respectively, when the meditated-upon,
> the goal, remains as the only objective and
> the mind becomes still like the flame of a lamp
> in a windless place –
> this is called samadhi, enlightenment.

Samadhi is the ultimate happening. The first three are the steps towards it, the fourth step is samadhi itself. Beyond that the world of words does not exist. Beyond that there is no world of speech. Only up to samadhi can anything be said. That which is beyond it, nothing has ever been said about it and nothing will ever be said about it.

Whosoever stands at the door of samadhi comes to see that which is invisible, comes to know that which is unknowable, meets that without which life was all misery, all pain and all anguish. That which is unknowable becomes known, and that which is a mystery is revealed and disclosed. All complexes shatter, the consciousness becomes one with the truth in its open sky.

Samadhi is something that comes after assimilation to one who has attuned his mind with the supreme statements like Tattvamasi, 'That art thou', *Aham Brahmasmi,* 'I am Brahman', *Soham,* 'I am that'. One whose mind and behavior have become expressions of these statements, one in whose movements there is the melody of 'That art thou', one in whose movements there is the gesture and the indication that he is moving in tune with Brahman – such a person is able to attain to samadhi.

When the meditator and meditation both are lost, only the meditated-upon, the goal, remains – this is samadhi.

Let us understand this. There are three words: meditator, meditation and the meditated-upon – the goal. For example, 'That art thou' is the goal, the meditated-upon. We are trying to grasp this supreme statement; this is the goal. This is worth achieving, only this is worth achieving. This is the goal, this is the final destination. Then 'I', the meditator, is the one who is thinking of this aim, is the one who is contemplating this aim, who is longing for this aim, who is thirsty for this aim; who is eager to attain this goal…. This is I, the meditator – the consciousness moving towards the goal. And when the meditator runs towards this goal, when all other running ceases and only this running of the consciousness towards this goal remains, this is called meditation.

When all streams of consciousness begin flowing towards the goal united and do not flow separately in dozens of streams any longer, when they are integrated into one, when the consciousness becomes a single stream and begins flowing towards the goal, constantly – flying straight like an arrow – this flowing consciousness is called meditation.

Samadhi – the Upanishad says that when the meditation drowns in the goal leaving not even a trace of life-energy behind, when the meditator's total energy and total consciousness becomes one with the goal, the moment comes when the meditator is not even aware that 'I am'. A moment comes when the meditator is not even aware that meditation is, that only Tattvamasi, only the goal, remains. That state is called samadhi, when not the three – the meditator, the meditation and the meditated-upon – when not the three but only the one remains.

Let this be understood a little more, because different spiritual disciplines have selected differently as to which of the three should remain in the end.

The Upanishads say that the meditated-upon, the goal, should remain; the meditator and the meditation should be lost. Mahavira says that the meditator should remain, the meditation and the meditated-upon should be lost; only the soul, the pure 'I' should remain. It all sounds contradictory. *Sankhya*, the path of nonduality, says both the meditator and the meditated-upon should be lost; only the meditation should remain, only the consciousness should remain – just the awareness.

It seems these are all very contradictory statements, but they are not contradictory at all. Scholars have always been having great debates, ludicrous debates. They have been debating hotly, and these debates are bound to arise. Those who understand only words will debate that these three are contradictory statements.

The Upanishads say that only the meditated-upon should remain, somebody else says the meditator should remain, and still another says the meditation should remain. What really is samadhi then? Is samadhi of three kinds? Moreover, if samadhi is when only the goal, the meditated-upon remains, then how can that be samadhi when only the meditator remains? So it will have to be decided as to which one is the right samadhi. Two of them will be wrong, only one can be right.

A scholar lives in words, not in experiences. The experience has a totally different taste to it: all these three are one and the same. Why? There is a very interesting thing about these three, that when any two out of the three disappear and only one remains, then a name for this remaining one is such a superficial matter that what name you give it is up to you.

Right now there are these three – the meditator, the meditation and the meditated-upon. For a seeker, for a seeker up to the state of assimilation, there are these three. When the three have disappeared and only one remains, then he selects for it any one name out of the three. This selection is altogether personal, it does not make any difference what name you give it. If you want you may select even a fourth name for it. Many Upanishads have in fact given it the name 'the fourth'; so all the three are lost, there remains no point of dispute. ...Because if any one of these three is selected, if two are dropped in favor of one, that may look like a bias, so they called it *turiya*, the fourth. They have not given it any name, just called it 'the fourth', so that no dispute arises.

But those looking for a dispute have no problem; they say that there were only these three, so from where has the fourth come? Which is this fourth? Which one of the three is this fourth? Or have all those three vanished and is this fourth something completely different from them? or it is a combination of the three? What is this fourth? It makes no difference – those who want to argue, they pick on anything to start an argument. But the one who is interested in real seeking, his journey is entirely different.

Out of these three, the Upanishads chose the meditated-upon as the one that remains; Mahavira chose the meditator as the one that survives; Sankhya, the path of nonduality, said it is the meditation that remains. But all these are just names. One thing is certain, that only one of the three remains. Names are all artificial, you may give it any name. Just remember one thing, that when only one remains there is samadhi, enlightenment. As long as there remain two, know well that all the three are there, because as long as the two remain, the third, adjoining them in the middle, is a must. Two alone cannot remain, two always means three.

So those who always think in mathematical terms do not call the world *dwaita*, dual, they call it *traita*, the triple, because when there are two the third is bound to be there, otherwise who will join or separate the two? The third becomes inevitable when there are two. Three is the way of existence.

This is why we have made *trimurti,* the three-faced statue representing Brahman, Vishnu and Mahesh: it is indicative of traita, that the world is made up of three. But the three faces are of the same person which is 'the fourth'. You enter through any of these three faces and when you reach within, the three faces no longer remain. But the seeker will admire the face through which he entered. Some seeker may enter through Brahman, some through Vishnu and some through Mahesh; each will name the experience after the face through which he entered, so he will say the fourth to be Vishnu or Mahesh or Brahman. But after reaching inside, all the three faces are lost. There is no space within, there everything is one.

This trimurti is not just a statue, it is the conclusion of our ultimate endeavors in seeking. The three are just before the final jump; they remain there – the meditator, the meditation and the meditated-upon. And whichever out of these three makes the jump, that one remains. Whatsoever name you want to give it, it is up to you; the name makes no difference whatsoever. If you do not want to name it, it is up to you. If you want to call it 'the fourth', beautiful. If you do not want to call it anything and you remain silent, that is the best.

Hear: turn hearing into listening.

Think: turn thinking into contemplation.

Contemplate: derive conclusions and let the conclusions become assimilation, to allow attunement.

And let attunement not remain mere attunement, let it ultimately become oneness.

Understand the difference. Attunement means the two still remain; though a harmony, an attunement has happened between the two, but still the two remain. Oneness means the two are lost and only the harmony has remained.

Attunement is assimilation; oneness is samadhi, the awakening.

Enough for today.

THE
SOUL'S THIRST

*During samadhi, the objects of the experiences
are not separate from the soul, hence they are not
experienced. But these glorified experiences
of the seeker who has come out of samadhi are
inferred through recollections of the mind.*

✳

*In this beginningless world, millions and millions
of karmas, action-impressions, are accumulated.
They are all destroyed by this samadhi
and pure dharma, self-nature, grows.*

✳

*The knowers of yoga call it Dharmamegha –
the raincloud of dharma – samadhi, because
it showers a thousand nectar-streams of dharma,
self-nature, like a raincloud.
In this samadhi, the network of desires dissolves
completely and the thickets of accumulated
karmas called virtue and sin are all uprooted
at their very source.
At first, this boundless statement – Tattvamasi,
That art thou – being true, is only realized
indirectly; then the direct knowledge, like a
myrobalan fruit kept on one's own palm, is born.*

his morning we talked about listening, contemplation, assimilation and *samadhi*. Samadhi, enlightenment, is the end of the world in you and the beginning of the truth. Samadhi is the death of the mind and the birth of the soul. Looked at from this end samadhi is the last step, looked at from the other end samadhi is the first step.

The mind goes on becoming reduced and dissolved more and more through listening, contemplation and assimilation; in samadhi, it is fully dissolved. And when the mind is fully dissolved, there begins the experience of what we really are. This sutra is about this samadhi. And in this sutra are some very deep things to be understood.

> *During samadhi, the objects of the experiences*
> *are not separate from the soul, hence they are not*
> *experienced. But these glorified experiences*
> *of the seeker who has come out of samadhi are*
> *inferred through recollections of the mind.*

Let this first thing be understood with your full attention. If not today, then tomorrow it will be useful to those who are meditating. There is no experience in samadhi – you will be troubled to hear this – there cannot be any experience in samadhi, and yet samadhi is the supreme experience. This is a paradoxical statement; it looks contradictory, but there are some reasons for it. In samadhi supreme bliss is experienced, but the seeker who is in samadhi does not come to know of it because the seeker and the bliss have become one, and there is no distance between the two for any knowing to take place.

We come to know only those things which are separate from us, at some distance from us. The realization, the experience of bliss in samadhi is not felt during samadhi. When the seeker comes out of the state of samadhi he infers that bliss had happened; it is a hindsight that ultimate bliss had happened, that the nectar had showered. That one had lived in a different dimension, that one had experienced some deeper state of life – all this is remembered afterwards when the mind is back.

Let us understand it this way. Listening, contemplation, assimilation and samadhi – these are the four steps. It is through these steps that the seeker reaches to the door of samadhi and realizes. If the seeker is not able to come out of samadhi and remains in it, he will never be able to relate his experience to anyone. Then there simply is no way of relating one's experience.

But any seeker who reaches the state of samadhi never returns the same person; he returns a completely new person. On the return all relationships are changed in his mind; however, he does return into the mind. Previously, when he used to live in the mind, he was a slave of the mind, he had no mastery over anything; the mind was able to get him to do anything it wanted. He had to agree to whatsoever mind was dictating, he had to run wherever the mind was making him run. It was a slavery by the mind; mind had the reins of the soul in its hands.

When a seeker returns from the doors of samadhi into the mind he returns as the master. Now the reins are in his own hands. Now he moves the mind where he wants to move it. If he does not want to move it anywhere, he does not move it. If he wants it to function, he makes it function, otherwise not. Now mind has no power of its own. But the seeker who has attained to samadhi can remember things only after he returns to the mind – of course, as its master this time. Because memory is a faculty of mind, that is why he can look back through mind to see what had happened.

This means that mind registers not only the events of the worldly life, but also registers what is happening when the seeker enters samadhi. Mind is a two-sided mirror. In it the outside world is reflected, in it the inside world is reflected. So it is only when the seeker returns to the mind that he is able to experience what happened. If he returns through the same three steps, then only can he express it.

While returning from samadhi, the first step of the seeker will be assimilation. It is at the step of assimilation that he will start experiencing what he has known in samadhi in a subtle form, at a deep level, at his own ultimate center. He will start seeing it reflected in his own behavior. When he lifts his foot, it will not feel as if it is the same old foot; the foot will have a sort of dance to it. When he raises his eyes and sees, the eyes will not feel as if they are the same old eyes, but fresh and clear like the morning dewdrop. When getting up he will feel as if weightless, as if he can fly in the sky. When he takes his meals he will see that the food is going into his body and he himself has never taken meals.

Now whatsoever the seeker just returned from samadhi does on that first step of assimilation, there will be the reflection of samadhi in his behavior; everywhere his behavior will have a new grace. That man of yesterday is dead. He is not the same person who was there before samadhi, standing within the boundary of assimilation. The step is the same, but this person climbing down is different. He has returned having known something, and he has returned knowing such a thing that his entire life is transformed. And in this knowing the old has died and the new is born.

At the step of assimilation he will see that which has happened in samadhi reflected. The juice that has flowed within him will be seen flowing in every direction in his behavior, from his every cell.

Mahakashyapa used every now and then to come to ask Buddha when samadhi would happen. Buddha would tell him not to worry, and that he would not need to come and ask him when it happened. When it happens you will recognize it, and not only will you recognize it, whosoever sees you will recognize it if they have even a little bit of ability to see, because when that revolution happens within its rays shine out, piercing their way through the person's body, being and everything.

On the step of assimilation the seeker will know that he is a different person, that he is new, that he is born again. He will know that he is not the same person who had gone into samadhi. Someone had gone in, somebody else has come out.

The next step below assimilation is contemplation. When the seeker comes into the mind further down from assimilation, the moment of contemplation will arise. Now the seeker will be able to think, look back and contemplate as to what really happened: "What did I see? What is it that I came to know? What did I live?" Now he will try to put his experience into thoughts, words and concepts.

It is those who have been able to put their experience into words at the step of contemplation who have given birth to the Vedas, the Upanishads, the Bible and the Koran. Many have reached the state of samadhi, but it is a difficult task to bring back to the step of contemplation what has been known.

Remember, the earlier journey towards samadhi is not as difficult as we think it is. If we compare it with the return journey it is very easy. This return journey is very difficult. Thousands attain samadhi, but only very few of them are able to come back and take a footing at the step of assimilation. Still fewer are able to descend to the step of contemplation, and still fewer make it to that first step called listening.

The name of this step is changed on the return journey, about which I shall talk to you later. Thousands reach to the state of samadhi, but rarely does one of them become a buddha. 'Buddha' means one who is able to climb down all the four steps and give to the world what he has known. Contemplation means putting all that is thoughtless into thoughts on the return journey. Putting that which cannot be spoken, cannot be thought, within the boundaries of words is the most impossible thing in this world.

You see it when the morning sun rises. Seldom is a painter able to catch that rising aspect of the sun in his painting. It is not very difficult to paint the sun, any painter can do that, but to catch the rising aspect of it is difficult. The phenomenon of rising, that quality of growth which is continuously growing – if that gets painted, so that seeing the painting one feels that the sun is about to move...now, now it is rising up, up.... This seldom happens. To catch a tree in a painting is not difficult, but to catch its aliveness is difficult. Looking at it one may feel that the leaves are about to flutter any moment, a slight breeze and the flowers will fall off. This is very difficult to paint – very difficult. And that is the difference between photography and painting. No matter how sharp a photograph may be, it portrays only the dead aspects, it does not portray the aliveness.

However, the sun, the trees, the flowers are experiences of ordinary life; they can be caught. Samadhi is an extraordinary experience – it happens to only one in millions. And what happens there, all the senses become incapable of informing about it. The ears do not hear there, eyes cannot see there, hands cannot touch there, and the experience that happens there is boundless. The vast immensity falling over your roof, or the whole sky coming down into your courtyard, the chaos, the dumbfoundedness that will come to you – something similar to this happens in the moment of samadhi. This tiny personal space of consciousness, and the whole ocean descends over it.

Kabir has said that first he figured that the drop had fallen into the ocean. But when he came to his senses he realized that the situation was just the opposite: it is the ocean that has fallen into the drop. So Kabir has said that at first he thought that he would be able to somehow tell something or other after returning – though that too appeared difficult. It *is* difficult.

Kabir's words are:

Herat herat hey sakhi rahya Kabir herayi
Bunda samani samunda men so kat heri jayi.

"Oh friend! Seeking and searching, Kabir was gradually lost. The drop has fallen into the ocean, how can the drop be sought out?"

The drop that fell into the ocean, how to bring it out again in order that it may narrate the happening to the world? This was already difficult, but Kabir afterwards changed the lines of the song, canceling the previous ones, and said, "That was a mistake committed because of haste. The experience was new. I could not quite understand what had happened. Out of the old habit I saw things the wrong way around." Then he wrote the verse differently:

Herat herat hey sakhi rahya Kabir herayi
Samunda samana bunda men so kat hera jayi.

"Oh friend, seeking and searching, Kabir was gradually lost. The ocean has fallen into the drop, how can the drop be sought out?

"The ocean has descended into the drop. Had it been the drop that had fallen into the ocean perhaps somehow I would have sought it out, but just the opposite has happened: it is the whole ocean that has fallen into the drop. Now even if I want to I would not know where to look for this drop. Now this drop cannot be found."

The mediums that have enabled us to know all that we have known in the world become useless in knowing what happens in the moment of samadhi. We ourselves become useless. Our very existence gets shattered. Some bigger existence, which has no limits, bursts forth on us – suddenly. We die in the process.

Samadhi is the ultimate death, bigger than the physical death; because in the physical death only the body dies, the mind survives, whereas in samadhi the mind dies. For the first time our entire relationship with the mind breaks; for the first time all the connecting strings of the mind snap, making us separate. And our whole knowledge was of the mind. So in samadhi, for the first time, we stand utterly ignorant.

Let me repeat it: in samadhi our knowledge does not help, because all that knowledge was learned by the mind, and that mind is left far behind, far away. We have gone beyond the mind. The one who knew is no longer a companion there. The one who understood everything, the one who had the knowledge of all kinds of words and doctrines, the one who had digested all the scriptures, is left far behind. It is not only the outer garment, the body, that is left behind, but the very mind is left behind. All that has been our deepest experience is left behind. Taking the jump from the mind, the seeker now stands at the very door of samadhi; now he has no way of knowing.

Whosoever enters the door to samadhi is suddenly totally ignorant. There is no way there for knowing anything, no system for knowing anything, no means for knowing anything; just the pure knowing remains. It is very difficult to give any information after coming back. Who is there to give information? Who is there to bring the news? But the information has been given. Some people have made untiring efforts to do this.

They are the most compassionate ones in this world who gave information after returning from samadhi. Why? Because even the desire to return from samadhi does not arise. Returning from samadhi is like returning from a situation where you achieved everything you wanted, where all wishes were fulfilled, where there remained no reason for even a slight movement, a slight activity... to return from such a place.

It is said that when Buddha attained samadhi he did not come out of it for seven days. It is a beautiful story. It says that all the gods gathered at his feet, Indra began to weep and Brahma put his head on Buddha's feet, and they all requested Buddha not to remain like that, "because," they said, "even we gods pine for the message that the person returning from samadhi gives. And so many people for so many lifetimes wait for someone to become a buddha and deliver the message after coming back from samadhi, to speak and tell what he has known. So please do not remain silent, please speak."

But Buddha said, "There is no one left here to speak, there is no desire left to speak. Moreover, what I have witnessed – it is hard even for me to believe that it can be spoken. Where then is the chance of listeners understanding it?"

When the gods did not agree, Buddha further said, "If you do not agree, I will speak; but I tell you that these things that I may say I myself would not have understood had someone else told them to me before my own realization. So how will anybody else understand? Through this experience I have also come to another understanding, that those who will be able to understand what I have to say can also reach without me; and those who would not be able to understand what I have to say – there is no sense in racking one's brain in front of them."

But the gods gave a very lovely argument. They said, "We do

understand, as you have rightly said, that those who would be able to understand are the very people who are standing on the verge of the experience, only a step away from it; they would somehow be able to cross this distance too even without you. No, we are not asking you to speak for them. And this too we accept, that there are people who have not taken even a single step on the path. Your voice will not reach to these people – they will not understand. We do not ask you to speak for them either. But there are such people also who are in the middle of the above two types – those who would not perhaps be able to understand if you do not speak, but can perhaps understand if you do speak."

The gods emphasized 'perhaps' though. But they also said one more thing to Buddha: "These people in the 'perhaps' category, they may understand, they may not. But if even one person who might have understood missed because of you not speaking.... You think about it. It will be a pain to you, it will be a pain on you. And such a thing buddhas have never done before." So Buddha spoke.

In the moment of samadhi it is very natural to feel that now all speaking, telling, explaining is useless. Who is there to tell? To whom to say it? Who will listen? But despite all this, some people have returned from samadhi.

On coming back to the contemplation step, a most difficult thing happens to such people. Hence great artists are not those artists who compose songs and poems, not those who create paintings and sculpt, but the great artists are those who at this step of contemplation put the absolutely invisible and imperceptible experience of samadhi into visible and perceptible word pictures. The great artists are those who make efforts that somehow, if even a few hints can be given...who create some devices, devise some system of thought, some corollary of thoughts from where you too can have at least a small glimpse, a slight sensation, a little thrill of that experience – even if at the mental level.

Many people attain even to this step of contemplation. But the last step – which was called *shravana*, listening, the first step while going – that same step now becomes *pravachan*, discoursing, when returning from samadhi. The step is the same – listening, speaking. What was shravana, right listening, on the way towards samadhi becomes pravachan, right speaking, on the way back from samadhi.

And remember, on that first step towards samadhi is the disciple, and on this last step on the way back from samadhi is the master, and the meeting that happens between the two is *upanishad*. Where the listener is rightly present and where the speaker is rightly present, the phenomenon of the meeting between the two is upanishad.

The word upanishad means that which one knew in being near the master, that which one listened to sitting near the master, that which came into one's experience in his presence, that which echoed in his nearness, that which was touched in his proximity.

Upanishad means sitting near, being near, having the closeness.

So the work of the disciples is just to listen, and the master should remain just the speech. The listener is not there, the speaker is not there; here remains just the speech, there remains just the capability of listening. Then upanishad happens.

The sutra says:

> *During samadhi, the objects of the experiences*
> *are not separate from the soul.*

Whether it is bliss being experienced, silence being experienced, peace being experienced, nothingness being experienced or emancipation being experienced, none of these experiences can be directly caught in samadhi.

> *...hence they are not experienced.*

These dispositions are not consciously experienced.

> *But these glorified experiences*
> *of the seeker who has come out of samadhi are*

inferred through recollections...

So even Buddha cannot say that it is so in samadhi. He too says only this much, that it is his inference that it is so in samadhi. Mahavira used to say anything only with the prefix 'perhaps' added. He would say, "Perhaps there is bliss there."

Nobody should deduce from this that Mahavira does not know. From his words it appears so – if Mahavira says 'perhaps', then it seems he also has some doubts. It is not due to any doubt but due to extreme loyalty to truth that he speaks thus. Mahavira's loyalty to truth is so untainted and so virgin that it is difficult to find such loyalty to truth elsewhere.

So what Mahavira is saying is that the mind through which he is knowing this was not present at the time of the experience. For the mind, this is news heard from a distance; where the happening took place, mind was not present. Mind is not an eyewitness. The mind was away. It has thought and used inference now, but the event happened far away. It is as if sitting here we can see the snow covering the peak of Gourishankar – from here! The mind was physically far away from that peak, and it has only inferred the cold prevailing there at the peak of Gourishankar.

Hence Mahavira uses the word *syat*, perhaps. He says that perhaps there is supreme bliss there. He does so because of his extreme loyalty to truth, because these are, after all, the inferences of the mind. Mahavira has known, for him it is not an inference. But the one who knows becomes so much one in the moment of knowing that nothing is experienced. When Mahavira returns into the mind, after knowing...

Let us understand it this way. It is as if you go to the peak of Gourishankar and become one with the cold there, you yourself become the cold. Or you become one with the snow there, you too get frozen like the snow and thus have no experience because the experiencer is not separate anymore. Then you come down from the peak, and after reaching the lowlands you pick up your binoculars and look again at Gourishankar through them. The experience of what has been known has remained reverberating inside. The closeness was such that because of the lack of distance necessary for knowing it could not be known. It has now attained a perspective because of the distance. Now picking up the binoculars of mind one has looked back. Now it feels through inference that there was ultimate coolness there, there was an expanse of absolutely spotless white snow. What a great height it was! It feels that all gravitation had disappeared, as if one had attained wings and could fly in the sky. What a clear sky it was! It feels that it was such a blueness that even the clouds were all left down below and only a cloudless empty sky had remained.

But all this is an afterthought when standing back on the low ground. Hence the sutra says: ...*are inferred through recollections of the mind.*

> *In this beginningless world, millions and millions*
> *of karmas, action-impressions, are accumulated.*
> *They are all destroyed by this samadhi*
> *and pure dharma, self-nature, grows.*

In this second sutra there are two very valuable words: karma and *dharma*, action and religion. What we do is action, and what we are is religion. Religion means our self-nature and action means what we are doing. Action means our self-nature reaching outside. Action means that we reach outside ourselves into the world. Action means that we connect with somebody other than ourselves. Self-nature means separate from the other, without relating to the world – the 'I am', the inner being. It has nothing to do with your doing. It is not made of what you do. It is present prior to all your doings. It is your nature.

There can be a mistake in karma, the doing; there can be none in dharma. Remember, the word dharma does not mean religion here. Dharma here means a quality – our self-nature, our inner self-nature, our being.

So the more the doing, the more the self-nature goes on getting covered. All that we do goes on burying our being. And there are so many layers of our doing that slowly, slowly we forget completely that there is any being of ours other than that of the doings.

If somebody asks you, "Who are you?" – whatever answer you give is about your doing, not about your being. You say you are an engineer, you say you are a doctor, you say you are a businessman. Do you realize that business is a doing? You are not a businessman, you are doing business. How can a person be a doctor? A person can do the work of a doctor. How can a person be an engineer? If a person can become an engineer, the person as such will be lost. The person can do the work of an engineer. Engineering is his doing, his work, not his being.

Whatsoever description you give about yourself, if you look deeply into it you will find that you are always saying what you do and never saying a thing about your being. And you cannot. You yourself know nothing about it, you know only what you do. You are thorough about the doing part – what you do, what you can do. All you are able to say is what you have done in the past and what you are able to do in the future. All those certificates you carry around say nothing but what you can do, not what you are. If you say you are a *sadhu*, a seeker, it means you are a doer of seeking. If somebody says he is a thief, it means that his work is the stealing of things. One's act is that of seeking the truth, the other's is that of stealing things.

But what is your being? What is within you? When you were not yet born from the womb of your mother, what did it mean to be a sadhu, a thief, an engineer or a doctor? Had someone asked you while you were in the womb of your mother who you were, it would have been difficult to answer, because you were not an engineer then, you were not a doctor then, you had not yet done any business. Had someone asked you in your mother's womb, "Who is in?" no answer would have been possible. Or do you think it would have been possible? You were still in the mother's womb – no answer could have come.

Now many methods have been discovered for brainwashing.

You say you are an engineer, but your brain can be washed, and after the brainwashing is done properly, if you are asked, "Who are you?" you will just remain blank, because your being an engineer was only in your memory system. You had studied, had received certificates, had done something, had received merits or demerits; it was all in your memory, which has now been washed out. Now you cannot give any answer as to who you are. But you still are. Your being cannot be effaced by washing out your memory, but the impressions of your actions can be washed out.

This sutra says:

> *In this beginningless world, millions and millions*
> *of karmas, action-impressions, are accumulated.*

Naturally, every day, each moment, the action-impressions are being accumulated. We are sitting, standing, breathing – action is happening. We are sleeping, dreaming – action is happening. Nobody can run away from action, because running away is also an action. Where will one go? Will you go and sit down in a jungle? Sitting is also an action. Will you close your eyes there? Closing the eyes is also an action. Anything you may do...where there is any doing there is karma, the action.

Each moment so many actions are being done. Their shadow, their memory, their impression, their conditioning, goes on gathering within us. Whatsoever you are doing is getting accumulated over your being. It is like grooves made on a gramophone disc: when you play back the disc, all that is stored in those grooves becomes alive and starts manifesting itself again. Your mind is exactly the same – a recorded collection of all your actions, everything accumulated. Whatsoever you have done, the grooves have formed upon you. And these grooves are of your endless lives. It is a big burden. And you go on repeating almost the same things over and over again. Your condition is almost like a worn-out disc where the needle has got stuck in the same groove and you go on playing it – the same line repeats itself again and again and again.

What are you doing? Yesterday you did the same thing, the day before yesterday you did the same thing, today you are doing the same thing, tomorrow you will also do the same thing – the same anger, the same greed, the same attachment, the same lust, everything the same...a worn-out record. The needle is stuck in the same groove, unable to get past it, and creating the same sound over and over.

This is why there is so much boredom in life. There is bound to be, because nothing new happens. The needle simply does not proceed further. Just look back on the past thirty, forty years of your life: What have you done? You are playing the same record, the same thing goes on repeating itself every day. This is what the seers of India have called *avagaman,* the cycle of birth and death. The same again, the same again; the same in this life, the same in the next life, the same in the life after that life – the story of the past is the same, the story of the future is the same. The same sexual desire, the same anger, the same hate, the same friendship, the same enmity, the same earning of money, the same making of a house – and after doing all this one finds one day that a gust of wind has come and this whole house of cards has collapsed.

But just as children immediately collect the cards and start building the house again, we also immediately take a new birth and get busy with building a new house of cards. This time we try to build a stronger house; but the plan of the house is the same, the structure is the same – the mind is the same. We end up doing the same again and go on sinking the same way again and again.

It is not only the sun that sets every evening and rises again in the morning – you also go on setting and rising in the same manner. It is circular, a wheel. The word *samsara* means a wheel, which goes on revolving on the same axis.

The endless karmas, the action-impressions that are accumulated, get destroyed by this samadhi. This is worth understanding, because many people think that if bad action-impressions have accumulated, we should destroy them by good actions. They are mistaken. Bad action-impressions cannot be destroyed by good action-impressions. Bad action-impressions will also remain intact and good actions will be accumulated – that is what will happen at the most. They do not cancel each other. There is no way for them to cancel each other.

A person commits a theft, then he repents and becomes a sadhu, a good man. By becoming a sadhu, those action-impressions of the theft that are lying within him are not canceled. There is no way for that. A separate action-impression, that of being a sadhu, forms. The action-impression of being a sadhu does not coincide with the action-impression of being a thief. What has a sadhu to do with a thief? You were a thief, you had drawn one kind of action-groove on the mind; then you became a sadhu. Now the action-grooves of being a sadhu do not get drawn over those of being a thief, because being a sadhu is the happening of a different part of your mind from that of being a thief.

What happens instead? Over the action-grooves of the thief are crammed the action-grooves of the sadhu; nothing is canceled. The sadhu rides over the thief, that's all that happens. This means yet another man, a thief-sadhu, is born. The goodness of being a sadhu cannot cancel the badness of stealing. The thief continues to remain within, only an imposition takes place – merely one more rider on top of it.

So even the thief was okay in a way, even the sadhu was okay in a way, but this hotch-potch of thief and sadhu that is created is the big trouble. It is a continuous inner conflict, because the thief continues his efforts and the sadhu continues his efforts. And God alone knows how many different forms we accumulate within us which do not cancel each other, which are created separately and remain so. Hence this sutra says that they are all destroyed through samadhi.

Action does not cancel action. Nonaction destroys action. Understand this properly: action does not cancel action, action makes action only more dense. Only nonaction cancels action. And nonaction is attained in samadhi, when the doer does not exist anymore.

When we reach that state of consciousness where there is only being, not the doing at all, where not even a ripple of doing has arisen ever, where only the being, the existence has always remained – the being, not the doing – in that moment of being, one suddenly realizes that all the actions that had ever been done by you were not done by you. Some actions were done by the body – let the body have the responsibility for them. Some actions were done by the mind – let the mind have the responsibility for them. But you had not done any actions at all.

Simultaneous to this realization the network of all action-impressions is destroyed. The soul-ness is the cancelation of all actions. It is on losing the soul-ness that the illusion, "I have done," is created.

When a person is stealing, it is either activated by his body or by his mind. Some people's bodies come to such a condition that stealing has to be done. A person is hungry, the body compels him to do the stealing. The soul never commits any theft. There is the body's hunger, its pain and its misery; or one's child is dying and there is no money for medicine – one commits the theft. All this is a theft because of the body.

Until now we have not been able to differentiate between the thief from the body and the thief from the mind. A thief from the body means that it is the society that is criminal. A thief from the mind is himself criminal – a thief from the mind is a different matter. He does not need anything, back home his coffers are full, but he finds a penny lying on the road and he picks it up and puts it in his pocket. Now, this man is a thief from the mind. It is not because of any physical need; his body is not imploring him to steal, but his greed. This one penny is not really going to add to his wealth but something will be added, at least one penny.

He may have millions of *rupees*, but the intention to pick up one *paisa* remains – this man is the real criminal. But he is never caught. It is the thief who steals because of the body needs who is caught. The real culprit is the other one, because he has no reason at all – on the body level – to steal, and yet he steals. Stealing is his habit, he derives juice from stealing.

Psychology talks about a disease known as kleptomania. It is a disease of the mind. Most people are suffering from this disease, but only some persons, whose disease becomes acute, come to the notice of psychology.

I used to know one professor, a rich man, very well off, who had everything one could desire, but he had only one son and this son was a kleptomaniac. He was suffering from this disease of stealing. He would steal anything – it did not matter what that thing was. If he came to your house and a button was lying on the floor, he would immediately put it in his pocket. He had no use for it. There might be even a sewing needle lying somewhere and he would put it in his pocket. He would be looking at a book of yours and he would tear off a page and put it in his pocket.

The professor once asked me what to do about him, because he did not steal such things that you felt that he was really stealing and was a thief. He just took trivial things. The boy was studying for his M.A. degree. He was clever. I developed a little relationship with him, so he took me to see his closet where he had kept everything that he had ever stolen. Each item was labeled as to who was deceived for a certain thing, from whose house a certain other thing was removed, etcetera. He was relishing the fact that until now nobody had been able to know who had taken away a certain thing and how. If he had stolen a button from your house, on the label was written, "I brought it from such and such person's house, right in front of his nose, but he could not have had even an inkling that such a thing was taking place."

Now this interest in stealing is of a different type. It has nothing to do with body-need. Thefts are either from the body or from the mind, there is no theft from the soul. So the day you enter your soul, you suddenly realize, "I have not done those thefts, I have not performed those actions; I was only present in those actions. It is true that those actions could not have been committed without me, but it is also true that I had not committed those actions."

Science uses a word, very valuable and significant – catalytic agent. If you split water you will get hydrogen and oxygen, nothing else. H_2O is the formula – two atoms of hydrogen and one atom of oxygen constitute water. But if you mix two atoms of hydrogen and one atom of oxygen you will not get water.

This is very interesting. When you split water, you get two parts of hydrogen and one part of oxygen. Naturally, when you mix these two in the same proportion you should get water. But that does not happen. There is one more thing whose presence is required for the making of water. It does not enter the actual formulation, but the formulation itself can take place only in its presence. That thing is electricity, in this case, and it is called a catalytic agent. When lightning happens in the sky it acts as a catalytic agent, and water is formed from the oxygen and hydrogen present in the air. It does not do anything, it does not enter the water, but its presence is necessary.

If you take hydrogen and oxygen and let an electric current pass through, water will be formed. But if you split that water you will get only hydrogen and oxygen, not the electricity. It means that electricity does not enter water as one of its constituents, but the water cannot be formed without its presence. Science calls this particular phenomenon a catalytic agent.

You cannot commit a theft without the presence of a soul. The soul is like a catalytic agent, its presence is necessary. The body alone – just the body alone – never goes out to commit any theft. Even if you slip money in the pocket of a dead body, it won't be called a thief when discovered. What does a corpse have to do with theft? Because it is a corpse, it cannot perform actions as such.

Mind alone also cannot be a thief. No matter how much a mind may think, it cannot commit a theft alone. Not only that, if there was no soul inside it could not even think. The presence of the soul is necessary, only then does the theft happen. But still, the day one reaches to the soul one finds that the theft had happened in the presence of the soul but the soul was not involved in the theft. The soul was only present. Its presence is so powerful that things start happening.

A piece of magnet is lying there; iron pieces are being attracted.

Perhaps you may think that the magnet is attracting them – you are wrong. The very presence of the magnet is enough. It does not have to attract, it does not have to make any effort to attract. The magnet does not have to contract any muscles to draw the iron pieces towards it. A magnet does not even know that it is attracting. The very presence of the magnet and the iron pieces begin to be attracted.

The very presence of the soul and actions begin; the body is activated, the mind is activated, and the actions begin their journey. The day you re-enter this soul, during samadhi, you are freed of all action-impressions – not because these actions had in any way bound you but because they had never bound you in the first place. You had never before attained to your inner self, where you would have understood that you are unbound.

This view of the Upanishad is in one sense very much against morality. Because of this, there has been great opposition towards the Upanishads deep within the mind. Whosoever is a moralist would ask you to cancel your bad actions with good actions, to do good deeds and not to do bad deeds. The Upanishads say that performing deeds as such is wrong. Whether you perform a good deed or a bad deed, that is a secondary matter. Your notion of doing, that you are a doer – that is the evil.

Evil is of two types: good evil and bad evil. But both are evils, because the belief that you do something is the fallacy. You are only present and the action is happening; action is happening only in your presence. You are only a witness, not a doer.

The day you taste this presence not as a doer but as a witness you will find out that whatever has ever happened only happened around you; whatever has ever happened you have not done, it only happened around you. Events had happened, had happened close by you, but still you had remained apart from them.

It is just as when you dream at night and you get up in the morning and you say, "I had a dream"; you remain separate from it. It may be that you committed a theft in the dream, it may be that you became imprisoned in the dream, it may be that you saved yourself from going to jail by paying a bribe. Anything can happen in a dream, but when you wake up in the morning the dream disappears completely – as if it had never happened. After waking up in the morning you don't regard yourself as a thief.

But did you ever give it a thought: could the dream have been there without you? The dream could happen because you were there. If you were not there...the dream would not happen to a dead body. The dream happened because you were there, your presence was a must for it to happen. Yet on waking up in the morning you do not feel concerned that you committed a theft. What to do now to offset it? Fast, do penance, give to charity, renounce? What to do? No, you do not feel to do anything. A dream does not even remain in the memory for more than two minutes after waking up. It disappears like a column of smoke.

In the state of right samadhi the whole of life feels like a dream, whatsoever has been lived...not just in this life but in the infinite lives lived in arriving to the state of samadhi. Just as in the morning when you come to the awake state from sleep, similarly, when you arrive in samadhi from this so-called waking state, that whole circle of the past, all that dream-stuff, disappears like smoke.

The one who has arrived in samadhi knows for the first time that, "I just am; all the actions that have happened near me are like dreams." And no anxiety or regret about them remains. Neither does any self-praise remain – "What great deeds I have done" – nor does any self-condemnation remain: "What mean deeds I have done." No, everything disappears.

In your dreams, whether you were an emperor, a great sannyasin, a murderer or a thief – none of these alter the taste of your morning tea. All the three become meaningless. It is not that if you were an emperor in your dream, then in the morning you are drinking your tea, dreaming of the dream – or if you were a thief, a scoundrel, a murderer in the dream, then you are feeling guilty and the tea tastes bitter. Nor do you give up taking tea because you were a sadhu, a sage in the dream. It also does not happen that you think, "I have been a saint all night long and now I am drinking tea the next morning – what a shameful act." No, when you drink your tea in the morning all your dreams have gone.

I have heard...Rinzai was a great Zen master in Japan, and once, when he got up in the morning, he told his disciple who was standing by, "I will narrate a dream I saw last night if you will explain it to me."

His disciple said, "Please wait for a couple of minutes, I shall first bring water for you to wash your face and hands."

The disciple brought the water. Rinzai washed his face and hands and smiled. By that time another disciple had come. Rinzai said, "I had a dream last night. I was going to tell the dream to this first disciple, asking him to define it, but he defined it before my telling him. Will you define it? Shall I tell it to you?"

The other disciple said, "Kindly wait a minute, let me first bring a cup of tea for you and then we will see."

After drinking the tea, Rinzai laughed and said, "I am very pleased, now there is no need to tell you my dream."

There was another person present who was watching all this. He thought there was no limit to the foolishness. He said, "There is a limit to everything. The dream has not even been told and the definitions have already been made, and everything is solved." He requested Rinzai to at least narrate the dream, so one could know what the dream was.

Rinzai said, "I was testing my disciples. Had they shown any readiness to define the dream I would have thrown them out of the monastery. Is there any need to define a dream? It was a dream, and the matter is over. This first one did the right thing. He was saying, 'There is still some shadow of the dream lurking, so just wash your face with cold water.' This second one also did the right thing: 'Perhaps the washing of your face was not enough. The dream is still lurking hazily in the mind, so have a cup of hot tea and wake up!' – and that is the definition of a dream. Can there be any other definition of a dream? Just wake up and a dream becomes meaningless. What is there to define in it? No one ever bothers to define what is meaningless."

What we call big deeds, small deeds, good deeds, bad deeds –
how many divisions have we not made – moral, immoral, good
conduct, bad conduct; they all become meaningless, futile, in
samadhi. On awakening in samadhi one finds out that it was all a
long, endless, infinite dream, and one was just present there. You
had not entered it, you were standing just outside. This is why all
action-impressions are destroyed, and dharma, self-nature, arises.
When all action-impressions are canceled, when all that we were
involved in is canceled, we come to know that which we are, that
which is our being, our self-nature. Self-nature is dharma, religion.

The knowers of yoga call it Dharmamegha –
the raincloud of dharma – samadhi, because
it showers a thousand nectar-streams of dharma,
self-nature, like a raincloud.

Dharmamegha is a beautiful word. Clouds we have seen. When
Ashadh, the first month of monsoon comes, clouds gather in the
sky. But we are not aware of the whole phenomenon. Those clouds
gather in the sky in Ashadh, and the peacocks start dancing. Big
cracks have developed in the vast stretches of land due to the summer heat, as if the earth has opened its lips, as if the earth has
opened its doors on all sides to drink the drops of water to its
heart's content. The thirsty earth has been waiting for so long, and
the thirsty trees have been listless like fishes thrown out on dry
sand. Then those clouds gather in the sky and the rains begin to
shower under the shadow of the dark clouds, and a dance, a song
spreads all over.

Dharmamegha is a phenomenon similar to Ashadh that happens
within you. It is as if your being was thirsty for lifetimes, cracks
had appeared in it, there was no trace of the water anywhere that
may quench the thirst. You were drinking water, but that only
increased the thirst rather than quenching it. You drank many
types of water and traveled to many water sources, and who
knows what you did not search for and hold onto. But every time

the hope turned into despair, nothing came to your hands. This thirsty and torn-apart earth of your entire being, full of longing... rainclouds gather over it for the first time in the moments of samadhi. Ashadh comes within, and a rainshower of nectar – it is only a symbol – a rainshower of nectar starts happening for the first time. For the first time, in the moments of samadhi, the soul is bathed and the nectar starts showering from those clouds in an endless number of streams.

This description is only symbolic. The actual happening is far bigger. Calling it nectar cannot actually give us any idea about it. But still we get some indication that the clouds gathered in the sky...rainshowers started from them and the soul, thirsty for lives upon lives, was satiated.

> The knowers of yoga call it Dharmamegha –
> the raincloud of dharma – samadhi, because
> it showers a thousand nectar-streams of dharma,
> self-nature, like a raincloud.

But why is it called dharmamegha? Because the self-nature for the first time showers upon oneself. Dharma means the self-nature.

Whatsoever we have known up to now was the nature of the other. Sometimes when beauty was seen it was in someone else. Sometimes when love was received it was from someone else. Happiness was received, unhappiness was received – it was always from the other. All information was through others; there was no experience of one's own. Someone else, someone else, someone else – always the other, and only that other was important. Now for the first time the other is removed and the self starts showering over the self. It is like our own springs have burst open, it is as though one found one's own source and the self began showering over the self.

Dharmamegha means the self-nature has started showering. You yourself become bathed in it, drowned in it; you become fresh, become new. All the action-impressions, all their dust, all the mess from the infinite journeys, all the rubbish that has gathered over one, is swept away. All that remains is naturalness, spontaneity; all that remains is oneself, nothing else.

In one sense we can call it the ultimate blessedness, in one sense we can say this is the ultimate treasure, and in another sense we can say this is the ultimate poverty. If we think of the divine, this man has attained the ultimate wealth. It is this dharmamegha samadhi that Jesus called, "Poverty of the spirit." When someone reaches this point he becomes poor in every respect. Now he has nothing else except himself, nothing else remains except one's own self. This is what will be called poverty.

This is why Buddha called his sannyasins *bhikkhus*, not *swamis*. It was because of the dharmamegha samadhi. Buddha said, "I will not call my sannyasins swamis, I will call them bhikkhus." But they mean the same thing. If you look from the side of the world they have become bhikkhus, beggars; if you look from the side of the divine they have become swamis, the owners, emperors.

Hindus were using the word swami from the other aspect: after attaining to samadhi one becomes for the first time an emperor, a master. Up to now one had been a beggar, begging all around, with folded hands and an outstretched begging bowl. Up to now your soul had been nothing more than a begging bowl. Whatever crumbs of bread someone threw in that begging bowl was your only treasure. Leftovers, defiled and stale food, crumbs fallen down from the dining tables – you were collecting it all and considering it your wealth. Until now you were a beggar.

Hence Hindus called the sannyasin attaining to this dharmamegha samadhi, swami. But Buddha said, "Whatever was there up to this time – all the riches, the empire, the whole world – has all been left behind. Nothing of the other has remained, only the self. The ultimate poverty has happened. When you are just alone without anything else, not even clothes, not even your own house, not even your own land – nothing is left as your own but only the self...who can be poorer? Even a beggar has something other than just his self. It may be little, but it is something; something other than his self. It may be just underwear, but that too is wealth." Even a beggar is not so much a beggar that he is all alone, without anything else.

Buddha told his bhikkhus that the world should drop from them in such a way that nothing remains, that not even a trace of the world remains. You become a total beggar as far as the world and its belongings are concerned.

But these two things are the same. One who becomes a beggar from the side of the world becomes a swami from the side of the soul. One who becomes a swami from the side of the soul becomes a beggar from the side of the world. That is why we have given so much respect to the bhikkhu, as never to any person with possessions. We have installed the bhikkhu on a throne on which we have never installed even an emperor. The word bhikkhu became respectable.

Now the meaning of the word bhikkhu is beggar, and if you call someone a bhikkhu he will want to fight with you. But Buddha called his most blessed disciples bhikkhus. Whosoever he called bhikkhu became blessed. Sometimes such people create problems even in the field of language. People like Buddha leave the language topsy-turvy. There had been a clear meaning for the word bhikkhu and he spoiled it. He gave it a totally new meaning – the bhikkhu became an emperor. If emperors bowed down at the feet of bhikkhus, that bestowed great dignity on the bhikkhu.

Dharmamegha samadhi makes one a beggar from one side and an emperor from the other side.

> In this samadhi, the network of desires dissolves
> completely and the thickets of accumulated
> karma called virtue and sin are uprooted at
> their very source.

Remember, both virtue and sin. This is the depth of the Upanishadic thinking. The thickets of virtue and sin, both; all the good you had done, that too, all the bad you had done, that too...the thickets of both are destroyed at their roots.

Do not think that when you attain God you will keep the bank balance of your virtues with you – "I built an inn for free accommodation. I built a temple. I gave food to a certain number of brahmins. Do you have a record of that?" If you arrive at the gates of paradise with an account of all this, it does not matter if the inscription at the entrance says 'Paradise', inside you will find only hell.

In the language of this world, virtue and sin are higher and lower. Sin is bad and virtue is good. This may be alright in the view of the society, but in the ultimate view of dharma, both virtue and sin are meaningless, because being a doer is sin and being a non-doer is virtue. There is one thing that is clear: only one who is a non-doer, one who is egoless, will be able to enter. Only he will be able to enter there who is not – one who has disappeared and is going there as a nothingness. If you as an ego are still there even slightly...the path is very narrow and you will not be able to enter.

There is a statement by Jesus which has never had its spiritual meaning explained. In fact, the West is not capable of finding the spiritual meaning; hence whatever meaning is derived turns out to be worldly. Jesus' words are, "It is possible for a camel to pass through the eye of a needle, but a rich person shall never be able to enter the kingdom of my Lord." But after two thousand years of Christianity not even once has anybody rightly interpreted the statement. Two thousand years is a long time.

The whole interpretation that has been given is that a rich person cannot go to heaven. Is there a possibility that a camel may pass through the eye of a needle? It cannot happen. How can a camel pass through the eye of a needle? But that which is not possible, Jesus says, may somehow happen; some trick may be devised, some way may be found for a camel to pass through the eye of a needle. But a rich person will not be able to gain entry past the doors of heaven. Christianity took only its superficial meaning, but that is not its true meaning.

What is meant by a rich person is, one who feels even slightly that he has something. A rich person is one who has the notion of having something. So if somebody feels he has earned virtues, he is a rich person. If somebody feels that he has been a sadhu, observing self-control, penance, he is a rich man. The meaning of a rich man is someone who says he has something about him other than himself. This is a rich man. If he says, "I performed this many prayers, observed this many fasts, have stood in the hot sun for this many days. For years I have been standing on my feet without sitting down. I did this much service to the poor, have visited this many hospitals, have done this, have done that" – if he has anything to claim, then this man is that rich man.

Now listen to the statement of Jesus again: "It is possible for a camel to pass through the eye of a needle, but a rich person shall not be able to enter the kingdom of my Lord."

Who is poor? One who has nothing to claim when standing in front of God. And if one says, "I have meditation, I have virtues, I have religion"? No, one who stands empty in front of God and says, "I have nothing, only I am. Whatsoever I am is all that you have given me, there are no accumulations of my own; my very being is my everything, I have no account of even my actions...." One who stands at that door with such an emptiness is the poor person. He is the bhikkhu of Buddha, the 'poor man' of Jesus. Such a person is able to enter the kingdom of God.

So the right meaning of being poor is, one who is empty. One who is empty is able to enter. And this is why Jesus talked of a camel. The eye of a needle is very small – there is no way for a camel to pass through it. The door to the kingdom of God is even smaller than the eye of a needle – only an emptiness can pass through it. Even if there is a little of something with you, even a little of the 'I', it will get stuck. You are trying to pass through the eye of a needle along with your camel. It is not possible. Drop the camel!

But it is very difficult to give up our vehicles, because on vehicles we look taller. This is how Jesus must have thought of a camel. Whosoever is riding on their ego is riding on a camel. And everybody knows how troublesome a camel ride is. The ego ride is like a camel ride: one has to bear with lots of jerks and jumps, it is continuously going up and down. However, one appears to be high.

One has to come down from the camel. Whatsoever you have, it has come from your doing – everything, whatsoever! Whatsoever you have because of your doing is limited by your mind; mind is its boundary. Nothing that has come from your doing reaches up to the soul.

...the network of desires dissolves completely.

Karmas – the action-impressions called virtue and sin – are all uprooted at their very source. Then this statement...

Tattvamasi, That art thou – being true,
is only realized indirectly...

Then for the first time it is experienced what these seers mean – what this Tattvamasi is, That art thou. It is for the first time experienced indirectly – indirectly! Even now it is not seen very clearly. Even now it only feels so, it is only touched, inferred; it is not yet directly experienced. When this dharmamegha showers over one, when the mind becomes absolutely empty and the poverty becomes ultimate and the seeker becomes nothing but an emptiness within, then for the first time this supreme statement, Tattvamasi, that you are the Brahman, is experienced indirectly.

These seers of the Upanishads are very wonderful people. Still they say it is not a direct experience. Still it is as if we are sitting with closed eyes, and the sound of somebody's footsteps is heard and we feel that somebody has come. But it is indirect. It is very dark and difficult to see, and suddenly the echo of a tuneful song spreads and we feel that somebody is singing. This is indirect knowledge. Indirect means, so far there is no face-to-face encounter, so far it is only being sensed.

The first thing that happens after the dharmamegha shower is the indirect experience of the statement: "Tattvamasi – That art

thou – that which is said by the seers, the Upanishads, is right."
That statement which you had heard – had listened to in shravana,
contemplated in *manan,* assimilated in *nididhyasan,* attained oneness with in samadhi, now on the showering of the dharmamegha
samadhi is found to be right. When you understand, "That is
right," this is an indirect knowledge. But today one comes to feel
it, one tastes it – that it has been said rightly.

...is only realized indirectly...

When this indirect knowledge becomes stabilized and there
remains not even a single ripple of the opposite of any kind anywhere, when it settles indubitably, becomes an implicit trust...

...then the direct knowledge, like a myrobalan
fruit kept on one's own palm, is born.

When the indirect knowledge becomes completely stabilized,
when the total being experiences and says that the seers were right
in saying, "Tattvamasi – That art thou"; when there remains not a
single ripple of any kind of the opposite anywhere, when it feels
wholly the truth – but still indirect – then the experience of Tattvamasi becomes direct and immediate, as if someone has placed a
myrobalan fruit on your palm. Such a man then does not say,
"What the seers had said is right." Such a man says, "Tattvamasi
is now my statement."

With indirect knowledge, this man says, "Because the seers have
said it, I can say that it is right." In direct knowledge, this man will
say, "I say it is right, hence the seers also must have been right in
saying so." Try to understand this difference properly.

In indirect knowledge the evidence was from the Vedas, the seers,
the scriptures. That is why the journey had begun with shravana –
listening. The master has said it, so it must be right – the search had
begun in this trust. It is indirect knowledge as long as you feel, "The
master has said it, so it must be right." And one who knows the

master accepts positively that the master must have said it right.

If somebody is with Buddha and Buddha says, "Tattvamasi – That art thou," then this man cannot even conceive of any falsehood. He has no idea if this statement is right or not, but he knows Buddha, so what Buddha says becomes authentic for him. That something unauthentic can come out of Buddha is out of the question for him, he cannot conceive of this.

For one who has lived near the master, has known the master, the master's words are the evidence for him. But, "The master's words are the evidence," is indirect knowledge, it has come from the other. This will be the first realization. When a disciple of Buddha attains samadhi, he will bow down at the feet of Buddha with folded hands and say, "Now I know that what you had said is right."

But when this realization deepens more and he drowns more and more, the situation will change completely. Then he will say, "I know it. And now I say that it is my experience that it is right; what the master had said is also right."

Now this person himself becomes the evidence, this person himself becomes the scripture. It is such persons we have called a buddha, a *tirthankara,* an incarnation, one who himself is the evidence – those who do not say that because it is written so in the Vedas it is right, but who say that because it is known by them to be right, it is right. And if the Vedas also say the same thing, then on the authority of their knowing, the Vedas are also right. And if the Vedas do not say so, the Vedas are wrong. Now the criterion is one's own experience. Now one's own touchstone is available.

This is the state of the *siddhas,* the fulfilled ones.

When samadhi enters from the indirect knowledge into the direct knowledge it becomes the state of siddha-hood. Only if a person having attained to such a state returns via samadhi, assimilation and contemplation up to the step of discourse, do we get the news of that world. So if we have given so much respect to the scriptures, it is because they are the words of those that were heard by the people living close to them and who had found that whatsoever this person says he can never say anything wrong.

Yet such people do not ask one to believe in what they are saying. Buddha says, "Think, reflect, contemplate, assimilate, practice, and if it becomes your own experience, only then accept it. Do not accept just because I am saying it, do not accept just because Buddha is saying it, do not accept just because the scriptures are saying it. No, you seek and search for it, and when it becomes your own experience then you will also become a witness for it."

A person who has attained to samadhi becomes a witness for all the scriptures – not a knower of them but a witness for them. A pundit becomes knowledgeable of them, an enlightened one becomes the witness. A pundit says scriptures are saying the right thing because it appeals to the logic; an enlightened one says scriptures are saying the right thing, because "That is my experience too."

Enough for today.

DIE
TO THE FUTURE

CHAPTER 12

When no desire arises for objects
worthy of being enjoyed,
know this as the ultimate in nonattachment.
When no I-ness arises,
know this as the ultimate in knowing.
When the dissolved desires do not arise again,
this is the ultimate in relaxedness,
and such a sthitpragya, a seeker,
stable in wisdom, ever remains in bliss.

✳

He whose self is absorbed only in Brahman,
the ultimate reality,
remains desireless and actionless.
When purified by its oneness with Brahman and
drowned in this one single rapture,
the activities of mind are choiceless and
remain only as the consciousness,
then it is called pragya, wisdom.
He who always has such a pragya is called
jivanamukta, the one liberated while living.

✳

One who has no I-ness for his body and the senses,
and no my-ness for other things, is a jivanamukta,
the one liberated while living.

When no desire arises for objects
worthy of being enjoyed,
then know this as the ultimate in nonattachment.
When no I-ness arises,
know this as the ultimate in knowing.

rdinarily *vairagya*, meaning non-attachment, is understood by people as *viraga*, meaning detachment. *Raga* and viraga – attachment and detachment – are opposites. Attachment means the arising of a desire to indulge on seeing an object. If beauty is seen, a tasteful food is seen, a comfortable situation is seen, then the desire that arises to enjoy it, to drown in it, to be lost in it, is attachment.

Attachment means a desire to become attached, a desire to become drowned in something by losing one's own self. If a pleasure is seen outside oneself, then the desire to drown oneself in that pleasure is attachment.

Detachment means a repulsion arises on seeing something enjoyable; a desire arises to go away from it, to turn one's back towards it. According to language, raga is attraction, viraga is repulsion. Where there is a desire to go towards a thing it is attachment, where there is a desire to move away from a thing it is repulsion. Viraga means inverted raga. In one we are drawn nearer, in the other we move away. Viraga, detachment, is not freedom from attachment, it is just inverted attachment.

Somebody desires money; if he gets money he thinks he has achieved everything. Someone else thinks that if he could give up money he would have achieved everything. But they are both focused on money. Somebody thinks there is pleasure in man or in woman, and someone else thinks there is pleasure in renouncing man or woman. But the central point to both of them is man or woman. Somebody thinks this worldly life is heaven, someone else thinks this world is hell, but the attention of both of them is on the world.

From the point of view of language, vairagya, nonattachment, is the opposite of raga, attachment, but for a seeker of the spiritual, vairagya is not the opposite of raga, it is the absence of raga. Please understand the difference properly. If you look in a dictionary, nonattachment is the opposite of attachment, but if you move into experience, nonattachment is not the opposite of attachment but its absence. The difference is subtle.

There is attraction towards women; this is attachment. If it becomes a repulsion towards women, it becomes difficult to bear their company, then a tendency is born in the mind to keep away from women. This is detachment, according to language and the dictionary; but according to *samadhi,* awakening, it is still an attraction.

From the point of view of samadhi, detachment is when there is neither attraction for women nor repulsion; neither the pull nor the push. It is when the presence of a woman or her absence are the same; when the presence of a man or his absence are the same; when poverty and richness are the same. When neither the gaining of a certain thing determines whether you are happy nor the losing of a certain thing makes you happy, when happiness has nothing to do with either gain or loss, when happiness has become one's own, with no requirement of outside stimulation – neither meeting nor not-meeting, they both become meaningless – then is vairagya, meaning nonattachment.

Nonattachment means that we simply don't look for the other any longer. We are neither in favor nor against; neither in attraction nor in repulsion. This complete freedom from the other is vairagya, nonattachment.

There can be two types of bondages with the other: when we meet a friend there is happiness, when we meet an enemy there is unhappiness; or when the enemy goes away there is happiness, when the friend goes away there is unhappiness. Buddha has said with deep satire, "Enemies give unhappiness, friends also give unhappiness; when friends leave us there is unhappiness, when enemies meet us there is unhappiness. What is the difference?"

There is some attachment to an enemy as well as to a friend. If your enemy dies, then too something breaks within, a place falls empty within. Many times the death of an enemy creates a bigger emptiness in you than the death of a friend because there was an attachment to the enemy also. It was inverted attachment; you were related with his presence as well. One is related with a friend as well as with an enemy. So you are related even with those things and people that you are opposed to.

Nonattachment means there is no relationship whatsoever; you have become unrelated, alone. So in this sutra the definition of the ultimate state in nonattachment has been given: *When no desire arises for objects worthy of enjoyment.*

In language, the word viraga, detachment, means renouncing and going away from the objects worthy of enjoyment. Whereas vairagya, nonattachment, means that no desire arises for enjoying an object even though it may be present; it means even if you are enjoying it there is no desire for it.

King Janaka, an enlightened man mentioned in the Ramayana, lives in his palace where everything is available that can be enjoyed, but there is no desire to enjoy. You may choose to leave and run away into a jungle where there is nothing to enjoy, but your desire for enjoyment will then turn itself into dreams, will excite your passions; your mind will go every now and then to the place where there are things to be enjoyed.

So the question is not of the presence or absence of the enjoyable things, the question is of the existence of desire. And it is very interesting to note that where there are no objects of enjoyment the desire is felt even more intensely; it is not felt so intensely where the objects of enjoyment are present. In the nonavailability the desire is more acute.

This sutra says that even if someone has renounced everything, still it is not the ultimate state in nonattachment. This too is not the ultimate form of nonattachment, because it is possible that the attachment may be there deep within. It is also possible that running away might have been just a form of attachment. What then is the ultimate definition? When everything enjoyable is present but there is no desire to indulge. Who will decide about it? Everyone has to decide it for himself. It is not a matter for others to decide; you are your own judge.

When no desire arises within, when the enjoyable objects may be present but no desire arises, neither in favor nor against, when mind simply does not run this way or that and you do not swing in any direction; you remain where you are, as if there is nothing outside – the object may be there outside but its reflection within does not create any attraction or repulsion – this then is the ultimate state in nonattachment.

This will look very difficult to us because so far we have understood detachment as the opposite of attachment. If a person renounces his wife and children, family and house and runs away, we call him a viraga, meaning a renunciate. But in his very escaping he shows that he is still in some way attached. When somebody escapes, he is not escaping out of fear of his house, he is actually escaping out of fear of his own inner desires. How can a house make one run away? And if a house can make one run away, then that inner state of nonattachment is not yet there.

One person is looking to buy a house; now the house is making him run in one direction. Another person is escaping to the jungle in fear of his house; here too it is the house that is making him run, but in another direction. He has his back to the house but he is still connected with the house. And there is yet another person...things do not cause him to run; such a person is not gripped by things any longer. But this nonattachment will mean being in the self, being settled within oneself. None of us are settled within ourselves.

There was a king whose life-force was kept in a parrot. These are old stories created for children where this kind of fantasy can still happen. Whatsoever anyone did to the king, the king would not die unless the parrot was killed. His soul was hidden in the parrot. As long as the parrot did not die, the king would not die. This is not only a story – it indicates that our souls are also imprisoned somewhere else, encased in something else. It may be that your soul is not imprisoned in a parrot but in your safe.

In 1930–31, when there was a sudden depression and the American dollar was devalued, many of the top millionaires of Wall Street in America committed suicide. The depression came so swiftly and acutely that most speculators and millionaires became poor overnight. Their bank balances suddenly disappeared. Many of them committed suicide instantly by jumping from the fiftieth or sixtieth floor of the buildings.

What happened to these people? What happened that suddenly there was no other option left for them but to die? Their souls were imprisoned in their safes. When the safe died, they died. This jumping.... Nothing else had happened, the whole world was unchanged; just some digits in the bank's ledgers had disappeared. Digits! In somebody's name there had been a ten-digit figure, now only two digits remained. Where there had been a long row of figures in credit to his account, now there remained none. All this happened in the banks, on paper, but their souls were imprisoned in those bank ledgers. Those ledgers were their lives. Any direct attempt to kill them would not have succeeded, but the safes became empty and they simply died.

Somebody is in love with someone. Then one of the two lovers dies and the life is finished for the other also. If we all search within ourselves we will find that our souls are also imprisoned somewhere or other, in some parrot or other. As long as your soul is imprisoned somewhere you are not settled in your self. Then your life is not present where it should be. It should be within yourself – but it is not there, it is somewhere else.

Now this being somewhere else can be of many types. One person thinks that his body is his soul; then this person is also somewhere else. Tomorrow he will start becoming old; then he will be in pain, he will feel miserable because his body is wasting away, becoming wrinkled, ugly, sick and aged. Such a person will feel himself dead before his actual death because the young body in which he had kept his soul is now fading.

There can be differences as to where you have imprisoned your soul, but if your soul is outside you, you are living in attachment. Attachment means your soul is not in its rightful place, it is somewhere else. You may run in a reverse direction, but still the soul will be somewhere else.

The definition of nonattachment is that your soul is within you, settled in yourself; nothing pulls you and nothing creates any sort of ripples or waves in you. Hence nonattachment is the door to bliss, because for one who has settled in himself...there is no way to make him unhappy.

Remember, those children's stories are saying the right thing. One who has settled in himself, one whose soul has come back within himself – there remains no way to kill him. Souls never die, it is only the parrots that die. Wherever else you put your souls, those things slip away, they die. Hence the person starts feeling himself as good as dead. The soul is immortal, but we attach it to mortal things. Those mortal things are bound to disintegrate – if not today, tomorrow. That is their very nature. When those things disintegrate you will have an illusion that you have died. This dying of the self is an illusion that is created by attaching yourself to mortal things.

Nonattachment is when in the breaking of all relationships one has come to know that which was relating – one's own self.

When no desire arises for objects worthy of being enjoyed... And is it okay for the opposite desire to arise? No, when desire as such does not arise – desire of any sort – then...*know this as the ultimate in nonattachment.*

This sutra is being given for *you* – do not go out judging others with it. We are very clever: if we are given definitions, then we use them to judge others: "Okay, let us see if so and so is really nonattached or not." It is none of your business. You have nothing to do with the other. If the other is in attachment he will suffer unhappiness; if he is in nonattachment he will be enjoying bliss. It is none of your concern. But we are so clever in deceiving ourselves that if we have a definition, a touchstone, we immediately begin to evaluate others without bothering to evaluate our own selves.

Test yourself; this sutra is for you. This sutra is not for making you think about others – whether Mahavira is a nonattached being or not, whether Krishna is a nonattached being or not. They may be or may not be, you have nothing to do with it. It is their own business. If they are nonattached they will enjoy bliss, if they are not they will suffer pain, but you don't figure anywhere in it.

Many people come to me and ask, "How to know that such and such a person is really enlightened?" Where is the necessity for you to know whether a person is really enlightened or not? If you can stay aware of whether you are enlightened or not, that is enough. Even if the other has become enlightened, this in itself does not make *you* enlightened. If the other has not become enlightened, this does not bring any hindrance to your enlightenment.

But why do we think in this manner? There are reasons for it. We want to make sure that nobody has attained to nonattachment. That gives us a sort of relief. Then there is no harm...if I have not attained to nonattachment then there is no harm, nobody else has attained it either! This gives a consolation to the mind, a support to the mind, that I am fine as I am because nobody has ever attained, and neither have I.

This is why our mind is never willing to accept that anybody has attained to nonattachment. We try to find all kinds of loopholes to show that the person has not yet attained. If somebody has attained to nonattachment it creates an inner discomfort within us. That discomfort is that if somebody else has attained, it only means that I can also attain but am unable to do so – and this creates anxiety and guilt. Hence nobody in this world accepts the other as right. It has nothing to do with the other, but in not accepting anybody as right it becomes easier to accept one's own evils.

If the whole world is a thief, then you don't feel any guilt in being a thief yourself. If the whole world is bad, then your being bad is only natural. But if the whole world is good, your being bad starts piercing you like a thorn. Then comes a self-condemnation, a sadness, a feeling of guilt, and one starts feeling that what should happen is not happening. And it creates a great uneasiness in your life.

In order that that uneasiness is not created and we can go on in deep sleep, we never see any good in the other. If someone comes and tells you that such and such a person has attained to the state of nonattachment, you will say, "No, he has not." You will try to find dozens of reasons to prove that he has not. This is part of a deep-seated conspiracy of our minds. It is necessary to become aware of this. The concern is not with the other at all.

A friend has been coming to me the last three days. He wanted a lot of time with me. He had been saying, "Yes, I want to take sannyas but before that I have a few very important questions to ask." I thought maybe he had some important questions, but not one question was important or necessary. The questions were about others, not about himself. He was here to take sannyas, and the questions were about others: "Was Krishna really enlightened? If he was, why have the Jainas put him in hell?"

The Jainas have put Krishna in hell in their scriptures because they have their own definition of nonattachment and Krishna does not fit into it. That one should renounce everything and escape from the world is their definition, and Krishna does not renounce anything to go anywhere. This is the problem.

But Krishna's own definition is that if you are renouncing and running away, you are not yet a nonattached person. This is why the Hindus have not mentioned Mahavira's name anywhere in their scriptures. He was not considered worth mentioning. But at least the Jainas have shown some love towards Krishna, putting him in hell! The Hindus did not even mention Mahavira's name. They did not even consider him worth talking about. Even in putting somebody in hell one is giving him some consideration. The Jainas could not ignore Krishna completely; some statement about him had to be made, some space for him had to be allotted – even if it is hell, it does not matter. The Hindus have not cared enough to put Mahavira even into hell, they simply dropped the matter. But if anyone clings to Krishna's definition of nonattachment, difficulty arises.

Remember, all definitions are for you, the seeker, so that you go on continually searching within yourself, so that there is a criterion, a touchstone in hand that you may go on testing yourself. But we are all very clever, we go on testing others with that touchstone. It has nothing to do with others; if Krishna is in hell, it is his business. What does anybody else have to do with it? You can be ready to take Krishna's place in hell and allow him to go free. If Krishna is liberated, it does not create your liberation. All your thinking about others is meaningless.

Another friend came and asked me that if a meeting between me and Krishnamurti was arranged, was I ready to meet him? This is a matter between me and Krishnamurti. What has this person to do with it? Then he also asked, "If a meeting of you two happens at all, who will initiate the greetings?" Now, this too is a matter between me and Krishnamurti.

Our minds are busy thinking about others and not thinking about ourselves at all. A seeker must decide that all thinking about others is useless, and "Nothing except me and my inner growth concerns me; all else is meaningless." Do not get entangled in questions arising out of your curiosity about others. It will not help you at all in changing your life.

Remember, these definitions are meant for you. The Upanishad has given you these measuring rods so that you may go on weighing yourself inside, so that you may not have any difficulty on the inner journey. Keep watching within yourself. As long as any desire arises within on seeing things, understand that nonattachment has not yet been attained. Direct all your energies toward nonattachment. We are slowly going to discuss these efforts.

When no I-ness arises,
know this as the ultimate in knowing.

These seers of the Upanishads are very strange people. They do not say that when you have seen God, know this as the ultimate knowing. They have maintained that even the seeing of God is not the limit of knowing; that when all your chakras have opened up, the kundalini has awakened and the thousand-petaled lotus has bloomed, know this as the limit of knowing. No, they don't say that. Nor do they say that when you have crossed all the seven heavens – and goodness only knows how many kinds of such calculations are prevalent – or when you have completed the journey of all the fourteen realms and entered the *sach khand*, the realm of truth.... No, the Upanishads say: these things have nothing to do with the matter; the only criterion is that I-ness does not arise.

Even kundalini creates arousal of the ego. The seeker feels that now he is not an ordinary person, his kundalini has arisen. Someone feels that his third eye center has awakened, he is able to see the light; now he is no ordinary person. Someone feels that his heart center is awakened, the blue diamond has appeared in the heart, the blue flame has been seen; now he is liberated, now there is no world for him.

Remember, whatever creates 'I' is still out of ignorance, no matter what beautiful names you go on giving it. The Upanishad says, as long as the 'I' is created – no matter what the cause – as long as one feels "I have become something," until then knowing has not ripened. No flowers have yet blossomed, no explosion has yet taken place.

The only criterion given is that no 'I' is created. So it is also possible that a person sitting in his shop whose kundalini has not awakened, who has not seen the blue light, who has not traveled to the realms of truth – who has done nothing, who is simply working in his shop but whose ego does not arise – has reached to the ultimate state in knowing. Even a great yogi standing on a high crest of the Himalayas, if his ego is also high like a peak of the Himalayas, if he thinks that only he has arrived and no one else, if he thinks that only he has achieved and no one else, then understand that knowing has not yet happened to him.

There is only one touchstone – that a state is attained inside where nothing whatsoever creates any ego. Then anything may go on happening – even if God himself comes the feeling will not arise: "How lucky I am, I have achieved even God! See, there is

God standing before me and I am seeing him."

When the very disposition of 'I' does not arise inside, then know it as the ultimate state in knowing. Keep watching within you, otherwise everything creates conceit – everything. Mind is very clever, it derives ego from anything. It is so clever that it can derive ego even from humility, and a person starts saying, "No one is more humble than I am. There is no one more humble than I." But that "No one more than I" still remains. It may be anything – it may be wealth, it may be prestige, it may be power, it may be knowledge, it may be liberation, it may be humility, but that "No one more than I"...that 'I' goes on surviving.

So go on searching within, checking within, otherwise even the spiritual search can turn into a worldly search. The difference between the spiritual search and the worldly search is not that of things but of ego. One person accumulates a large amount of wealth in the world, it strengthens his ego. Another person renounces all the wealth and strengthens his ego by renunciation. Both are on a worldly trip.

The spiritual journey begins with the dropping of the ego. There is only one renunciation worth carrying out and that is the renunciation of 'I'. All other renunciations are useless, because they too only inflate your 'I'.

Just yesterday one man came to see me. He told me, "I have not taken any food grains for fourteen years." And his pride was worth seeing. The amount of conceit that has been generated in him through not taking food grains is not possible even through the taking of food grains. This non-taking of food grains has turned into a poison. What conceit he has! He has not eaten food grains for fourteen years – conceit is bound to arise. Now who are you obliging by not taking food grains? Don't eat them if you don't want to. But he is going around declaring, "For fourteen years I have not taken food grains" – now this has become his ego. Even food grains don't fill the ego as much as this "No food grains" is filling it!

People come to me and say, "I have taken only milk for years."

For them this seems to be becoming a poison. They are not walking on earth, because they are only drinking milk! What real difference are you bringing through this? What great revolution is happening through this only drinking of milk? But there are reasons. Such people feel that they are doing something special – which others are not doing. But the moment one thinks of being special the ego begins building up – no matter what that special thing may be related to. You can create a speciality for yourself about anything, it only creates ego.

What is the meaning of being a seeker? Being a seeker means that one stops creating any speciality about oneself from within and slowly, slowly becomes a nobody. Then slowly, slowly you become so ordinary from within yourself that the feeling does not even arise that you are something, and you become a nothing. The day a seeker becomes no-thing, the ultimate state in knowledge has been arrived at – not through accumulation of knowledge but by dropping the ego, not through accumulation of information but by the death of the 'I'.

> *When the dissolved desires do not arise again,*
> *this is the ultimate in relaxedness,*
> *and such a sthitpragya, a seeker*
> *stable in wisdom, ever remains in bliss.*

When the dissolved desires do not arise again.... Many a time the desires dissolve, but they are just suspended for a while and return again and again. One day it feels that your mind has become completely peaceful, but the next day it again becomes restless. One day it feels that you are in great bliss, but the next day you are again being drowned in miseries.

There are certain laws of the mind which must be understood. One law is that the mind never remains constantly the same; change is its nature. So the peace which comes and goes, understand well that it is not spiritual peace, it is only of the mind. A bliss that is attained and then lost, understand well that it is not the spiritual bliss, it is of the mind. Anything that comes and goes is of the mind, but something that comes once and remains forever, which comes and settles and cannot go away by any means whatsoever, which cannot be removed even by effort....

Remember this difference. If your peace is the peace of the mind, however much you may try it will not remain for long, it will change. And if the spiritual peace comes, however much you may try to destroy it you will not be able to do so, it will remain there.

Constancy cannot be added to the mind even with effort, and in the soul it cannot be disrupted even with effort.

So if some desires stop arising, don't be in haste; do not conclude that you have arrived. Just wait and see if they do not arise again. If they do arise again, understand that everything is still going on on the mental level. And what is the value of the mental peace? That will come and go and restlessness will again follow.

With the mind, in every moment there is movement towards the opposite. When you are restless the mind starts moving towards peace, and when you are in peace the mind starts moving towards restlessness. Mind is duality, hence the opposite will always be there and it will keep moving.

How will you know that what is happening is of the mind? There is one basic difference. When the peace is of the mind and it has not reached to the deeper layers within, then immediately on becoming peaceful a desire will arise that this peace should continue to remain, that it should not go away. If this desire arises, take it that it was all mental, because the fear of losing is that of the mind. If peace comes and no fear of losing it follows, understand that it does not belong to the mind.

The second thing: mind gets bored with everything – *everything*. It gets bored not only with unhappiness, but also with happiness. This is another law of the mind, that it becomes bored with everything that is stable. If you are unhappy, it becomes bored with that and wants happiness. What you do not know is that it is the law of the mind that if it gets happiness, it gets bored with happiness too, and then it starts looking for unhappiness.

I see this constantly, when so many people are here doing the meditations: even if happiness settles with them for some days they start getting uneasy; peace stays with them for a few days and they start getting uneasy, because even that creates boredom.

Mind gets bored with everything. Mind is always asking for the new, and all the trouble arises out of the demand for the new. When you are beyond the mind there is no demand for the new, there is no feeling of boredom with the old; there is so much oneness with what is, that there is no demand for anything other than that.

The sutra says: *When the dissolved desires do not arise again, this is the ultimate in relaxedness.* Only then can you accept that you have attained to rest. If desires keep on arising again and again, understand that it has all been a trap of the mind. Why? Why is it necessary to understand this? – because our relations with the mind are so deep that we take the peace of the mind itself as *our* peace. That brings great suffering – because it disappears.

What can we do? It is helpful to use the principle of witnessing in this connection. Thereby a way of going beyond the mind is created and the ultimate relaxedness is attained. And what are we normally doing? When the mind becomes restless we want to get away from it, and when the mind becomes peaceful we want to cling to it. We want to save the peace and remove the restlessness. When the mind is miserable we want to get rid of it; when the mind is in happiness we embrace it and want to keep it with us. By continually looking for the opposite you will never be able to be free of the mind, because that is the very function of the mind: to be rid of the unhappiness, to catch hold of the happiness.

The way to be free of the mind is to remain a witness when the mind is giving you happiness, and do not try to hold onto it. For example, you are meditating here; suddenly, sometimes in meditation, a stream of peacefulness will arrive. Then don't just embrace it; keep watching it, standing at a distance: "Peace is happening and I am a witness." When a fountain of bliss rises up in some moment and pervades every fiber from within, then keep watching that too from a distance; don't hold onto it with your full force, that "Alright, now liberation has come." No, keep watching that too as a witness: "Bliss is happening and I will not catch hold of it."

The interesting thing is that one who does not hold onto happiness, his unhappiness also vanishes; one who does not hold onto peace, his restlessness vanishes forever. It is in the holding onto peace that the seeds of peacelessness are sown, and in holding onto happiness is the birth of unhappiness. Simply don't cling! Clinging is the mind. Do not cling to anything. The moment your fist is open you will be beyond the mind and you will enter where desires do not arise anymore – their ultimate dissolution happens. This ultimate dissolution has been called here *uparati,* relaxedness.

Such a sthitpragya yati, a seeker
stable in wisdom, ever remains in bliss.

Sthitpragya is a very beautiful word. Its meaning is: one whose wisdom has become stable in himself, one whose wisdom has become self-contained, one whose consciousness does not leave him and move anywhere else, one whose consciousness has become stabilized. Such a seeker, such a sannyasin, ever attains to bliss.

All dualities are created by the mind: happiness and unhappiness, peace and peacelessness, good and bad, birth and death. The moment mind recedes there is nonduality, bliss. There is no opposite word for bliss; it is beyond duality. And the seeker who is beyond duality ever attains to bliss.

We have a great problem: our problem is that we want to attain bliss very much, and hearing this kind of thing our greed is stirred up. If perpetual bliss can be had, then we too want to have it; if somebody can show us the way, we certainly want to have eternal bliss. But remember, this definition is only indicative of a certain state. If it gives birth to desire in you, you will never be able to attain to this state. Try to understand the difference well.

A friend came to me saying, "I want liberation soon; I want to have deep meditation, samadhi, soon." I told him that the more haste you create the more delayed you will be, because a hasty mind cannot become peaceful. It is the haste itself which is the restlessness. And we all know what sort of problems arise when we are in a hurry.

We have to catch a train and so we are in a hurry. Now those things which usually could have been done in two minutes take five minutes. The buttons on the coat get wrongly done up. You undo them again, you do them up again. You pick up your spectacles, they slip out of your hands and break. You are trying to lock your suitcase, the key keeps missing the keyhole. It's the hurry.... Haste always makes waste, because in haste your mind is very much topsy-turvy and you are bound to make mistakes. And if haste creates delay in small matters, it will create enormous delays in matters pertaining to the journey to the ultimate.

I told that friend, "Do not be in a hurry, otherwise things will be delayed. In this area, if you stay with the attitude that whenever it may happen you are willing, there is no hurry – then probably it will happen early."

He said, "Oh, is it so? So if I am ready to wait forever, that will make it happen earlier?"

If you are ready to wait it will happen fast, but that fastness is the outcome of a waiting mind. If you say you will wait so that it can happen quickly, it means you are not waiting at all, and it will never happen quickly. How can an awaiting emanate from the desire for haste?

This is an everyday problem. We all feel that we want bliss, so how can we get it? This thought and desire, "How to get bliss?" is the very obstacle to bliss. Bliss is an outcome. Please do not make it a desire – it will happen on its own. Just go on traveling silently and quietly – it will happen on its own.

Thus a great difficulty can arise, that on the reading of this sutra many people will become full of the desire for bliss. So many people down the centuries have become full of desire after reading such sutras, and these sutras are for freedom from desire. Instead a new desire catches hold of you: How to achieve bliss? How to become a sthitpragya, the one stable in wisdom? How to achieve relaxedness? How to achieve nonattachment? And then people go on running about with such desires birth after birth and this event does not happen in their life at all. Then they start wondering whether it could be that these talks are all lies, because they had been told that bliss will happen and so far it has not happened.

I would like to tell you one more thing in connection with this. We see that with each passing day the world goes on becoming more and more irreligious; people are losing their trust in religion. Do you know the reason for this? The reason is given here in this sutra.

Every one of you has already entertained the desire in many lives to achieve bliss, enlightenment, God; but you have neither achieved bliss, nor enlightenment, nor God. The result it was bound to bring is there. The result is that you have lost all faith in such sutras and now you feel that these are things that can never be achieved.

Man has known these sutras for the last ten thousand years. During these ten thousand years almost all the human beings that are now on the earth have gone through the desire for this bliss. Some were near Buddha, some were near Krishna, some were near Jesus, some were near Mohammed, and all have made efforts to achieve it; sometimes doing meditation, sometimes doing yoga, sometimes practicing tantra, sometimes using a mantra, and so on and so forth. You have done everything.

When I look at people on their inner plane, I have not found a single person so far who has not strived to do such things in some lifetime or other. Every person has traveled on the path of seeking – but full of desires. Because of those desires all endeavors have become fruitless, and this failure has become embedded deep in your consciousness. This is the reason why irreligiousness seems to be increasing in the whole world, because for most people religion has failed.

You do not even remember, but you have made religion a failure within you. And you are the cause of that, because you have committed a mistake by desiring something which cannot be desired.

So this is the outcome. But if you move on the spiritual path these things will happen, you don't have to bother about them. Neither you have to think about them, nor desire them, nor make haste for them to happen. It is due to that haste that all goes topsy-turvy.

Irreligiousness will go on increasing in this world as long as we form desires even for religiousness. And you are not new, nobody is new on this earth. Everybody is old and ancient. And all have trodden so many roads and paths, and having met with no success they have lost all hope. That despondency has settled deep into your being. The greatest difficulty today is to break that despondency. And if someone wants to break this despondency, the only feasible method seems to be that of exciting your desires once again very intensely and telling you that this will deliver the goods – only then will you gather some courage. But that very thing, the arousal of the desire, is the root cause of all the troubles in the first place.

Buddha has made a unique experiment. In his time also the conditions were the same as they have become today. They always become like this. Whenever people like Buddha or Mahavira are born in this world a sort of shadow-period follows their death for thousands of years. It is bound to be so. When a person like Buddha or Krishna is born, seeing him, being in his presence, in his milieu, thousands of people become full of desire for religion and they feel that it is possible also for them. A confidence arises seeing Buddha: "If it can happen to him, it can also happen to me." And if they make the mistake of turning it into a desire, then these people are tortured by that desire and, just because of that desire, they become irreligious for thousands of years afterwards.

Just understand the condition. Bliss can be attained, but do not make it a goal. Ultimate peace is possible, but do not make that a goal. That is not the goal. Make knowledge and understanding your goal, make meditation your goal, make stability within your goal, make stopping still and going within yourself a goal – and the bliss will follow as an outcome, it just naturally follows. Do not do the reverse, do not make bliss the goal. One who makes bliss the goal will simply fall into difficulty.

Outcomes are outcomes and not goals.

Let us understand it by taking an illustration from day-to-day life. You play a game – football, hockey, tennis or anything – and you find great pleasure in it. Now you are telling this to someone, that while playing these games you have great pleasure. That person says, "I also want pleasure. I shall come tomorrow and see if I can get pleasure." This man comes to play and keeps a constant watch to see whether pleasure is coming yet or not. Because of this desire for pleasure, the constant thought about whether or not pleasure is coming, he will not be able to get absorbed in the play. The play will become secondary and pleasure will become the primary concern. While playing he will be continuously searching within to see whether there is any pleasure. He will feel that he is not having any pleasure, and that pleasure should have been experienced by now if there was any to be had in the game. This man will only be exhausted by the end of the game and complain, "There is no pleasure here. What is this nonsense?"

One who goes to seek pleasure in the game will not only not get the pleasure but he will also spoil the game. Pleasure is a by-product. If you become fully absorbed in the game the pleasure happens. If the idea of pleasure dominates your mind and you are unable to be absorbed in the game, how can pleasure happen? Your whole life is like that. In life everything significant is a by-product. Whatsoever is significant happens quietly. Whatsoever is a deep experience is not to be turned into the goal. In the very making a goal of it, the doors close.

Bliss happens effortlessly, bliss is a spontaneous happening. If someone sits consciously to try to receive it, in that very conscious sitting so much tension is generated that the doors close; the tension becomes a barrier and bliss does not happen.

Keep this sutra in mind – this is a dangerous sutra. This sutra is present in all the scriptures. And all those who have studied the scriptures have had their desire aroused and they go out in search of how to gain liberation. No, self-realization cannot be grabbed: it is attained through dissolving. How to attain bliss? No, bliss is not attained that way. Do something in which you are drowned so deeply that neither you are remembered nor bliss is remembered. And on suddenly waking up it is found that only bliss has remained; that what you were searching for and not finding even after strenuous search, has been found.

This is very clearly shown in Buddha's life. Buddha was relentlessly striving for six years in order to achieve self-realization, to achieve peace, to achieve truth. But he could not. He searched at the feet of all the masters; even the masters became weary of him because he was really a seeker, a determined one. His was the obstinacy of a *kshatriya*, a warrior, for reaching the goal; his was the ego of a kshatriya. It was a challenge to him: How can a thing be and still not be possible to attain? A kshatriya never believes that anything is impossible – that is what is meant by being a kshatriya.

So to whichever master he went, they were all in great difficulty, because whatever the master would ask him to do, he would do it immediately. Howsoever difficult it may be, howsoever long he may have to stand in the hot sun or in the pouring rains, howsoever many fasts have to be performed – whatsoever was required of him he at once did it to the satisfaction of his masters, and nothing would happen. The masters became tired. They would say, "What more can we do?"

A so-called master is never tired of an ordinary disciple because an ordinary disciple never does totally what he has been asked to do. Hence such a situation never arises that the master may have to say, "Now what can we do? Whatsoever we could do we have done." When one has a disciple like Buddha great difficulty arises, because anything that the master asked, Buddha would accomplish. Even the master could not find any fault with it. And yet nothing was happening. In the end the master would say, "Whatsoever I could do, whatsoever I could show, I have shown. Now I myself don't know beyond this; now you will have to move on to somewhere else."

All the masters were tired of Buddha. And Buddha was really obstinate. For six years he did everything that anybody asked –

right or wrong, rational or irrational – and with great sincerity. Not even one master could say that it was not happening because he was not doing what he was asked to do. He was doing everything so fully and so well that the masters themselves asked for forgiveness and said, "If something more happens to you, inform us also, because we have told everything to you that we know."

Nothing did happen, however. Not that what they preached to Buddha had not happened to those masters. No, it had happened to them through that understanding. And Buddha was exactly following the same techniques his masters had pursued and attained with. So the master was also at a loss that this Buddha was following the same technique, even more accurately than he had – "And even I had not done it with so much sincerity. Why then is it not happening to him?"

But there was a reason. It might have happened to the master because he had done the technique without any expectation or preconceptions. Buddha's expectation was intense. He was doing it, but his eyes were set on the goal: when would the truth, the bliss, the self-realization be achieved? So he was certainly following all the techniques fully, but that goal-orientation was the obstacle.

Eventually Buddha also became tired. After six years, one day he left off doing everything. The world he had already left earlier; now he left sannyas also. He had left all sorts of pleasures before and had wasted six years in practicing yoga; now he left that too. One night he decided that he would not do anything further and that he would not search any longer. He simply understood that nothing was going to be achieved.

He had reached the maximum tension of the search. His endeavor, the effort, had reached the extreme. So he dropped everything. That night he went to sleep under a tree. That was the first night in many lifetimes that Buddha had slept in such a way as if nothing existed to be done the next morning. And there really was nothing left to be done. He had already left his kingdom, his family and any planning about the world; he had begun another plan of life, and that too had failed. Now there was nothing to do. If he woke up tomorrow morning, good; if he did not wake up, that too would be good. If he lived on, it made no difference; if he died, it made no difference – all was the same. There was absolutely nothing left to be done tomorrow morning, there simply was no meaning in tomorrow for him any longer.

And when someone goes to sleep at night in such a way that there is no plan for tomorrow, samadhi happens. *Sushupti*, the deep sleep, becomes samadhi. There was no desire for tomorrow, there were no goals remaining, there was nothing left to be achieved, there was nowhere to go. The question had been, "What will I do if I am here in the morning?" Up to now there was only doing and doing and doing, but now there was nothing to be done at all. Buddha slept that night so free of any purpose that there was no idea what he would do if he woke up in the morning. The sun would rise, the birds would sing, but what would he do? And there was a void as the answer.

When there are no goals the future dies, time becomes meaningless. When there are no goals all plans are shattered to pieces and the movement of the mind stops. For the movement of the mind plans are necessary, goals are necessary; for the movement of the mind something to achieve is necessary, a future, some time is necessary. And all these had vanished.

Buddha went to sleep that night as if he were a person that has died while alive. He was alive, yet death had happened. In the morning around 5 a.m. his eyes opened. Buddha has said, "I did not open my eyes." What would he do by opening the eyes? There remained nothing to be seen, nor anything to be heard, nor anything to be attained; there was no reason to open the eyes. Hence Buddha said, "I did not open the eyes, they opened on their own. They were tired of remaining closed; they had been closed the whole night and now the resting was complete and the eyelids opened on their own." Inside him was a void.

When there is no future, the inside turns into a void. In such a void Buddha saw the last morning star setting, and in that seeing he became enlightened. Along with that disappearing star disappeared the whole past of Buddha. Along with that disappearing star the whole journey, the whole search disappeared.

Buddha has said, "For the first time I saw a star purposelessly setting in the sky – it did not require a purpose." There was no purpose in it. And seeing was as fine as not seeing it would have been. There was no question of any choice either, this way or that – the eyes were open, so the star was seen. The star was setting, went on setting. "There the star went on setting, there the sky became empty of stars; here I was completely empty within, the meeting of two empty skies took place." Buddha has further said, "What I could not attain through incessant search was attained that night without any searching. What could not be attained by running after it was attained that night just sitting, just lying down. What could not be attained with effort was attained that night with restfulness."

But why did he attain at that time? Because bliss is the natural outcome of your being a void within.

When you run after bliss and by so doing are unable to become a void, the chase after bliss itself is the barrier; you are unable to become a void, hence its natural outcome does not take place.

> *He whose self is absorbed only in Brahman,*
> *the ultimate reality,*
> *remains desireless and actionless.*
> *When purified by its oneness with Brahman and*
> *drowned in this one single rapture,*
> *the activities of mind are choiceless and*
> *remain only as the consciousness;*
> *then it is called pragya, wisdom.*
> *He who always has such a pragya is called*
> *jivanamukta, the one liberated while living.*

Thus when the inner sky becomes one with the outer sky, when the inner emptiness merges with the outer emptiness, everything becomes desireless and actionless. Desires cannot arise without a thought: thought is disturbance of mind. Remember, a thought arises only because one wants to do something.

People come to me and tell me they are unable to be free of thoughts. You will not be free of thought; you have a desire to do something! And when you want to do something, how can you be free of thought? That desire to do something, that very plan, is thought. Even if you wish to be free of thoughts you won't be, because there will be thoughts engaged in planning it. People tell me that they sit and try hard to become thoughtless. But this planning to be thoughtless in itself is an opportunity for thinking. So the mind goes on thinking, "How to become thoughtless? Up to now you have not become thoughtless. Will it ever be possible for you to be thoughtless? When?"

Remember, as long as there is any desire – for heaven, for self-realization, for meeting God – thoughts will continue. Thoughts are not at fault. All that is meant by thought is that whatever you desire, your mind thinks about how to achieve it. As long as there is anything left to be achieved, thoughts will continue. The day you are willing to accept the fact that, "I don't want to achieve anything, not even desirelessness," suddenly you will find that the thoughts have started to disappear. They are not needed anymore.

When everything within becomes a void, when there are no plans, when nothing remains to be achieved and there remains nowhere to go, when all running about becomes meaningless and the consciousness settles down on the side of the road...dropping all concern for the goal, the goal has been attained.

> *He whose self is absorbed only in Brahman,*
> *the ultimate reality,*
> *remains desireless and actionless.*

Such a person remains desireless and actionless. Nothing arises within him; his mirror is empty, there are no images upon it. And he remains actionless. There remains no impulse to do anything. It does not mean that he goes on lying down like a corpse.

No, actions do happen, but there is no plan for them. Understand this difference rightly.

I came here, I am to speak on this sutra of the Upanishad. If I come after planning it, thinking about what is to be said, what is not to be said, then there will be movement of thoughts in the mind, it will be disturbed. Mind will go on working. But if I just come, see the sutra and begin to speak, and remain content with whatever happens to come out of my mouth, then the act of my speaking is not an act. If I leave after speaking and on the way I feel that what I spoke was not good, that it would have been better had I said this or that, or it would have been better had I not said this or that, then this is just pollution. But if the moment I finish speaking nothing remains within me regarding what I had spoken, no current of thought, then this is nonaction.

I have heard about Abraham Lincoln. He was returning home one night with his wife after delivering a speech. When he arrived home his children asked him, "How was the speech?" Lincoln said, "Which speech? The one that I had prepared prior to delivering it or the one that I actually delivered, or the one that I thought I should have delivered after having actually delivered it? Which one are you asking about? Three I have delivered so far – one that I was rehearsing within my mind before going there, the second that I actually delivered, and the third that I kept repenting afterwards that I should have said this and that and I forgot to say this, etcetera."

Now this speech is an act. The act is not in delivering the speech, it is in its pre-planning. So if the mind decides in advance, or if the mind thinks about it afterwards, it is pollution of the mind. If the act simply takes place – without any pre-planning or afterthoughts – then this action has come out of nonaction.

Action will continue. Buddha becomes a buddha, yet the action will continue – but with a difference. Krishna becomes a Krishna, the action will continue – but with a difference.

The Gita is valuable in this very respect, that whatever Krishna has said in it is totally spontaneous. Nobody goes to a battlefield prepared to give a discourse in the first place. Krishna would never have even thought, he would never have even imagined that he would be required to do this at the battlefield. It cannot be, even in his wildest imagination. There certainly can be no pre-planning about it. Suddenly, unexpectedly, accidentally, a happening, and Krishna's fountain spurted out.

This is not a speech, this is a speech coming out of non-speech. This is not an action, this is an action born out of nonaction. This is why the Gita became so valuable. Because it was so accidental, it became so valuable. There are many scriptures in the world, but none has had such an accidental birth as the Gita.

It is a battlefield, the calls for the deadly battle have already been given by blowing the conch shells; the warriors are ready to attack and kill or be killed...a religious dialogue there? There appears to be no relevance. Had the Gita happened in an ashram, a hermitage, or in the commune of a master, that would have made sense. But because it is so spontaneous it went deep into the very core of India. It is born out of nonaction, it is born without any plans. This is why we called it Bhagavadgita, Song of the Divine. In it there is no human planning. In it Krishna is simply not behaving like a human being. It is a message emanating from the divine.

When all actions are born out of one's inner nonaction, and the thoughts are arising out of one's thoughtlessness, and the words are born out of one's silence, such a person is called jivanamukta – one who is liberated while living.

In India there is the concept of two types of liberation. One type of liberated one is a jivanamukta, one who is free while living. The other liberated one is the one who is liberated at the time of his death. Both types of liberation do happen. A person goes on searching and searching his whole life – and then, just as I talked of with Buddha, he seeks and seeks and is one day tired of the seeking, and it happens.

Sometimes it happens that a person seeks his whole life – not just six years like Buddha but his whole life – and does not get tired.

He goes on seeking and seeking, and it is only when his death arrives that he realizes that all the seeking has been futile and he has attained nothing – and thus in the moment of death all his search relaxes. If just prior to death all the seeking relaxes and all the plans stop and no future remains, then what happened to Buddha under the *bodhi* tree – that same happens under the tree of death. Then death and liberation happen simultaneously, because death can relax one very deeply.

If all your searching has gone in vain, if it has become your firm experience that all searching is useless, that you have not attained anything anywhere – neither in the worldly life nor in the spiritual endeavor – nothing has been achieved…. Only then, if this becomes absolutely clear to you and there remains no demand of any kind for the future that you still want to achieve something…only then, when not even the feeling remains that if you do not die now and you live for a few more days that you may do something further, but instead you accept the approaching death….

If everything is futile, man accepts death. Just as Buddha slept that night – not even the question remained about what he would do next morning. Similarly, if someone dies to the future at the moment of death without thinking, "Now I am dying and certain things have remained incomplete. There was something to be completed but it could not be completed; should I get a couple more days I may complete it…." When no such feelings remain and the death descends naturally, the way evening descends and man goes to sleep, then such a death also becomes liberation. Such a person is called the liberated one.

But this happening sometimes takes place during life and the person survives even after liberation. This survival depends on other factors.

When you are born, your body has a certain in-built span of years – seventy years, eighty years. Now if this happening of liberation takes place at the age of forty years, the body is bound to complete those remaining forty years. You may have died at the age of forty, but the body will die only after completing eighty years. You as an ego are no more at the age of forty, but the body will last for forty more years. That is its own inbuilt plan; it has its own arrangements of its atoms. At the time of birth the body arrived with its own capacity to last for eighty years, and it will last for that long.

So Buddha and Mahavira died at the age of forty, but their bodies continued for forty more years. All the running within stopped, but the body continued to work. It is just like your wristwatch was wound up to run seven days and then you went to some jungle, got lost, fell down and died; but your wristwatch will continue to work for seven more days. Your watch was wound for seven days and your death makes no difference to it; it goes on running for seven days – tick, tick, tick.... Your body is a machine. You may attain to the ultimate awakening today, you may have died today, but your body will go on ticking.

This state of the inner consciousness becoming as if it is not, and the ticking of the body continuing, is called jivanamukta, liberated while living.

> *When purified by its oneness with Brahman and*
> *drowned in this one single rapture,*
> *the activities of mind are choiceless and*
> *remain only as the consciousness,*
> *then it is called pragya, wisdom.*

When the intellect does not think about the other, does not think at all and becomes thoughtless, when all thoughts are dropped and only the capacity to think remains within, when the intellect does not associate itself with any objects and remains pure – like a solitary lamp burning in the void lighting nothing – for such a state of consciousness the Indian word is *pragya,* wisdom. Then you have really attained the true flame of knowledge. The one in whom such a wisdom is always aflame is a jivanamukta, the liberated while living.

> *One who has no I-ness for his body and the senses,*

and no my-ness for the other things, is a jivanamukta,
the one liberated while living.

These feelings will certainly drop. 'Mine', 'I' – these have dropped long ago. It is at the dropping of the ego that enlightenment has happened. To such a person there is no 'I' or 'mine' associated with anything. Such a consciousness cannot even claim that "I am soul." He does not attach any sense of 'I' to anything; just the 'am-ness' remains. We use the expression 'I am'; such a person uses the expression 'am'. His 'I' drops, only the state of pure 'am-ness' remains.

This 'am-ness' has been called the state of jivanamukta. When the 'I' dies and only the 'am-ness' remains, you have attained to self-realization while living.

If our effort in this direction is free of desire, this happening can take place right now. If desire is still present, it takes time.

Enough for today.

SWEET FRUITS

CHAPTER 13

One who never knows any difference through
intellect between jiva, the embodied soul,
and Brahman, or between Brahman and nature,
the creation, is called a jivanamukta,
the one who is liberated while living.
Respected by the good or insulted by the wicked,
one who ever remains in equanimity
is called a jivanamukta.

✳

For the one who has known the Brahman essence,
this world no longer remains the same as before. If it
is not so, he has not known the Brahman state of
being and is still an extrovert.

✳

As far as happiness etcetera are experienced,
it is called prarabdha,
accumulated past action-impressions;
because the arising of any fruits is from actions in
the past. There is no fruit anywhere without action.
Just as the dream activity ceases upon waking,
similarly, past actions accumulated over billions
of eons dissolve instantly upon one's knowing:
"I am Brahman."

few more indications about the inner state of a *jivanamukta*, the one liberated while living. The jivanamukta is one who has known death while still living. As it is, death is known by all, but only at the time of dying. That too cannot be called the knowing of death because just in the moment of dying the mind becomes unconscious. So we never know our own death, we always know only the death of others. You have only seen others dying, you have never seen yourself dying. Thus even our knowledge about death is borrowed. When someone else dies what do we learn from this? We know that he has lost his speech, his eyes cannot see, his pulse has ceased, and that his heart has stopped. We just know that the body mechanism has ceased to work, but we do not know anything about what happened to the one that was hidden behind the body mechanism, or whether there really was anything hidden behind or not, or whether that hidden being is saved or not.

Death happens within, and all we are able to see is its symptoms on the outside. How can one know death by seeing others dying? We too have died many times, but we have never been able to see ourselves dying because we had become unconscious before dying.

So you may see many persons dying, but you never come to believe that you too are going to die. Have you ever believed that you too will die? Many people may start dying every day, the whole cemetery may become full of them; some epidemic may spread and you will see dead bodies everywhere – still one always feels that only others are dying. You never feel within that you are also going to die. Even if such an awareness of death comes it remains only on the surface, it never enters deep within. Why? Because we have never seen our own death, we have no experience of it, we have no remembrance of death. However much we may think backwards in the past we never come to find that we have died before. So something that has never happened in the past, how can it happen in the future?

All the calculations of mind are based on the past. Even when the mind thinks of the future it thinks only in the language of the past. What has happened yesterday, that alone can happen tomorrow – with a little difference here and there. But what has never happened before, how can that happen tomorrow? This is why the mind is never able to believe in death. And when death in fact happens the mind is already unconscious.

Thus the two great experiences of life, birth and death, we never experience. We take birth and we die, and if we are unable to experience these two great events of birth and death then how can we experience and what can we experience of the life that flows in between the two? One who is unable to know the beginning of life, one who is unable to know the end of life, how can he ever know the middle of life?

The stream that flows between birth and death is life. Neither we know the beginning nor the end; the middle is bound to remain unknown. There may be some hazy dim knowing – like something heard from a faraway distance, or like a dream that was seen. But we have no direct contact with life.

The meaning of jivanamukta is a person who has known death during life by waking up, by becoming conscious.

This word jivanamukta is wonderful. It has many different meanings. One meaning can be: one who is liberated during life. Another meaning can be: one who is liberated from life. The second meaning is deeper. Actually the first meaning is useful only after the second meaning is known. Only the one who is liberated from life can be liberated in life.

Who will be liberated from life?

Only he can be liberated from life who has known that the whole life is a process of death; one who has seen that that which we call life is only a long march towards death.

After birth we do not do anything else except die. We may be doing anything – the march towards death continues each moment. Evening comes after the morning and we have died for twelve more hours. Then morning will come again after this evening and we will have died for twelve more hours. Life goes on exhausting itself drop by drop; time goes on emptying itself away.

So what we call life is actually a long process of dying. After birth, whatsoever one may be doing, one is definitely doing one thing – that is dying, continuing to die. No sooner are you born than you have begun to die. In the very first breath taken by a child the arrangement for his last breath has been made. Now there is no way of avoiding death. One who is born will die sooner or later; the difference may be of time, but death is certain.

One who has seen life as a long process of death...I say has seen, not has understood. You can also understand, "So this is how it is?" – that you can also do. But by that you will not be a jivanamukta. No, one who sees, one who becomes a witness to it, is one who has seen that every moment he is dying.

One thing we never realize is that "I will die"; it is always the others who die. Secondly, even if we infer our death through the death of others, then too it is something that will happen in the future; for now it can be postponed. It is not happening now, today. Even a man lying on his death-bed does not think that his death is happening today, this moment. He too avoids, postpones – tomorrow. In avoiding we save ourselves. For us life is now and death is far away in time.

One who has seen that the whole of life is a process of death has also seen that death is not tomorrow but now, this very moment – "I am already dying in this very moment. How to see, how to realize this happening of my death this very moment?" If one is able to see, then one does not lust for life. Buddha has said that one who does not lust to live is a jivanamukta. One who does not demand that he should get more life, one who does not desire to live more, one who has no lust to live more, one who will accept death gracefully if it comes now, one who will not ask death for even one moment more – "Wait, let me tidy up matters" – one who is ever ready to live every moment, that person is a jivanamukta.

One whose lust to live is finished can be free from life. One who becomes free from life becomes a jivanamukta – then he is liberated while living. Then here and now he is with us but he is not like us. He too is sitting, rising, eating, drinking, walking, sleeping, but the very quality of all these activities is transformed. Doing everything as we do, he is still not doing what we do. This world as we see it remains the same but it looks different to him – his angle of perception is changed; the center in him that is seeing is changed; for him the whole world is transformed. The definition of and indications about such a liberation while living is in these aphorisms. We shall try to understand them one after the other.

One who never knows any difference through
intellect between jiva, the embodied soul,
and Brahman...

...Those few friends who are under the influence of coughing should leave from here immediately. Or else stop coughing and remain seated. But both things together won't do.

One who never knows any difference through
intellect between jiva, the embodied soul,
and Brahman, or between Brahman and nature,
the creation, is called a jivanamukta,
the one who is liberated while living.

The first characteristic: one who does not see through his intellect any difference between the soul that is hidden within oneself and the Brahman that is hidden within creation, is a jivanamukta.

There are two things in it. "No difference is seen through intellect." All differences are made by the intellect, the mind. The intellect is the mechanism which enables us to see things as different. Just as when we dip a stick in water the stick appears bent – pull it out of the water, and it looks straight again. Put it back in the water, it appears bent again. The stick does not become bent in water, it only appears bent because the path of the rays of light in the water and outside the water are different. In the medium of water the rays become bent and so the stick appears bent.

Dip any straight object in water and it will appear bent. The objects themselves do not become bent, they only appear bent. The interesting thing is that you are well aware that the objects do not actually bend – but still you see them as bent. You can make the experiment any number of times, the result will be the same. Put your hand into the water and you can feel that the object is still straight. And yet your hands and your eyes are giving contradictory information. The air medium and the water medium change the path of the light rays.

Let us understand it in another way. You may have seen a prism. If the sun's rays are passed through the prism the rays are divided into seven colors.

You may have seen a rainbow. That too is a play on the principle of the prism. What is really happening when you see a rainbow? The sun's rays are always coming towards the earth, but whenever there are tiny droplets of water in the atmosphere these droplets function as a prism and divide the sun's rays into seven colors and they are seen as a rainbow. A rainbow is nothing but the sun's rays passing through water droplets. There will be no rainbow if there is no sun in the sky or if there are no clouds and water droplets.

A prism, or drops of water, divide the sun's rays into seven colors; they are mediums. If you see the sun's rays passing through a water drop you will see seven colors. If you see it without water drops, it is white, it has no color. White is not a color, it is an absence of colors.

The mind, the intellect too is similar, it acts as a medium. As an object appears bent inside water and light passing through a prism divides itself into seven colors, the mind, the thoughts, are similarly a subtle medium. Whatsoever we recognize through it is split into two, a division is created.

Intellect creates division. If you look at anything through intellect...for example, when we look at light the mind divides it at once into two parts: darkness and light. In fact in existence there is no division between light and darkness; they are the progressive and regressive expansions of one reality. This is why some birds are able to see in darkness. If darkness was absolute darkness, the owl would not be able to see. It is only able to see because in darkness too is *some* light. It is only that our eyes are not able to catch that light and the owl's eyes can. The darkness is also subtle light.

If there is a very bright light our eyes cannot see it. Our eyes have a limited spectrum of seeing; they cannot see above it, they cannot see below it. Beyond these upper and lower limits there is darkness for our eyes. Have you ever noticed that if your eyes are suddenly confronted with a very bright light source everything goes dark before you? The eye is not able to see that much light.

So darkness is of two types. What we see as light is as far as the spectrum of our seeing capacity allows. Above that and below that there is darkness. If the capacity of our eyes is reduced the light becomes darkness; if the capacity of our eyes is increased the darkness becomes light. The blind man has no capacity at all to see, so everything is darkness; there is no light at all for him. But light and darkness are one in existence. It is because of our intellect that they appear as two.

Intellect divides everything into two. The way intellect looks at things, nothing can remain undivided. Intellect is analysis, intellect is discrimination, intellect is division. This is why birth and death appear as two to us, because of our seeing through the intellect; otherwise they are not two. Birth is a beginning, death is the end; they are two extremes of the same thing. We see happiness and unhappiness as two separate things; this is because of the intellect, otherwise they are not two. This is why happiness can turn into unhappiness and unhappiness can turn into happiness. What appears as happiness today, by tomorrow morning can become unhappiness. The morning is far away; what appears as happiness now can become unhappiness in the next moment.

This should be impossible. If happiness and unhappiness are two things, two separate things, then our happiness should never become unhappiness and our unhappiness can never become happiness.

But this change continues each moment. Now there is love, now it becomes hate. A moment ago there was attraction, now it becomes repulsion. A moment ago it was felt to be friendship, now it has become enmity. These are not two things, otherwise change from one to the other would be impossible. One who was alive a moment ago is dead now. So life and death cannot be two separate things, otherwise how can a living man be dead? How can life turn into death?

It is our error that we divide everything into two. Our very way of seeing is such that things are divided into two. When one puts this way of seeing aside, when one removes the mind from in front of one's eyes and looks at the world without the mind, all divisions disappear. The experience of nonduality, the experience of *vedanta* in essence, is the experience of those who have looked at the world putting their intellect aside. Then the world is no longer the world, it becomes God. Then what we saw as the embodied soul within us and God out there, they too remain as nothing but two ends of one and the same reality. That which I am here, inside, and that which is spread there all over, both become one: *Tattvamasi*, 'That art thou'.

You then experience that you are not only one of the ends of 'that'. "The same sky of this vast existence is also touching my hand here. The same expanse of air which is surrounding the whole earth is also entering me as my breath." The life-force of this whole existence is pulsating, and because of that all life is: the stars move and the sun rises and there is light from the moon, fruits come to the trees and the birds sing their songs, and man lives. "This life-force hidden within all – this great pulsation somewhere at the center of the universe and this tiny pulsation of my heart in my body, these must be the two ends of one and the same thing." They are not two.

But this can be experienced only when not seen through the intellect. It is very difficult to see keeping the mind aside, because we normally see only through the intellect. Our habit is well-entrenched. How will you see other than through the intellect? Whatsoever you see, a thought will arise.

Just stand near a flower. You have hardly seen the flower and your mind begins to prompt: "It is a roseflower, it is very beautiful! Notice how pleasant its fragrance is." You have not even properly seen the flower, the echo of it has not touched your being yet, and the intellect has started feeding information from its past experiences and their memories: it is a roseflower, it is fragrant and beautiful. The mind makes these statements and it has spread its curtain in between. The flower has remained outside, you have remained within, and a curtain of thoughts from your intellect has already been stretched in between. You now see the flower only from behind that curtain. All our seeing is like that.

So a great effort is necessary to transcend this intellect and to see directly. You are sitting near a flower: don't let the intellect come in between. See the flower directly, let not even a single thought arise that this is a roseflower, it is beautiful – let there be no word formation at all. Try it for a while, and sometimes you will have a momentary glimpse of a situation wherein you will be on one side, the flower will be on the other side, and between the two there will be no thought for a moment. Then you will be able to see a world in that flower which you have never known before.

Tennyson has said, "If one can see even one flower fully, he has seen the whole world. Nothing more remains to be seen." It is so, because the whole world is contained in one flower. What we call tiny is the imitation of the vast. What we call micro is nothing but a smaller form of the macro.

Just as the whole sky may be reflected in a small mirror, just as the millions of stars in the sky may flash through a human eye, the whole universe can be seen in a small flower. However this is possible only when your intellect is not standing in between.

Go on practicing it. You are sitting leisurely, the birds are singing: do not let the mind interfere – just be the ear, listen and don't think. In the beginning it will be very difficult because of habits; otherwise there is no reason for any difficulty. But slowly, slowly glimpses will happen. One day the bird will go on singing, your intellect will have no say; you will go on listening and a direct relationship between you and the bird will be established, without any medium. Then you will be very surprised; then it will be difficult for you to decide whether you are singing or the bird is singing, whether you are listening or the bird is listening.

The moment your intellect has moved away from being in between, you and the song of the bird become the two ends of one and the same thing. The throat of the bird is one end and your ear is the other, and the song becomes the bridging link. The flower that is blossoming there and your heart that is within, your consciousness that is within, they become part of one and the same phenomenon, and the vibrations that are running between the two become the bridge joining them.

Then one does not feel that the flower is blossoming there at a distance and you are seeing it standing here at a distance, then one feels that "I am blossoming in the flower and the flower is standing and seeing from within me." But this too you do not feel in that very moment, you feel it only when you have come out of that moment. In that moment even this much is not noticed because the entity who notices, thinks and contemplates – the mind – has been put aside. Then the experience in each moment becomes the experience of the Brahman, the ultimate reality.

Somebody asks Bokoju, "What is your experience of God?" Bokoju says, "God? I know nothing of God."

"What are you doing, what is your spiritual discipline?" asks the inquirer.

Bokoju was fetching water from the well at that time. So he said, "When I am fetching water from the well I am not quite sure whether I am fetching the water, or if it is the well which is fetching and I am the well. And when my bucket is going down into the well I do not know whether the bucket has gone in the well or I have gone in the well. And when the bucket is full and it starts coming up, believe me, I am not clear about anything as to what is what and what is happening. But now that you have asked me, I am telling you after thinking about it. Just because you have asked, I have thought about it and told you; otherwise I am no more.

I have no idea of God. I have no idea even of myself."

When you have lost all idea even about who and what you are, what is then known in such a moment is what God is. When does one lose track of who one is? When the intellect that attaches thoughts to everything no longer remains with you. The very work of the intellect is to attach thoughts, to label everything, to give words, name and form to everything.

When a child is born and it first opens its eyes it does not have any intellect. The intellect will develop slowly afterwards; it will form, be educated and conditioned. The scientists say that when the child first opens his eyes he does not see any divisions. Red color will look red to the child also, but it cannot experience that it is red because it has still to learn the word red. The color green will look green to the child also, because the eyes can see color so green will be seen, but he cannot say it is green. The child cannot even say that it is color. The child also cannot say where the red ends and where the green begins, because he has no knowledge of red and green yet.

In the eyes of the child the world appears as one integrated whole, where things are all mixed into each other and nothing can be separated. It is an oceanic experience, indivisible. But this too is our inference – it is difficult to say what happens to the child.

The enlightened ones, those who have again become child-like, who have again become as simple as they were when they had no mind, who have now become innocent and simple as they were when they had no intellect, have such experiences where everything becomes one. One thing joins with the second, the second joins with the third, and so on. The separateness of things ceases to be seen, only the inner connection between them is seen.

Our condition is such that we are able to see only the beads of the necklace; the string running through them and joining them is not seen. The intellect sees only the beads. When the intellect moves away the inner consciousness, free of intellect, sees that hidden thread that is running through all the beads. It sees the oneness that encompasses everything, that connects everything, that is hidden within everything and is the base of everything.

Whenever intellect functions, it divides. Science is the system of intellect, hence science divides, analyzes. Science has arrived at the atom after dividing and subdividing. Science only sees pieces, parts; it cannot see the oneness at all.

Religion gives up the intellect and then a reverse process begins: things go on joining together and becoming one.

Science has arrived at the atom, religion arrives at God. The intellect goes on breaking things into their components. 'God' is a name for the biggest thing that we could synthesize with the absence of intellect. In using the intellect to break things down, we have come to the atom – the atom is the power of science. On seeing without intellect we have experienced God – God is the power of religion.

Remember therefore that any religion that divides is not a religion – no matter where it divides, on what level it divides. If a Hindu becomes separate from a Mohammedan, understand that they are merely politics of two types, not religion. If a Jaina appears separate from a Hindu, understand that they are merely types of social systems, not religion. Understand that behind all of them intellect, which only has the capacity to divide, is working. And behind them there is no experience of the consciousness that has transcended intellect – where everything synthesizes and becomes one.

> One who never knows any difference through
> intellect between jiva, the embodied soul,
> and Brahman, or between Brahman and nature,
> the creation, is called a jivanamukta,
> the one who is liberated while living.
> Respected by the good or insulted by the wicked,
> one who ever remains in equanimity
> is called a jivanamukta.

Equanimity is the first thing, nonduality the second. Equanimity is a word a little difficult to understand, because we use it loosely to mean different things.

One person may abuse you and another person may bow down to you. Now what do we mean by equanimity in relation to these? Does it mean that you should make an effort and control yourself not to be angry with the one who has abused you and not to be pleased with the one who respected you? No, if there is any effort or control it is not equanimity; it is only an imposed self-control, it is a self-regulation, a discipline. Equanimity means there is no reaction at all within you, whether one abuses you or one respects you – a total absence of reaction within. Simply nothing stirs within you. The abuse remains outside and the respect remains outside; nothing at all enters within.

When will this happen? This happens only when there is a witness within.

When somebody abuses us there is a reaction. On hearing abuse we immediately feel that "I have been abused," and the suffering begins. When somebody respects us we feel happy because it feels that "I am respected." It means that whatsoever is done to you, you become identified with it. It is because of this that suffering and pleasure are created, disharmony is created, and balance is lost.

A moral person also tries to attain equanimity, but such equanimity is imposed, cultivated. That person consoles himself with, "What if somebody has abused me? There is no harm." And if somebody respects him, he thinks, "Okay, that is his desire. I shall remain in equanimity between the two." This sort of equanimity remains on the surface, it does not go very deep, because this man has no contact with his witness. His equanimity is character-oriented. So sometimes, in some not very conscious moment, he can be provoked; sometime when there may be a little crack in his character, his inner disharmony may become manifest.

In the eyes of the Upanishad, character-oriented equanimity has no value. In the eyes of the Upanishad, only equanimity derived from the being has value. Being-oriented equanimity means that whatsoever may happen outside, you remain the witness.

Some people abused and threw stones at Ramateertha when he was in New York. When he returned home he was dancing. A disciple asked, "What happened, why are you so happy?"

Ramateertha replied, "It is a matter of joy. Today Ramateertha was in great difficulty. Some people started abusing him, ridiculing him, and some people started throwing stones at him. It was great fun seeing Ramateertha being harassed and trapped. He was badly trapped!"

His disciples were puzzled and they asked, "Who are you talking about? Who is this Ramateertha?"

Ramateertha replied, keeping his hands on his chest, "This Ramateertha was badly trapped and I was just watching and enjoying seeing him trapped. I saw those who were abusing him and I also saw that man Ramateertha who was trapped and being abused. I kept watching the whole scene."

When you have attained this third perspective, only then is there equanimity. If you have only two perspectives there cannot be any equanimity; then there is only the abuser and the abused. You may try to remain harmonious – because that is a characteristic of a person who is trying to be a good man – but this is only a way of consoling yourself: "Never mind, if somebody abused me what harm does it do to me?" But this is only a self-consolation, and you are feeling the abuse, hence this self-consolation. You say, "The man has harmed himself by using abusive words; what have I lost through the whole thing?" But you did lose something, hence this self-consolation.

A 'good' man lives in consolation. He thinks, "It is okay, he abused me so he is creating his own bad karma, he will reap its fruits. Why should I say anything? He has abused me, he will suffer and go to hell because he has sinned." This man is consoling himself. He himself cannot create hell for the abuser so he is leaving it to God to complete the job. He is employing God in his service – but he is only consoling himself. He is saying that those who sow the wrong seeds will reap the wrong fruits. Those who sow good seeds will reap good fruits. "And I shall sow only good seeds, so that I reap good fruits. This man is sowing wrong seeds, so let him have his wrong fruits." He can even go to the extent of saying, "Even if somebody sows thorns for me, I will only sow flowers for him, because in the future the other will reap thorns and I will reap flowers." But this sort of thinking only reflects a calculating business mind. This is a sort of prudent, bargaining mind, it is not equanimity.

Where is equanimity? Equanimity is only when beyond the duality, beyond the two opposing points, the third perspective begins to be seen: "Here is the abuser, here is my body and name that are being abused, and here am I, the third party, who is watching the whole thing. If I am at the same distance from both the abuser and the abused, then there is equanimity. If there is even a slight difference in the distance – if the one abusing me appears at a greater distance than I, the abused – the equanimity has already been lost; disharmony has set in."

Equanimity means that the scale is balanced and you become the third in the middle, like the pointer of the scale: steady, neither leaning to this side nor to that; neither leaning towards the abuser nor the abused, standing beyond and just watching.

This witnessing is equanimity. And a jivanamukta will live in equanimity, because jivanamukta arises out of witnessing.

Understand this second sutra well: through self-consolation a good man is born, through witnessing a saint is born. And there is a great difference between a saint and a good man. A good man is a saint only on the surface, inside there is no difference between him and a wicked man. A wicked man is wicked both outside and inside. A good man is good outside and wicked within. So there is a big difference between a good man and a saint.

In one sense, the saint and the wicked man are similar. The wicked man is wicked both outside and inside. The good man is good outside and wicked inside, and a saint is good both outside and inside. The similarity is that the wicked man is uniform both inside and outside and so is the saint. Their forms are different but their uniformity is the same. And a good man is hanging between these two; hence there is no end to the misery of a good man, because his mind is like that of a wicked person but his behavior is like that of a saint. Hence a good man lives in a great dilemma. In his mind there is always a duality.

People come to me and say, "I have never done anything wrong, I have never committed a theft nor cheated anybody, and I am suffering so much. On the other hand, those who have committed thefts and have cheated others are well-off and enjoying themselves. So there is no justice in this world."

...Or the good man consoles himself that whatever may be his condition now, there is a divine law which prevails; there may be some delay in it but the law is there. He consoles himself, "There is a little delay and for now the dishonest are succeeding, but in the end it is I who will succeed." He is consoling himself that there is delay, but not the lack of divine law. But one point is clear, that he is experiencing a delay. And there is also a doubt lurking in his mind: "Could it be that something is not right about my assumption of the existence of a divine law? Could it be that I am going to miss at both ends, neither the material gain here nor any spiritual goal attained there? Could it be that I am losing material wealth now only to later discover that God simply never did exist? That the one who has succeeded in obtaining material wealth here wins in the end also?"

This nagging doubt is a constant companion of a good man. And being in doubt as to one's goodness clearly means only one thing, that one's inside desires are no different from a wicked man's. On the inside you desire to do and to gain the same thing that the wicked man is doing and gaining, but you have somehow maintained the behavior of a good man. Your greed is twofold. Your cart has bullocks harnessed at both ends and is being pulled in two directions. You are greedy to have money and fame to satisfy your ego – all the greeds of any wicked man are your greeds as well – and you are greedy also to attain to God, soul, liberation, peace and bliss; all the greeds of any saint are your greeds as well. Your greeds are twofold, and you are suffering between the two greeds. And this is why a good man is often found to be less at peace than anybody else.

If a good man becomes more at peace he becomes a saint. If a good man is not at peace, then if not today, tomorrow he will become a wicked man. He cannot carry on that way for long. From that middle position he has to either fall down or go up, but there is no way of remaining in the middle.

A jivanamukta is a saint. He is not doing any wrong to anybody, but not because not doing wrong will backfire on him someday; no, he cannot do any wrong because he is standing at that third point where no wrong has ever been done.

Alexander the Great wanted to take an Indian sannyasin to his own country; the name of that sannyasin was Dandami. But Dandami was not willing to go. Alexander drew out his sword and threatened him saying, "I will cut you to pieces if you do not agree. Even the Himalayas would have to come with me if I ordered it."

Dandami said, "Maybe the Himalayas would go with you, but you will not be able to take me."

Alexander could not understand the source of strength of this skinny fakir standing naked on the sands of the riverbank and talking so courageously. He ordered his soldiers, and suddenly Dandami was surrounded with naked swords all around. Dandami laughed hilariously at this and said, "You are not surrounding me, you are surrounding that which I am not. You have no capacity to surround me, because my expanse has become one with the expanse of the vast existence."

Alexander said, "I do not understand this philosophical talk, I only understand the language of the sword, and soon your head will be rolling on the ground."

Dandami said, "It will be great fun. You will see the head rolling down on the ground and I will also see it rolling down on the ground – we will both be seeing the same event."

Now this is the third perspective: "I will also see the head rolling down on the ground."

If you can see your own head being chopped off and rolling down on the ground it means that you have no identification whatsoever with your body, that you have become the witness of your body, that you are standing outside and away from your own body. Only at this point is the birth of saintliness, and only at this point is liberation while living.

> *For the one who has known the Brahman essence,*
> *this world no longer remains the same as before. If it*
> *is not so, he has not known the Brahman state of*
> *being and is still an extrovert.*

The world will remain the same. By your becoming changed the world will not change, but by your change, *your* world will be changed.

As I said earlier, we all have our own worlds. If I am ignorant the Mount Abu mountains will remain the same, and when I become awakened then too the Mount Abu mountains will remain the same. The sky will remain the same, the moon will remain the same, the earth will remain the same – this whole world will remain the same. But when I am ignorant, then the way I see the world, the way I choose it to be for me, the way I choose for it to appear to me.... I may like to feel the mountain is mine; when I am ignorant the mountain is not just a mountain, it is *my* mountain. But in the moment of awakening, in the experience of liberation, the mountain will just be a mountain, it will not be mine. That 'mine' which was imposed upon it will disappear. And on the disappearance of my-ness, the beauty and grandeur of the mountain will be fully revealed. My own my-ness, my own attachment was my misery and my pain. It was my own intellect that used to stand in between. So whenever I looked at the mountain, I felt, "My mountain." That my-ness would come in between and I would see through this screen. Now the mountain is a mountain and I am I.

In Japan, Zen masters have created ten pictures. Those pictures have been used for centuries for meditation. These pictures are worth understanding, they will be useful in understanding this sutra.

In the first picture nothing can be seen, but on a closer look one can see in it a mountain, a tree and a bull hidden behind the tree. Only the back of the bull, its two legs and its tail, can be seen. In the second picture, the person who is looking and searching for the bull here and there has also appeared on the scene. It is evening, the darkness is descending, and he is not able to see clearly. The tree is there, some creepers are there and the bull is hiding behind it all; just a little bit of the tail and the hind legs can be seen – of that too one can only see the outline.

In the third picture he can see the bull clearly. In the second picture he appeared sad and his eyes were full of an anxious search with no glow in them. But now that he has seen the bull a glow has come into his eyes and movement has come to his feet.

In the fourth picture the whole bull is seen and the person searching for the bull has come closer to the bull. In the fifth picture he has caught hold of the bull's tail.

In the sixth picture he has caught the bull by its horns. In the seventh picture he has managed to turn the bull to be facing towards home.

In the eighth picture he is riding the bull. In the ninth picture he is in full control of the bull and is returning home, and in the tenth picture there is nothing – neither the bull nor the rider, its owner, are there. The forest is there, the mountain is there, but the bull and the owner have both disappeared.

These ten pictures are used for meditation in the Zen tradition. They are depictions of the search for the soul, the self. In the first depiction the seeker is nowhere to be seen. In the second depiction the seeker is roused, the desire has arisen to know the soul, for the search. In the third depiction a little glimpse of the soul has begun to appear. In the fourth depiction the soul is seen in full view. In the fifth picture, not only a full view of the soul is seen, but its tail has also been caught, meaning the right of ownership has been established in a tiny corner of it.

In the next depiction a face-to-face encounter has happened, the soul has been caught by its horns. In the depiction after this the soul has not only been caught by its horns, but it has also been turned around on the journey back home, towards Brahman. In the next two pictures, not only the soul has now been turned towards home but the seeker is in control of himself, is now riding the bull, and has started moving towards home. And in the last depiction both are lost; neither the seeker is there nor the search, the world has become a void. The mountains are still standing, the trees are still standing, but the seeker and the search have both disappeared.

This is the discovery. The way this world appears today when one sets out on the search is not the way it is after the awakening. All my-ness will disappear. All accumulated concepts will disappear. All one's projections within the world will be destroyed; all one's expectations of the world will drop. No demands will remain; all one's ideas of finding happiness in the world will vanish, even the illusion that the world gives unhappiness will be destroyed. Any feelings that one has any transactions with the world will also end.

So this sutra says that for the one who has known Brahman, the supreme essence, the world does not remain the same as before. The world remains, but not the same as before. And if the world is still remaining the same as before, then understand that Brahman is not yet known. This is for testing one's own self. One has to go on checking oneself. There is the wife.... People come to me and say, "The wife is there, the children are there, family, conflicts, business; nothing is possible in this mess. Should I leave everything and run away?"

I tell them, "Do not run away. After all, where will you run away to? – the world is there everywhere. And if you remain as you are now, someone else will become your wife, some other home will be created, some other business will be started. There are businesses of many kinds, there are even religious kinds of businesses: you may not open a shop, maybe you will open a monastery; something or the other is bound to happen. What can you do? If the person residing within you remains unchanged, he is bound to do only what he knows."

Do not run away. Remain where you are and go on plunging deeper and searching within. Take the search to be complete the day you are sitting in the market, and the market is there but it is no longer a marketplace for you. Your wife may be sitting near you – in the mind she will remain a wife; let her be, but for *you* she should not remain your wife. That feeling of my-ness must disappear, only the woman remains.

And she will appear as a woman only as long as there is the desire for sex. As meditation deepens, the sex desire will also vanish; then she will not even remain a woman for you, she will cease to be a body. Just as the feeling of my-ness within you goes on withering away, your outer projections about the woman, your feelings about the woman as a wife, as a woman, will also go on disappearing. A day will come when wherever you are sitting you will become void and empty. All around you the world will remain the same, but you will not remain the same. Your whole outlook will be changed.

One has to go on constantly searching within: "Is everything the same to me as it was before? Is everything running the same way in my life?" Names may change, things may change, but if one's inner attitude towards everything continues to be the same as before, and everything appears the same as before, then understand that jivanamukta is far away, the glimpse of truth is far away.

The very meaning of the glimpse of the truth is that the relationship between you and your world is changed. The world will remain the same as before, and the relationship with it will change only when you change.

As far as happiness, etcetera are experienced,
it is called prarabdha,
accumulated past action-impressions;

> *because the arising of any fruits is from actions in*
> *the past. There is no fruit anywhere without action.*
> *Just as the dream activity ceases upon waking,*
> *similarly, past actions accumulated over billions*
> *of eons dissolve instantly upon one's knowing*
> *"I am Brahman."*

Happiness and suffering happen due to our past actions. So do not think that physical suffering or happiness will not happen to those who have become liberated while living.

Ramana Maharshi died of cancer. It was very painful, naturally. It was a deep malady – there was no way of escaping it. Many doctors came, and they were very puzzled because the whole body was torn with pain but there was no sign of any pain in his eyes. His eyes remained the same serene lakes as ever. Through his eyes only the witnessing self arose; it was the witnessing self that looked, that observed.

Doctors would ask, "You must be in great pain?" Ramana would reply, "Yes there is great pain, but it is not happening to me. I am aware that there is great pain happening to the body; I know that there is great pain happening. I am seeing it, but it is not happening to me."

A question arises in the minds of many people as to how a man like Ramana, who is liberated, enlightened, got a disease like cancer. This sutra has the answer to it. Happiness and sufferings will be happening to the body, even to those who are liberated while living, because these are related to past actions and their impressions, they are related to whatsoever has been done before becoming awakened.

Understand it this way: if I have sown some seeds in a field and then I become awakened, the seeds are bound to sprout. Had I remained sleeping, then too the seeds would have sprouted, flowered and come to fruition. Now too they will sprout, flower and come to fruition. There will only be one difference: had I been still asleep I would think it to be my crop and keep it close to my chest.

Now that I am awake, I will understand that the seeds were already sown and now they are reaching their destiny; nothing of it is mine, I will just go on witnessing. If I had remained asleep I would have harvested the crop and preserved the new seeds so that I could sow them next year. Now that I am awake I will just go on witnessing: seeds will sprout, flowers will come, fruits will grow, but I will not gather them. Those fruits will grow and fall off on their own accord and die. My relationship with them will snap. My relationship with them before was of having sown them – now I will not do that again. Thus no further relationship will be formed.

So happiness and suffering keep coming to the liberated one also, but such a person knows that these are part of the chain of his past actions and now he has nothing to do with them: he will just go on witnessing.

When somebody comes and offers flowers at the feet of Ramana, he just goes on watching – it must be a part of some past chain of actions that prompts this person to give him happiness. But Ramana does not take the happiness; the person gives, but he does not take it. Should he take, the journey of a new action will begin. He does not prevent the person from offering flowers – that "Don't give happiness to me, don't offer flowers to me, don't touch my feet" – he does not prevent him, because that prevention too would be an action and another chain of action would begin.

Try to understand this. This man has come to offer flowers to Ramana; he has put a garland round his neck, he has put his head at his feet. And what is Ramana doing within? He is just watching: "There must be a past transaction with this man, some past impressions of action; the man is now completing it. But now the transaction has to come to an end, no further chain has to be created. This matter is finished here, it will not continue."

So he will just sit there and will not prevent that man from doing anything...because what will 'preventing' really mean? It will mean first that you are not ready to take back the past action where you had given, and which you would have to take back when preventing this man's action. And second, you are creating another chain of relationship with this man by asking him not to do a certain thing. Now when will this new relationship end? You are creating another action; you are reacting. No, Ramana will just go on watching, whether a man brings flowers to him or cancer comes. He will even watch the cancer happening.

Ramakrishna also died of cancer. He had throat cancer. Even water would not go down his throat; food would not go down his throat. Then one day Vivekananda asked Ramakrishna, "Why don't you tell mother Kali? It is just a matter of your telling her and in a moment your throat will be cured." Ramakrishna just laughed and said nothing.

One day, when Vivekananda had insisted too much, Ramakrishna said, "You don't understand. It is necessary to be finished with whatsoever is one's own doing, otherwise one will have to came back again just to finish it. So it is right to allow whatsoever is happening to happen; it is not right to hinder it."

Then Vivekananda said, "Alright, if you do not want to ask to be cured, at least ask her that as long as you are in the body to let the throat be good enough to allow water and food to pass through. Otherwise it is unbearably painful for us to see you in such a condition."

Ramakrishna agreed to ask. When he woke up the next morning he said, "It was great fun. When I told the mother she said, 'Has this throat a monopoly on your work? Is there some difficulty in eating through others' throats?'"

Ramakrishna further said, "Because of listening to your advice, I acted like a great fool. You harassed me unnecessarily. And this is right – does this throat have any monopoly? So from today onwards, when you take food, understand that I am also taking food through your throat."

Ramakrishna laughed continuously all day long. When the doctor came he said, "Why are you laughing? The body is in such a painful condition, and no other condition can be more painful than this."

Ramakrishna said, "I am laughing because I don't know what

happened to my mind that I failed to remember that all throats are mine, that now I can take food through all throats. Why be obsessed with this one throat?"

Howsoever supreme a state an individual may attain, the past that is attached to the body will complete itself. Happiness and sufferings will come and go, but the liberated person will know that it is only the accumulated past actions. Knowing so, he will stand apart from them too and his witnessing will not be affected by them in any way. His witnessing is now steady.

Just as the dream activity ceases upon waking,
similarly, past actions accumulated over billions
of eons dissolve instantly upon one's knowing,
"I am Brahman."

We have discussed this earlier. Just as on waking up from sleep dreams disappear, similarly upon the real awakening it becomes clear that all that one had done in the past, one had not done in reality – all of it disappears. But even after coming to know this, the body does not come to know it. The body continues to move on mechanically, it completes its destiny. Just as an arrow that has left the bow cannot be brought back, just as a word that has left the lips cannot be called back, in the same way the body is just a mechanical arrangement. Whatsoever has happened through it in the past will be completed. Until the arrow reaches its target, until the word touches the farthest bounds of the sky, it is not destroyed. So the body will have to suffer and endure.

It will be good to tell you one more thing in this connection. You may have perhaps felt too that it is strange that Ramakrishna and Ramana both should have cancer – such a sinister disease.

Buddha died of some poisonous food, his blood became full of poison. Mahavira died of a deadly dysentery – he suffered unbearable abdominal pain for six months, which could not be cured. So one starts asking why such deadly diseases should catch hold of the purest souls – what could be the reason? If these diseases catch us, the sinners, the ignorant people, one can understand that, "Yes, we are reaping the fruits of our wrongdoings." But when it happens to Mahavira, to Buddha or Ramana or Ramakrishna, we start wondering what is the matter. But it has a reason.

The person who becomes a jivanamukta, the liberated while living, has no further journey; this life is his last life. But *you* have a long journey ahead, you still have lots of time. You can finish up all your sufferings in small doses, bit by bit – you have lots and lots of time for it. Buddha, Mahavira or Ramana had no time left. They may have just ten, twenty, thirty years to go. You may have lifetimes upon lifetimes still to go.

So in such a short period of time all the accumulated past actions and impressions are intensely compacted and give their fruits. So the events happen in a twofold manner. On the one hand, Mahavira has the honor and respect of a *tirthankara* – that too is an intensely compacted experience of all the accumulated happiness. And on the other hand, he has to suffer unbearable pain – that too is an intensely compacted impact of all the accumulated sufferings.

Thousands and thousands of people have immense respect for Ramana in their hearts; that is a collection of all the happiness. And then he has a disease like cancer; that is a collection of all the sufferings. Time is very short: everything is completed in its totality, at full intensity and at great speed. Thus such people go through experiences of extreme happiness and extreme suffering simultaneously. Because of lack of time, everything becomes concentrated and intense. But they have to be undergone: there is no other way but to undergo them.

Ma Anand Madhu suddenly gets up and asks: "Can someone who has more time absorb such diseases from them or not? If yes, what is the method?"

No, there is no method and no way, and they cannot be shared, because if disease can be taken by somebody, that would mean that somebody else can take the fruit of my doings. Then there will be anarchy. And if somebody else can take the fruit of my doings, then there will remain no law, no rit – the natural law. Then my freedom can also be had by someone else, my liberation can also be had by someone else. My happiness, my suffering, my experience, my knowing, my bliss – anything becomes transferable.

No, nothing in this world is transferred. There is no way for it, simply no way, and it is only proper that there is no way. Yes, such a feeling of sharing arises in one's heart; that too is good, that too is right. Somebody loving Ramana may desire to take his cancer. This desire creates happiness, and out of this desire the person will earn fruits of goodness. This becomes an accumulated good action on the part of this person. Try to understand this.

Ramana is dying of cancer: somebody may pray in full sincerity and feeling of heart that he should absorb Ramana's disease. Still he cannot do so, but the very fact that he has felt this way, has felt like taking this disease on himself, becomes an action, a good deed, and he will receive happiness for it.

This is very strange: this person had asked for suffering – but he is doing a wonderful, virtuous deed; he will receive its fruits of happiness. But nothing of Ramana's disease can be transferred. This feeling which he is having is becoming his own action-impression for which he will get the benefit.

Someone else now stands up and begins to ask: "About Arvind...."

No. Madhu, you created a bad precedent. This will be harmful.

Your intentions are good, but here there are so many people sitting.... Do not start any such thing, it will make everything difficult. It will create disorderliness.

Enough for today.

TO FLY
IS YOUR
BIRTHRIGHT

CHAPTER 14

Knowing oneself as unattached and indifferent
as the sky, a yogi is not attached at all after that
to any future actions.
Just as the sky present in a pot full of liquor is not
affected by the smell of the liquor, the soul
remains untouched by all happenings
in spite of being present during all of them.

✳

Just as an arrow released will not stop before piercing
the aimed-at object, the actions done before the
happening of enlightenment will not cease to yield
fruits after enlightenment happens.
An arrow released taking an animal to be a tiger,
cannot be stopped midway if later on the
understanding dawns that the animal was instead a
cow. The arrow will hit the target with its full
strength. Similarly, action already done comes to
fruition even after enlightenment has happened.

✳

One who understands that he is deathless and ever
young remains one with the soul and has no
relationship with the fruits of his past actions.

n this sutra some deep hints are given regarding the nature of consciousness. Only a *jivana-mukta*, a person liberated while living, passes through such experiences. Only a jivanamukta comes to experience these sutras. We do not have any direct experience of consciousness; whatsoever we know about consciousness is from its reflections in the mind. First let this be properly understood, then we shall go into the sutras.

Mind is a wonderful mechanism. Now it has also been confirmed by science that mind is nothing more than a mechanism. A computer works even more efficiently than mind. It is not necessary to send a human being to the moon, computers can be sent instead. Russia has already sent such computers to the moon and they collect data and transmit it to Russian ground stations. They are machines, but receptive and subtle like our minds, and whatsoever is happening around them is accumulated and transmitted.

I said to you earlier that when a jivanamukta returns from *samadhi,* the happening of enlightenment....

A friend has asked me that since when consciousness enters the experience of samadhi mind is left far behind – and since it is only mind that can remember – who recalls the experiences that have happened to the consciousness? It was consciousness that had entered the experience, but consciousness neither keeps any memory nor does it allow any trace of memory to be left over it; and the mind did not enter into the experience, it was left behind. Who then is remembering? Then who is looking at the experience in retrospect?

Yes, though the mind had not entered into the experience and was left just standing at the door, it is still able to catch glimpses from a doorway. It catches glimpses of events happening in the outer world as well as in the inner world. It observes on both sides whatever is within its periphery. It is not necessary for the mind to enter into the experience itself. If a camera is kept at a distance over there, it will go on catching all that is happening here. Or if a tape recorder is kept at a distance over there, it will go on recording all that I am saying – the song of the birds, the rustle of the wind passing through the trees, the sound of the dry falling leaves.

Understand it well that mind is only a machine; it has no soul to it, it is only a biological machine developed by nature. Mind is something in between our soul and the world outside. Mind records all that happens in the world. For that it has five senses as its doors.

The senses are the doors of the mind. For example this microphone placed before me can convey the sound to a tape recorder placed hundreds of miles away. Your senses are like this microphone conveying various types of information to the mind. The five senses are like five doors to the mind. To convey anything that happens in the outside world of light, color and form, the mind has the eyes as its extension on the outside of the body; they go on recording everything like a camera.

Whatsoever happens in the world of sound such as music, words or silence, is caught every moment by the ears. And what is being caught is also being relayed to the mind and the mind accumulates this information. The hands touch, the tongue tastes and the nose smells, and all this is being relayed to the mind.

The five senses are all doors of the mind. There is one more sense, and that is your inner sense. This sense catches whatsoever is happening within you. It is also a sense. Whatsoever is happening within you, for example in the state of samadhi, this inner sense goes on recording all that is happening. Peace? Silence? Bliss? Realization of God? Whatever is happening, it keeps track.

This inner sense is like a microphone that is directed inwards. It is the receptivity of the within. Inside, one sense is enough, five senses are not required there. Outside, five senses are required because there are five basic elements and to record each one a separate sense is required. Inside, there is only one Brahman – five senses are not required, only one sense is enough to register the inner experiences.

Thus man has six senses – five extrovert and one introvert – and mind is the mechanism in between, connected to all of them. Just this one branch goes within and catches all the inner experiences.

Whatsoever is happening within is passed on by this inner sense to the mind. Mind need not go anywhere. Thus when a person returns from samadhi the mind itself hands over all the records to him, that such and such a thing happened when you were not here.

If you leave your tape recorder here and go away, then when you come back after an hour the tape recorder will give you a complete record of all the words spoken here and the various sounds that happened. It is not necessary for a tape recorder to have life. Mind is not consciousness; it is matter, and a subtle mechanism. This mechanism goes on collecting data from either side. Hence a seeker returning from samadhi infers through mind what has happened.

The more clarity of mind, the more authentic the information given by it. The more confused the mind is, the more incorrect the information. For example, if your tape recorder is defective it may record things but the recording will not be clear; the sound will be distorted, mixed up or deformed. Some parts may be clear, some parts may not be.

Hence the mind is first to be purified through right listening, right contemplation and assimilation. When the receptivity of the mind becomes pure, so that it can produce an authentic copy of whatsoever is happening, only then occurs the entry into samadhi.

So the inner sense records everything. But it is because of their allegiance to truth that seers have called it inference of the mind, because the mind was not present there and whatsoever it is now saying is information supplied to it by its inner sense. And mind is aware that there is a possibility of flaws in that information.

Hence there is one more interesting point to be properly understood. When a Hindu returns from samadhi, or when a Mohammedan or a Christian or a Jaina returns from samadhi, their minds give a slightly different version of the information because there are differences in the make-up of the devices which are their minds. The experience of samadhi is the same, but the make-up of the minds is different.

A person who is born in a Jaina family has a conscience developed in the manner of Jainism, and his being a Jaina has entered the mechanism of his mind. He has heard since his very childhood that there is no God, so it has become a built-in process in his mind that there is no God. His mind has also heard that the ultimate experience is that of the soul and not of God. This mind is manufactured and conditioned, so when samadhi happens it is this very mind which will record the event.

Samadhi is the same to whomsoever it happens, but our minds are different – and it is the mind that will record the experience. A Jaina mind knows that there is no God, the ultimate experience is that of soul, there is no experience beyond it; or, this experience itself is God, there is no other God than this experience itself. Now such a mind will immediately record the samadhi experience as, "The ultimate experience of soul is happening."

A Hindu has heard about the experience of God and has the information that what the experience is when the soul dissolves within is the experience of God. His mind will record, "This is seeing God." The happening is the same, but in this case it is God being experienced.

The mind of a Buddhist who believes neither in the soul nor in God will record neither of the two. His mind will say, "Nirvana has happened, you have become a void, a nothingness."

This is the reason scriptures differ, because scriptures are records of different minds, not of the actual experiences. This is why there will be differences between the Hindu scriptures, the Jaina scriptures and the Buddhist scriptures. Sometimes the differences will even look contradictory, because the mind is limited by the words available and they are learned. Mind is knowledge, a learned thing, a manufactured thing.

Let us understand it this way, putting religion aside. Let us say you have learned Sanskrit or Greek or Arabic, so your mind has known one language. Now there is not even a question of any language during the happening of samadhi, but the mind will record the experience in the language it knows. The one who knows Arabic can never say that it was the happening of samadhi – the very word samadhi is not known to that mind. So a Sufi will say *fana* – he has remained no more. But the meaning is the same.

You are aware that the grave of a sannyasin is called a samadhi – for the same reason. Not everybody's grave is called a samadhi, only the grave of such a person who has annihilated himself. He has annihilated his ego while living; there is nothing left for death to annihilate when it comes, the person has annihilated himself on his own.

So a Sufi will call it fana, a Hindu will call it samadhi, and a Buddhist will call it nirvana. These words are there in the mind. So whatever will happen within the mind, it will immediately translate it into its own language. We find it difficult to understand how a mechanism could translate, but this only says that you don't know much about mechanisms.

The latest discoveries in mechanisms and instruments are very amazing. All that mind can do can also be done by machines. There is nothing that a mind can do that cannot be done by a mechanism. This has brought a very dangerous attitude: if a machine can do everything that a mind does, then mind is nothing more than a machine. So for those who believe that there is nothing beyond the mind, that there is no soul, then man becomes a machine, nothing else remains. If it is true that there is no soul, then man is just a machine – and not a very efficient one either. Machines can be made more efficient than man.

Soon speeches will be simultaneously translated. If I am speaking here in Hindi, my speech will be simultaneously translated into the five major languages. No human translators will be required for this, only machines. When I speak the word *prem* in Hindi, the English language translating machine will immediately translate it as love. The impact of the sound of the word prem on the machine electronically will convert it into other sound waves that produce the sounds for the word love.

So there are machines that talk, machines that calculate and machines that have memory; machines have started doing everything that the mind of man can do. When the yogis, the *tantrikas* and the Upanishads said for the first time that the mind of man is just like a machine, people all over the world did not understand it. Now science has devised machines that do similar work to that of the mind, and there is no problem in understanding it.

The human mind stores data from either side – from the world as well as from samadhi. It is the mind that gives information about the world as well as about Brahman.

Now we shall enter the sutra.

When one comes to experience that all reflections form only on the mind, and as one moves deeper within oneself to one's very center, that there are no impressions, that all conditionings form only on the mind, not on the self – only then will this sutra be understood.

> *Knowing oneself as unattached and indifferent*
> *as the sky, a yogi is not attached at all after that*
> *to any future actions.*

There are many things to be understood here. *Knowing oneself as unattached and indifferent as the sky....* We see the sky every day. A bird flies in the sky, but leaves no traces in the sky. When one walks on the ground, footprints are left behind. If the ground is wet the footprints are deeper; if the ground is rocky the footprints are very light, but if you try they can be made deeper there too. But in the sky, when a bird flies, no footprints are left behind. The sky remains the same as it was before the bird flew by. There is no way of knowing from the sky that a bird has flown across it. Clouds gather in the sky, they come and go; the sky remains as it was.

There is no way of contaminating the sky – of making impressions on it, marks on it. We can draw lines on water, but no sooner are the lines made than they disappear; yet if lines are made on stone they last for thousands of years. Lines just cannot be drawn in the sky, so there is no question of their disappearing.

Please understand this difference. Lines cannot be drawn in the sky – I may move my finger across the sky, the finger passes but the line is not drawn and the question of the disappearance of the line simply does not arise. The day a person goes beyond the mind, when the consciousness transcends the mind, he experiences that, like the sky, so far no marks or lines have ever been drawn on the soul. It is eternally pure, eternally enlightened, no pollution has ever happened to it.

Unattached – asanga – like the sky.... The word *asanga* is very valuable. Asanga means one is in the world but unattached, unaffected by anything. The sky is present all around; it is encompassing trees, it is encompassing you. It is encompassing the pious man as well as the impious man; it is present where a good deed is happening, it is present where an evil deed is happening. You sin or you earn virtue, you live or you die – the sky is present, but unattached. It is present with you, but it is not your companion. It does not make any relationship with you. It is present but its presence is unattached. It is always present, but no friendship is created with you, no relationship is formed with you.

Asanga means unrelated. It is there, but unrelated. If you disappear the sky does not even notice that you disappeared or that you ever were. How many earths appear and disappear again, how many people are born and die, how many palaces are built and collapse into dust again – how much has happened under the sky, but the sky keeps no account. You inquire and the sky has kept no history; it is empty. The sky is as if nothing has ever happened.

You may look back at millions of years – it is said that our earth was born some four billion years ago. During these four billion years how much has happened on this small earth – how many wars, how many love affairs, how many friendships, how many enmities, how many conquests, how many defeats and how many people – but the sky has no account of any of it. It is as if nothing has ever happened; no traces of any happenings are left on the sky.

Indians have never been concerned with history. Westerners wonder why this is so, why Indians do not have a sense of history. We do not know exactly when Rama lived, we do not know the exact date of the birth of Krishna. Nothing is certain. We have mythical stories about them, but no historical records.

The credit for making history a part of the human world goes to Christianity. In the sense that Jesus is historical, Buddha, Krishna or Parashuram are not. With Jesus, human history is divided into two parts: the world before Jesus Christ is considered unimportant and the world after Jesus Christ is considered important. Hence it is only proper that the Christian dating method should have become prevalent all over, because it is with Jesus that history enters the world of man. So we say before Christ and after Christ; a line is drawn.

India has never written any history; there is a reason for it. The fundamental reason is that India has felt that, when the very sky within which everything happens does not keep any account, why should we keep such a useless account? When the one within which everything happens does not bother to keep any account, why should we unnecessarily keep account of who was born when and who died when?

So we did not write any history, we created the *Puranas,* mythology. Mythology is an Indian phenomenon. It means we did not bother about dates and years, birthdays and death days, we bothered about the essence – that a Rama could happen. We did not bother to tie down when he was born, what year and date, where he went for his studies, when he married, etcetera, because keeping the record of all these seemed to be of no consequence at all. But the inner phenomenon that made Rama a Rama, the fact that one individual became a Rama, that one lamp was lit and there was a flame, was remembered. We did not keep any account of the happenings to his shell, the body. We remembered only this much – that an extinguished lamp can be lighted; we kept account of only this much, that a man's life is not just a stink, a fragrance can also happen to it. All the remaining useless details have been left out.

So we do not consider it essential to have kept a precise historical record of Rama; that is of no consequence. A Rama is possible – just that is enough. The phenomenon of being a Rama can happen;

this much we have remembered, and that remembrance is enough. A Krishna is possible – whether he has existed historically or not is secondary. Even when we keep an historical record of this kind of person it is only to remind ourselves that such a person is possible, that such a flower can bloom within us also, that such a spring of bliss can flow within us also.

Purana means, only that which is essential.

On entering into consciousness it is discovered that no line, no traces are drawn on the sky, but what is of the essence in you is left behind in the sky.

Try to understand this properly.

No traces are left behind in the sky but your essential fragrance is. And that happens because that essential fragrance is not in any way foreign to the sky; it is the sky within you. When you die it is the sky within you that is released into the sky – the rest of you gets lost. We call that outer sky the sky, but we call our innermost sky the soul.

There is one expanse outside and there is one expanse within. In the outer sky too clouds gather and it becomes covered. In the rainy season, in the evenings of July and August, all is covered with clouds and one cannot even conceive that there was once a blue sky, or conceive that one may be able to see that blue sky again. When dark clouds cover the sky, the blue sky cannot be seen, only the clouds can be seen.

Similarly, like the dark clouds covering the outer sky, the inner sky also gets covered by clouds. The clouds of the inner sky are called thoughts, choices, desires – or whatsoever we want to call them. When such clouds cover the inner sky, there too one feels there exists no cloudless sky behind it. Removing these inner clouds and seeing into the inner blue sky is meditation.

Seeing into this inner sky is the attainment, the ultimate fulfillment.

This sutra says: *Knowing oneself as unattached and indifferent as the sky....* The sky neither laughs with you nor weeps with you. When you die the sky does not shed any tears; if you live and rejoice the sky does not tie anklets on its feet and dance for your joy. The sky is absolutely indifferent. It does not express any opinion about what is happening. Whether a dead body is being taken to the crematorium, or a great celebration is going on due to the birth of a new child, the sky remains indifferent. Whether a marriage ceremony is taking place and the houses are decorated with flowers and garlands, or a loved one has just died and living any longer appears meaningless to you, the sky remains indifferent. It has nothing to do with whatsoever is happening.

Similarly, as one enters the inner sky he becomes indifferent. He does not have any relationship with whatsoever happens; he begins to see the world just as the sky sees it.

When such an experience happens, know that you have become a jivanamukta, one liberated while living. This is when no traces form on your inner sky, when whatsoever happens outside remains just a drama to you, when everything happens only on the circumference and your center remains untouched. When the mind is put aside, such a thing happens.

Knowing oneself as unattached and indifferent
as the sky, a yogi is not attached at all after that
to any future actions.

Now the second part of this sutra: when a person comes to know that none of his actions have ever touched him.... If he was defeated, his soul was not defeated, and if he had won, his soul had not won; if he was honored, his soul had nothing added to it, if he was insulted, his soul had nothing taken away from it – with such a realization future actions naturally lose their preoccupation for such a man. He knows that if his actions in the past could not touch him, his actions in the future will also not touch him. Hence all planning for the future will stop. He no longer worries whether he will succeed or fail, whether his prestige will sustain him or someone will dishonor him. For the one who has seen his own self, his whole past becomes disassociated from him and so does his whole future.

The future is just an extension of the past. Whatsoever we have known in the past, either as pleasant or as painful, we continue planning the same for the future. What we have found pleasant we desire to repeat in the future; and what we have found unpleasant we desire to avoid in the future.

What is our future? It is only a projection of our past, a little improved version of it. Yesterday we did something which brought unhappiness – we do not want to do it again in the future. Yesterday we had done something that gave us happiness – we want to do it again in the future.

If one sees that in his whole past, its pleasures and pains, its good things and bad things, that nothing has touched him, he has remained as empty as the sky, utterly void, the future becomes meaningless. Nothing has left any mark on him, he has remained unconditioned; now this whole journey is completed and he has remained untouched and virgin within, now the whole future has become meaningless to him.

Remember, for a jivanamukta there is no future. Even if a little of your future has remained, understand that the inner sky has not yet been experienced. If some meditator is still thinking how to attain enlightenment or how to see God, understand that the experience of the inner sky has not yet happened to him. These are still plans for the future; the future is still there. Even an inch of future remaining is enough. Even an inch of future remaining indicates that one has not yet experienced that no action touches the soul. Neither enlightenment nor God can touch the soul. In fact it is this untouchability, this eternal untouchability which is the reality. This eternally remaining, untouched consciousness is godliness, is God. There is no other meaning of God.

If we call Krishna or Mahavira or Buddha, *bhagwan,* the blessed one, what do we mean by it? Has Buddha made this universe – that is why he is bhagwan? What is the meaning of 'bhagwan'? Buddha also falls sick, he gets old, he dies, his body comes to an end – what sort of a bhagwan is he? Sufferings come to him, sickness, old age and death come to him. A bhagwan should not become old, a bhagwan should not get any disease, a bhagwan should not die. Buddha also becomes hungry and thirsty. If one were to cut his body with a knife, blood would come out – what kind of bhagwan is he? What does it mean to be a bhagwan?

What it means to be a bhagwan is that all this can happen and the one hidden within the body knows that nothing ever touches it. All this can happen: if a hand is cut, blood will definitely flow out; the body will become hungry and feel thirsty, old age will come and so does death; but the inner sky of the buddha within knows that nothing touches it. Neither death touches it nor life. Life passes, death passes – youth as well as old age – but the inner virginity remains untouched; there is no break in it, not even news of what is happening outside reaches it.

The name of this experience is godliness.

So if somebody is seeking to see God, he has a future. He who has a future never has a meeting with God. The future means the world. The future means that the truth of the past has not yet been seen, that it has not yet been experienced that one is like the sky.

This sutra says that for a *yogin,* a meditator, no interest whatsoever remains in any future actions. For a yogin there exists no tomorrow, only today. Even today is a long time; one should say there is only this moment. Here and now is the whole existence; there is nothing left in him moving towards the future.

> *Just as the sky present in a pot full of liquor is not*
> *affected by the smell of the liquor, the soul*
> *remains untouched by all happenings*
> *in spite of being present during all of them.*

When an earthen pot is full of liquor, it is affected by the liquor. The clay of the pot actually drinks the liquor, all the pores soak up the liquor. And if some pot has been used for a very long time for the storage of liquor, then one may get intoxicated even by chewing the clay of that pot. The clay of a pot is affected by the liquor, becomes soaked with it. Why? Because clay is porous.

Try to understand this. The clay of the pot has many pores, the liquor fills up those pores and hides there. The earthen pot drinks the liquor and becomes a drunkard...the pot gets intoxicated. But the pot is full of one more element, and that is sky – the emptiness of the pot.

Now this is very interesting. One is pouring liquor into the emptiness of the pot, not into the clay of the pot. The liquor collects not in the clay of the pot but in the emptiness – the sky of the pot. Are we pouring liquor into the clay of the pot? No, the clay is there only to surround that emptiness from all sides. The sky is very big, the liquor is very little. Hence we choose a small area of the sky and enclose it with clay walls, ending up with a small sky within. Then we pour liquor in it.

Liquor is thus poured into the sky, not into the clay. But the interesting thing to note is that the clay becomes intoxicated and drunk and the sky in which liquor is actually poured remains untouched by it. If you remove the liquor from the pot the emptiness in the pot retains no smell of the liquor but the clay pot does. The clay becomes drunk due to the proximity – just the *satsang*, being in close company, brings results – and everything is actually contained in the sky but the sky remains untouched.

So whatever you have done has touched only your body, nothing else. It has gone into your clay, the body, but it has not touched your inner sky, the soul. You may have committed sin or have done good deeds – good things or bad things; everything has touched only your clay, the body.

Your mind is clay and your body is also clay. The emptiness, the void between these two is your soul – nothing has ever reached there. To have known this, to have experienced this, is going beyond all disturbances. All disturbances are of the body and of the mind, not of you. But whatsoever the clay has absorbed, the clay will have to live it.

Even the body of the enlightened person will have to live all that has been absorbed by it. The good, the bad, the sorrows...all that has been done and all that has happened – the whole past is there in every cell of the body. So even when enlightenment happens and the person awakens and becomes like the sky, whatever was happening to the body will complete its journey.

It is as if you were riding a bicycle and you just stopped pedaling because you came to realize that all journeying was futile and that you have nowhere to go. But the bicycle has gathered a momentum. You have been pedaling the bicycle for thousands of miles and it has gathered a force of its own. Even though you have stopped pedaling the bicycle will not stop then and there. Even without further pedaling it will move on for some distance, because the bicycle has momentum. Until that momentum is fully exhausted the bicycle will continue to move. Once the momentum is spent it will fall, but if you go on providing momentum it will never fall. If you stop providing momentum it will not fall immediately, but after some time.

We have been riding our bodies and minds for innumerable lifetimes: if we become awake today and separate ourselves from the body and mind they will not fall immediately. Body and mind will have to exhaust the momentum they have acquired.

Just as an arrow released will not stop before piercing the aimed-at object, the actions done before the happening of enlightenment will not cease to yield fruits after enlightenment...

So, be it Buddha, be it Krishna, or be it someone else, whatever has been done in the past has to come to fruition; the arrow will go the full distance. It means that the fruits of previous actions have to be endured even after enlightenment. Past actions are not destroyed by enlightenment. Enlightenment brings the experience that one is not the doer, but it does not destroy the past actions. Whatsoever has been done will come to fruition.

It can be explained through the example of an arrow which has been released after taking aim. After the arrow is released, even if one realizes that he is doing violence and that he should not do it, nothing can now be done, the arrow will complete its journey.

I utter a word, and immediately after uttering it I realize that I should not have uttered it, but it is too late now, the word will complete its journey. The momentum the word has received in its utterance will keep it on the move until the momentum dissipates.

When we throw a stone, we are giving our energy to the stone; the stone moves on while that energy lasts and then falls. After throwing the stone, even if we realize we should not have thrown it there is no way of calling the stone back.

Actions are like arrows released from the bow. Any after-thoughts are of no use, the arrows will complete their journey. Until the journey of all previous actions is finished there will be only jivanamukti, nirvana while living, but no *mahanirvana*, the ultimate merging with existence.

Try to understand this. A jivanamukta will live in a state of lib-eration, but around him the activities of his body and mind will continue. Nothing new will be fed, but until the old feelings are exhausted the activities will continue.

Understand it this way. Suppose you decide to leave your body by fasting. You won't die the very day you begin your fast, it will take you at least about ninety days – it may take even longer, but ninety days are a minimum before death can happen. Why? You fasted today, you should die today. But no, your body has an accu-mulation of flesh from the past and it will take about three months for that flesh to be consumed. You will have become just a skele-ton by then, all the flesh stored in the body will have been con-sumed. This is how when you fast for a day you lose weight by nearly a pound.

So the fatter a person, the longer he will last when fasting, because he has a larger accumulation of fat. Thus one goes on los-ing a pound or so every day, and you will not die while the stock of accumulated flesh lasts. It will take about three months.

Similarly, when the consciousness is fully awake, one should attain to mahanirvana, the ultimate merging, at once. But that does not happen. Once in a while it has happened that way, but

such events are very rare – as good as nonexistent – that a person
has died immediately upon becoming enlightened. It would be as if
someone was already a skeleton, there was nothing at all of any
accumulation, and the person died the very first day he fasted. It
would mean that such a person was just ready to die, he had no
savings at all. But it is difficult to find such a person; even a hungry beggar's body keeps savings, some accumulated stock necessary for any emergencies.

Such a coincidence may happen sometime that a person's actions
also come to completion at the same moment as enlightenment. It
is, however, a very rare phenomenon. Normally they have stayed
and lived for many years after enlightenment – be it Buddha or
Mahavira or someone else.

What is the reason for continuing to live?...because liberation
has already happened. It is the burden of past actions, its momentum, that goes on pushing the body ahead on the journey for some
time. When that momentum is dissipated, jivanamukti, liberation
while living, will become mahanirvana.

But it is necessary and useful too that such persons live on after
enlightenment, because if they die immediately upon enlightenment, whatsoever they have known they will not be able to tell us.
A person liberated while living is able to tell us, share with us,
because there is this interval of time.

Buddha lived for forty years after his enlightenment, Mahavira
also lived for forty years after his enlightenment. It is these forty
years which became useful to us. In these forty years their minds
could communicate to us whatsoever they had experienced and
known.

An arrow released taking an animal to be a tiger,
cannot be stopped midway if later on the
understanding dawns that the animal was instead a
cow. The arrow will hit the target with its full
strength. Similarly, action already done comes to
fruition even after enlightenment has happened.

So if an enlightened person is seen by you to be suffering some-times, do not wonder why existence should torture such a pure and peaceful, such an enlightened person. Nobody is torturing anybody. However great an enlightened person one may be, one still has behind him a long journey of ignorance. The very fact that one is enlightened means that one has traveled long in ignorance. Whatever dirt and dust has been gathered during that long journey will have to be dealt with. The enlightened one now lives it with his sky-nature. But the people who gather around him may not be able to deal with it in the same way.

When Ramakrishna was suffering from cancer, Vivekananda still used to weep. Vivekananda had not attained to enlightenment, his sky-nature. When Ramana Maharshi had cancer, the people in his ashram were unhappy because those who had gathered there had not known the sky-nature.

At the time of his death, almost as he was breathing his last, somebody asked Ramana, "Now what will happen to us?" Ramana replied, "What will happen? I will be here."

People's tears stopped. The assurance had come that he would remain. They thought he was not going to die – and he died! People had misunderstood the statement. When Ramana was saying, "I will be here," he was talking about the sky that he was. Where can the sky go even when the pot is broken?

It is only the pot that breaks. Ramana is saying, "I will be here; why do you weep?" But these were the words of the sky, not of the pot. Those who were around him understood that the words were of the pot, that the pot would remain, but then the pot broke. They thought, "Has Ramana deceived us? Did he say all that just to console us? Was that just a consolation?"

This was not a consolation, this was a truth. But you have no way of experiencing Ramana as the sky as long as you have not experienced yourself as the sky. As long as you think yourself to be only the pot, for you Ramana is gone.

When Ramakrishna was dying his wife, Sharda, started weeping and wailing. Ramakrishna said, "Why are you weeping? You will

not become a widow." And Ramakrishna died – leaving the message, "You will not be a widow, and how in the first place can I
die?" But Sharda was no ordinary woman. Ramakrishna died, his
body was cremated, but there was not even a tear in her eyes. People gathered and, according to the tradition in Bengal, wanted to
shatter and remove the bangles from Sharda's wrists. But she asked
them not to, "Because," she said, "I am not a widow." People
asked her to put on the traditional clothes of a widow, but Sharda
asked them not to even mention it, that she trusted in the words
that had been said to her by Ramakrishna, that they had not been
said to her as a consolation.

What happened is a very sweet story. As long as Sharda lived
after his death, she never accepted even in her dreams that
Ramakrishna had died. People wondered if she had gone mad. But
she was not mad, there were no other signs of madness. On the
contrary, the truth of the matter is that from the very day Ramakrishna died and Sharda did not accept that he had died, she herself became deathless and sky-like.

For Sharda the experience of Ramakrishna's death remained
only an experience of the death of the pot, the body. And there
had never existed any transaction between the pots – the marriage
of Ramakrishna and Sharda was an extraordinary marriage. During their married life the pots never met. Ramakrishna always
treated Sharda like his mother; there was no bodily transaction in
it. Their marriage was nothing but a meeting of two skies.

It is really a very beautiful and amazing story. Sharda lived for
many years after Ramakrishna's death, but she used to prepare
food as she had in the past and then go near Ramakrishna's bed
and say, "Paramahansadeva, the food is ready" – all continued as
it had before. She would still prepare food, go near the bed –
where there was nobody – and address Ramakrishna as usual.

People used to see this and weep at her condition. She would
call him for food and even wait as usual for him to get up, and
then, when he began walking, she would follow him. Only she
could see all this happening, no one else could. She would make

him sit for food, she would fan him while he would be eating. She would make him go to sleep at night and would wake him up in the morning. All continued as usual.

Somebody asked Sharda whom she was waking and whom she was feeding and whom she was putting to bed – what was going on? Sharda replied that it was the same person she had served before. Now the body had gone, but the sky has remained. Sharda did not become a widow even after her husband's death. It was a unique experience for any wife in the whole history of mankind. This is the only event of its type. It is difficult to find another woman like Sharda.

Past actions come to their completion even after enlightenment, but after this experience of the inner void the person watches all that is happening as a witness. He has no desires, no will as to what should happen and what should not happen. He accepts whatsoever happens.

Witnessing means suchness. Whatsoever is happening or not happening is good. The inner trust in the experience is constantly present – that nothing has ever happened or can ever happen to the sky within.

One who understands that he is deathless and ever young remains one with the soul and has no relationship with the fruits of his past actions.

Understand this. This sutra appears a little contradictory but it is not. Past actions continue, but the enlightened person remains unrelated to them. The enlightened person comes to know that he is sky-like – deathless, ever young, unconcerned, unattached, indifferent and neutral. He knows, "I have never gone outside myself, nothing has ever come inside me, neither was I born nor will I die; only being is my state." To such a person actions go on happening because of their chain in the past, but the person has no relationship with them. When unhappiness and pain or age come to the body, he does not identify and say, "I am getting old," he only says that he is seeing the body getting old, or he is seeing the body getting sick, or that happiness has come or unhappiness has come.

He who is settled in the self does not identify. And when one does not identify, past actions dissolve after exhausting their momentum; the body drops after completing its journey, its desires, and tires out, and the witness becomes one with the empty sky.

As long as the body is there, there is only jivanamukti, liberation in life, and when the body also drops, there is mahanirvana.

Enough for today.

WAKE UP!
THIS IS A DREAM

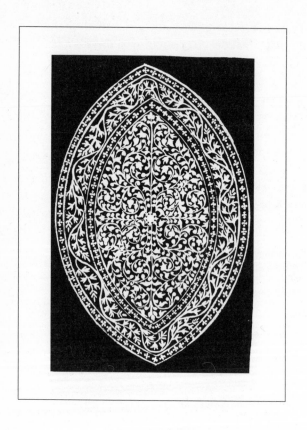

C H A P T E R   1 5

Karma, past actions, bear fruits only when we have
a feeling of my-ness for our bodies. It is never
desirable to have a feeling of my-self for the body.
Thus, by giving up the feeling of my-ness for
the body one gives up the fruits of past actions.

✳

This fallacy that the body is myself is the cause of
creating in the imagination the idea of past actions.
But how could something be true
that is imposed or imagined about a fallacy?

✳

From where can a thing be born
which is not real in the first place?
What has not been born, how can it be destroyed?
How can a thing that is unreal have past actions?

✳

The my-ness with the body is the result
of our ignorance and it is destroyed totally by
enlightenment. Then how does the body remain?
It is to satisfy this doubt of the ignorant
that the scriptures have outwardly attributed
the continuance of the body to past actions.

ne or two questions have been asked. It will be good to discuss them first. A friend has said that what I have been saying is understood by him, but still it is not understood. So, what is he supposed to do about it?

This question is valuable. Everybody must be feeling like this, because understanding has two levels. One is that what I am saying is understood by your intellect; it appears logical to your intellect and your intellect thinks this must be so. This understanding is superficial, it cannot penetrate to the inner core of your being. This understanding is not from your being – it is not from your soul. It appears outwardly that you understand, and as long as you listen to me sitting here you feel you have understood completely. But then you go away from this place and the understanding begins to fade. This is so because as long as whatever has been understood is not practiced also, it cannot become a part of your being. Whatever has been understood, if it does not become assimilated in your blood, flesh and bones, it will fade away like some coloring done on an outer surface.

Your entire past understanding is lying underneath that which you have now understood, and as soon as you go away from here it will begin to create conflict with this new understanding. The old understanding will fight it and push it away. The old ideas will resist the entry of the new idea, will make everything topsy-turvy, will raise thousands of doubts and objections. If you become lost in those objections and doubts, the glimpse of the new understanding will be destroyed.

There is only one way – that whatsoever has been understood by the intellect should be transformed into your life energy, it should be practiced. A harmony should be created with it. It should not remain just a thought, but deep down it should become your action too. And not only your action, but your whole inner being should become recreated by it. Only then slowly, slowly what has reached the surface will go deeper in you and become a practiced truth which your old ideas won't be able to destroy. Rather, because of its presence the old ideas will slowly recede and vanish on their own.

So this is right – this is a natural question for a seeker. Although we understand, we remain as we were. And if we remain as we were, this new understanding will not last for long. Where, in what space, can it stay? If you remain the same old person, all the new understanding will be eliminated, soon forgotten.

And this is the way you have understood many times, this is not the first time. Many times you have turned back from the very doorstep of truth. Many times you have found the door and it was only a matter of knocking when again you have moved away towards the wall. This is where an error is made, that whatever is understood is not immediately translated into life.

In this context it is worth remembering that if someone calls you names you become angry immediately, but if someone gives you an understanding of truth you do not begin meditations immediately. If anything wrong is to be done we do it immediately; if something good is to be done we think about it. Both of these are very deep tricks of the mind, because whatsoever is to be done can be done only if it is done immediately – whether it is a question of being angry or doing meditation it does not matter. We want to express the anger, hence we do it immediately. We do not even wait for a moment, because if we wait we will not be able to do it.

If somebody calls you names and you tell him that you will come back and reply to him in twenty-four hours' time, you will never be able to reply at all. Twenty-four hours is a long time – if you wait even for twenty-four moments in silent consideration perhaps you will not have any desire to become angry. Perhaps you may laugh, perhaps you may see the foolishness of that person, or perhaps you may even see that the names he was calling you were right. So you think it is not right to lose time, it is necessary to retaliate in anger at once when the abusing words strike. As far as repenting is concerned, you will do that later on.

Have you noticed that all angry persons later repent? They

repent after the act of anger. Had they waited a little the repentance would have come before the anger, and then the anger would
never have happened. One who repents after anger will never be
able to become free of anger. Only the one whose repentance pre-
cedes the anger can become free of anger, because whatsoever has
already happened cannot be undone.

But where is the gap? There you called me names and here I
become angry. Where is the time gap between the two so that I may
think, consider and reflect, so that I may look into all the vows I
took in the past not to become angry again, so that I can search in
my past to see how many times I have already repented after
becoming angry? But there is not that much opportunity, time or
space. There somebody called me names and here the fire of anger
is spitting.

Create a little gap and anger will become difficult. However, we
do not create a gap when it is a question of anger, but we do create
a gap when it comes to meditation. So meditation becomes difficult.

When there is an impact of something that is good and right, we
do not immediately engage ourselves in doing it, we wait. That
intervening time spoils everything. It is necessary to strike while
the iron is hot. While we are thinking about it the iron becomes
cold and then it brings no results.

One friend came today. He said he wanted to take sannyas, but
he needed some time to consider the matter. I asked him how
many other matters in his life he had thought about first before
acting. Had he given prior thought to other matters sannyas would
have happened long ago, because sannyas is nothing but the end
result of thinking. All indulgence in life is going to become meaningless to anybody who thinks and deliberates.

So I asked him what else in life he had thought about beforehand.
How many other things had he done after thinking about it? Or
was it only about taking sannyas he wanted to think and deliberate?
How long do you intend to depend on these deliberations? And it
is you, after all, who is deliberating – do you think you are going to
be more intelligent tomorrow? Just look back: your intelligence

may have even become less sharp, it certainly does not seem to be growing.

Scientists say that ordinarily between fourteen and eighteen years of age people's intelligence stops growing. And only in the case of special individuals does intelligence grow up to the age of eighteen, otherwise it stops growing much earlier.

During the last world war, recruits for the army were tested for their intelligence and the average age of intelligence was found to be thirteen and a half years. After thirteen and a half years intelligence does not continue to develop in the average person.

You may say that that does not seem to be right because you feel that you have definitely become more intelligent than when you were younger. Even if you do not feel that way, you definitely go on making your children feel that you are more intelligent. You are an old man, experienced...certainly you are more intelligent.

You may have more experience, but you do not have more intelligence because of your age. Experience is only an accumulation of information. Intelligence is use of that accumulation, and that is entirely different.

A child has less of an accumulation of experience, you have more. But how you use that accumulation is intelligence. Intelligence is not experience. So it can be that a child has more intelligence than an old man, but it can never happen that a child has more experience than the old man. The child is bound to have less experience, but he can have more intelligence. The old man has more experience.

I said to that friend, "Do you think that tomorrow, or the day after tomorrow, you will have more intelligence? No, all that has happened is that right now an urge has arisen in you in this atmosphere, in the waves of meditation surrounding you, under the impact of the bliss and freedom of so many sannyasins here, but by the time you are going down Mount Abu – as your bus is descending towards the plains – you too will be descending from your idea of taking sannyas. It will be amazing if this idea remains with you to the Abu Road railway station at the foot of Mount Abu. Getting down from your bus at the railway station you will take a deep, cool sigh of relief that it is good that you are returning the same as you had come, that you did not lose anything here, that you did not venture into anything that will create unnecessary trouble. After a month you will not even be able to remember it.

"This atmosphere, the presence of so many people, the collective effort of so many people, raises you also to an unaccustomed height. You are dancing in the *kirtan* meditation: are you sure you will be able to dance with the same totality and the same drowning feeling all by yourself? It is not so much that you are dancing, but that the dancing of so many people becomes infectious – it touches you. Their vibrations begin to stimulate your heart; their movement, their steps create an opportunity for the movement of your steps too. And, above all, the pattern of your thinking is always the same as others. So where all are dancing, one thing is certain: nobody is going to say anything to the one who is dancing – but someone may say something to the one who is only standing by. So it creates a stimulus; you feel free – it is alright, there is no problem, one can dance here.

"As you get down from the bus in the crowd of the marketplace, this glimpse you had of a certain height, the jump you had taken that raised your eyes towards the sky, will fade. Now your eyes will again be focused towards the earth. So why do you hope that tomorrow or the day after tomorrow you will be able to make a decision? It is you who has to make the decision, and that can be done today."

But that friend said, "It is not that I have not made any effort to make a decision. Ninety-nine percent of my mind is decided, it is just a matter of the one percent more."

I asked him, "Haven't you done anything in your life where ninety-nine percent of your mind was ready and one percent was not? Have you ever before not made a decision because of that one percent?" I also asked him, "Do you understand what you are saying? Your mind is ninety-nine percent decided to take sannyas, only one percent is not, and you are deciding in favor of the one percent."

And don't think that you can avoid making a decision. There is no way in this world to avoid making a decision. You may decide against, but that too is a decision. You may decide to postpone it for tomorrow, that too is a decision. In the world you have the freedom to make any decision, but you don't have the freedom not to make a decision. That is not possible.

One is bound to make a decision. But one interesting thing is that we think our decision not to do something is not a decision. It is a very amazing concept. That friend had no comprehension that to take sannyas is a decision and not to take sannyas is also a decision. If both are decisions, then the mind is very amazing when it sides with the one percent and does not gather courage to go with the ninety-nine percent in favor.

We are very clever in deceiving ourselves. Even if the understanding is only on the surface, the mind understands what sannyas means and we are afraid. So we think if somehow some time can be gained...not time to allow that one will be able to make a better decision, but time for the impact to fade away so that the ninety-nine percent will turn into one percent and that one percent will then have become ninety-nine percent.... And when it was ninety-nine percent for and one did not decide for sannyas, do you think you will decide for it when the urge remains only one percent?

Your understanding can never go deep because you never translate it into life, you never turn it into a decision. Understand this properly. Many times you listen, you understand, but you still remain the same as you were. This even has a danger of its own, and that is: whenever you have listened many times, understood many times, if you still remain the same as you were, you gradually become like a slippery pot. The more things slip over you, the more slippery the surface becomes. So many thoughts make an impact on you, but you remain as you were. Those thoughts slip over and fall away from you, and you, the pot, remain sitting undisturbed. The pot has become too slippery.

So the more often you remain unchanged after listening, the more difficult your transformation goes on becoming, because now the impact slips off you almost as it touches you. The pot has become absolutely slippery; ways to slip have developed all over it.

It is better that you not only listen to good things but when you listen be courageous and take the decision to transform yourself. Then you will find that your understanding has not remained only on the surface, it has become the melody of your being.

But until the day understanding becomes your very breathing it has no value. It has only one value – that you may have learned to talk cleverly. We all know about it – our country is so clever in pious talk. We are ready to talk about spirituality at any time. But it is only talk, not deeper than that. One may ask anybody in this country; everybody has knowledge of God. Everybody!

The condition of the mind of this whole country has become like that of a slippery pot. For thousands of years the only use we have made of the *tirthankaras,* the incarnations and the sages, is that by hearing them repeatedly we have become slippery pots.

In one town somebody was saying to me that India is really a sacred land because all the incarnations of god, all the tirthankaras and all the buddhas have happened here. I asked him to reconsider his statement. Is India really a sacred land, or is it that the sinners of this land are so amazing that despite the existence of all these people they have remained unchanged? Have all the incarnations come and gone without being able to draw a single line on our slippery pots? Or did the tirthankaras come and we said, "You may come and go, but we are not such fools that we will be disturbed by your talk."

What does it mean in fact? If all the doctors of the town come to visit just the one house, it will mean that house has the maximum number of patients and is the most sick of all the houses. It is the same when all the incarnations have to incarnate here. And Krishna has said in the Gita, "Whenever religion declines and sins increase and the evildoers are on the rise, I will come." And all these incarnations only came here to India. So what does it mean? Does it mean this is a sacred land?

If Krishna's statement is right, then where he was not required to incarnate must be the sacred land. But all incarnations only happened here in this land. It is very clear that the soul of this country has become very slippery. We have heard such beautiful words for so long and have lulled ourselves into such a sleep that we have never bothered to do anything whatever.

No understanding will be complete and deep until it penetrates to your very inner being. Only when you make a decision does understanding penetrate to your inner being. The decision is the door.

Even small decisions are very revolutionary. What is important is not what you decided but that you made a decision. In making a decision your being becomes integrated. The moment you make a decision you become a different man. That decision can be very trivial.

I ask you not to cough for ten minutes. It appears very inhuman: you feel like coughing and I am preventing you from doing so. It looks like wickedness. You are attending a meeting and I tell you you are not to cough at all, to stop it altogether. But you have no idea...even such a small decision on your part gives birth to the soul within you. If you decide not to cough for ten minutes, and if you are successful in not coughing, a wave of joy passes throughout your body; you come to know that you can carry through a decision to completion.

Sneezing and coughing are very nasty things: if you try to prevent them, they persist with greater force. If you try to prevent them, your whole attention becomes centered on them. If you try to prevent them, they rebel. They seem to tell you, "You have never done this before. What is this new whim? What is the matter? So far our relationship has been that you have never prevented me when I came. Before this, even if I had not come and somebody else was coughing, you would begin to clear your throat also. Even though you were not coughing, you would just become infected by others, as it were. What has happened now?"

But if you can prevent your coughing even for ten minutes your relationship with your body will already begin to change, with this small decision.

For example, I call out to you: "Stop!" Gurdjieff has made great use of it in meditations. He had given it a separate name: the stop meditation. When you are ready some time we will do that complete experiment. When I ask you to stop.... In this stopping I am not at this point putting much pressure on you. Gurdjieff also used to say, "Stop!" but it meant that whatever was the position, the situation of your body, it had to stay as it was. If you were dancing and one foot was in the air and another on the ground, you had to stop just like that. Or if your neck was bent one way, or your body was twisted, it had to remain in that position, no changes or adjustments of the body were to be made at all. The body may fall down flat, but you are not to make any change to its position. And if it happens that one foot is a little twisted and you fall down, you straighten it and then lie down – no, make no change to its position either. Gurdjieff called this the stop meditation. Thousands of people had deep experiences through it.

This is a very valuable experiment, just stopping suddenly. And if one deceives, there is no question of anyone else, it is purely deceiving your own self. If one of your legs is in the air and you quietly bring it down, who is watching you? Nobody is watching anybody. But you lost an opportunity. There is no need; it is your leg, you can put it where you like. But within you, you lost an opportunity. Here it was possible to change the relationship between the soul and the body, where the soul could have won over the body and confirmed that the soul is the master. If you carefully brought your leg down to a comfortable position and declared to the world, "Look, I am doing the stop meditation," then you are not deceiving anybody else, your own body has deceived you.

Small decisions, very small decisions can also bring forth great results. The question is not of size, the question is of your decision, of decisiveness. Then your understanding will slowly go deeper within you.

So whatever I am saying to you, you should not only listen to it but also put it into practice.

The Upanishads are very practical lessons. They have nothing to do with theories, they have to do with the alchemy of transforming you. These are simple and direct sutras capable of creating a new man out of you.

But the difficulty is that nobody else can create you with a hammer and chisel. You are the sculptor, you are the stone, and you are the hammer and chisel. All the three things have to be done by you. With the hammer and the chisel of your own decisions, with your own willpower, you have to sculpt your own stone. You have to carve your own statue according to your own understanding. Even a moment of postponement becomes a postponement forever; he who says he will do it tomorrow postpones forever. It would have been better if he had said he will never do it, because that would have been a decision.

So I suggested to that friend who had come to at least make the decision that he would never take sannyas – never. Then too he would have benefited. But he says he will think about whether to take sannyas or not – this is indecisiveness. Even if he makes a clear decision in favor of no, at least he made a decision. Or if he wants to take sannyas he should be clear about it, and then he has also taken a decision. His inner feeling is that he should not take sannyas, but he does not allow this to be a clear-cut decision either. About this too he says, "No, I definitely will take sannyas but I require some time." This way he deceives himself.

Sannyas is a decision, a resolution which brings results. It is beneficial. People ask me what is going to happen by switching to orange clothes. I say, "If you think nothing is going to happen, then wear them for three months."

They say, "People will laugh at us."

I say, "Certainly that will happen. And if you can tolerate their laughter for three months with a cool mind, much will happen to you. Don't bother about the laughing of others...and it triggers the beginning of many things."

People ask me, "What is going to happen by these external changes? Please show us how inner transformation can happen."

I tell them, "You do not have the courage for even transformation of the outer, and you dare to talk about inner transformation? You begin to die, as it were, when only your clothes have to be changed; it will be very difficult if I begin to change your skin. And you talk of the inner?" But we are clever at deceiving ourselves. And one who is deceiving himself can never become religious.

Remember, a person who deceives others may become religious, but one who deceives himself can never become religious because then there remains no way for transformation.

Another friend has asked, "You say good deeds do not nullify the bad deeds, rather they cover them up. So it is inevitable to endure the fruits of bad as well as good deeds. Do the bad and good deeds yield fruit in the same order as they occurred? Or is there no order in the giving of fruit? If bad deeds cannot be destroyed by good deeds, there cannot be any reason in doing good deeds. Is such a doctrine useful for the society?"

Let us understand this. If good deeds cannot destroy bad deeds, that makes this friend anxious – why then would anybody do good deeds? This would really create a big danger for the society.

The situation is just the opposite. If you know that bad deeds can be destroyed by good deeds, you will go on doing bad deeds without any worry – because anytime good deeds can be done and the bad ones counterbalanced. When the medicine is with you, where is the fear of the disease? "We will go and take a holy dip in the Ganges and all our sins will be washed away. We will receive blessings from some saint and all the bad deeds will be wiped out. If I have committed a theft I will give a donation" – from the same money. Other than that where would the money come from anyway?

A big thief will become a big donor. He will steal one hundred thousand rupees and donate ten thousand rupees. Then there can be no fear in stealing, because you can donate to destroy the effect of the theft. You can murder someone and then give birth to a child. You have taken one life and you are giving back one life.

This world has become so bad only because you think that bad deeds can be nullified by good deeds. When I say that there is no way of nullifying bad deeds by good deeds, then you will have to think twice before doing a bad deed. Every deed will yield its fruit, and it will have to be endured, it is inevitable; it cannot be nullified. There is no way out; neither any good deed, donation or virtue will help, nor will any holy Ganges pilgrimage, master, god or blessing be of any help. The fruits of what has been done will have to be endured.

So at the time you do anything you have to think clearly, because the deal is being sealed and there will be no way out of it. It is not that you will weep and cry in front of God, "You are the savior of the sinners, and we are sinners. Now do something. If you don't it won't harm us very much, but your name will be spoiled because you are the savior of sinners. And we have been committing sins only for you, because unless we do that how can you remain a savior of sinners? So now prove your saviorhood."

A woman came to me the day before yesterday. It was very crowded and in that crowd she abruptly said, "Bless me!"

I said, "Fine."

The next day she came back again and asked, "Will the blessings come true? – because the blessings of good saints *do* come true, and you have blessed me."

I said, "This seems to be difficult. It appears you will drag me to a court of law if they don't come true! At least let me have some idea in what connection you want my blessings to come true."

She said, "But you should know that whenever a good saint blesses someone, the blessing does come true."

I said to her, "There is one escape for me in it, that at least you cannot drag me into the courts. If the blessings do not make what you want come true you may understand that I am neither good nor a saint – and the matter is over. This way you created one escape route for me. Now I don't even want to know what it is that you wanted my blessings for. If it does not come true you can understand that neither was I good nor a saint, and the matter is over."

We call this being religious! The woman believes she is religious.

In this universe there is a law, an inner discipline that we have

390 FINGER POINTING TO THE MOON

called *rit* in the Vedas, and Lao Tzu called Tao. There are no excep-
tions under that law. Whatever you do, you will have to endure its
fruit. If this understanding goes deeper in you, you will have to
change your way of living and your actions. It is a truth. And if this
truth becomes clear it will be good for the society. For how long
have you been preaching this to each other, but the society does not
seem to be changing. On the contrary, sins are increasing because
we are aware of the loophole, that there is a way out. If I commit a
sin, the house of sin does not only have a door of entry but a door
of exit as well. It is possible to get out as well; one need not be too
afraid to enter.

The meaning of what I have said to you is that there is no exit,
you will have to live the outcome. You can be free only after living the outcome. There is no way of nullifying, living the outcome
is the nullifying. There is only one way of being cleansed, and that
is to live the outcome. There is no other way of getting free of it.

The second thing he says is, what is the rationale then of doing
good deeds? It is very clear from his question itself that, in his opinion, good deeds are done only to nullify the bad deeds. The questioner says that when I say it is not possible to annihilate bad deeds
with good deeds, the whole rationale of doing good deeds is lost,
the only reason for doing good deeds is lost. His mind also believes,
as is clear from his question, that good deeds such as giving to charity are useful only to offset the thefts committed. In this case the
theft becomes more important, the giving of charity is secondary. If
there were no thefts in the world charity would not be possible.

One so-called thinker, Karapatri, has written in his book that
if socialism becomes successful religiousness will decline – because
if nobody is poor, to whom will you give charity? That means
poverty must remain so that charity is possible, and without charity there is no entry to paradise.

Do you understand the meaning? It means that hell must remain
and the naked, hungry beggar on the road must also remain...
because if there are no hungry people, to whom will you give
food? And if no one takes the food you offer as charity, you are in

trouble; then how will you gain paradise? So according to you, the reason for doing good deeds is dependent on the existence of bad deeds? This would mean that a good deed is being benefited by a bad deed, that it is a good man who is exploiting a bad man.

No, the rationale for doing good deeds is not in nullifying the effects of bad deeds. Bad deeds result in unhappiness and good deeds result in happiness. A good deed brings happiness – that is its rationale. One who wants happiness does good deeds. One who thinks he will attain happiness by doing bad deeds is being foolish. He is going against the law and will have to suffer. The rationale for doing good deeds is in their fruits, and bad deeds result in their fruits. How can the rationale for doing good deeds lie in bad deeds? They have no relationship at all.

A good deed brings its fruit and that is happiness; a bad deed brings its fruit and that is unhappiness. If we can understand this properly, and if this understanding goes deep into the mind, then whosoever desires happiness will have to do good deeds, then it will be beneficial to the society. Whosoever does bad deeds will have to suffer the resulting misery. If he thinks that by doing some good deeds afterwards it will be possible to wipe out the bad deeds, he is mistaken.

You may understand it this way. If I have abused you, I have hurt you and made you unhappy; that unhappiness has already happened. Then later I ask for your forgiveness and make you happy. Do you think that because of the good feelings and happiness that I now create by my request to be forgiven, that the earlier unhappiness which had already happened can be said to have never happened? No, it has already happened; that unhappiness that I caused you has already happened. This dressing upon the wound does not, by now bringing some happiness, annihilate the unhappiness that occurred before, it only brings a little soothing.

I abused you, I did a bad deed – I suffered the unhappiness that comes with it. I asked for forgiveness, I did a good deed – I enjoyed the happiness that comes with it.

The bad deed leads to unhappiness, the good deed leads to

happiness. The more good deeds, the more the happiness grows. The more bad deeds, the more the unhappiness grows. One who wants to remain happy has to slowly go on dropping bad deeds and continuing to do good deeds.

But religion has nothing to do with happiness either because, ordinarily, to avoid unhappiness is the desire of everybody. As long as you are full of desire to avoid unhappiness you are an ordinary person, not a religious person. So far your desire is only for happiness – this is the rationale for doing good deeds. You should be urged to do good deeds; you want happiness, you will have it. You do not want unhappiness; then do not do bad deeds because that brings unhappiness.

If the inevitability of a bad deed resulting in unhappiness is seen just as clearly as that one's hand is burned if held in a fire, people will stop putting their hands into fire. If the inevitability of becoming happy for having done good deeds is also as clearly realized as that one's hands become fragrant if flowers are held by them, people will do good deeds.

But religion has nothing to do with this as yet; it is still morality, it is still at the level of morality in society. But a person who experiences happiness slowly comes to realize something new, that not only is unhappiness meaningless, but happiness too is meaningless. While unhappiness does make one unhappy, even happiness available in full measure begins to give unhappiness. Happiness too is boredom. The unhappiness from happiness is boredom.

Have you ever seen any animal bored – a bored donkey or a bored buffalo? Except man, no other animal on the earth ever becomes bored. Why? Because an animal's day is spent just in attaining its day-to-day life's requirements. It is never able to accumulate that much happiness and comfort that it can become bored. The question of boredom arises only when there is excessive happiness.

This is why a poor man is also not bored – only the rich. If you look at the face of a rich man it looks bored, as if declaring that there is no meaning, that one is dragging on but there is no purpose. The legs of a poor man have a sort of movement. He may be weak, tired and anemic, but the movement is there. He has some goal to reach; there is a hope in his eyes that tomorrow he will have a house, or the day after he will have a shop, that his son will be able to complete his education – he has a heaven projected in the future. But those people whose sons have come home duly educated know the things that follow, how he also brings unhappiness. Those who have built their palaces come to realize that they have become a prison.

When all happiness is achieved one realizes for the first time that happiness too is creating boredom. Our minds get bored with happiness too. Thus, Mahavira, Krishna and Rama were all born as the sons of kings. It is not possible to become a tirthankara or an incarnation of God by taking birth in the house of a poor man. The reason is that there is no possibility of being bored with happiness.

All the twenty-four tirthankaras of the Jainas are sons of kings. Buddha, Rama, Krishna – all are sons of kings. It is in the affluence of the palaces of kings that one realizes that all things are meaningless. You only come to realize this if you have everything you want; how would you realize this before? When Buddha realized that there was nothing worthwhile in the body of a woman it was because his father had gathered all the most beautiful girls of the kingdom in his harem. Only then did he realize that there was nothing in them.

You find a thing to be worthless only when you have it in plenty. This is why America is the most bored country in the world today. And the young boys and girls of America are running around the whole world in the hope of getting rid of this boredom. It does not matter how – it may be marijuana, opium, drugs, or whatever works – but the boredom has to go.

When one becomes bored with happiness and one's whole being is filled with a quest to go beyond happiness, religion is born.

So the rationale for doing good deeds are two: one, the outcome of good deeds is happiness. So those who desire happiness – and everybody desires, be he an atheist or a theist, be he a Hindu or a Mohammedan, anybody – the rationale for doing good deeds is that they bring happiness. The second rationale for doing good deeds is that once happiness has been achieved its futility is also seen. And when happiness becomes futile, then man sets off on the journey towards religion.

The journey towards religion means how to go beyond happiness too. The journey towards the world means how to get rid of unhappiness, and the journey towards nirvana means how to get rid of happiness also.

Now we go into the sutra:

> *Karma, past actions, bear fruits only when we have*
> *a feeling of my-ness for our bodies. It is never*
> *desirable to have a feeling of my-self for the body.*
> *Thus, by giving up the feeling of my-ness for*
> *the body, one gives up the fruits of past actions.*

Actions stick to us only when we feel that this body is 'mine'. All actions stick to the body, not to us. But when we cling to our bodies the actions naturally cling to us also. The actions cling to the body from the outside and we cling to the body from inside, thus we become connected with the actions.

Actions cannot cling to the soul, they always cling only to the body. It is like somebody wanting to cut something with a knife: a knife can only cut matter; if you want to cut the sky with a knife it is not possible. The knife will make the cutting action, but the sky will remain uncut.

The effect of actions, or the result of actions, or the knife of actions, can cut matter only. Body is matter, mind too is matter. Matter can encounter matter. But the consciousness within you, that empty sky within you, cannot be cut or touched by any action. But one thing can happen: if the consciousness within you believes the body as 'mine', which it is free to do, then all the sufferings of the body will start happening to you too.

Let us understand it like this. I have heard that once a house caught fire. Its owner, seeing this, began to weep bitterly. But one of his neighbors told him that he had seen his son in the fire insurance office yesterday; the building was already insured against fire. Where was his son? The son had gone out to do some work. But meanwhile the father had stopped weeping; because the house was insured, there was no reason to weep.

His tears dried up – and the house was still burning, the same house. But now that he thought it was insured, the relationship of 'mine' had shifted from the house to the insurance money. But then the son came running to the scene and saw his father standing in front of the burning house laughing. The son said, "I certainly did go to the fire insurance office, but the transaction was never completed."

Immediately the man began to weep bitterly again, "I am ruined, I am finished!" The house is the same, but what happened in between? The my-ness was detached from the house and then attached itself to the house again.

The feeling of my-ness with the body is the cause of all our miseries, or our happiness – of all our fruits of karma. If that my-ness is removed, the effects of all actions on the body become unrelated to us.

This sutra says that to keep the feeling of my-ness is to help create the process of all actions, is to cooperate with this process. As that feeling of my-ness is gone, as you come to realize who you are – that you are not the body – then you remain unconcerned, just the way that the man remained unconcerned with the burning house once he knew it was not *his* house. Buddha and Mahavira realized that the body, the house, was not theirs and they became unconcerned with its burning. They went inside. They had come to know the one who lives in the house. They had come to know the one who certainly lives in this house but is not the house itself.

The disappearance of my-ness is the renunciation of the fruits of all past actions. Then past actions are of no consequence, the renunciation has happened.

This fallacy that the body is myself is the cause of

creating in the imagination the idea of past actions.
But how could something be true
that is imposed or imagined about a fallacy?

It is all imposed, imagined; it only appears that it is yours. There is your son – you are doing everything in your power for his upbringing. You are ready even to give up your life for your son. And then one day suddenly you find a letter hidden in an old book from which you learn that your wife was in love with another man. Now this creates doubt as to whether the son is yours or is not yours, and everything is disturbed.

A father always remains a little doubtful, because the father is a very irrelevant phenomenon in the birth of a child – not very important. The father is no more important than an injection. Only the mother knows with certainty that the child is hers; the father always has a lurking doubt, that he is not the father. It is only to get rid of that feeling of doubt that we have created such strict systems of marriage so that the very question of that doubt does not arise, otherwise it will cause trouble for one's whole life. If one remained doubtful whether the children for whose upbringing one has to labor hard are his own or not there would be great chaos in life. This is why a very strict code of marriage has been evolved, and all movement of women has been curtailed so that they do not come in contact with other men. If coming in contact is prevented, then there is no fear.

This is also why there is so much fuss about the virginity of the girl – that marriage should be only with a virgin girl. And this is also why those who were extremely worried about such matters started child marriage, so that there remains simply no way for any fear: "It is certain that the child is mine."

If the child is mine, the my-ness is easily projected; if there is any doubt, the projection becomes difficult. Wherever there is projection of 'mine', I have become identified and now I can do everything for it, even suffer pain for it. When the projection of 'mine' shifts away, I have become disidentified, separated from it.

All this feeling of 'mine' is just a projection. In this world there is nothing that is 'mine'. Even your body is not 'mine'. That too has come from the parents – and their's is not their's either, they received it from their parents. If we go deeper in our search the tiny atom of which our bodies are created has a journey of billions and trillions of years behind it. Neither the bone is yours nor the flesh nor the marrow – none of these are yours, neither is the mind yours. Only you are yours. But you have no inkling of that 'you'.

Who is that within you whom you can call 'mine', or 'I'? If you go on removing your idea of 'mine', dropping it, eliminating it – the Upanishads call the process *neti, neti:* "I am not this, I am not that"...just go on doing this, breaking away from all kinds of 'mine', then suddenly one day you will experience, just as a flame of light may leap out of the darkness, who you are.

On being free from 'mine', the self is experienced. By increasing the expanse of 'mine', the feeling of self goes on diminishing. So the bigger the expanse of 'mine', the smaller the experience of self.

This is the reason why Buddha and Mahavira ran away from their families and houses. The trouble was not the house – they had extensive empires, they had lots of things they could call 'mine', but the extension of the 'mine' was so vast that their self was untraceably lost; they could not trace, "Who am I?" So they moved away from the whole empire of 'mine'. Mahavira has made the ultimate effort in this moving away. He even dropped his clothes and became naked so he could have nothing to call his; now not even his clothing is 'mine'.

And why? Because of only one reason – that in this vast expanse of 'mine' the self is not experienced and felt at all, and if I run away from it all and remain totally alone, perhaps I may know who I am.

It is easy to know the self when you break away from everything you call 'mine'. It goes on becoming more difficult to know the self as you add more to what you call 'mine'. So the more things you go on accumulating, the more the possessions go on increasing, the more their expansion, the more the center of self goes on disappearing, getting covered.

The entire network of 'mine' is imaginary. The self is the truth, 'mine' is an untruth.

> *From where can a thing be born*
> *which is not real in the first place?*
> *What has not been born, how can it be destroyed?*
> *How can a thing that is unreal have past actions?*

Very thought-provoking things have been said in this sutra. *Which is not real*...which does not exist. From where is the feeling of 'mine' born? When is it born? How will it come to an end? It is a difficult matter, because we feel that when there is this 'mine' it must have been born somewhere, otherwise how could it be? And if something is mine, it must also die sometime, otherwise how would you be free from it? To understand this, we shall have to go back to the category of the 'almost true' that I discussed with you earlier. Understand this once more.

There is a rope; it appeared to be a snake. Then you went for a closer look and discovered it was only a rope, not a snake. Now the question is that, since the rope was seen as a snake, a snake certainly was born from the rope – how else would it be seen there? But we know no snake was born there. How can something which is not there, a falsehood, be born? Afterwards, when you approached with a lighted lamp, you could see clearly that there was no snake. So the snake died, but where is the dead body of that snake?

What is seen but is not actually there has neither any birth nor any death, it is only an illusion. But illusions can happen, do happen. An illusion is a projection. In that rope no snake was ever born; your own mind had just projected the snake on the rope and you were able to see it.

When you sit in a movie theater you never turn around to see anything behind you. There is actually nothing there to see. Everything is seen on the screen in front of you. The flow of colors, forms, songs and music is all on the screen in front. But the interesting fact is that there is actually nothing on the screen; the screen is empty, it is only rays projecting light and shadow on the screen. The screen itself is empty, everything is behind your back where the projector is installed.

This word projection is very good. It is the translation into English of the Sanskrit word *kalpit* or *prakshepit,* meaning imaginary, or projection.

The projector is installed behind you. From there things are being projected onto the screen, and we are seeing them on the screen where they actually are not. And you don't look where they are, you keep your back to them. You saw a snake in a rope, but the rope is functioning only as a screen; it is your mind which is projecting a picture of a snake on the rope. And then you are running away from that snake.

When three-dimensional pictures were made for the first time very interesting things happened all over the world. In London, in one of the very first three-dimensional films, a man riding a horse is shown rushing forwards and then he throws a long spear. A three-dimensional picture shows things in their real form. If it is a horse, it appears as natural as a real horse – in all its three dimensions.

The horse comes charging forwards, the sound of its hooves becoming louder and louder, and then the rider throws a spear.... The whole audience put their heads down and leaned sideways in an attempt to avoid the approaching spear and give way for it. Fearful shrieks were heard and a few women became unconscious.

What happened? In actuality there was no spear at all. But on the screen it appeared so real. As the picture was three-dimensional, it appeared that the spear would pierce them. In that moment the instinctive ducking happened, because the mind did not know if the spear was real or unreal. It only appeared to be real, but it was not real. The heads leaned away out of instinctive habit, to save themselves from being hurt. This happened in a split second – one does not need time to think. Afterwards one would have laughed at oneself: "I must have looked mad!" But it happened.

When a buddha becomes enlightened, he also laughs at his previous madness.

There is a story about Rinzai. When he became enlightened he began to laugh hilariously. When his disciples asked him why he was laughing, he replied that he had become enlightened. The astonished disciples asked, "Enlightened? We have never heard that a person laughs like this when he is enlightened. Why are you laughing?"

Rinzai was rolling and shaking with laughter and trying to say how he had been befooled – and that, too, meaninglessly. There was nothing: what he had been catching hold of was not there, and what he had been trying to give up was also not there. He alone was there. It was as if he had been holding onto something and he had caught his own hand.

Sometimes it happens at night that your hands are lying on your chest and you start dreaming that somebody is forcibly sitting on your chest, and when you wake up and open your eyes you are trembling and perspiring from the nightmare. Your own hands were lying on your chest, and it is their weight that created the dream. During sleep all the senses become very sensitive, hence a little weight feels to be very heavy. One's own hands...and it appears as if someone is sitting on the chest.

You may try it sometime. When someone in your house is sleeping, slowly rub a piece of ice on the soles of their feet. Soon they will begin to have a dream, something like climbing a mountain covered with snow and getting frozen. It is very, very cold...a real crisis would have begun within the person. Or bring the flame of a burning lamp near the soles of the feet and the person will start dreaming of hell: wild flames, huge cauldrons full of boiling oil, and the person is being taken out and then thrown back in again.

What is happening within? The mind already has its concepts and ideas: even a slight hint and it begins to project them...just any screen and your projector is switched on.

Even while we are awake, what we are doing is the same thing. When somebody becomes really awakened – not our wakeful state, but the awakening of a buddha or the seers of the Upanishads – he laughs, and that laughter is because he realizes how foolish he has been. He has been seeing what was never there. He has been clinging to something that was never there. He has even been trying to renounce that which was never there. And the whole game was his own creation. It was only him – his mind – from all sides. If you properly analyze any event of your life, you will come to experience the truth of what I am saying. If you do not analyze, the activities of your mind continue being at your back; the world remains as a screen and the whole play goes on – which is visible on the screen.

No, this illusion has neither any birth nor any death. The false is neither born nor does it die.

> *The my-ness with the body is the result*
> *of our ignorance and it is destroyed totally by*
> *enlightenment. Then how does the body remain?*
> *It is to satisfy this doubt of the ignorant*
> *that the scriptures have outwardly attributed*
> *the continuance of the body to past actions.*

This is a very difficult matter. And what I was saying to you two or three days ago will have complicated the matter even more for you. I said to you that Buddha has to tell a lie, Mahavira has to tell a lie, because of you, because you understand only the language of lies, you understand no other language.

This sutra says that in actuality there is neither body nor past actions. In fact, the truth contains neither body nor past actions in it, neither good deeds nor bad deeds in it, neither happiness nor misery in it. In fact, the world is not.

This is the reality, but it cannot be said. This sutra says that it cannot be said to ignorant people. If you tell ignorant people that you are not the body, they will say, "Get away! Is your mind alright? Go and get some treatment for your mind!" If you tell ignorant people that there is no world, they will send you to a madhouse.

An enlightened one among ignorant people is in the same situation as a man with eyes among a race of blind people. If he says there is great light, all the blind people will laugh at him. They will say, "What are you talking about? Is your mind alright? What light?" He says, "I am seeing the light," and the blind will laugh again and ask him what he means by 'seeing'. They have never heard of a thing like seeing. Was there such a thing as seeing? Neither such a thing as seeing had ever happened to their parents nor their grandparents; certainly the person with eyes has gone out of his mind.

Do you understand what the condition of a man with eyes among blind people would be? If he has any intelligence he will not even by mistake talk about things that blind people cannot see. And if he wants to bring the blind to the ways of the people with eyes he will have to create and use many devices. It will not be good for him to tell them directly, "I have eyes and you are blind, and I am going to treat your eyes. What you are is false; there is something else, which is only seen when the eyes open – you are living in a sort of falsehood."

If such a thing is done, instead of his treating their eyes the blind people will conspire to treat *his* eyes. This has happened many times. We crucified Jesus, we cut Mansoor to pieces, we poisoned Socrates. The only reason why this was done was that these people started saying the truth directly, but they were not understood. If we are to follow what they say, we cannot survive the way we are. So we are also not at fault.

You will be amazed to know that in India we have not crucified any Buddha or Mahavira or Ramakrishna. Jesus was crucified in Jerusalem, Mansoor was killed by Mohammedans, Socrates was poisoned by Greeks. In this country we have not killed, crucified or poisoned or hanged any Buddha, any Mahavira, any Krishna. Do you know the reason? The reason is very amazing. The reason is that Krishna, Buddha and Mahavira are more skilled than Jesus and Socrates in talking with blind people. This is the sole reason – that they are more skilled. And there is a reason for this skill.

For thousands and thousands of years in this country, Buddhas and Mahaviras have talked to blind people, so they have developed methods and devices for it.

Jesus was in a great difficulty. The entire teaching of Jesus took place in India; he had no inkling of what he was stepping into when he went back from here. When he returned and began to speak in Jerusalem, there was no place for him in the traditions there. Jesus appeared to be totally alien; what he said appeared to be madness.

In the Old Testament it is said that if someone takes one of your eyes, then you take both his eyes. This is the language of the blind. And Jesus arriving there began to talk in the language of the people with eyes – all of a sudden, out of nowhere, there was no bridge in between. He said, "If someone hits your left cheek, offer him your right cheek also; if someone takes your coat, give him your shirt also; if someone asks you to carry his luggage for one mile, carry it for two miles – maybe it is out of shyness that he asked you to carry it only one mile."

This language of the people with eyes was completely beyond understanding in a place where the rule was to answer a brick with a stone. Actually, Jesus made a mistake by plainly and directly speaking of the experiences of the people with eyes to the blind people.

Buddha and Mahavira were more skilled. And there can be no comparison to them as far as the art of inventing 'almost truth' is concerned. And this is what this sutra of the Upanishad is saying very clearly. It is saying that neither are you the body nor is there any past action, but for the satisfaction of the ignorant people the mention of body and past actions is outwardly and superficially made. In actuality, there is neither body nor past actions.

Now this is very difficult. All the scriptures are ninety-nine percent untrue. This had to be so for the sake of the blind, to explain things to them. Otherwise they understand nothing and they will just get confused if the truth is told directly.

It is just as when we teach children the alphabet we make them repeat 'g', for god. The letter 'g' is not the monopoly of god; 'g' can also stand for goat. But now that India has gone secular, I hear 'g' stands for goat in the schoolbooks. It used to stand for god when I was a student...a goat is a more secular animal. God belongs to certain religions, the goat does not; it is found in all the religions. This technique of emphasizing 'g' on the mind of a child with the help of a picture of a goat is sound, but if the child gets stuck with it and always utters the word goat whenever it reads 'g' it will create a problem.

The picture of a goat was only an aid for understanding something abstruse like the letter 'g'. Because a child can understand 'goat' easily but not the letter 'g', the picture of a goat was associated with 'g'. The picture of the goat was just symbolic. After some time the symbols will be gone, the pictures will be gone; the child will begin to read the letter 'g' directly.

Thus, if ignorant people have to be made to understand, in the beginning they have to be talked to in the language they know. They have to be told, "This is happiness, that is misery. If you desire happiness, do good deeds; only if you want misery must you do bad deeds. Even if you don't want misery, bad deeds will still bring it. If you transcend them both you will reap no fruits. And when you reap no fruits you are liberated."

In this whole thing we are proceeding with the one assumption that everything is real. But when a person becomes awakened, when he is utterly conscious, when he disidentifies himself with the body and his ignorance is destroyed, he can't help laughing. He sees that all that was left behind was not real, but a big dream. And the methods and devices that have been given to him were also dreams within dreams.

It will be easier to understand it this way. Ramakrishna was a devotee of the mother goddess Kali, and he was also very humble. If anybody wanted to teach him some path other than that of devotion, he was ready to learn and follow.

Once a *vedantin* master named Totapuri was visiting him. He began to question Ramakrishna about the superficiality of dancing and chanting and singing devotional songs. These were of no use, he said. If Ramakrishna really wanted to know the ultimate, he should search for the one absolute. This duality of a devotee and his god was incorrect.

Ramakrishna was a very humble and unique person. He immediately bowed his head to the feet of Totapuri and asked him to teach this path of nonduality. So Totapuri taught him how to sit in meditation. Ramakrishna would sit with his eyes closed and he would soon be feeling very blissful. Totapuri asked him what was happening. He said he was seeing the mother goddess. Totapuri would not accept this as defeat. He said that if Ramakrishna was seeing the goddess Kali, what was there in it to be so overjoyed about? "All this is imagination – this mother and this goddess – all this is your own projection."

Ramakrishna said, "It might be so, but it is immensely blissful." Totapuri said that if he wanted to remain satisfied with this bliss he would never know the ultimate bliss. Ramakrishna then asked him what he should do. Totapuri suggested that there was a method: "When you begin to see Kali, immediately take a sword and cut her into two pieces." Ramakrishna asked from where he would get a sword.

It is natural to ask from where would one suddenly find a sword within. Even if there was a sword actually lying outside, how could it be taken within to kill Kali when he saw her? Totapuri said that the mind that produced Kali within could also produce a sword: "When you have succeeded in producing Kali within you, won't you be able to produce just a small thing like a sword?"

This is a technique of a dream within a dream. Do you understand me? Kali too is imagination. An ecstatic dream, but imagination. It is one's own mental projection, it is one's own feelings that have taken a form; it is one's own desires, one's own colors that one has spread within. Kali standing within him and Ramakrishna lying at her feet also within himself...interestingly enough all that is Ramakrishna's own imagined feelings.

So Totapuri rightly asked him, "Will the sword have to be taken from the outside when you have already taken Kali from within? When you have created a Kali within you, you can also create a sword within. And you appear to be very skilled at it. When you become so ecstatic on seeing Kali within you, that only means you have created a very solid Kali within, so much so that you have no doubts at all about her being real. So just create one more thing – a sword!"

Ramakrishna became very sad: "How can this happen, how can I myself kill mother Kali?"

Totapuri said, "If the sword cannot kill Kali, we will think of something else, but at least make an attempt."

Ramakrishna again wondered how he would manage to cut Kali. Totapuri then threatened to leave. "You have accepted to learn the path of Vedanta, nonduality; you should gather some more courage. What is the use of weeping like a child?"

Totapuri brought a piece of glass and asked Ramakrishna to sit in meditation. He said, "When I feel that you have begun to see Kali within, in order that you do not forget – because as hypnotized as you have become with her you will forget to use the sword.... Even if you remember, it seems you will not have the courage to lift the sword. You appear so filled with love for her: how will you pick up the sword? I understand how difficult it will be for you, almost like a mother who has to cut her own child. So I will assist you, don't worry.

"When I feel that you have begun to see Kali within, I shall cut a deep wound with this piece of glass on the location of your third eye. As soon as you feel the cut and blood begins to flow and you feel the pain – and I will continue to cut with the glass – right at that moment you too have to gather courage and, lifting the sword, cut Kali into two pieces."

This is right. If a cut is made on the location of the third eye with a piece of glass from the outside – because it is through that third eye that one sees the visions of Kali or Rama or Krishna or whoever it may be – and simultaneously one gathers courage, then with this experience of the cutting of the third eye any inner image whatsoever will fall to pieces.

Ramakrishna did gather courage, and the image fell into pieces. Ramakrishna, after coming out of his experience, said, "The last barrier has fallen."

But these are all devices. What I was explaining is that Kali is one untruth within and the sword is another untruth within – but one untruth cuts the other untruth.

All the seers of the Upanishads are giving devices for cutting that which is not, because we maintain a belief in what actually is not, as though it is. So some devices are being given to us that may cut what does not exist. A false disease demands a false medicine. Our whole psychological world is false – this is why so many devices are required. And for that very reason any device can work...any device, provided you get the knack of it.

There is a dream within a dream: the dream has to kill the dream, there is no other way. Truth is not killed with truth – it is not possible. Untruth is also not killed with truth – that too is not possible, because the truth and untruth can never meet anywhere so how can one kill the other? Only untruth kills the untruth. One untruth kills the other untruth, and when they both fall, what remains is the truth.

Understand it this way: your foot is pierced by a thorn. You pick up another thorn from the ground and remove the one in your foot with its help. Then you throw them both away.

So this sutra is saying, neither you are the body, nor is there karma, action, nor accumulated karma, past actions – nor the world in fact. It is, however, not asking you to believe that, because by so doing you will fall into difficulty, right now.

No, for you it still is, because *you* are not yet. You do not yet know the truth, hence all untruths are truths for you. The day you know your own truth all untruths will vanish.

On knowing one's own self, the world becomes false. It is because we do not know ourselves that the false world appears to be true.

Enough for today.

ONLY THIS IS

CHAPTER 16

It is not to explain to the knowers
but to satisfy the ignorant
that the scriptures say that "Body etcetera is true,"
and that there is accumulated karma, past action.

✳

Actually there exists nothing else
except the one and nondual Brahman,
which is perfect, beginningless and endless,
immeasurable, unchanging, abode of truth,
abode of consciousness, abode of bliss,
eternal, indestructible, omnipresent, uniform,
whole, infinite, with head in all directions,
impossible to be lost or to be found,
supportless, independent, devoid of all attributes,
actionless, subtle, choiceless, spotless, indefinable,
beyond mind and speech, truly affluent,
self-evident, pure, conscious and
unlike anything we know.

✳

Thus, knowing through your own experience
that the soul is indivisible, be fulfilled and
dwell blissfully in the changeless soul.

It is not to explain to the knowers
but to satisfy the ignorant
that the scriptures say that "Body etcetera is true,"
and that there is accumulated karma, past action.

hatsoever is said is not related only to the sayer, but relates also to the one to whom it is said. In fact the one to whom it is being said is more important. It has to be something that can be understood by him, that will not go over his head, that will not confuse him but rather bring clarity, that will become a path for him, not a mental disturbance – something that will not become just a journey into thinking but may become a discipline for transforming his life.

This sutra says that the scriptures speak to the ignorant in one language and to the knowers in a different language. The reality is that the enlightened ones speak with every individual in a different language. This is why you find so many inconsistencies in the scriptures, because the statements were addressed to different individuals. Buddha says one thing today, another tomorrow and a third thing the day after – and it becomes difficult to understand how the same individual would have said all these three things which are contradictory and opposite. There is no inconsistency, but a believer in Buddha tries hard to manage some sort of connection among them so that Buddha does not appear inconsistent. But the real fact is only this, that the speaker in all of them was the same but the listeners were different – and the statements were made keeping the listener in view.

The physician may be the same, but if the patients are different the medicines will be different. The statements of Buddha, the statements of the buddhas, are not doctrines but medicines. Hence it is always necessary to know to whom the statement was made.

The scriptures say one thing to the ignorant and another to the knowers. To the knowers it says that there is nothing like a body, only you are; to the ignorant it says that the body is there, but you are not the body. Now these statements are contradictory. If there is no body then there is no body; it has to be so whether you are talking to a knower or to the ignorant. And if there is body, then what difference does it make whether the listener is a knower or an ignorant person? Let us go into this more minutely.

There are some truths which are objective facts, such as, "This is morning." Whether a person is a knower or ignorant makes no difference; morning is morning for both. Or if the sun has set and it is now night, it is night for the knower as well as the ignorant.

Science explores facts, hence it has to speak in a consistent language. Science deals with things that are outside, hence there is a great consistency in it. Religion is a subjective phenomenon. It uses a language in accordance with the inner; its emphasis is more on the subjectivity, less on fact.

So depending on who is seeing, differences arise. When a knower looks, the body is not seen by him at all. When an ignorant person looks, the soul is not seen at all. The ignorant man looks in such a way that he sees only the body, a knower looks in such a way that he sees only the soul. For the knower it is impossible to see the body and for the ignorant it is impossible to see the soul.

This is the reason sages like Shankara could say that the world is false, it is not there at all...and materialists like Brahaspati could say that soul and God are all untruths, only matter exists. There is no inconsistency between these two, because there is no meeting ground for them. These are two statements seen through different perspectives. The whole way of looking at life is different. No world is seen from the point where Shankara looks at it; only the world is seen from the point where the materialist Charwak looks. This is a difference of perspectives. These are statements of people who have looked entirely separately and whose ways of looking are different.

It is like this: if smell is the only mode of detection for you, if you only have the nose as a sensory organ.... There are some animals, birds and insects who do live only through smell, who find their way through smell. Now such insects who find their way only through smell have no way of knowing what sound is, what music is, because there is no way to detect music through the sense of smell. Music has no smell whatsoever – if it is good music it is not fragrant and if it is bad music it is not stinking. Smell has nothing to do with sound. So someone who is equipped only with the detection system for smell will not know sound. For him sound does not exist. Something only exists in our world when we have the means to detect it.

Remember, we have five senses, hence we are able to recognize five elements. If we had ten senses we would be able to recognize ten elements. Below man on the ladder of evolution are animals; some of them have four senses, some have three senses and some have two only. Their world is limited to the number of senses they have.

For an animal that does not have ears, though he may have the rest of the senses, sound does not exist. Not that sound is not there, but if you do not have the medium to catch the sound, the sound becomes nonexistent for you, this world is soundless for you. If there are no eyes, there is no light in the world. So you will know only that for which you have a medium.

Your world is your medium.

An ignorant person searches through his body medium. This is the reason an ignorant person always asks, "Where is God? Show me." What he is saying is, "As long as my eyes do not see, I will not agree." When you say that as long as you have not seen God with your own eyes you will not believe, what is it that you are really saying? You are saying that as long as God does not become an object that you can see, you cannot agree about his existence. But who has told you that God is an object for the eyes to see? And if God is not an object that can be seen by the eyes then you will never encounter him, because your very insistence about seeing him through the eyes will become the barrier.

Form is what is seen by the eyes, and all knowers say that God is formless. But you say that you would believe only after seeing with your eyes. It means you have decided not to see him. There simply is no way that you can see him through the eyes, because how can you see the form of what is, by its nature, formless? And remember, if you ever do see God in a form you will immediately say that this cannot be God because the scriptures say that God is formless.

Marx has jokingly said that he does not and cannot believe in God because he can only believe in such things that can be proved scientifically. If he can examine God in a test tube in a laboratory, if he can dissect God by laying God on a laboratory table, if he can investigate God from all angles, only then can he believe in God's existence. But he immediately makes a joke – that if God ever made the mistake of materializing in a test tube or becoming ready to be examined on the laboratory table, he would cease to be God. Certainly whatsoever you could capture and examine in a test tube would become less than you. What you can dissect and analyze in a laboratory will become only matter, it cannot remain God.

So our demand is such that there is difficulty if it is fulfilled and there is difficulty if it is not fulfilled. People say, "We shall not believe in God until we see him before our eyes." It means that they have decided that whatsoever is available to their eyes is their whole world, and whatever is not before their eyes does not exist.

But the world is vast, so what is the knower supposed to do? He who has seen that which is not seen with the eyes, he who has heard with closed ears that which is not heard through open ears, he who has touched within his innermost core that which cannot be touched – what language shall he speak so that even the ignorant person can understand? He will have to say it in a certain way. If he speaks to a knower in the same way, the knower will laugh.

A Mohammedan fakir, Sheikh Farid, and Kabir once met. There was no talk between them. They stayed together for two days, they laughed, they embraced, they sat together for hours, but without a word. A big crowd of devotees of both Farid and Kabir and many other curious people had gathered. They thought that when two such eminent saints have come together there will be some very valuable conversation, they will all benefit from it. But two days passed just like that. Then came the moment of their departure. All were very disappointed. Those who had gathered to hear became very sad. They could not understand what was the matter. Two men of tremendous experience had met; had any conversation between the two taken place it would have been so beneficial. But nobody had the courage to ask anything in the presence of them both.

When Farid set out on his journey again, his devotees asked him why they had not conversed with each other. Farid said, "Whoever had spoken would have been proved ignorant. And then what was there to say? What I know, Kabir also knows; from where Kabir is seeing, I am also seeing."

Kabir was also asked by his devotees, the inmates of his ashram. Kabir replied, "Are you people mad? At the most we could have laughed at the fact that the two who are not are meeting; that the two who have already met inside are meeting. With whom was one to speak?"

Kabir has explained about the phenomenon of speaking. Two ignorant persons speak a lot with each other, though neither of the two understand each other at all. Two ignorant persons debate non-stop, endlessly, with no outcome – just the argument, with no conclusions, with nothing to be shared.

The talk between two ignorant persons is in words, though words do not take one anywhere. Two enlightened ones also meet but the use of words becomes impossible. Their meeting happens in silence, without the exchange of any words, because what they have seen is the same, what they have known and experienced is the same. What is there to be said?

When does meaningful speaking happen? It happens when an enlightened one and an unenlightened one meet. Then one knows and the other does not; there is some meaning in speaking. When both know, speaking becomes meaningless. When both do not know, speaking cannot be prevented. A lot will be said, but without any meaning and purpose. These are the only three possibilities.

When a knower meets one who does not know, what will he say? One way is that he goes on saying all that he knows without bothering about who he is talking to. In that case he is talking to the walls. Nobody will listen, nobody will understand – one will at the most misunderstand. Just the opposite of what has been said will be understood. It will cause some harm. It would have been better to remain silent, or say only that which an ignorant person can understand. An ignorant person will misunderstand.

Then is there any method to say something in such a way that the ignorant can be made to turn towards the truth? All this is necessary to be kept in mind. There is no body, but for the ignorant there is nothing but body. Then what is to be done? A middle way has to be found, devised, so that an ignorant person can be told, "The body is and you are also, but you are not the body and you should set out in search to find out this truth."

If you tell an ignorant person that he is nothing like the body his search ceases. He will say, "Now be quiet. I am not the body, you say. But I do not experience anything else but body. I feel that there is only body, there is nothing like a soul." He is not saying anything wrong, he is speaking of his experience. The knower is speaking of his experience, the ignorant is speaking of his experience.

Have you ever known yourself to be anything but the body? Have you ever had any glimpse that may make you realize that you are not the body? Are you completely sure that if your head is cut off it is not you who will be cut? Have you even a little understanding that when your body will be burned on a funeral pyre it is not you who will be burning? Impossible! – because whenever a small thorn pierces the foot it pierces you; if the hand is burned, you feel you are burned, so when your whole body will be burning, it is an impossible hope that you will feel that it is not you who is burning. When even the slightest hurt, even a small abuse pierces you and affects you, then you cannot think that when death penetrates you, you will remain unaffected, untouched.

You have no experience that you are anything other than the body; your only experience is that you are the body. Yes, you may believe that you are the soul and that you will not die, but that is only your belief – and a belief that is very deceptive and a belief that is part of ignorance.

Every man likes to believe that he will not die. Nobody wants to die. Take note of this simple thing – that nobody wants to die. And whosoever does not want to die knows for certain that he will have to die; that is the reason why the feeling arises in the first place that he does not want to die.

The knower wants to die, the ignorant does not want to die. The knower wants to die because he knows that nothing dies at death. A knower wants to enter death because he knows that on entering death he will have the purest experience of deathlessness.

Where the opposite is present, the experiencing becomes easier. You draw a white line on a blackboard: it shines more clearly. When there are dark clouds and the lightning flashes, it is seen more clearly. Let it flash in white clouds during the day and you may not even see it.

A knower wants to enter death – insistently, blissfully and celebratingly – so that that white line of deathlessness that is hidden within can flash clearly against the backdrop of the dark clouds of death that come to surround it, and for the experience to become very clear that death happens always around one and never within one. The ignorant man fears going into death, because he is convinced that death means an end of everything, that nothing will remain.

Now this is a very interesting thing: an ignorant person believes that the soul is immortal so that he may not be annihilated completely. This belief is not because of his knowing but because of his fear. This is the reason a young man does not believe very much in matters of the soul, etcetera. But as he grows older he begins to believe more and more, because as death comes nearer the fear grows bigger. A person lying on his deathbed normally becomes religious. Whosoever remains irreligious even on his deathbed is a man of some courage. Even the greatest atheist becomes a little shaky at the time of death as he realizes that he does not know what reality is, and then comes the fear of death, of entering into that darkness. Out of fear he falls back to all the old beliefs and doctrines.

You also believe that the soul is immortal, although you know that you are nothing more than a body. But what is this soul you are saying is immortal when you have no experience of it? You say that it is immortal, yet it is something about which you have no experience whatsoever. Your fear becomes your doctrine.

The more fearful people are, the more they become believers in the soul. This is why this phenomenon is seen only in India, that the whole country believes in the soul and yet everybody is afraid of moving into darkness. They believe strongly in the existence of a soul. Their whole being trembles for fear of death and yet they have a firm belief in the existence of the soul.

This country of believers in the soul remained in slavery for a thousand years. Over this race of believers in the soul any small outside community could rule. And these believers in the soul continued to believe in the immortality of the soul and also continued to fear war.

Fear, not experience or knowing, is within the foundation of your belief. Otherwise it would be impossible to turn a believer in the immortality of the soul into a slave. A knower will have no fear, and slavery only comes out of the fear that, "If we do not become slaves we will be killed." Thus a man prefers to remain alive even at the cost of becoming a slave.

Had this country really believed in the soul as everybody goes on claiming, it could never have entered slavery. The whole country might have preferred to be killed, and would have quoted from the scriptures: "The soul cannot be pierced by weapons or burned by fire – so let them kill and burn." It would have been impossible to place this country in slavery had it been a believer in the soul. But this country is a complete believer in the body, not in the soul. Just due to fear it goes on saying it believes in the soul.

Your conviction is that you are the body, and the knower's realization is that you are not the body. So where, on what ground, is it possible to meet where you may understand each other's language? The scriptures have found a device, a technique. So in the beginning they do not deny you completely and say that there is no body at all; that denial would shut your doors and it would become even more difficult for you to understand – so for your sake they say that there is a body. This makes the ignorant a little assured that he is not entirely wrong, that the body is, that his belief is also right. This creates a yes mood in him.

An American thinker, Dale Carnegie, has done a lot of work on this yes mood. It has nothing to do with religion, he is an expert in salesmanship: how to sell things better, how to win friendships. His book, How to Win Friends and Influence People, is next only to the Bible in sales throughout the whole world. How to win friends and how also to influence people? – it is a secret formula for creating the yes mood in the other. Once that yes mood has arisen, it becomes more and more difficult to say no.

So Dale Carnegie says that if you want to influence somebody, or convert or change somebody's mind, do not say anything at the very outset which that person might deny right away. If he has said no to something in the very beginning, his no mood becomes strong. Then to the second thing that is mentioned, to which he could have said yes had it been mentioned earlier, he would only say no. Hence, in the beginning talk about a few such matters to which he naturally says yes and only then raise the matter to which ordinarily he would have said no.

After saying yes three or four times, the feeling to say no becomes weak. Once we agree about four things and say yes, a tendency arises to say yes to whatever a person says in the fifth instance also. But if we have said no to the first four things the person mentioned, the feeling to say no for the fifth time also grows stronger.

Dale Carnegie has written in a memoir that once he had gone to a town and stayed with a friend who was an insurance agent. That friend said to him, "You talk and write a lot about how to influence people and win friends. There is an old woman in this town:

if you can sell her an insurance policy I will agree with your theory, otherwise it is all mere talk."

Dale Carnegie began his investigations about that old woman. It was a tough job, because it was very difficult to even enter her office. As soon as any one of her employees knew that a visitor was an insurance agent he was driven out. That old woman was an eighty-year-old widow, a multi-millionaire, had everything one could desire, and she was dead against insurance. Where it was difficult even to enter, the matter of influencing her seemed impossible.

Dale Carnegie has written, "After gathering as much information as possible about the old woman, I went at five o'clock for a morning walk near the wall of her garden. That old woman used to get up at six o'clock. She came out into her garden and, seeing me standing near her garden wall looking at the flowers, she asked, 'Are you a lover of flowers?' I replied, 'Not only am I a lover of flowers, but I am an expert. I have seen many roseflowers all over the world, but these roseflowers that you have in your garden are matchless.'

"The old woman asked me to come inside through the gate. She took me around the garden, showing each and every type of flower. She showed me the chickens, the pigeons and the pets she had in the garden." Dale Carnegie managed to create a yes mood in her.

This became a routine every morning. That old woman would stand at the gate ready to welcome him. One day she offered him tea and breakfast. The next day, while they were walking in the garden, the old woman said, "You seem to be a very intelligent man and an expert on many subjects, what do you think of insurance? The insurance people are always running after me. Is getting insured a right thing or not?"

Then Dale Carnegie discussed the subject with her, but still did not allow her to know that he was an insurance agent because that could create a no mood in her. On the seventh day, Carnegie got her insured.

Once a relationship of yes begins with a person, a sort of trust in that person begins to grow. When a feeling of trust is created, saying no to that person goes on becoming more and more difficult. It is possible to hold the hand only after holding the fingers.

So the scriptures speak to ignorant people in such a way that a yes mood is created; only then is it possible to proceed further. If one was directly told that neither is there body, nor you, nor the world, the ignorant would say, "Enough of this! There is nothing reliable in what you are saying."

This is why the scriptures say to the ignorant that *"Body etcetera is true."* The ignorant person immediately sits up with straightened back, confident that he is not absolutely wrong and that this man is not dangerous. It is very painful for anybody to know that he is absolutely wrong. One likes to feel that one is also right a little bit. And it is on the basis of this little bit of right that further progress in the journey is possible.

But you are absolutely wrong. The experience of all the knowers is that you are completely wrong, one hundred percent wrong. But saying this to you would mean that there could be no further relationship with you; hence the knower says that you are right to a great extent. The body is there, the world is there, everything is there – you are not wrong at all. The misunderstanding is only a slight one, that you have taken your body as the soul.

In this way a yes mood is created in the ignorant. He feels, "I am also right to a great extent. The difference between me and the knower is very small, and that is that I have taken my body to be the soul." And the ignorant also wants that he should not understand the body to be the soul, because the body does not give anything but suffering. And the body also has to die. So he also wants to search and know that which is not the body so that he comes to know deathlessness also. Then the knower says that there is supreme bliss in knowing the soul, which is not the body. So this arouses the ignorant person's greed also. He becomes keen to know that supreme bliss – and thus the journey begins.

But the journey is such that as the ignorant person makes progress, he realizes that the body whose existence the knower had earlier confirmed actually does not exist; the world whose existence the knower had earlier confirmed actually does not exist. As the ignorant person moves deeper, the knower goes on adding conditions. He says that if you become greedy for bliss you will never have it – though this man had set out on the journey out of greed in the first place.

But all this comes later on, when one has set out on the journey, when one has already covered some distance and going back has become impossible. This path is such that going back on it is not possible; whatever you have come to know on the path cannot be undone. There is no returning from knowledge. It is possible only to go forwards from where you have reached, not backwards.

And the most interesting thing is that as the ignorant person moves ahead on the path, he falls into more troubled waters than he was ever in, because whatever he knew earlier, though wrong, was all clear cut. As he proceeds all previous knowledge becomes a blur and is futile, and he hangs in a limbo.

He cannot go back, there is no alternative but to go ahead; hence whatever conditions are brought in by the knower have to be fulfilled. Now the knower says to give up greed and there will be bliss, though in the beginning the knower had aroused only your greed: "There is supreme bliss. Why are you lying here in hell? Why are you suffering in misery? The fountain of nectar is near by – come along!"

So in the hope of getting rid of his miseries, in the hope of getting happiness, he happily engages in the venture. There will be great happiness there – in this hope he moves ahead. Now this is greed. But only some time afterwards the knower says, "Give up greed. Do not ask for bliss, otherwise you will never get it." Now one is in a fix. One cannot go back. Mind thinks that one was better off with the previous happiness – but now one cannot see any happiness there, the unhappiness of all that existed before is now so clearly visible. So what was in his hands is dropped, and that which he was hoping for does not seem to be coming into his grasp, and on top of it all the knower now asks him even to drop the hope of getting anything. One has to drop it! One cannot go back, one just has to drop it.

Thus the knower shatters your false illusions inch by inch and slowly, slowly, takes you to a place where, if you had been asked to go in the very beginning, you would not have gone.

Buddha made such a mistake. There have been very few people who could say the truth so directly and simply as Buddha. This is why Buddhism could not survive in India. There is a reason for this, which is only that Buddha did not adopt that skill which should be adopted when dealing with the ignorant. Buddha had attained to the experience and he expressed it in direct terms. And the reason for this is that Buddha was not born in a brahmin family.

Brahmins are the ancientmost clever ones, the tradition of their profession is long – the oldest. In this world, since time immemorial, they have been in this business of knowledge. They are skilled in it, they know from where to begin the matter. Buddha was the son of a *kshatriya,* the warrior caste; his forefathers had never been in this business. He had no expertise in it, he had newly entered the business. It was a new shop; he had not the least idea what to say to the customer, how to persuade the customer. So he fell into trouble. He said the truth plainly and directly.

Do you know what Buddha said? If someone came to Buddha and said, "I want to realize the soul," Buddha would say, "There is no soul, how can you realize it?" The man would run away. He would wonder about this whole situation. At least the soul has to be there. One could have understood if told that there was no body, but you are saying there is not even the soul!

Somebody would come to Buddha and say, "There must be great bliss in enlightenment." Buddha would say, "What enlightenment? What bliss? Only nothingness remains. There is no bliss and there is no enlightenment, because as long as one is able to experience bliss, the misery will also remain. It has to be there, because it is only the contrasts one becomes aware of."

So Buddha says there is no bliss there. Thus that person who had come to him with some greed, some hope, is completely shattered at the door itself. He simply does not enter inside. He says to himself, "When there is not even bliss there, then these transient pleasures that I have are not so bad. Here there is no eternal happiness, but at least I have these transient pleasures." The knowers had always tempted him to give up his transient pleasures in order to get that permanent happiness.

Buddha said there is simply no permanent happiness. Happiness as such does not exist. Neither is there transient happiness nor permanent happiness; you are in an illusion about their existence. That man would ask to be excused and would think it is better to preserve what little he had. Half a loaf of bread here is better than a whole loaf of bread in heaven: "And then you say there is neither any heaven nor any loaf of bread. Why should I then give up the half loaf of bread that I have?"

People would go to Buddha and ask whether they would attain God. Buddha would say that there is no God. When Sariputta, who was a son of a brahmin, who was learned and knowledgeable, came to Buddha for the first time, he said to Buddha, "If there is nothing, if there is nothingness and only nothingness, then we should try to save our world we have, where at least we have something. You are saying very astonishing things. You want to snatch away everything and promise nothing. Who will come to you?" That son of a brahmin asked, "Who will come to you? You want us to renounce everything. And when we ask what shall we get in return, you tell us there is nothing to get. Why then would anybody give up anything? People renounce something in their greed for getting something else."

Buddha said, "One who renounces to get something has not renounced at all. What is the meaning of renunciation? If renunciation is done to get something it is a business transaction, not renunciation. A person renounces his palace so that he may get a palace in heaven – it is a business deal. A person does a virtuous deed to become happy – it is business. A person donates, renders service, becomes religious, only in the hope of having a better next life in some world. It is business – where is the renunciation in it?"

Buddha said, "There is renunciation only if there is no expectation of getting anything in return."

Sariputta said, "Maybe it is so, but where will you find such renouncers?"

We are all business-minded people. Even when we desire to have a relationship with God, it is business. An ignorant person cannot do anything else.

So Buddhism could not survive in India. And when it could not survive in India, where else could it survive? It did survive in other countries, but when? – when the followers of Buddha had learned all the tricks that were known to the brahmins, then it survived.

You may be surprised to know that Buddha himself was a kshatriya but all his senior disciples were brahmins...and they managed the survival. But in India Buddha had already spoiled the matter; in India he had already said things directly, so even the brahmin disciples could not impose anything different. Buddhism could not survive in India. It did survive in Sri Lanka, Burma, Japan, China, Tibet, Thailand and Korea – in the whole of Asia – but not in India, because Buddha himself had said things directly, that there was nothing to gain. Hence in India it was difficult to revive that hope of getting something. But that could be managed outside India.

The Buddhist religion that exists outside India is just another version of the Hindu religion. It is not the original words of Buddha, it is not real, that is why it survived. Where it was real it did not survive at all. You know that Mahavira was a kshatriya, but all his eleven chief disciples were brahmins. They are the ones responsible for the survival of Mahavira's teachings. It was beyond the capacity of Mahavira.

A kshatriya has no idea – it is not his profession. He may be good in the art of swordsmanship but this world of scriptures, the play of words...he has no know-how in this area. So all of the eleven chief disciples of Mahavira who were brahmins helped Jainism to survive. And there was a loophole for them. Buddha spoke himself, so it was not possible even for his disciples to spoil it. Mahavira did not speak, he remained silent; only the chief disciples spoke. This gave a loophole. Because Mahavira himself did not speak, whatever his chief disciples spoke as interpretation of his silence was taken as the Jaina religion. Thus Mahavira's religion somehow survived, but it does not seem to have gained any wide base.

There are only about two and a half million Jainas, twenty-five centuries after Mahavira lived. Even if twenty-five persons had been influenced by Mahavira and if they then had married, they would have multiplied to the present number of Jainas in these twenty-five centuries. So this present number does not speak very highly of its survival. What is the reason for it? The same – that a kshatriya does not know the language that should be used with the ignorant people. It takes centuries for it to develop.

This sutra says:

> It is not to explain to the knowers
> but to satisfy the ignorant
> that the scriptures say that "Body etcetera is true,"
> and that there is accumulated karma, past action.

> Actually there exists nothing else
> except the one and nondual Brahman,
> which is perfect, beginningless and endless,
> immeasurable, unchanging, abode of truth,
> abode of consciousness, abode of bliss,
> eternal, indestructible, omnipresent, uniform,
> whole, infinite, with head in all directions,
> impossible to be lost or to be found,
> supportless, independent, devoid of all attributes,
> actionless, subtle, choiceless, spotless, indefinable,
> beyond mind and speech, truly affluent,
> self-evident, pure, conscious and
> unlike anything we know.

Everything else is actually unreal. We see a thing as true only because we do not have the eyes that can see the truth. We only have that mind which gives birth to untruth. We have the mind that produces dreams, but we do not have the eyes that see the truth. Hence we are able to see what is false and what does not exist and we miss that which truly exists. How to give birth to that eye, the third eye, through which we can see the truth?

There is a small child: he lives in the world of toys, toys are a reality for him. Hence if the leg of his doll breaks, he weeps the same as if a real person had a broken leg. He is not able to sleep at night if the doll is not with him in his bed. He feels the same kind of missing as any lover would for his beloved.

For a child his toys are a reality. He will laugh at himself after he becomes adult about how foolish he was. As he grows up he will forget them completely. Those toys might be lying in some junk corner; even when they are thrown out he will not weep for them. What has happened? Those toys are the same, but what has happened to this man? His intelligence has risen higher, he has become able to see more.

But this alone will not make much of a difference. Some other living toys will replace these toys, the dolls. Previously he clasped the doll to his chest while sleeping, now he will be sleeping clasping a living woman to his chest. The dolls will have changed, but the mind? But there are methods to rise above this mind too. Very few of us do that. Everyone grows from childhood to youth. Why? Because to grow into your youth nothing is required to be done by you, it is a natural growth.

If it was necessary for you to do something so as to grow to your youth, only a handful of people would attain it in this world, all the others would remain only children. But you do not have to do anything for it; youthhood is unavoidable, you just go on growing. In fact you cannot stop it, you cannot prevent it – that is why you attain to youth. But spiritual consciousness does not grow that way, for that you have to do something. That growth depends on your decision. Nature does not impose that growth on you, it is left to your own freedom and choice. Hence it is only a handful of people who are able to become a Buddha, a Krishna or a Christ ...because it is a matter of hard work and endeavor.

The day you look with awakened eyes, the whole world will appear to you like a child's play. At that level of maturity, all things of the past become false to you.

This sutra says that in reality there is only one Brahman. And about this Brahman a few very important hints are given in this sutra. Many of these attributes are familiar to us, and I will not discuss them.

> *...perfect, beginningless and endless,*
> *immeasurable, unchanging, abode of truth,*
> *abode of consciousness, abode of bliss,*
> *eternal, indestructible, omnipresent, uniform,*
> *whole, infinite, with head in all directions...*

These are familiar words that we have used for the Brahman. But two or three of them are wonderful attributes.

Impossible to be lost or to be found...is a very important statement. Something that cannot be dropped or caught hold of: what does this mean?

People come to me and say, "We want to search for God." I ask them, "Where and when have you lost him?" Because anything that is lost can be sought for, but if something is not lost at all, it is a difficult question. They say they do not know if it is lost at all and when or where. I ask them to first ascertain if they have ever lost it, because if you have not lost it and I tell you the ways to search for it, you will be in more difficulty. You would have set out on a journey to search for that which you have never lost; how can you succeed? Your very search will lead you astray.

God is our nature – how can we lose him? We may forget him but we cannot lose him.

Try to understand the difference. It is possible you may have forgotten – you may not have paid any attention to who is hidden within for a long time. It is so near us that it is possible that there may have been no need to give any attention to the one within. One's focus may have been set on faraway objects, forgetting what is within. All this is possible, but to lose the one inside is not possible.

This is why all the saints have said that just the remembrance is enough, a search is not necessary. This is why Nanak, Kabir, Dadu, Raidas, all have put emphasis on *nam smaran*, remembering his name. Nam smaran only means that there simply arises no question of searching for that which has never been lost, only try to remember him. It is not even a remembrance, it is more like reminding yourself of that which is always there.

This sutra is very revolutionary.

...impossible to be lost or to be found...

That which can never be lost is our essential nature. If it can be lost, it cannot be our essential nature. If fire can lose its fieriness, its heat, then it was not its essential nature. If fire is cool, it is something else, not fire.

To be hot is the nature of fire. To be empty is the nature of sky. Nature is something that cannot be separated from us, whatever may happen. Anything from which we can be separated is not our nature. Let this truth sink deep into you.

Something from which we can be separated is not our nature. Something with which we can be united is not our nature. We can break away from that with which we can be united. Our very being is that which we cannot be separated from nor united with. Brahman is our being. There is no way of escaping from it, there is no way of avoiding it, there is no way of losing it, there is no way of finding it. But if such things were told to the ignorant person, he would say, "It is okay; then where is the need to search for that which has never been lost? And where is the need to find that which is always there? It is okay – then let us remain in our worldly life. What is the need – why try any crazy idea?"

No, it cannot be said to the ignorant. The ignorant will have to be told, "You have lost him; you have lost your real being – search for it. As long as you do not find it, you will remain in misery. As long as you do not find God your life will be nothing but anguish, worry, an agony."

The ignorant person understands this language of searching, he feels alright with it. He has been searching for everything – for money, for position, for prestige – so he says, "Fine, at least the search will continue; now I will search for religion instead of money."

The ignorant person understands this language. Throughout this life, in fact many, many lives, he has done only one thing – searching. He has known only one profession: today search for this, tomorrow search for that. So he says, "Alright: before I searched for money, prestige and position; and you say there is no happiness in them – and I also experience that there is no happiness in them, so now I will search for your God. It fits."

After he has begun the search, he will then be told later on, "God cannot be reached; unless you give up all searching you cannot find him." Now he is in difficulty. He gave up his search for money, position and prestige because they were futile, and in the hope that he would now be searching for something meaningful he entered the search for God. And when he has come quite far in this search and cannot go back – now he cannot go back to the search for money, that has all become meaningless; in fact that is why he turned in the direction of this new, meaningful search – his master tells him to give up all searching.

First he gave up money, position and prestige, but he saved half of the coin – the search itself. He had renounced money, but saved the search. Money was on the outside, the search was inside. It was easy to give up that which was on the outside, but now the master asks him to give up all searching, because, he says, "What you are searching for you have never lost at all."

When someone gives up the search also, he immediately enters into that which he has always been. God is our very being. Hence this sutra is very revolutionary and very valuable.

...impossible to be lost or to be found...

When Buddha became enlightened somebody asked him, "What have you attained?" Buddha replied, "I have not attained anything. I only came to know what I already had." To say to you, "I have not attained anything," was a mistake of Buddha's. With such a statement you will immediately react and say, "Come, let us go back to our own work. We unnecessarily wasted our eight days with this man...and now he says he did not attain anything when he became enlightened. Why are we then doing this hard work, all this jogging and jumping and getting tired?...and this man says nothing is attained in the end."

Buddha said, "I have not attained anything." The questioner said, "You did not attain anything? Then what are you teaching to the people?" Buddha replied, "This very thing, that you come to such a state where there remains nothing to be attained or to be lost, and this becomes your own experience – that nothing can be attained and nothing can be lost."

But this is something that can be understood only by a knower.

> *...supportless, independent, devoid of all attributes,*
> *actionless, subtle, choiceless, spotless, indefinable,*
> *beyond mind and speech, truly affluent,*
> *self-evident, pure, conscious...*

There are also words familiar to us. *Unlike anything we know....* It cannot be compared with anything; it is unique, matchless. Any comparisons that are made are makeshift arrangements. We say, "It is empty like the sky." But this is also not right, because the sky also is contained in him. It is bigger than the sky, it cannot even be compared with the sky. We say, "It is shining like a super-sun." But this also is small talk, because even super-suns are nothing but tiny lamps before it. It cannot be compared with suns.

We say, "It is bliss itself." When we say this, somewhere in our mind we are measuring it with happiness. It has nothing to do with happiness. We say, "It is peaceful." Then in our minds we have somewhere the idea about peace being something opposite to peacelessness. No, it has never experienced peacelessness; hence it does not have any idea of our peace.

Our comparisons are of no use. For that experience all analogies are inadequate. The seers have described it as only like itself – not like anyone or anything else, but only like itself. There is no way of describing it using the analogy of anything known to us. But still it is described for the ignorant that it is like such and such. It is only at the end of the search that it is found that it is not like anything.

Actually there exists nothing else
except the one and nondual Brahman...

Thus, knowing through your own experience
that the soul is indivisible, be fulfilled and
dwell blissfully in the changeless soul.

In this way...*knowing through your own experience that the soul is indivisible, be fulfilled....* It will not do to know the scriptures – scriptures may say anything, that will not do. The solution will not come to you by listening to them, nothing will happen. You have to be fulfilled through your own experience.

A fulfilled one, a *siddha,* is one for whom there is no further journey, no further movement – one for whom the last camp, the last destination has come. All roads end here.

An unfulfilled one, an *asiddha,* is as we are now. An asiddha means one who has still something more to do, something has yet to happen for him to become happy, something has yet to be achieved after which happiness is expected to follow.

The happiness of the unfulfilled one is dependent on something else. He has to meet a certain woman, a certain man; has to own a certain house, a certain piece of land; he has to have a certain position, has to become a president, a prime minister, or this or that. His happiness is somewhere in something, in some object, and when that is achieved he will have happiness.

A siddha, the fulfilled one, means one who is happy in his own

being. Whether he gets something, whether he does not get something, that is not the question. Whether something comes to him or
something is taken away from him...his happiness is not dependent on anything else but his own being: it is enough that 'I am'.
There is no other condition of any sort. One whose happiness is
unconditional is a siddha. His happiness is here and now.

Your happiness is always sometime and somewhere in the future;
your happiness is never here and now. Have you ever seen a person who could say, "I am happy here and now"? Here and now
everybody is unhappy, their happiness is somewhere in the future.

I have a friend who was a deputy minister of one state. He was
very unhappy. I inquired, "What is the matter with you?"

He said, "Until I become a minister I will not be happy."

He became a minister after some time. Later when I met him he
was still unhappy. I asked him, "What is the matter now? You
have already become a minister; now you should feel fulfilled."

He said, "Fulfilled? Until I become the chief minister there is no
happiness. I am trying my best – sometime I shall reach there."

He became the chief minister also. I again inquired of him
whether he was now fulfilled. He said, "Why are you after me?
Fulfillment seems nowhere around. I have become the chief minister but nothing has been resolved in my life. And at the same time
many more positions have now become visible; perhaps when I
reach there...."

Happiness always goes on receding from you. That is the characteristic of an unfulfilled person. The characteristic of a fulfilled
one is that happiness is here and now. No matter what the situation, no matter what happens on the outside, there is no change in
the flow of the inner stream of happiness. And there are no conditions attached to it. Whosoever makes conditions is bound to be
unhappy. No condition ever gets fulfilled. And even if conditions
laid down are fulfilled, that condition-creating mind creates new
conditions.

It is like the leaves of a tree: old leaves fall – it makes no difference
because new ones come. In fact, because the new leaves want to

come, the old leaves fall. New ones start pushing from within to come out, and the old ones begin to fall. As soon as the old leaf has fallen the new one sprouts. The old condition falls only when a new condition begins to push from within to come to the surface. On the trees leaves grow; in the mind of man conditions grow.

Whosoever's life is conditional, unhappiness will be the outcome. Whosoever's life is unconditional, whosoever is happy here and now without any reason – meaning whose happiness does not come from outside but from within, whose stream of happiness flows from within his own self, the source, the fountain – is a fulfilled one. It is not something to be begged for from others. Even if this whole world disappears, even if all the stars and the moons disintegrate, even if the whole of humanity is finished, there will be no change in the happiness of a fulfilled one.

But for you there will be no difference in your unhappiness even if the whole world is made as desired by you. Perhaps you will become more unhappy. When all one's demands are met one comes to realize: all that labor, all that hard work and nothing has really been gained. One becomes more unhappy.

In order to be a fulfilled one, the sutra says:

> *Thus, knowing through your own experience*
> *that the soul is indivisible, be fulfilled and*
> *dwell blissfully in the changeless soul.*

Be in it, remain in it, stay in it and be settled in it. Just be one with it. Do not look outside. Just remember, rising up or sitting down, look for the unconditional happiness. Walking, sleeping, waking, eating and drinking – whatsoever may be the situation, look for the unconditional happiness. Just be happy.

This appears to be very strange to us, to say to somebody, "Just be happy." The person will ask, "How to be happy?" ...Because we all have an idea that happiness comes from the outside. To be happy from within! – this is something that we are unable to understand. We have never known the inner happiness.

Just search for it. Your inside is full of happiness. Gather some courage and go within. Just remove that veil of conditions and you will find that you become filled with happiness...so much so that if you want you can fill the whole world with your happiness. It will go on spreading all over and all around.

We are always demanding from others. We are demanding from those who are themselves demanding from us. It is a crowd of beggars, standing in front of one another with our begging bowls hoping that something may be received – and all are begging. Have you ever thought that this whole world is a community of beggars?

I come to you so that you may give me some happiness, you come to me so that I may give you some happiness. Neither have I ever found any happiness within me, nor have you ever found any happiness within you. Hence all our relationships give only unhappiness. Nobody gives happiness – nobody can – because how can you give something which you do not have? We are out giving others what we do not have.

The father is giving happiness to the son, the wife is giving happiness to the husband, the son is giving happiness to the mother. In the whole world, everybody is giving happiness to one another and everybody is bitterly wailing that he is unhappy. Nobody seems to become happy. You yourself do not have happiness, and you are going around giving it to others?

In this world, there is only one way of becoming happy and that is not to go to anybody asking for it. It is not with others, it is within you. Dropping all your demands you just stop seeking it. Even if you are feeling unhappy you stay in it, you wait; do not go begging from others. One day, suddenly you will realize that because you have dropped the habit of begging, a stone within is removed and the stream pours out, filling every cell of your body with happiness. This happiness is uncaused. Nobody can take it away from you, it is coming from within you. And then it is possible that others coming into contact with you may get touched by the stream of your happiness.

It is very interesting to note that we are demanding happiness, and we also want to give happiness. We are not able to give happiness and we are not able to get happiness. Such a person whose own stream of happiness has burst forth, whose own source has opened up, does not demand happiness from others, nor does he desire to give happiness to others; but from such a person happiness is simply received – by many.

No buddha ever goes out to give happiness to anybody, but just his presence.... The flowers that have blossomed in him, their fragrance, the fountain of happiness that has opened up within him, its murmuring sound – all these resonate and reach out to anybody who comes near him, who is open and is not sitting with the doors of his heart closed.

And anybody sitting near someone like Buddha with open eyes is also able to see that Buddha's happiness does not seem to be coming from somewhere outside, it does not seem to be dependent on anybody, it seems to be flowing from within his own self. His rays are not borrowed, they are his own. He is not like the moon which reflects the rays of the sun; he is like the sun who has his own light, his own rays emanating from him directly.

This we have called *satsang*. Sitting near a person like Buddha is satsang. Perhaps this may shake us too from our foolishness, perhaps our obstructing stone may also reach to the point of shifting, perhaps seeing that someone can be happy in himself, our illusion that others can give us happiness may shatter. We go on demanding happiness from others and keep holding to the illusion that it will come someday – if not today, then tomorrow, or the day after – but it will come from others.

Make yourself unconditional, drop all demanding, give up all hopes that happiness will come to you from others; then one day happiness is attained. This is the state of a siddha, the fulfilled one, when one's own stream of happiness is attained.

Enough for today.

I AM THIS!

CHAPTER 17

*Listening to these teachings from the master,
the disciple became enlightened and began to say:
I had seen the world just now, where has it gone?
Who has taken it away? Into what has it become
dissolved? It is a great surprise! Does it not exist?
In this great ocean of Brahman which is full of
the nectar of infinite bliss, what have I
to renounce now and what have I to take?
What is other now and what is extraordinary?
Here I do not see anything, I do not hear anything
and I do not know anything, because I am always
in my blissful soul and I myself am my own nature.
I am unattached, bodiless, genderless;
I am God myself; I am absolutely silent,
I am infinite, I am the whole and the most ancient.
I am not the doer, I am not the sufferer,
I am unchanging and inexhaustible.
I am the abode of pure knowledge,
I am alone and I am the eternal godliness.*

*This knowledge was given by the master to
Apantaram, Apantaram gave it to Brahma, Brahma
gave it to Ghorangiras, Ghorangiras gave it to
Raikva, Raikva gave it to Rama and Rama gave it to
all living beings. This is the message of nirvana and
this is the teaching and discipline of the Vedas.
Thus ends this Upanishad.*

Listening to these teachings from the master,
the disciple became enlightened...

hat is stated in this sutra is not only difficult to understand, it may appear impossible to us. How can one become enlightened just by listening? Our logical minds cannot understand it. If listening has really happened it is not impossible, but because we do not know how to listen, it appears impossible that just by listening the disciple became enlightened.

Let us first understand this before we enter into the sutra. There is one fundamental difference between the present era of science and the era when the Upanishads were born. In those days when the Upanishads were born the basis of the mind was trust. Now the basis of the mind is doubt. In those days trust was as natural as doubt is natural today. The mind has undergone a revolutionary change. With the birth of science, doubt has gained a sort of dignity. Why? Because science is born out of doubt.

Science only doubts. Right doubt is the key for the development of science. Scientific facts can be discovered only if one goes on doubting. Doubt is a process of discovering the truths of science.

When the discoveries of science started becoming useful to man, when it spread all over from the smallest needle to the atom bomb, science started acquiring prestige. And when it became impossible for man to live without science and science began to win in all fields and its victory flag began to flutter in the material world, naturally doubt also acquired prestige, because science is born out of doubt.

When science became victorious in the material world, doubt also gained prestige. Today, throughout the whole world, whatever education we impart is the education of doubt. Right from the first grade to the last degrees of the university we teach doubt, because without doubt there is no thinking. If one has to think, one should doubt. The sharper the thinking is to be made, the sharper the edge of doubt required.

The whole structure of the modern world is created around science. Science has entered into everything – our eating, drinking, sitting, getting up, walking and living. But because science exists on the foundations of doubt, doubt has also become the foundation stone of the present man's mind. Today nobody can accept anything quietly. Trust is not the word of the day.

When the Upanishads were written, trust had the same prestige as doubt has today. Just as doubt is the basis for science, trust is the basis for religion. Let this be properly understood. Just as thinking cannot exist without doubt, the no-mind state cannot arise without trust.

Doubt and trust are opposites. If one wants to think, right doubt is necessary. One should then doubt courageously, every inch of ground should be put to the test, and nothing should be accepted without its passing through the test of logic. Whatever the consequence, logic has to remain the only shelter and doubt the only boat if one has to make any progress in thought processes. And if any conclusion has to be arrived at through thought, doubt is the way.

But religion has nothing to do with thought. The very process of religion is the opposite. Religion says one has to go beyond thoughts. And because one has to go beyond thought, there is no place for doubt, there is no use for doubt; the boat of doubt is useless here. If one is to go beyond mind, something that is the opposite of doubt will be of use, because doubt is the basis for thought.

Trust is the opposite of doubt; it is acceptance, faith. These are two different boats, their journeys are different. If somebody wants to become a scientist, he cannot do so through trust. If somebody wants to become religious, he cannot do so without trust. Just as today science is at its height and has spread over our whole life, similarly, in the old days, religion was at its height and had permeated every cell and tissue of our life. In those days attainment of success in religion was the goal. No matter how great a scientist one would become in those days, still it would not appeal to people as a status worth achieving. The greatest achievement in those days was that of a Buddha, a Krishna, an Angirasa, a Raikva. In those days we held such people in high esteem. Just as today science is at the pinnacle of its glory, in those days religion was at the pinnacle of its glory.

When science is at its height, the number of things increases, the number of machines increases, efficiency increases and the means of enjoyment increases. When religion is successful, consciousness increases, soul develops, and the unique mysteries of desirelessness are attained. When science develops, the journey into external objects increases; when religion develops, the inner journey increases. These two are opposites, their directions are opposite. In those earlier days there were high beacon lights of religion and the minds of entire masses were influenced by these lights. There were the schools, universities, the universities of the masters in the forests – all teaching trust. So trust was flowing in our blood. It was natural to accept, nonacceptance was very difficult. One had to make great effort in rejecting something, but acceptance was effortless.

Today the situation is just the reverse. Today no effort at all is necessary for rejection; that is our natural tendency. For accepting something one has to make tireless effort, and still something within you goes on continuously telling you that it may be right, it may not be right; it may be a trick, a deception. "I have not known it myself, somebody else has known it – who knows how true it is?"

When science wins, doubt wins. This is why science could not be born in India. It could not have been. Where trust is deep, there just cannot be any journey in science. This is why the days of the Upanishads were the days of no science; there was no development of science. This is also why there cannot be any development of religion in the West today, because science has become successful there and doubt has won. The two journeys are opposite.

The East has given religion, because it gave to mind the base of trust; the West has given science, because it gave to mind the base of doubt.

I do not say that doubt is wrong, nor do I say that doubt is right. I do not say that trust is right, nor do I say that trust is wrong. Understand my viewpoint rightly.

If somebody uses trust for science, it is wrong. If somebody uses doubt for religion, it is wrong. If someone uses trust in religion, it is right; if someone uses doubt in science, it is right. Doubt has its own capabilities.

For knowing about matter, doubt has its accepted use; for knowing oneself it is impotent. Trust has no capabilities for knowing about matter, but for knowing oneself, trust alone has the capability. When we try to use a means from one world in the opposite world we are in difficulty. There is no need to do such a thing. If I want to go out of my house I have to keep my face towards the outside of the house and my back towards the house. If I want to come into my house, my face has to be towards the house and my back towards the outside of the house.

Trust is to face towards the house, doubt is to face away from the house. Trust and doubt are two sides of the same coin, but their uses are different and their achievements are different. One who is in confusion about the two falls into difficulty.

In the days when the Upanishads were born, trust was the foundation; what was heard was assimilated instantly. Trust means receptivity, trust means loving acceptance.

This acceptance was intrinsic to the society. It was not that somebody casually told something to someone while walking on the road; one had to sit with the master for many years. One had to drink in the master for years, one had to live with the master for years. Slowly, slowly the rhythm of the master's breathing would become the rhythm of the disciple's breathing too. Slowly, slowly the sitting and the rising of the master, the movements of the master, would become the sitting and the rising of the disciple too. Slowly, slowly an attunement, an inner harmony would be created between the two, and then the disciple knew from his innermost being that the master was right.

This recognition used to commence slowly. It was not like asking someone passing on the road, "Is there a God?"

I come across such people. I am going to catch some train and they stop me in the middle of it, on the platform, and say, "One moment please, is there really a God?"

What are they really saying? – as if an answer can be given to you whether God is or is not. As if there is no necessity for any preparation to receive an answer to this question. As if this is some routine question about some day-to-day dealing, like asking a shop-keeper, "Have you got a packet of cigarettes?"

Is there a God? To ask this, years of awaiting are necessary; to ask this a sort of fitness and worthiness are necessary. A right kind of mind has to be created so that when the answer comes one may be able to hear it, understand it.

This story is of a time when a disciple used to just sit near the master for many years. Just sitting, just watching the master...if the master said something, he listened to it but did not ask. He would ask only when he was convinced that he was in tune with the master, when he felt that some inner relationship between them has developed, when a bridge between them was established: "Whatsoever the master says now will not stop at my ears, it will sink deep into my heart."

Until a connection is established with your heart and the heart of the master there is no sense in saying anything to you. But this Upanishad must have been told in such a moment. This is why this sutra says intimacy with a master can become a spiritual discipline. But we are unaware of any such thing today. Today we have no intimacy even with those whom we love very much. We feel a distance even from those who may be very close to us. Today everybody has become closed within themselves, and the reason for this is doubt. How could intimacy happen with those about whom one has doubt? Intimacy can happen only with those about whom one has no doubt. Doubt closes the doors, locks itself up within; it needs security.

Trust is insecurity. Trust does not need security. The very meaning of trust is: "If you push me into a ditch, I will fall happily into it. If you are throwing me into a ditch there must be some secret reason for it."

What matters is not the ditch but who is throwing you into it. If the master was pushing the disciple into a ditch, a disciple from the days of the Upanishads would simply touch the feet of the master and fall happily into it. The question is not that it is a ditch, the question is who is the person throwing you.

If someone whom you have loved so much, one with whom such an intimacy has happened, is pushing you into the ditch, it must be for some benefit and for your welfare: this attitude is called trust. When something is listened to with this attitude it sinks down to one's innermost being. And then no other spiritual discipline is necessary.

Spiritual disciplines are actually a way of compensating for the lack of trust. That empty space, which is there because of the absence of trust, has to be filled by means of spiritual endeavors. They are substitutes; otherwise they are not necessary, because the very viewpoint of the Upanishads is that whatsoever is to be achieved is already there within you. There is no question of seeking and searching, no effort is necessary, because what is to be achieved is already the case – you have only to look towards it.

If you have deep trust and if you are ready to open your eyes into the unknown at the hint of your master, the matter is over.

Marpa, an amazing monk of Tibet, has said, "I never meditated, I never made any effort, I did only one thing: I trusted my master."

The story of Marpa is very interesting. When he came to his master he said, "I have come prepared to trust you."

The master asked him, "Is this trust total?"

Marpa replied, "I have never heard that trust could also be fragmentary – how could that be?"

If there is trust it is total, otherwise it is not there. Let this be properly understood.

Some people say, "We have a little trust." They do not know what they are saying. Trust cannot be in parts. If you say to somebody, "I have a little bit of love for you" – what does it mean? Or if you say, "I speak a little bit of truth" – what does it mean? A little bit of truth?

These things are indivisible, nobody can divide them. Either there is trust or there is not. A little bit means none. But you are not even honest enough to accept that you have no trust so you say, "I have a little bit."

Marpa said, "Trust is always complete. I have not heard of incomplete trust. I have trust."

So his master said, "Then jump off the cliff into this valley in front of us."

Marpa immediately ran and jumped into the valley. The master became anxious that one life was unnecessarily lost. He had not thought that Marpa would jump. The master and all his disciples ran down into the valley and saw Marpa sitting in deep meditation at the bottom of the cliff.

The valley was very deep and frightening, and there was no possibility of surviving after the fall – but Marpa did not have even a scratch on his body. The master thought that probably it was a coincidence: some other test would have to be taken.

There was a house on fire and the whole village was running towards it. The master went with Marpa, and he asked Marpa to enter into the raging fire. Marpa ran into the fire, he ran deep inside the house, and there he sat in meditation. The whole house was reduced to ashes. The master and his disciples thought Marpa must also have been burned to ashes. When the fire was extinguished they went inside; there was Marpa sitting amidst smouldering ashes. He had not been touched at all by the fire. The master then asked him, "What is this trick you have done? What is the power you have that you can do all this?"

Marpa replied, "Power? All I have is trust in you."

Then the master asked him to walk on water. He walked on the water too. The master then thought, "When Marpa can do such miracles in my name, what is there that I cannot do?" So the master tried to walk on water and started drowning!

It is not a question of being a master. The master had no trust that one can walk on water, that one can save oneself in fire, that a fall into a valley will also not hurt. The master himself was at a loss to understand how it was all happening. He was thinking that Marpa must know of some trick that he was not aware of, otherwise how could one walk on water?

Even after seeing Marpa walk on water, the master did not trust that someone could do this. He felt that there must be some mystery, some trick which was not known to him: "Marpa is only deceiving me by saying that he is doing everything just due to his trust. And if there is any truth in it, that he can walk on water because of his trust in me, then I myself should certainly be able to do so."

That was the mistake. Marpa was walking on water due to his trust. In whom the trust was placed is not the question – there was trust in his heart. All he felt was that if the master was asking him to walk on water, he would be able to – there was not even an iota of doubt about it. Had doubt entered even for a moment, Marpa would have drowned.

Trust is a boat, but if there is even one small hole in it, the boat will sink. The master tried to walk and he started drowning. The master then said to Marpa, "You are deceiving me; you certainly know some tricks. You walked on water in my name and I myself could not do it!"

Marpa said, "Now you have made even my walking on water doubtful. Since I saw you drowning the matter is over, my trust is broken. Now even by mistake don't order me to do such things, because now I will not be able to carry them out. If I did, I would not come back alive. I have seen you drowning, now it will be difficult for me. The boat I moved in is broken." From then on Marpa could not walk on water.

This is a very beautiful story, and useful. Trust has its own power. If there is trust, spiritual disciplines are unnecessary – trust is enough. If there is no trust, techniques are absolutely necessary.

A very interesting thing happened.... In the Middle Ages, the saints in India felt that people were becoming more and more atheistic and that nobody was becoming interested in religion. Nobody wanted to do the long spiritual practices, perform the austerities, practice yoga or follow tantra. They saw that people were becoming uninterested in religion. So they said that, in this *Kaliyuga,* the era of darkness, chanting the name of Rama was enough. They thought that in this age of Kaliyuga people would at least do this much. This act would not cost them anything.

But it was a great mistake. This advice was against the science of religion. In Kaliyuga, spiritual disciplines are needed the most because there is no trust.

Let us understand this, because what I am telling you is a very contrary statement. I say that in this Kaliyuga spiritual practices are most necessary; in *Satyuga,* the era of truth, they were not. Since there is now no trust, how can one compensate for it? The name of Rama can work, but only for those who have trust. So chanting the name of Rama would have been the right thing in Satyuga, but not now.

So I affirm that in this Kaliyuga nothing is going to happen just by repeating the name of Rama, because the trustful heart that could be helpful does not exist. Now a great effort will have to be made, now rigorous spiritual practices will have to be gone through, a lot of effort will have to be put into it; only then can something happen. Why? ...Because what else can compensate for the lack of trust?

Trust means faith in someone else: in a master, or in God or in something else. Trust means such a deep faith, that what the other says must happen. When there is no trust, one has to have faith in himself.

Spiritual endeavor is to place trust in one's own self: "Nothing will happen through others' help, I will have to make the effort myself."

In this Kaliyuga rigorous spiritual practices are necessary; nothing will happen through chanting the name of Rama. It was happening in Satyuga – merely saying the name of God was sufficient then. All these were excuses, and any excuse would have done because people were ready and trustful – just a spark and the dry gunpowder would explode. Now that dry gunpowder of trust is not there in man so that a spark from the name of Rama could explode it. Now there is only the cold water of doubt within man. What to say of a spark – you could throw a big bomb in there and it would be extinguished in that water.

This sutra is worth understanding.

> *Listening to these teachings from the master,*
> *the disciple became enlightened and began to say...*

Whatever the master has said has become evident to him. Whatever the master has said was not only heard by him, but had begun to be experienced by him. Whatever the master had said, he did not think or reflect, he had begun seeing it so. He began to say:

> *I had seen the world just now, where has it gone?*

He had heard that the world is an illusion, he had heard that beauty is our own projection, he had heard that all attraction is our own dreaming...but if one had really heard, one would immediately realize that whatsoever dreams one had been seeing up to now had disappeared. They would have broken.

A dream breaks the moment you know it as a dream. Even if you can hear somebody who is awake saying to you that it is a dream, it will break. The master says that the world is an illusion, a dream; you hear it but say, "Let it be, who knows?" How can you believe that the world is a dream, when it is so clearly present all around? It does not appear convincing that the world is a dream. Even if it may appear to be convincing, we do not want our own minds to be convinced because we have a big investment in our dreams, we have invested a fortune in them.

All our happinesses lie in our dreams. If the world is a dream, then what will happen to our happinesses? And what will happen to our lifelong investments in them, in the hope that someday they will come true? All that invested capital will become a waste. And suddenly somebody is saying the world is a dream....

For example, you have become an emperor in your dream and

you are enjoying it immensely; you are sitting on a throne studded with diamonds, pearls, and diamonds are surrounding you in abundance. By that time your wife begins to shake you and tells you that you are dreaming. You tell her to keep quiet, she is spoiling the whole pleasure. After such a long time this dream has come.... It seems difficult to break such dreams.

We are all dreaming. The master goes on saying that all this is a dream, an illusion. But who wants to agree with this? Only the one who is ready to put aside his happinesses and unhappinesses, his greed and his attachments, and then look into this truth and inquire whether it is really so.

Is this world really nothing but a rainbow that vanishes as you get nearer to it? Is it only from a distance that it looks so colorful, as if it has stolen all the colors of the butterflies for itself, as if all the flowers have flown above to form a rainbow? But as you get closer to it, it is nowhere. If you try to hold it in your hands all you get is a few drops of water, which contain neither any colors nor any beauty in them.

The disciple had heard everything and began to say: *I had seen the world just now....* He had seen it before he heard the master, he had seen it before he met the master. He had seen it so much that he had felt that he should go on seeing it more and more and more.... Everything was there up until now, now where had it gone?

This statement is very deep. The disciple is saying to the master, "What have you done? You have shattered everything like a dream. Where has that world gone which I had seen until just moments ago, which I had believed was there, which I had thought was there? Today, suddenly, that world has slipped away from my hands and I have become empty. Who took it away from me?" There is in it a sort of pain also – of its being taken away. There is in it a sort of awakening also – that now he will not have it again. An understanding has grown. A happening has taken place. And:

...Into what has it become dissolved?
It is a great surprise! Does it not exist?

Certainly, what greater surprise can there be than knowing that whatever we had known, whatever we were living and were busy in, and whatever we had cherished – all our dreams of happiness and heaven – have all suddenly disappeared? *It is a great surprise!*...does it simply not exist?

Still the disciple is standing at the midpoint. The world which was there on that side is now lost, and he has not yet quite settled with the new one. It is like a sudden coming of light and the disappearance of darkness: the darkness is dispelled but the eyes have not yet adjusted to the light – they blink.

When the world that has been known to us for birth after birth disappears in a flash, the world is lost but we do not yet see the Brahman. It will take a little time; the eyes will have to become adjusted to seeing the light. Our long habit of seeing darkness creates a hindrance in seeing the light. The eyes are dazzled. For this reason also there is usefulness in spiritual practices, in that the light may come gradually so that the eyes are not dazzled.

If the truth comes directly in front of you, you will go blind, because eyes cannot see the truth as they are; they will have to develop the capacity to see the truth. It is such an immense explosion of light that your tiny eyes will not be able to bear it, they will lose their sight and go blind. It is like approaching the sun with open eyes.

The disciple is now able to see that what he believed to be there has disappeared, but he has not yet been able to see that which should be seen in its place.

It is a great surprise! How did such a big mistake become possible? How was such a great illusion possible, that the whole of life was nothing but a dream? We will also feel this if the same happens to us someday, that there can be no bigger surprise than this. But it happens, it has happened many times, it has happened to many people. It is in the present age that such happenings have become less and less frequent. There are many reasons for this. One reason is a lack of a sense of wonder. Our capacity to wonder has declined. That too has a reason.

Science has opened up many mysteries for us. And with every mystery decoded it is not only that the mysteries become fewer, but our capacity to wonder also becomes less.

Children are full of wonder. Everything looks miraculous to them. We scold them and tell them to be quiet, and say that whatever they are questioning has no big surprises in it. We explain things away to them. But are you aware that by doing so you are snatching away from them their world of wonder where every small happening...? A small butterfly flying by gives so much happiness to a child which later on even the whole world of science cannot give. A small blossoming flower, or a shooting star in the sky, fills the child with such a thrill that when later on the whole wealth of the world is given to him, or even if he is made the owner of all the stars, that childhood thrill cannot come back.

A child sees everything with wonder. Why? Because he is still ignorant, he does not know anything. Now that science has made so many things known, you have a feeling that you know this, that and the other, and this has reduced your sense of wonder. It does not need to be so, but in order to arouse, and in order to maintain your sense of wonder, you will need to go very deep into science – there is no other way.

At the time of his death Einstein said, "I am dying as a mystic. I had thought that I would be able to unlock all the mysteries of the world. I did unlock many mysteries, but upon the unlocking of each mystery, greater mysteries confronted me." It is just as a magician takes out one box from within another box, and goes on taking out box after box – there are mysteries within mysteries, but in order to know them now one will have to go beyond many boxes.

When the genius of an Einstein starts cutting through all the boxes, it finds the mysteries have not lessened. But we who have accumulated some petty knowledge, our sense of wonder dies. We begin to explain everything, we think we have all the answers.

But when everything has been defined and given a meaning our sense of wonder declines. And when the sense of wonder is lessened, the possibility of our being religious disappears. Religion is a mystery, the ultimate mystery; it is the supreme wonder. The greatest miracle that can happen in this world is to become religious. Why? Because on becoming religious, one begins to talk like this disciple who is saying: *"It is a great surprise!* Is the world which was here a few moments ago, the world that I had known a few moments ago, not there? Where has it gone? In what has it dissolved?"

But immediately after that the second statement comes. The first statement is of wonder, the second is of bliss. The bliss hides right behind the wonder. One who has lost his sense of wonder will never be able to attain bliss, because wonder is the door to bliss. He whose door of wonder is closed will not be able to enter the palace of bliss. The second statement follows immediately.

> *In this great ocean of Brahman which is full of*
> *the nectar of infinite bliss, what have I*
> *to renounce now and what have I to take?*
> *What is other now and what is extraordinary?*

"If the whole world has turned out to be false, then I don't have anything to renounce. Whatsoever could have been renounced has already disappeared. Now I do not have anything to indulge in either, because whatsoever I could have indulged in has also disappeared." Nothing is to be clung to and nothing is to be renounced. Nothing is to be taken and nothing is to be removed; that whole world of indulgence and renunciation has disappeared.

Let this sutra be properly understood. Do not think that with the disappearance of the world only indulgence disappears; renunciation also disappears, because indulgence and renunciation were both part of that world which is no more.

One person was accumulating money, he was an indulger; one person was renouncing money, he was a renouncer – but for the one for whom the world itself has disappeared, the wealth itself has disappeared...what is indulgence and what is renunciation? Hence the sages of the Upanishads were not renouncers by your definition; by your definition they were not indulgers either.

452   FINGER POINTING TO THE MOON

The sages of the Upanishads were of a totally different kind, a third category of people.

What we mean today by someone who renounces is in opposition to someone who indulges. The sages of the Upanishads who have given these statements were not people who had given up and run away from everything, going about naked. They were not roaming around here and there. They were neither renouncers nor indulgers, they were extremely ordinary and simple people, living like children. For them the whole world where renunciation and indulgence both happen had disappeared. Neither of them had any value.

When the ideology of renunciation became popular in this country, under the influence of the Buddhist and Jaina religions, it came to be understood as the opposite of indulgence and slowly, slowly the sages of the Upanishads started fading away from our memories, because they were an entirely different kind of people. We cannot call them indulgers, because they were never eager to accumulate anything; we cannot call them renouncers, because they were not eager to give up anything either. If anybody gave them anything, they would take it; if anybody took anything from them, they were not going to chase him. I shall tell you one anecdote that may give you some idea....

Kabir had a son called Kamaal. Kabir did not accept any gifts or money, whereas Kamaal was like the sages of the Upanishads. Kabir's disciples asked him to throw Kamaal out of his place. They said, "When somebody offers you gifts or money you tell him that you don't need it, just keep this rubbish yourself, but this Kamaal sits outside and accepts all those things from the people that you have refused. He blesses them and then keeps the things. This boy is a trouble."

I don't know if Kabir made this statement – I don't believe Kabir could have done it, it must have been some follower of Kabir who also was familiar with Kamaal – the statement is: "A son called Kamaal is born and the whole pedigree of Kabir is drowned forever." The statement means that Kabir's son Kamaal spoiled the name of his whole family.

So Kabir told Kamaal what people were saying about him and asked him what he thought about it. Kamaal then suggested that he would go and stay in a separate hut, that was no problem.

Kamaal moved into a separate hut. The king of Kashi came to know of this. The king had never felt that Kamaal was an indulger. That he did not follow renunciation was clear, but the king also doubted that he was an indulger. The king thought that it would be better to check it out, so he came with a very valuable diamond and presented it to Kamaal. Kamaal said, "What sort of a gift have you brought me? It can neither be eaten nor drunk."

The king was surprised to hear the remark. He had heard people saying that Kamaal kept everything that he was offered, and here he was giving him a diamond worth millions of rupees and this Kamaal was calling it just a stone. Thinking that the talk of the people was not correct and that Kamaal would not take the gift, the king took back the diamond and began to put it in his pocket. Kamaal stopped him, saying, "Are you mad? First you carried this burden here, and now you will also carry it back? Leave it here!"

Now the king became very suspicious, thinking something was fishy about this man. But do you see how our minds work? What Kamaal did was the perfectly logical thing: "If it really is just a stone, you have suffered the trouble of carrying its burden to this place...and now you want to bear its burden in carrying it back. Just let go of it."

But the first idea had appealed to the king. Any idea of renunciation always appeals to the indulger. Kamaal's second remark about letting go of the diamond did not appeal to him at all – now he became suspicious. Still the king asked, "Where shall I leave it?"

Kamaal said, "Now you are asking where to leave it – it means you do not take it to be a stone. Then you had better take it back with you. Why does the question arise as to where to put it? It is just a stone after all – just let it remain anywhere."

To test the matter further the king said, "Okay." The hut was made with a straw roof, so the king pushed the diamond into the roof and said, "I will leave it here."

Kamaal said, "Fine. Do as you like, but I don't see the point of trying to keep such an account of a stone."

The king came back after a month. He was sure that the very next day the diamond would have been sold or hidden away elsewhere. So he came back after a month and asked Kamaal, "A month ago I left a diamond here. Is it still there?"

Kamaal said, "I told you at that time that it was only a stone. Now you are creating a difficulty. Where did you put it? Maybe somebody has taken it away, maybe it is there – just find out."

The king thought Kamaal was trying to be clever in saying, "Maybe somebody has taken it away." But when the king actually looked for it the diamond was still there in the same spot, in the straw of the roof.

The sages of the Upanishads were like that. For them neither indulgence nor renunciation had any meaning. All the respect for renunciation is there because of one's indulgence. This is why a renunciate appeals highly to an indulgent person – because opposites attract. One's attention is drawn to it, one feels that one cannot do such a thing and this man is doing it.

So indulgers touch the feet of renouncers. And there is a reason for it: they feel that they cannot skip even one meal and here there is this man who has been fasting for a month. "Bow down, bow down at his feet. We cannot renounce our homes, and here there is this man who has renounced everything. We cannot remain without clothes, and here this man is standing naked on the road. Bow down to him!"

If somebody does what we cannot do, we feel he deserves our respect. All our respect for renunciation is because of our indulgence. Hence a very interesting thing happens: the more affluent a society, the more indulgent a society, the more it respects the renouncers. The Jainas are wealthy, they have all the amenities of life, so they expect a very strict conduct of renunciation from their monks. It is very interesting that a society of indulgers, of affluent people, expects renunciation of a high order from their monks, otherwise they cannot give them respect.

Hindus do not emphasize renunciation so much – that renunciates should renounce this much, should do this, should do that; therefore no Hindu renunciate stands a chance if he is to be compared with a Jaina renunciate. The whole reason for this is that the Hindu society by and large is not as rich as the Jaina society. Comparatively it is a very poor group, and a poor society does not expect a very high degree of renunciation from their renunciates.

So the more affluent a society, the higher the criterion for renunciation will be. Only with great renunciation will it accept that yes, this man has done something, he has renounced something. We evaluate according to our own minds.

The Upanishads say that as long as there is a value placed on renunciation, know well that there is a value placed on indulgence as well. As long as there is respect for renunciation, understand well that you also have an attraction towards indulgence. This respect is only a reflection of the attraction. The sages of the Upanishads say that for an awakened person, for a conscious being, the whole world – both renunciation and indulgence – disappears.

The disciple says, "What shall I renounce? What shall I take and what shall I give up? I am already drowned in an ocean of infinite bliss."

It happens simultaneously: no sooner is the world lost than the new immortal world is attained. This happening takes place in the same moment, although a time gap may appear to be there in seeing it.

*Here I do not see anything, I do not hear anything
and I do not know anything...*

The disciple says, "In this ocean of the nectar of infinite bliss in which I am drowned, I do not see anything. I do not see anything because only things that are separate from *this* can be seen. I do not hear anything because only the sound of the other can be heard. I do not know anything because even knowing is also of the other. I am only experiencing bliss."

I am always in my blissful soul...

"Neither do I have any other knowledge, nor do I have any sight, nor do I hear anything; none of my senses function anymore. Now only one thing is happening within me and that is, I am constantly experiencing bliss. And what is being experienced by me today is unique and unparalleled. There is no way, there is no symbol with which to explain or define it. *I myself am my own nature.*"

I am unattached, bodiless, genderless;
I am God myself; I am absolutely silent,
I am infinite, I am the whole and the most ancient.

The disciple is experiencing this. These experiences begin the moment this world disappears. The moment the dreaming is broken the realization of this truth begins that...

I am unattached, bodiless, genderless;
I am God myself; I am absolutely silent,
I am infinite, I am the whole and the most ancient.
I am not the doer, I am not the sufferer,
I am unchanging and inexhaustible.
I am the abode of pure knowledge,
I am alone and I am the eternal godliness.

This declaration is from the disciple.

The master had said so, had explained to him that it was like this. The disciple could have taken it in two ways. Had he made it a part of his intellectual knowledge and said, "Okay, I agree with you; whatsoever you have said makes sense to my intellect," and then given these statements, this Upanishad would have become useless. But the explanation also became the experience of the disciple and he said, "Whatsoever you are saying is being seen by me. I am also experiencing it." And the disciple announces further, "I am God myself; I am the most ancient and I am eternal godliness."

This knowledge was given by the master to
Apantaram...

The name of the master is not mentioned. The name of the first seeker is not given. Who the first person was to have known this is not known.

This is very interesting and should be properly understood, because spirituality is not something new. Spirituality is most ancient, eternal. Spirituality has been here ever since man has been here. We cannot imagine a time when spirituality may not have been here. We can imagine a time when there was no science, we can also imagine a time when there were no art forms – when thousands of things were not there – but we cannot imagine a time when man may have been there but no spirituality, because the spiritual thirst is the basic characteristic of man.

Even if there is no science, man can be man. Even if there is no money, man can be man; even if there is no education, man can be man – an illiterate man is also a man and a man of an unscientific society is also a man. But if there is no spirituality man is not a man, he becomes an animal. Spirituality is the basic characteristic of man.

In defining man, Aristotle has said, "Man is a rational being." This definition is not so correct because, after all, even an irrational man will have to be called a man. Rationality is not an invariable characteristic of man. Machiavelli has said, "Man is a political being." If we look at men of today his statement is right; man is a completely political being. Politics is his food, politics is his drink; the newspaper is his first need early in the morning and discussing about politics till late in the night is his last – politics seems to be his life. But politics is also not the fundamental characteristic of man. Research now shows that politics is found even among monkeys and wild animals. Just as there are presidents, prime ministers and their cabinets in the nations, similarly there are chiefs, prime ministers and their cabinets in groups of monkeys also.

There is not much difference between politicians and monkeys.

Among men it is those who have more monkeyness in them who become attracted towards politics.

But man is a spiritual being. And that is his true characteristic.

So whoever discovered this knowledge first, his name is not given. And this is a very good thing. It means that this knowledge is so ancient, so eternal that the name of the first man who became the knower is not known. In place of the name of the first man all that has been said is that...*the master gave it to Apantaram.*

Apantaram too is a wonderful word. It means a disciple whose name is not known. The master gave the knowledge to a disciple whose name is not known. The name of the first disciple is not known, hence his name is nominally given as Apantaram.

The first master who came to know is not known and the first disciple who heard from him is also not known, because when it is the first master, the first disciple also does not know that he is a disciple, or who is a master. Being a master and a disciple are all later developments.

When the first master came to know, the first person who came to him must have been a disciple. We call him a disciple only for the sake of a name, but he would not have been aware of it. He must have come, just drawn towards the magnet as it were, and the knowing was transferred. Hence the sutra says:

> *This knowledge was given by the master to*
> *Apantaram, and Apantaram gave it to Brahma...*

Brahma is the creator of the universe. It is interesting to note that the one who created the universe is also ignorant, has also to receive the knowledge from someone. In this respect it becomes difficult to fathom the depth of Hindu thought. We call Brahma the creator, but we do not consider him also a knower, because if he were a knower he would not have created this dream world. If this world is a dream, its creator cannot be a knower. The work of Brahma is just to develop the dream world – just spreading the dreams.

This is why we did not make many temples of Brahma; there is only one temple in India. They should have numbered more than any other, because the one who created this world should be installed in more temples for worshipping than any other deity. But there is only one temple. Why? – because we came to understand that this world is a dream, and the one who created this dream does not deserve many temples.

We have made the most temples for Shiva, because he is the destroyer of this world. In every town, in every village, you will find a *shivalinga* – the phallic symbol of Shiva – installed virtually under every tree. We have filled the whole land with Shiva, and there is a reason. Why remember Brahma? – he is the one who has unnecessarily put us in this trouble. We have remembered Shiva more often, and on purpose, because he is the destroyer, he will destroy everything.

> ...*Apantaram gave it to Brahma, Brahma*
> *gave it to Ghorangiras, Ghorangiras gave it to*
> *Raikva, and Raikva gave it to Rama...*

Thus in that chain there have been thousands, but a few important names have been selected. There have been thousands whose names are not even known. Some of the most well-known names have been selected here. Ghorangiras is one of the greatest of knowers from the Upanishadic period and he passed on the knowledge to Raikva. Raikva too is an amazing sage: he gave it to Rama, and Rama in turn gave it to all living beings.

Through Rama this knowledge grew widespread, reached to the masses. Before that this knowledge was esoteric and a master would only pass it on to a disciple in secrecy. Rama made it available for all living beings. In the hands of Rama it no longer remained esoteric, it became open for all.

> *Rama gave it to all living beings.*
> *This is the message of nirvana...*

The message of nirvana is that of dissolution of the 'I'. Just the way a lamp is extinguished the 'I' is extinguished. He who extinguishes himself attains to that absolute reality which cannot be extinguished in any way.

What can be extinguished within us is our ego; what cannot be extinguished is the Brahman within us. So extinguish that which can be extinguished so that the non-extinguishable can be experienced.

This is the teaching of the Vedas. This is the essence of all the Vedas. And this is the discipline of the Vedas.

Thus ends this Upanishad.

This Upanishad ends in a very unique way. It does not end with the teachings of the master, but ends with the attainment of the disciple. It does not end on what the master said, but on what happened to the disciple. And as long as a teaching does not become a living phenomenon it has no value. As long as a teaching is not alive it is only a mind-play.

This Upanishad is not a mind-play, it is a transformation of life.

The master gave it...to Apantaram, Apantaram
gave it to Brahma, Brahma gave it to Ghorangiras,
Ghorangiras gave it to Raikva, Raikva gave it to
Rama and Rama gave it to all living beings.

...And we have again tried to enliven this wonderful teaching, this experiencing and this spiritual technique within ourselves. We have again stimulated the flame by moving the wick.

After going from here, continue to stimulate this flame. One day that moment will definitely come in your life when you will also be able to say, *I had seen the world just now, where has it gone?... Does it* simply *not exist?* And the day this will be experienced by you, you will also be able to say, "I am God myself, I am the eternal godliness, I am infinite, I am bliss, I am Brahman."

As long as this has not happened within you, what use is this message of nirvana, what use is this essence of the Vedas? And until then, though this Upanishad ends here, it has not ended for you.

May there be a day when you can also say, "The teachings of the Upanishad end here for me."

Enough for today.

About
The Author

M OST OF US LIVE OUT OUR LIVES in the world of time, in memories of the past and anticipation of the future. Only rarely
do we touch the timeless dimension of the present – in moments of
sudden beauty, or sudden danger, in meeting with a lover or with
the surprise of the unexpected. Very few people step out of the
world of time and mind, its ambitions and competitiveness, and
begin to live in the world of the timeless. And of those who do,
only a few have attempted to share their experience. Lao Tzu,
Gautam Buddha, Bodhidharma...or more recently, George Gurdjieff, Ramana Maharshi, J. Krishnamurti – they are thought by their
contemporaries to be eccentrics or madmen; after their death they
are called "philosophers." And in time they become legends – not
flesh-and-blood human beings, but perhaps mythological represen-
tations of our collective wish to grow beyond the smallness and
trivia, the meaninglessness of our everyday lives.

Osho is one who has discovered the door to living his life in
the timeless dimension of the present – he has called himself a
"true existentialist" – and he has devoted his life to provoking
others to seek this same door, to step out of the world of past

and future and discover for themselves the world of eternity.

Osho was born in Kuchwada, Madhya Pradesh, India, on December 11, 1931. From his earliest childhood, his was a rebellious and independent spirit, insisting on experiencing the truth for himself rather than acquiring knowledge and beliefs given by others.

After his enlightenment at the age of twenty-one, Osho completed his academic studies and spent several years teaching philosophy at the University of Jabalpur. Meanwhile, he traveled throughout India giving talks, challenging orthodox religious leaders in public debate, questioning traditional beliefs, and meeting people from all walks of life. He read extensively, everything he could find to broaden his understanding of the belief systems and psychology of contemporary man. By the late 1960s Osho had begun to develop his unique dynamic meditation techniques. Modern man, he says, is so burdened with the outmoded traditions of the past and the anxieties of modern-day living that he must go through a deep cleansing process before he can hope to discover the thought-less, relaxed state of meditation.

In the early 1970s, the first Westerners began to hear of Osho. By 1974 a commune had been established around him in Poona, India, and the trickle of visitors from the West was soon to become a flood. In the course of his work, Osho has spoken on virtually every aspect of the development of human consciousness. He has distilled the essence of what is significant to the spiritual quest of contemporary man, based not on intellectual understanding but tested against his own existential experience.

He belongs to no tradition – "I am the beginning of a totally new religious consciousness," he says. "Please don't connect me with the past – it is not even worth remembering."

His talks to disciples and seekers from all over the world have been published in more than six hundred volumes, and translated into over thirty languages. And he says, "My message is not a doctrine, not a philosophy. My message is a certain alchemy, a science of transformation, so only those who are willing to die as they are and be born again into something so new that they cannot even imagine it right now...only those few courageous people will be ready to listen, because listening is going to be risky.

"Listening, you have taken the first step towards being reborn. So it is not a philosophy that you can just make an overcoat of and go bragging about. It is not a doctrine where you can find consolation for harassing questions. No, my message is not some verbal communication. It is far more risky. It is nothing less than death and rebirth."

Osho left his body on January 19, 1990. His huge commune in India continues to be the largest spiritual growth center in the world attracting thousands of international visitors who come to participate in its meditation, therapy, bodywork and creative programs, or just to experience being in a buddhafield.

Suggested Further Reading

HEARTBEAT OF THE ABSOLUTE
Discourses on the Ishavasya Upanishad

IN THESE DISCOURSES Osho gave during a Mount Abu meditation camp, sutras from ancient Hindu scriptures are transmuted into stunning insights that can open the reader's eyes to his own inner reality. Osho speaks on issues that touch the heart of every intelligent individual – on love, possessiveness, God as another name for existence, our investment in forgetting the phenomenon of death, karma, the nature of the mind, and meditation. In addition, he gives practical suggestions about how to prepare for meditation and how to extract the most from meditation techniques.

The Tantra Experience

Discourses on 'The Royal Song' of Saraha, the founder of Tantric Buddhism, a lineage which bears fruit to this day in Tibet. "Saraha is one of my most loved persons; it is my old love affair. You may not have even heard the name of Saraha, but Saraha is one of the great benefactors of humanity. If I were to count on my fingers ten benefactors of humanity, Saraha would be one of those ten. If I were to count five, then too I would not be able to drop Saraha."

The Mustard Seed
Commentaries on the
Fifth Gospel of Saint Thomas

Osho brings to life these excerpts from a scroll found at Nag Hammadi, Egypt, contributing a new understanding to these little-known sayings of Jesus – the man he calls "a revolutionary of the inner world."

No Water No Moon

Osho breathes new life into many familiar Zen stories.

"I found No Water No Moon one of the most refreshing, cleansing and delightful books I could imagine," wrote the renowned violinist Yehudi Menuhin. "It is a book which will never cease to be a comforting companion."

Tantric Transformation

In this second volume of discourses on Saraha's Royal Song, given by a contemporary Tantric master, Osho, we are given a detailed map of Tantra: inner man, inner woman; the meeting of man and woman; the transformation of energy through sex and other techniques. "Tantra is freedom: freedom from all mind-constructs, from all mind games; freedom from all structures, freedom from the other. Tantra is a space to *be*. Tantra is liberation."

Tantric Transformation is a very alive, concrete book for exploration of our own energy, of our own inner space.

THE HEART SUTRA

DISCOURSES ON the Prajnaparamita Hridayam Sutra of Gautama the Buddha reveal his essential teachings: the merging of negative and positive, the non-existence of the ego and the buddha-nature of mankind. In addition, Osho speaks on the seven *chakras* and the corresponding facets in man – the physical, psychosomatic, psychological, psycho-spiritual, spiritual, spiritual-transcendental and transcendental.

JOURNEY TO THE HEART
Discourses on the Sufi way

THIS IS A JOURNEY towards the heart, on the path of the Sufis. Here Osho speaks on some of the ancient teaching stories of the Sufi mystics, including those of Bayazid, Bahauddin, Dhun-Nun and Maruf Karkhi. This is the path of love: the lover and the beloved. The search for the beloved, the godliness that is within us all.

"Sufism is *the* religion. Whenever a religion is alive it is because Sufism is alive within it. "

Osho Commune International

THE OSHO COMMUNE INTERNATIONAL in Poona, India, guided by the vision of the enlightened master Osho, might be described as a laboratory, an experiment in creating the "New Man" – a human being who lives in harmony with himself and his environment, and who is free from all ideologies and belief systems which now divide humanity.

The Commune's Osho Multiversity offers hundreds of workshops, groups and trainings, presented by its nine different faculties:

Osho School for Centering and Zen Martial Arts
Osho School of Creative Arts
Osho International Academy of Healing Arts
Osho Meditation Academy
Osho Institute for Love and Consciousness
Osho School of Mysticism
Osho Institute of Tibetan Pulsing Healing

Osho Center for Transformation
Osho Club Meditation: Creative Leisure

All these programs are designed to help people to
find the knack of meditation: the passive witnessing
of thoughts, emotions, and actions, without judgment or identification. Unlike many traditional
Eastern disciplines, meditation at Osho Commune is
an inseparable part of everyday life – working, relating or just being. The result is that people do not
renounce the world but bring to it a spirit of awareness and celebration, in a deep reverence for life.

The highlight of the day at the Commune is the
meeting of the White Robe Brotherhood. This two-
hour celebration of music, dance and silence, with a
discourse from Osho, is unique – a complete meditation in itself where thousands of seekers, in Osho's
words, "dissolve into a sea of consciousness."

For
Further
Information

MANY OF OSHO'S BOOKS have been translated and published in a variety of languages worldwide. For information about Osho, his meditations, books, tapes and the address of an Osho meditation/information center near you, contact:

Osho International Foundation
P.O. Box 2976
London NW5 2PZ, UK

Osho Commune International
17 Koregaon Park
Poona 411001, India

Chidvilas Inc.
P.O. Box 17550, Boulder
CO 80308, U.S.A.